D1143191

THE SPIN DOCTOR'S DIARY

THE SPIN DOCTOR'S DIARY

LANCE PRICE

INSIDE NUMBER 10 WITH NEW LABOUR

HODDER &
STOUGHTON

First published in Great Britain in 2005 by Hodder and Stoughton
A division of Hodder Headline

A Hodder & Stoughton Book

2

A CIP catalogue record for this title is available from the British Library

ISBN 0 340 89822 4

Typeset in Monotype Sabon by
Rowland Phototypesetting Ltd,
Bury St Edmunds, Suffolk

Printed and bound by
Clays Ltd, St Ives plc

Hodder and Stoughton Ltd
A division of Hodder Headline
338 Euston Road
London NW1 3BH

To James

Contents

Introduction   ix

Prologue   1

1998   5

1999   67

2000   182

2001   280

Epilogue   365

Acknowledgements   367

Index   371

Introduction

The prime minister's eyes lit up when he saw me. That had never happened before and, if I'm honest, I'm not sure it has ever happened since. But on one occasion, in a crowded hotel room in central London, he was definitely pleased to see me.

I was a BBC political correspondent and this was the Labour Party gala dinner, a glittering fund-raising occasion full of the great and the good, business leaders, pop stars and actors. They were there to get close to the man who had been prime minister for just a year. He was there to get as much money out of them as he could. I was there for a job interview. To see if he wanted me to join his staff at Number Ten Downing Street.

The interview went something like this:

'Lance, hi!'

'Er . . . hi.'

'Well . . .'

'Er . . .'

'How's it going, Lance?'

'Um . . . fine.'

'Great. Great. So, what are you doing?'

'Well . . . er . . . um . . . I've been speaking to Alastair.'

'Great.'

'Um . . . er . . . is that okay with you?'

'Yup. Absolutely. Great.'

That was it. He had been pushing his way through the crowd, shaking hands left and right. Those crushing around him must have been bemused by this conversation and would have forgotten it immediately as he moved away. But the most powerful man in Britain had just told me he wanted me to take on the most important job of my life. At least, I thought he had.

The Alastair in question was, of course, Alastair Campbell, Tony Blair's official spokesman and later the Number Ten director of communications. The job I'd just been told it was 'okay' for me to have was essentially that of Alastair's deputy in the Downing Street press office. That was how he had described it to me in a recent conversation that had lasted at least a little longer than the one with Tony Blair.

For the next two years I would have a desk just outside the door to Alastair's spacious office overlooking Downing Street. I would be one of the political staff at Number Ten, a so-called 'special adviser'. I would have to learn to work alongside the press office civil servants, career men and women with no political affiliations. They would carry on if Tony Blair was ejected from office but I, like Alastair and the rest of the politicos, would be out on my ear.

In May 1998, however, when I had my 'interview' with the prime minister, that didn't look likely. Tony Blair had been swept into office a year earlier with a majority in the House of Commons of 179. Nobody, with the possible exception of the prime minister himself, thought there was the slightest prospect of him being evicted any time soon.

I knew Tony Blair a bit already, but not exactly well. We'd first met when he was a new member of the shadow cabinet under Neil Kinnock. We got to know each other a bit better, I remember, over lunch in a nice little French restaurant near the House of Commons. He was the party's employment spokesman, not a particularly senior job but he was already being described as a man to watch. He stood up to leave after a frank and interesting discussion, and I think I got on with settling the bill. When I looked up he had been called across by some people at a neighbouring table. He straightened his back, obviously pleased to have been recognised. Maybe it was his white shirt and dark trousers, but this must have been the first and last time that the future prime minister was mistaken for a waiter and asked to fetch the coats.

I found Tony Blair then much as I find him today: very clever, charming and good company but at the same time extremely ambitious, not just for himself but for the Labour Party. Back in the mid-eighties he stood out, along with Gordon Brown and Peter Mandelson, not yet an MP, for his single-mindedness of purpose. You had the sense that whatever it took to make the Labour Party electable again he was prepared to embrace.

Tony, Gordon, Peter and Alastair – who joined them when Blair became leader in 1994 – created New Labour. It was a daring, difficult and ultimately hugely successful project. It wrong-footed the Conservatives, who couldn't decide whether to claim that Labour hadn't really changed and that it was all just clever PR, or that it had changed but into something that was still a threat to Britain's way of life. It was immaterial in the end. The electorate believed Labour *had* changed and rewarded them handsomely for having done so.

Labour supporters were delighted at the Tories' discomfort but were faced with a slightly different dilemma, in particular those like me who thought of themselves as being on the liberal wing of left-leaning politics. We rather hoped Tony Blair wasn't as close to traditional conservative thinking as he appeared to be. We would have supported him whatever his motives, but we liked to think he might be secretly one of us, stealing Tory clothes only for good tactical, election-winning reasons. We were wrong.

When I joined the staff at Downing Street the Conservatives put down questions in the House of Commons about me, seeking to suggest that I had been a Labour mole inside what they liked to call the Blair Broadcasting Corporation. In fact, although my private sympathies had always been with Labour, I hadn't been a party member since my Oxford student days and was strict about keeping my personal views out of my work. Besides, the Tories didn't need Blair sympathisers at the BBC to help destroy their reputation in government. They were doing a perfectly good job of it for themselves. It wasn't difficult at that time to be an impartial journalist and also to hope fervently for a change of government. All you had to do was report the truth and let the electorate take care of the rest.

As a journalist my views weren't allowed to matter. All shades of political opinion had to be treated with equal respect, without fear or favour. Once I was working at Number Ten there would be only one view that mattered: 'the line'. In effect this amounted to whatever Tony Blair thought on any particular issue, even if Alastair had to remind him of what his view was from time to time. My job had switched dramatically from balancing all opinions to pushing just one and selling it as hard as I could. It was easier than I had expected, helped by the obvious sincerity of Tony Blair and an early decision of my own. I'd seen previous journalists turned spin doctors suffer horribly and end up resigning or being sacked because they tried to hang on to some of their detachment. I was sure that the only way to do the job was as a 100 per cent Blair loyalist. Fortunately it was a part I was happy to play. I believed in the guy and, for what it's worth, I still do. No doubt those with a slightly more sceptical view of the prime minister's politics – John Prescott, Robin Cook, Clare Short and the rest – saw me as just about as Blairite as you could get. I know my old friends in the media, too, found it a bit hard to take because they told me so.

As I pondered the huge change that was about to take place in my life I thought a lot about the truth. Would I have the same relationship with it that I had enjoyed while I was employed by the BBC? I had seen the Labour spin doctors at work close up so it seemed unlikely. Not that they were habitual liars. They weren't. Get caught out lying as a spin doctor and your reputation is dead in the water. But most spin doctors would stand uneasily in the dock with a Bible in their hands. They might just about manage 'the truth and nothing but the truth'. The bit about 'the whole truth' would be more of a problem.

The reader of these diaries, kept during my two years at Downing Street and a third as the Labour Party's director of communications at Millbank up to and during the 2001 general election campaign, can judge for themselves how I fared.

When I left on the morning after the 2001 general election it was with a sense of a job done, if not well then to the best of my ability. I didn't feel that I was walking away as somebody who had compromised his integrity. The only thing that stopped me holding my head high was exhaustion.

I decided to leave not because I was disillusioned but because I had always said to myself and to my partner, James, that I would do the job only up until the next election. I predicted, correctly, that it would take up almost every waking hour. To have stayed would have meant another four years of being unable to go to the cinema without sitting in an aisle seat with my pager set to vibrate, to invite friends for dinner in case I had to cancel at short notice, to take a weekend break abroad without prising myself out of the clutches of a voracious creature with a firm grip. And yet I walked away with real regret that while everybody else was going back into government, eager to get on with the job, I was . . . well, I was walking away.

So has the worm turned again? From impartial observer to Blair loyalist and now to loose cannon freed from all constraints? It is a reasonable question to ask.

Two general elections have been and gone since I worked for Tony Blair and he has said he will not be fighting another. Most of the men and women who appear in these pages have already moved on to other things or are about to do so. Some people will say that it is still too soon to reveal anything about what went on away from the distrustful eyes of the media and the public. Indeed, some already have. That was certainly the view of the cabinet secretary, Britain's most senior civil servant, when I first showed him the manuscript of this book. I disagreed then and I disagree now. I passionately believe that unnecessary secrecy about how our government works is bad not just for the people in whose name it operates but for government itself. Greater transparency, in my view, makes for better government, not worse.

The same is true of party politics. Individual party membership is falling. People feel disengaged. More openness, more honesty about where we've gone wrong, rather than simply trumpeting the things we've got right, is surely one route towards better engagement with those whose support we seek. The voters of this country are grown-ups. They don't expect politicians to be perfect and they are prepared to let them learn from their mistakes. The pages of these diaries detail many of those mistakes in the first term. But to his credit Tony Blair has been able to admit it when he's got things wrong – over the Dome, for example, or Ken Livingstone, or Rhodri Morgan in Wales. A fair reader will conclude, I hope, that most of those mistakes were born of the best intentions.

We should not forget that Tony Blair had been prime

minister only just over a year when these diaries begin. Before that, Labour had been out of office and in the wilderness for eighteen years. If he was slow to realise that devolution meant just what it said on the can, and that he couldn't go on running everything from the centre, it was because he wanted the right policies for all parts of the UK. He was determined that 'Old Labour' – what the papers loved to call the 'loony left' – should never reassert itself in London or anywhere else. If he appeared to be circumventing cabinet government and adopting an almost presidential style, and he has been accused of both, it was because he was a man in a hurry. His frustration at how slowly decisions could be turned into results appears on almost every page. We all became obsessed by 'delivery', but isn't that what we were there for? To deliver? And if he spent more time than he should worrying about how the government was perceived in the media, then it came of his bitter memories of how Labour had been maligned and misrepresented in the past.

To some readers this book will confirm what they have believed all along: that Tony Blair's government is and always has been obsessed with 'spin'. But that, too, is a lesson that has been learned.

When I first sat at my desk in Downing Street I stuck a cutting from the *Sun* to my computer screen. It was from Mystic Meg, the paper's astrologer. It said (I can't remember why) 'Spin and Win'. I was obviously quite proud to be a spin doctor. When I left it was still there, but yellowed by the sun, appropriately enough, and about ready to fall off. We had long since concluded that spin not only made for bad government but for bad political communications. It's a statement of the obvious that, like a magician's trick, once people can see how it's done it doesn't work any more. And the media's relentless attention on spin had rendered it useless. The papers weren't ready to give up that particular stick with which to beat us, however. Whenever we complained that we were 'more spinned against than spinning', and we did it a lot, they rejected our arguments as just more spin. It was a circular argument that we couldn't win so we gave up trying.

There are a lot of definitions of what 'spin' actually is. The *Encarta Dictionary* describes a spin doctor as 'somebody whose job it is to present the actions of a person or organisation in the best possible light, especially via the news media'. That makes it sound innocent enough. In politics, however, spin became synonymous with every sort of news management and manipulation, whether legitimate or not. The very same journalists who would call asking for help and 'exclusives' to keep them one step ahead of their rivals would happily accuse us of spinning if the same help was ever offered to anybody else. Again, let the reader be the judge. Yes, there are examples in this book of our strenuous efforts to shape the news agenda in our favour. There are even examples of downright lies. But lies aren't spin, they are just lies. They were rare and not always wise. Perhaps they were never justified but I was very aware of them when they happened – becoming a spin doctor didn't turn me into an habitual liar – and I hope there was always a reason for them. There are at least as many examples, however, of a government trying vainly to get its message across in the face of a cynical and often hostile media.

And yet what follows is not an attempt to defend spin doctors or the politicians they serve. It is a straight account of what I saw and what I did. Or as straight as was possible in the circumstances. Other than for the reasons given below, I have deliberately not changed it in any way, other than to correct punctuation and grammar and to add the occasional note to explain the otherwise opaque or even incomprehensible reference.

The civil service is infected with a love of initials and it's a disease to which politicians fall victim very quickly. It is at its worst when referring to people. I have had to administer an antidote to make the following pages comprehensible. Only TB and AC remain as they were. The rest have been re-humanised. And so GB, as he appeared in my original notes, is back as Gordon Brown, or frequently just Gordon. There is only one, after all. PM is Peter Mandelson, sometimes just Peter. Somehow JP sounds more affectionate than John Prescott, but for consistency's sake he, too, has been given back his real name. It also solves the problem the civil service had with Jonathan Powell, the chief of staff with the same initials. Mr Prescott has suffered some humiliations in office but at least it was Jonathan who had to make do with being known as JPo.

The civil service has other rules, too, including those of confidentiality. In July 2005 the then Cabinet Secretary, Sir Andrew Turnbull, described this book as 'completely unacceptable'. In September the Cabinet Office requested a small number of changes. Where these appear justified and to avoid inaccuracies they were accepted. Otherwise, at my own decision, I have taken out references to official information contained in confidential documents and notes that crossed my desk and I have omitted anything that might fall foul of the Official Secrets Act. On legal advice I have also deleted some passages and amended others, but the number of such changes was modest. I have also removed references to career civil servants who have the right to give advice in confidence and are not able to defend themselves in public. Politicians, on the other hand, are used to taking criticism and more than capable of answering their critics. Without exception they will have survived far worse than anything that appears here. The same goes for the likes of Alastair Campbell, who is now free to say what he likes and often does, and others for whom life as a temporary civil servant was, like mine, temporary.

What follows is the truth as I saw it. An account of the events I witnessed and took part in, written sometimes on a daily basis, sometimes less regularly, depending on how busy or tired I happened to be. It wasn't written with the intention that it should be published and that may be a strength or a weakness. I gave no thought or time to polishing phrases or worrying about how my words might one day appear in print. This diary was intended as nothing more that an *aide memoire*. And my memory needs all the help it can get. It was my greatest weakness as a journalist, and later in the many political meetings that I attended and conversations that I had, that I could rarely remember precisely what had been said to me unless I made a note of it. So I have always made copious notes.

I had a vague idea that one day there might be a book on my experience of life behind that famous black front door. So few people get to see what really goes on there and no doubt everybody who does has their own perspective on it. This happens to be mine.

There are certainly omissions. When I wasn't able to write an entry every day I undoubtedly forgot things by the time I did sit down to catch up. One occasion, however, that is etched painfully in my memory never made it into the diary. Maybe I was too embarrassed about it at the time to commit it to paper.

There weren't many quiet moments but when there were, especially at weekends, I would try to slip away from the phones to go for a walk or spend a couple of hours at the gym. Mobile phones were quite rightly banned at my gym so I left it behind the reception desk. My pager I carried surreptitiously in the palm of my hand, set to vibrate. One afternoon it went off as I was sitting in the sauna: 'Call Downing Street.' I rushed to the desk and recovered my phone, naked but for a towel round my waist. The operator at Number Ten – the infamous 'Switch' – said as soon as I got through, 'I've got the prime minister for you.' In retrospect I should have asked her to tell him I was busy and would call back shortly, giving myself time to dress and find somewhere private to take the call. But I didn't. You tend not to ask the prime minister to hang on.

It was an excruciatingly embarrassing call. The girl at the reception was listening to every word. 'How's it going?' he asked. 'Fine,' I said, 'not much happening but we're doing our best.' He wanted a quick, concise run-down on what the media were up to and any political difficulties we might be in. What he got was gibberish as I tried to find a form of words that wouldn't give away who I was talking to. We were pushing an NHS announcement from Alan Milburn, so I remember burbling something about Alan having a good story to tell on cancer. At one point the prime minister asked me rather pointedly if I was on duty that day. He obviously thought I was completely incapable of telling him anything remotely useful. I put the phone down aghast. 'So,' asked the girl behind the desk, cheerily, 'are you a doctor or something then?'

By the time I got back to the office the following Monday, life had moved on and I never made the time to explain to him why I had sounded so incompetent. Maybe it was a mistake to try to have something of a life at the same time as doing a job like that, but it was the only way I could have done it. So if Tony Blair and Alastair Campbell occasionally thought that, for a special adviser, my advice wasn't always that special I couldn't blame them. Fortunately nobody, with the possible exception of my mother, is likely to buy this book hoping to read *Tony Blair – my part is in his triumphs*. It would be thin pickings indeed.

So, I hope these pages don't echo with the sound of too much trumpet-blowing, either on my own behalf or, indeed, on his. For somebody whose job it was to sell the virtues and achievements of the first Blair administration, I didn't spend a lot of time writing about them. I would have driven myself crazy if I'd come home each night only to list for my own benefit all the positive things about the government that I'd spent all day explaining to journalists. It was the frustrations and setbacks along the way that I tended to write down and these are well chronicled here. As a result some of those featured will find their portrayal unfair, I'm sure. But I left after three years with no lasting enmities and I have no wish to damage anybody's career or undermine their reputation for the sake of it.

Life in the public eye is difficult enough and I don't want to make it any harder. I believe we are lucky to have so many people of talent and integrity who give up so much to try to make Britain not just a better place but a better-governed country. I wish the Labour Party well and look forward to it achieving even more in office under whoever takes over from Tony Blair as prime minister. But there would be no point in publishing sanitised or bowdlerised diaries and these are certainly not that.

Almost as soon as I left, on election night 2001, I came to the house we had bought here in the South of France where I am writing this today. James and I went off on a holiday – we thought we deserved it. When we got back there was a letter from the prime minister in the box at the end of the drive. It had rained while we were away and the envelope was still wet. Tony Blair had taken the trouble to write in longhand thanking me for all I had done, but the ink had run and it was barely legible. It seemed to symbolise something, although I was never quite sure what. I found the letter up in the loft when I was digging out the original pages of these diaries. Luckily they had avoided a similar fate. Whether they will stand the test of time any better than the prime minister's letter is for others to judge. I've no doubt other diaries and memoirs of the Blair government will soon emerge. They may well have a different take on the events described here. But this is mine and I take full responsibility for it.

Prologue

For anybody remotely interested in politics, election night 1997 was an occasion they will remember quite possibly for the rest of their lives. I was still a BBC political correspondent and was sent to report on the count at Enfield, Southgate in north London. I had spent much of the previous week complaining that I'd drawn a short straw. There was never going to be much news in Enfield. Michael Portillo, the Conservative defence secretary, was hardly likely to lose his seat. Not for the first time, or the last, my judgement proved lamentable but my luck was good. I had the best story of the night.

The faces of Portillo and the man who defeated him, Stephen Twigg, said everything you needed to know: the Tory, tired, defeated, uncomprehending; the New Labour victor, young, energetic, exhilarated.

The statistics are well known. Labour won the election with a majority of 179. They had a lead of more than 12 per cent, the biggest for any party since 1935. Labour's tally of 419 seats (including the speaker, Betty Boothroyd) was the largest in the party's history. The Tories had 165 seats, just one more than their previous worst tally way back in 1906. Seven cabinet ministers had lost their seats. There was no longer a single Conservative MP in Scotland, Wales, Manchester, Liverpool or Newcastle.

Tony Blair's first cabinet contained few surprises. Gordon Brown was made chancellor, Jack Straw went to the Home Office and Robin Cook was foreign secretary. John Prescott combined being deputy prime minister with responsibility for the environment, transport and the regions. Lower down the ranks, David Blunkett was at Education, Frank Dobson at Health and George Robertson at Defence. There were more women in the cabinet than ever before, including Mo Mowlam (Northern Ireland), Harriet Harman (Social Security) and Margaret Beckett (Trade and Industry). Peter Mandelson was outside the cabinet, but still influential as a Cabinet Office minister.

Labour's majority may have been huge but, on paper at least, its ambitions were modest. Its famous pledge card contained just five promises:

- to cut class sizes to thirty or under for five-, six- and seven-year-olds;
- fast-track punishment for persistent young offenders;
- to cut NHS waiting lists by treating an extra 100,000 patients;
- to get 250,000 under-25-year-olds off benefit and into work;
- to set tough rules for government spending and borrowing; ensure low inflation; strengthen the economy.

I would spend my time at Downing Street and later at Millbank Tower (the Labour Party headquarters) insisting that good progress was being made in meeting these pledges, as well as much else besides. But in Tony Blair's first year in office, before these diaries begin, I was still at the BBC. Like everybody else, I was taken by surprise at the decision immediately after the election to make the Bank of England independent of political control. I watched as the government became embroiled in the so-called Ecclestone Affair, which looked to many like a rich man buying influence on behalf of his Formula One empire through a generous gift – later repaid – to Labour's coffers. It was in the wake of this that Tony Blair famously appealed to the public to continue trusting him, saying, 'I am a pretty straight sort of guy.'

There was great progress in Northern Ireland, culminating in the signing of the Good Friday Agreement, and early evidence of government splits over policy towards the single currency. The ups and downs in both areas continued after I joined and continue still.

Progress on the economy was good, although critics said Gordon Brown was merely building on what he'd inherited from the Tories. The government had committed itself to sticking to Conservative spending limits for the first two years, something many of the new ministers deeply regretted. Welfare reform was being pushed heavily, but by a social-security department that was at war with itself. Already some Labour backbenchers were feeling restless. Their suspicions about what their leader was up to were compounded when they saw him flirting so openly with the Liberal Democrat leader, Paddy Ashdown. The government got on quickly with its plans for devolution to Scotland and Wales, no doubt remembering that this was the issue that had brought down the previous Labour government eighteen years previously. There were urgent talks, too, about a new assembly for London to be led by Britain's first ever directly elected mayor.

Relations between the prime minister and his chancellor excited much media interest from the start. The tensions were too well known to be denied convincingly and they would break to the surface repeatedly in the years to come. The low point, although there were many, came in January 1998, when the respected *Observer* journalist Andrew Rawnsley wrote that 'someone who has an extremely good claim to know the mind of the Prime Minister' had told him that Gordon Brown 'has these psychological flaws'. I got a small scoop of my own the same day, when one of those at the very heart of New Labour told me Brown's position might not always be as strong as it seemed then. 'Nobody is indispensable,' he said. Alastair Campbell rang me, clearly trying to find out whom I'd been talking to. 'I've narrowed it down to Jack Straw or Peter Mandelson,' he said. I never told him which.

So, by the time I walked through the front door of Ten Downing Street as a special adviser to the prime minister much had already happened to set the tone of the Blair government. On the other side of the House of Commons William Hague had been elected to replace John Major as leader of the Conservative Party. Aside from the politics there had been some major events of a more personal nature, some far more significant than others. Diana, Princess of Wales had died in a car crash in Paris. President Bill Clinton was embroiled in the consequences of his relationship with Monica Lewinsky. The foreign secretary, Robin Cook, had left his wife for his secretary.

On Monday, 8 June 1998, the day I started my new job, the news was reporting Tony Blair's assurance that everything possible would be done to stop substandard surgeons operating on patients after a scandal involving the death of twenty-nine babies at Bristol Royal Infirmary.

The story continues . . .

1998

Monday, 8 June 1998

I told the BBC today that I'd been offered and had accepted the job of special adviser to the prime minister. Inevitably it means I'll do no more broadcasting. Both Ric Bailey [head of News, BBC Westminster] and Richard Ayre [deputy chief executive, BBC News] were surprised and, I believe, impressed. Certainly both warmly congratulated me. I think the announcement will be made by Downing Street tomorrow morning, although Alastair [Campbell] is with Blair in Sweden today. It still seems amazing that I'm going into such a high-powered job on the basis of three or four very brief conversations with AC and a few cryptic words with Blair. They know very little about me and can have no way of knowing whether I'll be any good at the job. But it's immensely exciting and not a little daunting. I'm not even a member of the Labour Party at the moment. On one level it's all very liberating. But everything I say from now on will be constrained by 'the line'. And, today of all days, the government is pushing through a policy that I have some difficulty with – the end of student grants and introducing tuition fees. I'm sure it won't be the last time either.

Tuesday, 9 June 1998

My first bit of spinning and a small triumph. Lead piece in the Londoner's Diary in the *Evening Standard* – 'Price is Right for Number Ten' – announcing my appointment. I called Simon Edge [a friend who worked on the diary] last night and it turned out to be as flattering a piece as I could ask for. Rather old BBC photo, unfortunately, but that's the least of my worries. Several calls as a result, including congratulations from John Sergeant, Paul Gambaccini, Carolyn Quinn, John Kampfner. I'm told there was a fair bit of astonishment in several BBC offices yesterday. But I'm not 100 per cent sure an announcement was made. It didn't appear on PA [the Press Association news agency] and there have been no calls from journos. Either that or I'm not really news. Tried and failed to choose a new suit and shoes.

Wednesday, 10 June 1998

Apparently Godric [Smith, number two in the Downing Street press office] did announce my appointment verbally at the eleven o'clock lobby meeting yesterday. AC decided a press notice would be a bit OTT. But I, of course, want as many people to know as soon as possible just to make my life a little easier – and to help me do my job properly. So far as I can see, only the *Independent* ran a piece on me today. Heard that the BBC took me off the payroll on Monday. I don't believe they were entitled to and I shall contest it.

Saw Peter [Mandelson] in his office in the Cabinet Office this evening. Brief chat but useful. He says I should get AC to make absolutely clear what the job is I'm being asked to do. Fair point. He warned me again about Gordon Brown and Charlie [Whelan, Brown's press spokesman, also a special adviser]. They're 'wicked' and are in a state of almost open warfare. Be nice to them but don't trust them an inch, says Peter. He also claimed that he never speaks to journalists, these days – seconds after putting the phone down on what was clearly some hack, having briefed him on the government's energy policy and the position of Geoffrey Robinson [paymaster general and key Brown ally]. AC, says Peter, is very good, usually but not always right, gets ratty when he's tired especially at the end of the week, is a dreadful delegater and works far too hard. Ben W-P [Wegg-Prosser, special adviser to Mandelson] calls Gordon, Charlie, etc., 'the forces of evil'. He and Peter are very worried about a biography of Peter being done by Paul Routledge, who's very close to Gordon.

Thursday, 11 June 1998

Spent a couple of hours in Number Ten and I think I'm going to love it. Anji [Hunter, special assistant to Tony Blair and his long-time friend] very welcoming and helpful. She's very protective of TB and makes sure he gets days 'off', time with the family, etc. He's in the flat [over Number Eleven Downing Street] by seven thirty most evenings, still likes to read widely, see friends, etc. She gave me a run-down of the staff and roughly who does what, then a tour. Says I'll be in a good position to pick up on what TB is thinking through AC because he has to pass my desk to get back to his own. She lunched with Jon Sopel [BBC political correspondent], whom she's mates with and overheard Alan Duncan [Tory MP] saying to Sopel, 'Great for Number Ten, great for Lance. Bastards!' She warned me that the security check is very thorough . . . were you promiscuous in your youth, does your eye stray up to the top shelf in newsagents?! I told the head of security today that my partner was another man and she didn't blink an eyelid. I've now got three security forms to fill in.

Anji said AC and Peter Mandelson now have a good relationship, though it was very shaky for a while. Peter admits he got things wrong last summer [when he and John Prescott jousted publicly over who was in charge while TB was on holiday]. 'He's brilliant at media advice for everyone but himself,' says Anji, and he wants to have this summer off.

AC gave me a decent job description at last: 'case building' and rebuttal on running stories, political spinning, Prime Minister's Questions, the Sunday papers, liaison with the Strategic Communications Unit, etc. He apparently has his bleeps put through to me or Godric at weekends and doesn't like to be bothered. And Tim [Allan, whom I replaced at Number Ten] used to refer things up to him more than he would have liked. AC was on the phone to PA who had inadvertently been sent not only this weekend's honours list on disk, but the also-rans, those who weren't included, as well. He was pleading for their return, but seemed surprisingly unperturbed.

I met the rest of the press-office team and the atmosphere in there was much more relaxed than I'd expected. Peter Hitchens had been on the phone asking if I was in the Labour Party when I worked at the Beeb. The *Guardian* Diary ran a piece this morning saying I had got off to a great start by not returning any of their calls – not that any were ever passed on to me.

Gordon Marsden [gay Labour MP and personal friend] came out properly yesterday and was in all the papers.

Had a bit of a chat with Godric, who seems great. Days will start around eight in the morning and finish about seven or eight in the evening, I guess. But I intend to throw myself into it 100 per cent or more, there's no other way of doing it. The morning in Brighton was pleasant and relaxed with James [Proctor, my partner]. I wonder how often I'll be able to say that in future?

Sunday, 14 June 1998

Spent much of Friday in Brighton [my weekend home] filling in my vetting forms, a fairly complex business. I put James down as my partner but then had to get details of his mortgage, parents, etc. Up to London mid-afternoon to take the forms into Downing Street and return my equipment to the BBC. Had a drink with John Pienaar [BBC political correspondent], who, no doubt, will be the first of my former colleagues to put me down on his expenses. Picked up my letter from BBC Personnel saying my resignation was put through on Monday, something I intend to challenge. Indeed I wrote back a letter saying I'd been available for work all week and questioning why they felt they had a right to sack me.

James went to Cardiff for the European summit. [He was then a presenter on BBC Five Live, covering Europe.] I got a mention in the *Daily Mail*, 'Conservatives voiced alarm at the resignation of BBC political correspondent Lance Price to become a full-time spin doctor for Tony Blair.' Peter Mandelson told me that another of my former BBC colleagues had wanted this job but that he, Peter, had told Blair he was untrustworthy.

Monday, 15 June 1998

First day at Number Ten. TB and AC in Cardiff for the Euro summit so James will see more of them than I will. Also England's first World Cup match today, so it wasn't the busiest of days in the office. Probably no bad thing. Attended my first lobby briefing from the other side, which was very strange. Sat there wondering how I would respond to the various questions. Decent chats with Peter Hyman [another special adviser attached to the press office] and Godric on how best to go about the job. Generally the atmosphere inside is pretty impressive, if eerily calm.

Wednesday, 17 June 1998

Getting more into the swing of things. Blair is back and greeted me very warmly this morning. Took part in my first Prime Minister's Questions preparations – and even had some effect. I pressed the line that employers should be encouraged to take action against hooligans identified during the World Cup [there had been trouble with British fans in France], including an RAF man. TB used it and it was the lead item on the ITN teatime news. Triumph. So, a fascinating day. TB very decisive and clear in pre-PMQs session. He wanted a plan of action on thugs, though the Home Office not keen to admit they hadn't already got one, so not much emerged. Hence the stress on the employers' line. I have started briefing journos a bit and so far have managed to avoid misleading anybody.

Yesterday had useful chats both in Number Ten with David Miliband [head of the Policy Unit] and at Labour Party HQ with Tom Sawyer [general secretary], who said I could always go for a seat at the next election: 'There are always a few that come up.' Sadly he won't be gen. sec. by then.

Saturday, 20 June 1998

Very strange to see myself quoted, though not by name, of course, in all the papers. I did the lobby yesterday as both AC and Godric were off, so my words crop up in all sorts of stories – new working peers, did Number Ten doctor Hansard (no, as it happens), Lord Neill [then chairman of the Committee on Standards in Public Life] signed up as a brief for Lady Porter [ex-Tory leader of Westminster Council with legal problems]. 'No concern in Number Ten' – perhaps my first exercise in less than 100 per cent veracity. It was a really fun day as I felt almost in charge at the end of my first week. Also feeding the lobby journalists about Peter Temple-Morris [ex-Tory MP] joining the Labour Party. All good fun. I was completely knackered by the end of the day.

Currently Mo [Mowlam, Northern Ireland secretary] is trying to get the parliamentary oath changed so Sinn Féin can take their seats. George Robertson [defence secretary] is worried about his defence review being seen as a huge cuts exercise and Robin Cook [foreign secretary] wants to butter up Gerhard Schröder [opposition leader in Germany] because he's worried about a Jospin-Schröder alliance if he becomes chancellor.

I see so much and get so many calls that I started to worry I'd lose track of it all. I'm going to have to be a lot more methodical in my note-taking, etc. Thursday seems a long time ago now, but that was when I spent the longest so far with TB – sat in on a forty-five-minute chat with Phil Hall, editor of the *News of the World*. No real surprises.

Thursday was the minimum-wage statement – a clear victory for Brown over Margaret Beckett [Trade and Industry Secretary], though quite a few people in Number Ten seem to think it was an unnecessary row and that we could happily have done what she wanted and accepted the recommendations in full. Policy Unit lunch on Thursday with Andrew Dilnot of the Institute of Fiscal Studies – a bit like an Oxford economics seminar. But he did say that our tax system is far more progressive than most people realise. The top 1 per cent of taxpayers pay 18 per cent of the tax bill or something. But that income distribution is getting ever more unequal and nothing we're doing, including the minimum wage, will do much about it.

Tuesday, 23 June 1998

The weekend wasn't too badly disrupted but I can see we'll be spending a lot of our Brighton time stuck in the house from now on. Peter Temple-Morris's defection to Labour got a good showing and we managed to keep it going for two days. I was dealing with it by phone from the garden, which was fine.

Yesterday was fairly quiet in the office. No real crisis at the moment. Last night the Commons voted to reduce the gay age of consent to sixteen, at long last. James in for the debate, which was actually a bit dull. Ann Keen [Labour MP] was great and Gordon Marsden made a powerful speech. But because the result was a foregone conclusion it was a bit flat somehow. We had a drink on the terrace afterwards with Ben Bradshaw, Stephen Twigg [gay Labour MPs] *et al.*

Bit tired today and fighting off a cold, and again not much going on. AC appeared before the Public Administration Committee this afternoon – great theatre. He was masterful and very entertaining, and gave few hostages to fortune. Denied politicisation of the Government Information Service. I'm not a member of the GIS and nor is any other special adviser. But I was used on *Channel 4 News* as an example of journalists being brought into Whitehall, some (though not me) at the expense of career civil servants. AC skirted around leaks from ministers. But before going in he took a ranting call from Harriet Harman [social security secretary], obviously very worried. He refused to take her calls all morning. TB came in after his appearance. AC called him a 'dickhead' and said the only problem had been his – Blair's – comment at Prime Minister's Questions that AC was very good at attacking the Tories, something he, and I, are not really supposed to do.

Wednesday, 24 June 1998

PMQs and what is clearly a regular mad scramble trying to get stuff for TB that he doesn't generally use. I am going to have to get myself fully attuned to the way he likes to do things. This morning the *Sun* did a heavy number on the single currency with a pic of TB, asking 'Is This the Most Dangerous Man in Britain?' And in the past week both Murdoch and the new editor of the *Sun*, David Yelland, were in Number Ten for dinner – not something we've been advertising.

I am now feeling part of the team and able to offer advice and ideas pretty much without fear or favour. The job is there for me to make of it what I will, and provided I'm prepared to put in the effort it will be great.

Government in a bit of a mess today over student fees in Scotland, which I said at the strategy meeting was a daft policy and bound to give problems, and so it proved.

Thursday, 25 June 1998

Foreign policy headaches. Only now getting to grips with the landmines issue, which we in the press office have been warning all week will be a problem. It was starting to look as if legislation to ban them wouldn't be introduced before the anniversary of Diana's death. Now the papers are on to it things are moving, but we could and should have pre-empted them. Also the 'ethical foreign policy'. TB clearly thinks Cook has been grandstanding too much.

Wrote my first speech for TB for tonight's Newspaper Press Fund meeting. It included a bit about him meeting the nominees for the Police Bravery Award in the Downing

Street garden and wondering if they were there to arrest him for being 'the most dangerous man in Britain'. I told him I'd left out a risqué joke about George Michael. 'What's that?' he asked. 'What did the policeman say when he first saw George Michael in the toilet cubicle? – Are you going to come quietly, sir?' TB groaned but said it was a good one.

I travelled with him to the speech in the Daimler, looked after him and brought him back. First decent opportunity to talk to him alone. He wants me to take some of the pressure off AC, especially at weekends. He did say I was quite capable of taking over from him whenever necessary, so I must have done OK today. I told him that AC had heard from Alan Clark [Tory MP] that many Tories were very unhappy with [William] Hague who is off sick at the moment and would like to replace him as party leader. I assumed he already knew, but he didn't. So we discussed what it might mean. I suggested maybe Michael Howard as an interim leader with the intention of getting Michael Portillo in place as soon as possible. He said Hague had got every major decision wrong so far – appointing Cecil Parkinson [as party chairman], listening to Alan Duncan, and policy on the single currency.

There was a Policy Unit lunch today on Europe. Quite clear there is no coherent strategy. Roger Liddle [in the Policy Unit, a close ally of Peter Mandelson] hugely in favour of the single currency, but many sceptics around the table. One idea is to have a Europe minister who reports directly to the prime minister. A general feeling that TB won't want the next election fought on the single currency, but I said that having acknowledged that the referendum would be shortly after the election, that was all but inevitable.

Tuesday, 30 June 1998

Nice quiet weekend in Brighton and this week has got off to a quiet start too. The whole government is gearing up for a series of big announcements: health spending, Defence Review, Comprehensive Spending Review. The immediate decisions are how much to make of recent small reductions in NHS waiting lists, and how far Blair should go in trailing extra cash for the Health Service – £18 billion over three years. A lot more than Major managed but a little less than the Tories after the '87 election.

Reshuffle speculation abounds. Peter [Mandelson] says it'll be more extensive than originally planned and he's obviously trying to carve out as big a role for himself as possible.

Friday, 3 July 1998

The week has passed with astonishing speed, which suits me fine. I love to be busy and fully engaged in something that I feel is important for the first time in a long while. I'm writing this at Edinburgh airport about to fly back down to London after meeting the Scottish party staff and attending a strategy meeting with Donald Dewar, Gordon Brown and others for the Scottish Parliament elections. Planning is at a pathetically early stage given that the election is next May. But Matthew Taylor [Labour Party head of policy] is now here four days a week and he's clearly brilliant. Also it looks as though Lorraine Davidson [a political journalist] is about to join as Scottish director of media, which would be excellent for all concerned. Matthew and I had lunch with her and she seems very keen, despite knowing full well what a nightmare it could be.

The key seats strategy is built on an assumption that we

and the SNP are neck and neck and is very sophisticated. It recognises that in some seats, because of the top-up list system, it doesn't matter if you win or lose, because if you lose you get an extra top-up seat anyway [the top-up list system elects most members in constituencies and then adds so-called 'top-up' seats to make the overall result more proportional to the votes cast]. Donald has come in for a lot of crap of late, but at least it has helped concentrate his and others' minds. So they are now open to a Millbank-style operation being drafted in – though the word McMillbank has been banned. Gordon looked very tired, but all his contributions were very sharp. So, things are looking a lot better than they might have been. It took me away from Number Ten for a day, but that's probably no bad thing.

Yesterday was a bit manic. We had strategy meetings on what to do in August, with Jonathan Powell [chief of staff], and then on the Child Support Agency with Harriet Harman. Two hours after the latter the whole CSA announcement due next Monday was on PA – not part of the strategy. It seems Patricia Hollis [minister of state in the Department of Social Security] briefed some backbenchers who then spilled the beans. Harriet, whom AC won't talk to, has now taken to calling me to complain that she's being unfairly treated and wrongly accused of leaking. Then, just as we were getting on top of that, we heard John Major was making a speech attacking TB for dumbing down politics and being more ready to discuss his views on the World Cup and the Spice Girls rather than the future of manufacturing industry. A bit pathetic on the day TB gave a major speech on the NHS and then flew to Northern Ireland.

We've been in a spat with the BBC all week since AC wrote a letter to *The Times* criticising an article in the paper suggesting ministers were avoiding tough interviews.

In the letter, which I helped a bit with, he was particularly rude about the *World At One* and *Newsnight*. Quite fun to see some of my words taken up in a Labour row with the BBC. AC seems to think it's a great thing to do, although I'm not sure I understand what we get from it, apart from, I guess, keeping the broadcasters a bit on the defensive. PMQs on Wednesday were OK. Hague still off with flu and sinusitis.

Monday, 6 July 1998

Bit of a crisis for the past two days over connections with lobbying companies. The *Observer* did a big exposé on Derek Draper [former aide to Mandelson and Blair in opposition] and other former Labour 'insiders' now running lobbying firms. They had them all claiming to be able to fix meetings, get hold of advance copies of reports, speeches, etc. Roger Liddle, a former business partner of Draper's, was alleged to have said, 'You tell us who you want to see and Derek and I will make the calls.' He now seems unsure whether he said it or not, having had a few glasses of champagne at the reception where he's supposed to have made the offer. David Miliband, his boss, agrees that if it's true and he did say it, he'll have to go.

I dealt with it all day on Sunday from Brighton. Fortunately James was away in Sarajevo. Glen and Tracey [my brother and sister] were down with their kids for tea. They didn't seem to mind the disruption and were very impressed when a call from Blair came through. Opinions very divided in Number Ten about what to do. Everybody agrees Liddle has been a fool, but should he be sacked? I was among those who said he should go on the grounds that it looks as if influence can be bought. Peter M strongly against. Blair so far backing him, but agrees that if he's going to have to go, he should go now. That partly depends on whether the *Observer* have any recordings. At first it seemed they did, now it appears they don't have the killer quote on tape.

Peter is in trouble himself because Derek said he sent his newspaper column to him every week. The papers are now going through them suggesting that whatever Derek said was authorised by Peter. At TB's political strategy meeting this morning he said he was very concerned to put an end to Blair-Brown split stories. Unfortunately Gordon's lot fuel them all the time. It seems the reshuffle may be more extensive than originally planned. AC says Mo simply isn't up to the job and he's amazed that she has been so highly praised. I suggested she might make a good party chairman, but AC said she just didn't have the political nous for it.

Friday, 10 July 1998

End of an amazing week. Claimed by some, including sympathetic outsiders, to be TB's worst week in office. Hague, back from illness, said that despite his sinus problems he could smell the stench from the lobbying allegations. He was making generalised charges of cronyism, and virtually all the specific allegations have now been rebutted with greater or lesser success. Most people probably still believe that Roger Liddle was willing to make calls and arrange meetings with and/or for Draper. I certainly believe that, despite spending all week defending him. I think he should have resigned saying he'd done nothing wrong but acknowledging that his presence was damaging the government. AC certainly wants rid of him and seems to think it's only a matter of time. Peter has been in full Peter-mode trying to defend him. TB says he thinks Roger is gabby and naïve, but not corrupt or dishonest. But he's more than just gabby and naïve: he's also willing to help his friends in the lobbying business. He doesn't stand to gain, so it's not corruption, but it's plainly unacceptable. Anyway, TB said he wasn't going to ruin his life and his livelihood by sacking him based on unproved allegations. So it's all been highly damaging and we're just waiting to see what happens with the papers this Sunday. Peter must be feeling very exposed. Ben Wegg-Prosser, and possibly Peter too, has been advising Draper on how to play it. Sadly Draper won't disappear quietly and will be on *Newsnight* again tonight, having already done it once this week.

I've actually very much enjoyed the week. I had a gossipy chat with Mo when she left a meeting with Orangemen at Number Ten because she just couldn't take any more. Met [culture secretary] Chris Smith's PPS [parliamentary private secretary], Fiona McTaggart, for lunch and said he should toughen up his act.

On the reshuffle, Michael Meacher [environment minister] has been told – after Draper claimed he would be out – that he'll be staying. Makes me wonder whether the reshuffle will be earlier than expected. It's pencilled in for the last week in July.

Wednesday, 15 July 1998

Heading down to Brighton for my mega positive vetting. Should be fun. The weekend was pretty busy. Lots of calls related to the *Observer*'s second week of 'revelations' – made far easier by the fact that they didn't have any. But I was still on the phone a lot.

By Monday Peter was feeling very vulnerable and exposed, because the best the *Observer* had come up with was that his office had been regularly sending (unclassified) faxes to Draper. Derek and Ben Wegg-Prosser were obviously in very close contact, but at the time it must have seemed perfectly above board. Draper has now been dropped by *Progress* magazine [a New Labour journal] but still seems keen to do endless interviews. But at today's Prime Minister's Questions there was no mention of sleaze or cronyism, so I guess we're winning.

TB did loads of interviews this morning, including the Nicky Campbell phone-in on Five Live at my suggestion, and it was barely raised. Attention is now focused on yesterday's Comprehensive Spending Review, which added forty billion pounds to health and education spending over the next three years. That went very well. The markets didn't think it was extravagant, but it sounded like loads of dosh.

I've been getting involved in the NEC [National Executive Committee] elections – a bit outside what I should really be doing, but we have to stop a left-wing slate getting elected in the constituency section. Also trying to help Lorraine in Scotland as much as possible.

Thursday, 16 July 1998

The vetting man turned out to be a pussy cat. Easily convinced that I am and always have been a fine, upstanding member of society.

Monday, 27 July 1998

Back at work after a week's holiday in Sweden. It wasn't particularly relaxing, lots of travelling around islands, staying in youth hostels, etc. The weather was a bit mixed, but it was good fun and a real joy to have a week with James free of pagers and mobile phones.

The reshuffle has been fun, but I've felt a bit outside it all. It was hard not to give anything away when former BBC colleagues and others rang to find out who was in and who was out. Harriet Harman is out completely, along with David Clark, Gavin Strang and Lord Richard (who took it very badly). Peter has gone to the Department of Trade and Industry. Very good for him. 'The secretary of state for Smugness,' says AC, as pictures of Peter walking down Whitehall appear on TV. Margaret Beckett took her move to leader of the House badly – she was being comforted by Anji Hunter in the gents' when I went in for a pee. Jack Cunningham is the new head of the Cabinet Office, so I'll be having a lot to do with him. I like him and he knows how to deliver a message. Ann Taylor is chief whip and Baroness [Margaret] Jay is leader in the Lords. Nick Brown goes to MAFF [the Ministry of Agriculture, Fisheries and Food]. It's a very good team, I think, though it's being portrayed as a reverse for Gordon. He's refused to do a photocall with Peter and Stephen Byers (the new chief secretary to the Treasury). Peter was very keen to do it, which kind of suggests he just wanted to crow. But it hasn't all gone against Gordon. This morning Geoffrey Robinson was to be sacked. Now it seems he has survived – a clear climb-down by Blair. Frank Field has resigned in a flounce because he wasn't offered a cabinet job. Otherwise things have gone pretty smoothly.

Tuesday, 28 July 1998

Quite fun to see my briefings on junior ministerial appointments being used on the media. Robin Oakley on the BBC: 'I have been able to discover that . . .' etc. Gordon apparently blames AC completely for the coverage suggesting it's all a triumph for Blair over Brown. It was inevitable that it would be portrayed that way, and actually it's not such a bad message to get across.

Today was Jack Cunningham's first in charge of the Cabinet Office, and first chairing the 09.00 morning meeting. It was a real embarrassment with little personal anecdotes, comments on the likes of Barbara Castle and Jim Callaghan, little spiels about Sellafield (in his constituency) and MAFF (his former department), but very little focus on what we were there for. AC and I exchanged exasperated glances and everybody was pretty horrified afterwards.

Monday, 3 August 1998

AC and TB are now on holiday and Godric and I are running the show. Not a particularly heroic start with a rather fluffed announcement that Gus Macdonald is to be the new Scottish industry minister and inadequate trailing of another story on sex tourism.

TB went off on Saturday, penning a note to me in mid-flight about answering a *Times* editorial accusing the government of lacking direction. Stephen Byers instantly wrote a response but *The Times* weren't interested in carrying a piece. So it may end up as a letter.

Much of the last week has been overshadowed by Frank Field's departure from government. We tried to have a fairly measured response, but anonymous cabinet ministers gave the papers some pretty damning quotes. So it looked like Number Ten coming heavy, which was never the intention. It occurs to me we now have three gay cabinet ministers: Chris [Smith], Peter [Mandelson] and Nick [Brown].

I've been dealing directly with more and more ministers as the best way of getting things done quickly. Alistair Darling [the new social security secretary] over welfare reform, Peter, of course, Margaret Jay on Lords reform, Byers. John Prescott came in today for his first day 'in charge'. His political judgement seems very sound.

Monday, 10 August 1998

One week on and we're still surviving. No real August horrors at all so far and we've managed to keep a steady stream of quite good stories going. A row involving Peter and the proposed BA/American Airlines merger continued all week, with allegations of a conflict of interest because of [BA chief executive] Bob Ayling's involvement with the Millennium Dome, for which Peter is also responsible. Peter briefed me by phone so at the morning meeting with Prescott I had a different line from the official one. Not surprisingly John said that wasn't good enough. Oops. He clearly still sees me as a Mandelson stooge. But we've been getting on fine and I continue to be impressed by his political judgement. On Wednesday I urged John to get involved in a photo opportunity with some kids in the Downing Street garden. Others said it was too risky, given his ability to speak before he thinks, but it went off very well.

Some of the press officers have complained to Godric that I was going over their heads to departments and that I was asking them to do things when I wasn't their boss. I've backed off a bit, but if I didn't push things they wouldn't happen.

Tuesday, 11 August 1998

Fairly rocky twenty-four hours, although with surprisingly little damage done politically. Job losses continue to fuel the story that manufacturing industry is in recession. Five hundred jobs went today at BOC. Last night no minister was willing to go up on the media to put the government's case. Peter at the DTI was about to go on holiday and, besides, apparently he has some BOC shares that he's trying to dispose of. Byers argued that we shouldn't put a cabinet minister up every time, and there was effectively nobody else available. I spoke to Byers twice, including a final call on my mobile outside the Albert Hall at ten thirty last night, having been to the Proms at the invitation of the BBC. But he wouldn't budge. In the end Prescott was doing interviews on another matter and handled the jobs story very well. But, as expected, he was furious at the buck-passing and spoke to Byers personally this morning. So the overall effect was good. Prescott did the business on the *Today* programme, Byers has been doing interviews ever since and everybody has got the message that they can't shirk these things. We were left with nobody on *News at Ten* last night, which isn't good, but that was the only real casualty.

The Prom was fun with Richard Ayre and Guy [his partner], Ben [Bradshaw MP] and Neal [his partner], George Alagiah and his wife, Frances. Very hot and a mixed bag of stuff, but enjoyable none the less. I broke it to Ben that I'd stolen Phil, his researcher, to be press officer for the NEC election campaign and he wasn't too happy. We continue to run a clandestine campaign from Number Ten and Millbank, but Phil is needed to give us cover.

Wednesday, 12 August 1998

Nice afternoon/evening yesterday in Brighton – I even got to the beach, the gym and to have a drink with Mum and Dad. A bit weird talking to a cabinet minister while on the beach, but I'm sure Mr Byers wouldn't have minded if he'd known! I had to be up very early to get the train back to London this morning.

A little ploy worked wonders overnight. Rehashing some old figures on 'fat cats'' pay in the utilities, so that when the Bank of England report came out today suggesting the minimum wage would cause a blip in inflation we could talk about fat cats instead. In fact the Tories didn't pick up on the minimum wage anyway. Long chat with Blair on the phone from Tuscany. He's very exercised about a *Telegraph* reporter who's been writing rubbish about him from over there.

Friday, 14 August 1998

Travelling home to Brighton rather later than expected, having had to deal with a minor crisis. TB was on the phone again this morning from Tuscany complaining about the *Telegraph* reporter, Bruce Johnston. He's been writing what Blair regards as complete lies about their relationship with their hosts, Prince Strozzi and his wife, and about the reaction they've been getting from local people. I helped rewrite a letter from the prince to the *Telegraph* this morning. TB is also thinking about complaining to the editor. One of the garden girls [secretaries] out there phoned me to say the Strozzis have been videoing everything (including, apparently, Tony during communion until the Special Branch detective blocked the shot), and trying to get him to meet high-ups in the Catholic Church.

Then tonight we heard that the *Telegraph* were planning a story alleging that TB had told the Archbishop of Siena that 'in my heart I feel more of a Catholic'. I phoned both Tony and the American priest who acted as interpreter and both said it wasn't true. TB quite agitated, saying Johnston had really gone too far this time and saying he'd take them to the Press Complaints Commission if they printed it. I duly came on very heavy with the acting editor of the *Telegraph*, Sarah Sands, and she subsequently pulled the story. Triumph. TB had already said that if August continued to go this well I wouldn't be allowed to go on holiday again. I'm sure we haven't heard the last of it, though.

TB also called me in the afternoon to ask if he should invite Fergie for dinner as she'd been pestering him. I said not as she was very publicity-conscious these days. He agreed and said he'd have her to Chequers with Andrew another time. So, an interesting day.

In between I was writing a speech for Tessa Jowell on public health and helping keep control of the party row over the NEC, which was leading the bulletins this morning. We have successfully branded the so-called Grassroots Alliance as hard left, but haven't had as much success raising the profile of our own candidates.

Switch [the Downing Street switchboard] have just rung to say that Derek Draper wants to speak to me before going on *Channel 4 News* to talk about the NEC. I said to tell him I was on the train and couldn't be reached. When all the fuss over lobbyists blew up, one of his boasts was that Number Ten briefed him before interviews, so how he has the gall to ring now beats me.

Monday, 17 August 1998

Quiet weekend, despite (or partly because of) an appalling bomb in Omagh. Twenty-eight dead and two hundred injured. The prime minister went over yesterday and again today. He'd called me on Sunday, before it went off, to thank me for dealing with the Catholicism story and to say how well he thought things were going back home – although he continues to worry about how the economy is being covered. There has been a bit of criticism today about him leaving Northern Ireland early, but it's not a major concern. With Clinton now giving evidence [in his impeachment proceedings] it's hardly big news. But TB was worried about a tip-off we had that the *Sun* is due to criticise him for it tomorrow. More of a concern was the failure of Mo and the Irish justice minister to come up with much by way of a security response. TB, by then continuing his holiday in France, ordered them to go back and come up with something tougher. But when Mo came to deliver it, it didn't come over at all well. AC, who's elsewhere in France, had a bit of a row with her by all accounts. He gave her two out of ten and said she was no longer talking to him.

Thursday, 20 August 1998

The repercussions of the Omagh bomb continue. Both TB and Mo are now back on holiday, and one priority has been to ensure that they can stay there. The Irish have decided to send both the president and Aherne [the prime minister] to a family memorial on Saturday, which has really put us on the spot. Mary McAleese [the Irish president] has already been to one in Madrid for the two Spanish victims and we just sent the ambassador. We hope to be able to cover it with an announcement about a full memorial in a few weeks' time. The Irish cabinet agreed a lot of 'draconian' measures yesterday, some of which will involve recalling the Dáil [the Irish Parliament]. We want to avoid a recall of Parliament, but we may have to do it in order to pass the same stuff. It looks bad, though – some total nutters get lucky with a bomb and Parliament is recalled.

Saturday, 22 August 1998

Slightly fraught couple of days. Mainly over who should attend the Omagh remembrance today. It's not a proper memorial service and the families didn't want loads of VIPs. We were going to send Paul Murphy, [Northern Ireland office minister] not even a secretary of state, but I said that would look awful. I wanted Prescott to go, but others thought that would just raise questions about why TB wasn't there. I thought I was losing the argument but then it was agreed yesterday that John should go.

Clinton launched air strikes against Afghanistan and Sudan on Thursday night. TB gave immediate support, but Robin Cook refused to go on the *Today* programme to defend it, saying there might be collateral damage and it could be difficult. Prescott was furious and did an interview clip himself and phoned Robin to tell him just what he thought. Prescott was very nice at our last meeting, thanking us all for how we'd helped him. I have to say, he's been excellent throughout.

Discussions about proportional representation, etc. Paddy Ashdown [the Liberal Democrat leader] has been in touch with TB in France to talk about proportional representation with a view to keeping the Tories out for a very long time. By all accounts, Ashdown doesn't think he can keep his party in 'constructive opposition' for a whole parliament and wants to be sitting on our side of the House sooner rather than later. He doesn't want us and them fighting each other at by-elections as this will only drive us apart. The plan is for a system of single member constituencies, as now, but with a national top-up to provide 'broad proportionality'. If any party gets 45 per cent of the vote they should be able to have an overall majority – that's broadly proportional apparently. There's a bit of a dispute over how the first batch of MPs should be elected. TB wants first past the post, as now, and Ashdown favours the Alternative Vote, which is more proportional.

The other point of dispute is whether to have a referendum next spring or at the time of the next election. Paddy wants the earlier option obviously. The other option, the Adonis option [Andrew Adonis was the Policy Unit member responsible for the subject] would slow the project down and Paddy believes long-term realignment will only happen if the two parties start working together on the same side of the House as soon as possible. He also argues that it would be wrong to have the referendum with the next election because it would give the Tories the dangerous combination of the single currency and the constitution to campaign on. Absolutely fascinating stuff. Maybe TB is just stringing Paddy along with no intention of going as far as he wants. But it does sound as if a pretty detailed strategy has already been agreed.

Monday, 24 August 1998

A fairly busy weekend on the phone, mainly about Ireland and the US bombings. George Robertson [defence secretary] rang me twice, furious about Robin Cook's refusal to come in behind the government's support of Clinton's missile strikes on 'terrorist targets' in Sudan and Afghanistan on 20 August. The *Mail on Sunday* had some obviously Foreign-Office-inspired stuff about ministers having doubts. AC, who's now back from holiday, less than impressed.

I had a chat with Sally Morgan [head of the Political Office] this morning about PR. She reckons Jenkins [Lord Jenkins was heading a commission on the subject] may not be able to produce a report that we can accept and Labour members on the Jenkins Commission may have to produce a minority report.

Tuesday, 25 August 1998

Parliament was finally recalled today, with TB in Omagh. Much discussion, but he clearly felt it was necessary to make changes to the law watertight. We said it would need to be a pretty substantial package to avoid criticism that we were bringing back MPs for only minor changes. It will now include a Home Office Bill on international terrorism. I spoke to Jack Straw [home secretary] about it. He was the only person able to explain all the legal niceties in layman's language. Mo rang too, concerned that the package shouldn't be dominated by measures against Arab terrorism. Discussions still going on about whether to have phone-tap evidence available in court. Jonathan Powell has been talking to the FBI about it. [It was decided not to change the law in this respect, but to keep the matter under review.] I had a decent chat with Cherie [Blair] for the first time. She's a delight and thanked me for ensuring their holiday wasn't as disrupted as last year.

Bank Holiday Monday, 31 August 1998

I've been on call all day and constantly on the phone. It's mainly Ireland stuff. Trying to reassure people that the new security measures aren't a threat to civil liberties. I've got to the stage where I completely submerge my own views – to such an extent that I sometimes lose contact with what they are.

Tuesday, 15 September 1998

First day back at work after a fantastic holiday in Cape Town to help celebrate my fortieth birthday. TB has been on the phone to Ashdown again. 'Selling the constitution down the river?' I asked, but Sally Morgan said it was quite the reverse.

Monday, 21 September 1998

Watching Clinton's evidence live on TV, with TB just landed in New York and due to see Clinton later today. We've called it TB's 'day trip from hell'. Lots of speeches, to the UN and the NY Stock Exchange, with lots of good stories to try to deflect at least some attention from the Bill/Tony relationship – all to no avail, I'm sure. There's clearly a worry that TB will be tarnished, although I'm not sure that it's a serious problem. We've said he's not a fair-weather friend, and I think most people accept that. So far the Clinton tapes haven't been too damning, but there's a good bit still to come. I didn't do too much briefing this weekend because I didn't want to be asked too much about it all.

Thursday, 24 September 1998

Ready for Conference [the annual Labour Party Conference] and leaving in the morning. But Conference itself is less ready. TB's speech so far is pretty crap and the theme is just 'making progress'. No really fancy announcements so leaving the journalists to write about NEC election reverses, PR, the House of Lords and lots of other unhelpful issues. My week is going to be fairly awful, I think. Mind you, the Liberal Democrats had a rough conference week despite trying to put pressure on us. And the latest opinion poll puts our lead up another eight points – Labour 56 per cent to the Tories' 24 per cent. So we're in a better state than the others.

The PR debate remains fascinating. It seems TB will welcome the Jenkins Commission as the best alternative to first past the post, but there'll be no referendum until after the next election. [The Jenkins Commission had written a report recommending a highly complex system that attempted to provide a more proportional system of electing MPs, without destroying the link to the individual constituencies. The report had been sent to the Prime Minister but was not yet public].

Saturday, 26 September 1998

In Blackpool since yesterday for Conference. It's hard work keeping track of what all the papers are doing. Of course they're looking for defeats and rows. They may well get one over PR as well as the NEC elections.

I found myself in a bit of hot water today, trying to place a story about zero tolerance and crime. AC said to give it to the *Mail on Sunday* but only if they splashed with it. They wouldn't guarantee to do that so I gave it to the *Express* who would. The *Mail on Sunday* has a new editor and we got a bit worried that they'd do a spin doctors' story, so I ended up giving it to them and asking them to attribute it to the Home Office to cover my tracks. Nothing too wicked in that, I suppose.

Wednesday, 30 September 1998

Conference is certainly far more fun on this side of the fence and so far it's been hugely successful. TB's speech yesterday was widely hailed as his best ever. Tough message of no backing down and lots of from-the-heart stuff from Tony about his values, community, etc. He and AC have a regular score sheet of whose soundbites make the news and as usual Alastair won by more than two to one. The speech-writing process wasn't as fraught as I'd expected.

Much hilarity as jokes were bandied about. AC, Peter Hyman and David Miliband are the main contributors. I didn't suggest much or get anything in, although I did advise against bits and edit stuff out. Good to get closer to TB and I have got to know Cherie much better too. On Sunday she said I was looking tanned and handsome, to which Tony said she meant *he* was looking tanned and handsome!

Getting along very well with Margaret McDonagh [the new general secretary of the Labour Party] too. She liked it when I said I didn't like rude people but I did like direct people. She seemed to take it as a huge compliment because everyone says how rude she is. Met Waheed Alli [Labour peer and close friend of McDonagh's], who seems very nice and we exchanged boyfriend stories.

It was the Labour Party gala dinner last night where I met the new woman high commissioner for South Africa, who was charming and very interesting indeed, and Liz Dawn who plays Vera Duckworth on *Coronation Street* – none too bright but quite fun.

As for the politics of the conference, lots of deal-making with the unions behind the scenes to make sure we don't lose votes on the renationalisation of the railways and on PR. On the latter the mood music is all quite hostile with us almost saying, but not quite, that we'll put it off until after the election. Huge ovation for Mo. Farcical scenes this morning as we tried to keep TB and Gerry Adams from bumping into each other while they were both doing interviews for the *Today* programme, breakfast TV, etc. It all worked – I just hope it doesn't become a story.

We've been snubbed rather by Gerhard Schröder, who defeated Kohl in the German elections on Sunday. TB personally invited him to come to Conference when he spoke to him to congratulate him. But he's gone to Paris instead to see Jospin [French prime minister]. So we lied and said we hadn't invited him.

We didn't do too well in the NEC election – two places in the constituency section to the left's four. But we put the results out on Sunday rather than today as would have been usual so it wouldn't drag on as a story and it was pretty much a one-day wonder.

It's been a triumph for spin all week, really. Lots of good stories on the morning of TB's speech, all selectively leaked by me. In fact, an almost universally good press yesterday and today. Trebles all round.

Thursday, 1 October 1998

Pretty knackered all day after a very late night. Went with TB to a dreary Radio 1 reception and to Welsh Night at Conference. Then met up with the BBC crowd for a drink and went to Flamingos [Blackpool's gay club]. Then early this morning I had to deal with a stupid story about some Lloyd's Name 'lunging' at TB last night. In fact, she never get closer than ten feet.

Monday, 5 October 1998

Back in Number Ten after a very nice weekend in Yorkshire with James's family. The conference ended well. Dinner on Thursday night with some key Downing Street people, Bill Bush [BBC head of research] and others. Jonathan Powell, along with Pat McFadden and James Purnell [both in the Policy Unit] and I were rather antisocial at one end while the rest were being jovial at the other end. We discussed London where the chief executive of Lambeth Council is now a front runner for the mayoral candidacy. Ken Livingstone will be excluded at the short-listing stage because we will ask everybody to apply by CV. There's a danger of a write-in campaign for him, though.

Pat says nobody really knows what TB is planning on PR because he has private meetings with Paddy and when he's asked what they discussed he just says, 'Nothing much.'

Jonathan Powell said he'd have liked to be an MP but he reckons it's too late now if he wants to be a cabinet minister.

Friday, 16 October 1998

Politics starting to get back to normal after the conference season and TB's visit to China. It's been a busy week dominated by the Neill Report [into party funding] and House of Lords reform. We're gearing up to the publication of the Jenkins Commission Report too, so all the stuff I'm really into is high on the agenda. Neill was OK, but we let the Tories get away with too much. Mainly because TB and AC decided our response shouldn't be too 'political'. Neill's unexpectedly tough line on referendums was a bit of a shock. He thinks the government shouldn't be able to throw its weight unfairly on either side of the argument. Not helped by Peter Shore [former shadow chancellor] being Labour's person on the committee. He's still smarting at being on the losing side of the referendum [on membership of the EEC] in 1975. So Jack Straw, whom I helped brief, says we'll have to look carefully at that. The main problem will be the referendum on the single currency, although PR could be affected too. Jack himself agrees that both sides should receive equal funding. He says he urged that in Scotland and Wales but Ron Davies [secretary of state for Wales] would have none of it.

I went up to Scotland on Wednesday. It's in a real mess. I did a note for TB about it today. Basically Helen Liddle [minister in the Scottish Office] is not bashing the nationalists enough. Everything is too low-key. She does no interviews and holds no news conferences. The plan is for TB to tell her things have to change in a private meeting on Wednesday and then go straight into a wider strategy meeting when he announces it publicly so she can't wriggle out of it. She'll have to attend party HQ every morning, chair proper Scottish strategy meetings and generally do the business.

The House of Lords reform was debated in the Lords

itself on Wednesday and Thursday. Margaret Jay is being very effective and we're getting the debate back on to our territory.

Jenkins remains fascinating. Paddy is threatening to leave politics if we put off the referendum in this parliament. This seems to be having some effect on TB and risks leaving us with a rather confused response when the report comes out. TB wants to say that while he's still not persuaded, he's more persuaded than he was because Jenkins has produced a very 'persuasive' report. It's basically the Alternative Vote-plus, but with two votes, which I reckon is far too confusing for most people. It's obviously a fudge. Peter Mandelson has been having talks with Richard Holmes [a key ally of Paddy Ashdown in the Liberal Democrats] and others, and nobody on our side really knows what he's been saying.

Monday, 19 October 1998

The serialisation has begun of [Labour's polling guru] Philip Gould's book *The Unfinished Revolution*. He's very anxious about how it's going down and calls regularly. In fact, because it plays down personality splits and is very helpful in saying Peter Mandelson was genuinely torn over the Blair/Brown succession, it hasn't generated a lot of interest. I don't know yet if Gordon's crew will buy that line but it fits in with my recollection of events.

Helen Liddle also rang me today, clearly worried about what people had been telling me last week and, not very convincingly, trying to convince me that she wasn't the problem. I've got a horrible feeling that I'm going to get drawn into all their internal squabbles in Scotland and I'm not interested in them.

Peter rings me to say there's no truth in the rumour that he's lurching to the left by applauding the arrest of [Chilean ex-dictator General] Pinochet in London at the weekend. [He had said most people would find what Pinochet did when in power 'gut-wrenching'.] 'There's method in everything I do,' he says. Unfortunately, it seems the Spanish, who've requested Pinochet's extradition to Madrid, may not have a very strong case. So it could all prove very embarrassing.

AC went off to a meeting on the honours list saying, 'Who can we give gongs to to get a good story?' or words to that effect. He also reports back on a meeting with Martin McGuinness. A new adviser to Sinn Féin asked TB for a signature on a piece of Number Ten notepaper for a friend. TB signs: 'Dear John, Good luck, Tony Blair.' AC says: 'Let's hope it's not for someone with a contract out on Paisley'!

Wednesday, 21 October 1998

Much speculation about who briefed the *Sun* and others that TB had slapped down Peter over his Pinochet remarks. Suspicion inevitably falls on Charlie [Whelan], who was a bit shifty this morning. It's a story that damages both TB and Peter, so it would suit Gordon and his allies very well. They have been out rubbishing Philip Gould's account of the leadership battle, which suggests they still don't accept what happened. We prepare for PMQs today. The accepted wisdom is that Hague is good at it and TB is crap. So we decided to suggest quietly about the place that Hague is actually a rather sad bastard who focuses solely on PMQs and tries to score some points rather than focusing on what people really care about or, indeed, getting the big decisions right with respect to his own party. In the event he wasn't great today and PMQs was a bit of a draw.

It's Peter's birthday so I sent him a pager message saying, 'I hope you're drinking Chilean wine.'

Thursday, 22 October 1998

Still trying to get the line straight on next week's Jenkins Report. It can't be done because TB hasn't agreed it. But it's clear he wants to be a lot warmer than Straw wants to be on behalf of the whole government. Peter is clearly playing an important role in urging him towards a more positive response.

There's a bit of a problem developing over the briefing Margaret Beckett [leader of the House of Commons] does on the record after PMQs on a Thursday. Today she strayed into dangerous territory on referendums and Peter's comments on Pinochet. I phoned her but she got very snooty, telling me she had a reputation for not putting her foot in it and generally implying I was some little eek who shouldn't be telling her how to do her job.

AC's ideas for honours included Naomi Campbell or Kate Moss, David Bowie, Sebastian Faulks, David Hare and one of John Humphrys, Jeremy Paxman or Jon Snow! My suggestions included Helen Rollason, the TV sportscaster who's dying of cancer.

Saturday, 24 October 1998

Papers full of the fuss over an article by Carlos Menem [president of Argentina] in yesterday's *Sun*. Allegations that AC either wrote it or had a big hand in it. It ran under the headline 'Argentina Says Sorry', but then Menem in Buenos Aires said expressing 'deep regret' (which he did) was different from saying 'sorry' (which he didn't). Unfortunately the article bore some very strong resemblances to one by the Japanese prime minister, Hashimoto, back in January, which AC also helped 'facilitate'.

Wednesday, 28 October 1998

In the middle of probably the most exciting week since I came into Downing Street. The resignation of a cabinet minister, Jenkins on PR, Pinochet and a variety of other stories. Not an easy week so far but a strangely enjoyable one.

On Monday TB was just back from a fairly uneventful European summit in Austria. He's very keen to step up efforts to build alliances in Europe. Doesn't want to be isolated long-term and accepts that we can't be wholly involved until we join the euro. He says the rest of Europe is expecting us to join. Jonathan [Powell] and AC are seen as the best people to go off to other capitals and send the message on behalf of TB himself. So AC is off to Germany on Friday. Even so we have had to heavily water down a speech Peter is planning to make in the North West. The original, drafted by Roger Liddle, is incredibly gushing about the euro, even implying that people would be better off investing in the euro area. I did the editing, at first against Peter's will and then with his acquiescence after Jonathan had spoken to him.

On Jenkins, TB who, until now, has been officially 'unpersuaded' of the need for change, says, 'I believe there is a case for reform.' But he acknowledges there's no enthusiasm for it either in the party or the country. In fact he says, 'The country doesn't give a fuck about PR.' TB, Jack Straw, John Prescott and Robin Cook are the key players but the only thing they agree on is that there can be no change until after the next election. TB's attitude to what Lord Jenkins has proposed is basically 'yes, unless we look at it and conclude that it's not a good idea', whereas Prescott takes exactly the opposite view. TB's long-term aim is to see Labour and the Lib Dems move closer together. His short-term aim is to get through the parliament without a referendum while keeping the Lib Dems on board. But none of the big beasts want a row. The report comes out in just over twelve hours' time and the line is still not agreed, even though we've been talking about it for weeks.

I saw Paddy in the House today and he seemed very chipper, said his party wouldn't do anything stupid and he believed the goodwill was there on the part of the government.

I had to go and see Margaret Beckett on Monday evening because apparently my phone call last week upset her. But she was sweetness and light when I saw her.

Tuesday was going fairly calmly until it became obvious that something big was about to break. All very hush-hush, but I managed to work out it was about Ron Davies and was personal. My mind immediately went back to a conversation I had with a Welsh guy in Flamingos during Conference. He said to me that Ron regularly cottages in a service station on the M4 on his way back to Wales on a Thursday night. When I said I didn't believe he could get away with it, so it couldn't be true, he said, 'Find out if Ron Davies has a G-reg gold Granada.' Well, on Monday night he left his G-reg gold Granada near Clapham Common, went for a walk, met a total stranger, agreed to go off with him, picked up two of the guy's friends and ended up being robbed at knifepoint, losing his wallet, mobile phone and car. He reported it to the police straight away.

On Tuesday morning Jack Straw heard about it from the police and alerted Downing Street. Ron was called in and said he went for a walk because he was under pressure, his wife was ill, he'd been dealing with floods in Wales and needed some fresh air. At one point he said, significantly, that when he's in his own car he feels he's just plain Ron Davies and not the secretary of state for Wales. TB and AC quickly conclude that he must resign for a 'serious lapse of judgement', although Ron denied it had anything to do with gay sex or drugs. He fiercely resisted but was eventually persuaded that he had to go.

The story we put out was significantly different. That the first we'd heard about the incident was from Ron himself and that he concluded he should resign, which TB then agreed to. The media all knew there must be more to it than they'd been told. It took until lunchtime to convince them that actually we agreed with them, but that we didn't have any more salient facts than they had. Which was true.

There's also now the question of whether he can still be the party's candidate for first secretary in Wales in next year's elections. As of now he apparently still thinks he can be, although we all know it's not tenable. He's hidden away somewhere with Hilary Coffman [another special adviser in the press office] to keep him from the press. But he plans to tell his constituency party on Friday that he has a mandate and intends to carry on. The question is how to stop him. There are no rules, but we don't want a divided Welsh Labour Party to turn against interfering London and either back Ron or the candidate he beat for the nomination, Rhodri Morgan. Alun Michael, Ron's successor as secretary of state, is trying to avoid being drafted in as first secretary, but it seems the most likely option.

In the wake of it all, Peter Mandelson was outed on *Newsnight* last night by Matthew Parris. Incidentally I hear that Nick Brown [agriculture minister] has denied to TB that he's gay too, going directly against what I've been told by gay journalists. There's a lot more to come out, with no pun intended.

Friday, 30 October 1998

Things have been moving on apace. Late yesterday Ron announced he was standing down as candidate for first secretary. As before, we said it was entirely his own decision, but AC played a big part in it, asking him if he really could stand up to all the media questions he'd have to face. He's been holed up at a Center Parcs place with his wife and daughter and Hilary, sleeping badly and pretty low. Refusing to read the newspapers. Hilary described it as being a bit like being in *The Prisoner* – lots of chalets and no real communication with the outside world. She's been making him wear a hood or hat when he goes out for walks, which he's been doing a lot. His wife, Chris, has been brilliant and very supportive but worried about what Ron might do to himself. Lots of lurid tales on the grapevine and from journalists about what he has been up to but none have appeared in print yet.

The political problem has been how to replace him as Labour candidate [in the first Welsh Assembly elections]. Rhodri Morgan, who ran him close, is so unacceptable to TB that he's out of the question. So Alun Michael has been told it will have to be him. Not a happy man. Just got his place in the cabinet only to be told he's going to be exiled to Wales from next May. *If* we can get him selected. Efforts to buy off Rhodri are mooted and TB will speak to him on Monday. Officially, of course, Number Ten is keeping out of it. One of those occasions when telling the whole truth has not been an option.

Interestingly, Ron was interviewed by the Beeb tonight and refused to deny he was gay, saying he'd never preached about morality and thought everyone was entitled to a private life. He still insisted that sex and drugs were not involved.

The general outing of Peter has continued in the papers,

which may be no bad thing. I also got involved in advising David Clelland, one of the Labour whips, in announcing that he'd left his wife for his secretary. And today we were briefing the Sunday papers on next week's Green Paper on the family!

John Birt [director general of the BBC] has been in touch. He wants to stop BBC Scotland doing their own *Six o'Clock News* on TV and wants help leaking an internal BBC survey that shows most Scots don't want it.

The publication of the Jenkins Report went down fairly well in the end. TB was pretty warm about it, Paddy was happy, but Jack Straw did most of the interviews and was negative about the timing of the referendum because of the complexity of the scheme.

Monday, 2 November 1998

Sunday papers pretty ghastly on Ron Davies. The *News of the World* had various eyewitness accounts of his cottaging and cruising – notably at the place off the M4 that the guy at Conference told me about. The *Sunday Times* said he was approached by his assailants again the morning after the attack. The *Express* tracked down Reinaldo [da Silva, Peter Mandelson's partner] in Japan where he's studying and did a totally gratuitous number on 'Peter's Friend'.

Today Ron is about to do a bizarre personal statement to the House of Commons about his 'moment of madness', which will do nothing to resolve the matter. He faxed it to us this morning and it's mainly an attack on the press without any explanation of what really happened. AC has been talking to him but without much success, trying to get him to change the tone of it. Endless comment pieces in the papers about Peter and coming out, fuelled by a memo from Anne Sloman [chief political adviser at the

BBC] saying there should be no more on-air discussions of Peter's private life. Norman Tebbit has a letter in the *Telegraph* this morning, saying homosexuals are like the masons, helping each other get jobs (and yet he says we should keep our sexuality to ourselves) and there should never be a gay home secretary.

Very little discussion of all this in the office, though. TB more concerned that Rhodri should be dealt with. The Welsh Executive [of the Labour Party] may be called upon to impose Alun Michael. TB has offered Rhodri the post of deputy to Alun but he rejected it, so Prescott may have another go. There's always the danger, of course, that he'll accuse us of trying to cut a deal. But he must be feeling very confident of success if we're reduced to bargaining with him.

TB is also concerned that we're not getting our message across on the New Deal [Labour's programme to get people off benefits and into work] and welfare reform. He described coverage of the Jenkins Report as a 'master of spinology', but he's worried that in the longer term what we said was so impudent that it was unreasonable. He wants to avoid that by moving quickly to offer something more to the Lib Dems – notably extending the remit of the Joint Consultation Committee [a cabinet committee that, unprecedentedly, included Liberal Democrats and which mainly discussed constitutional reform] to include maybe education and pensions reform. He wants a proposal he can send to Paddy tonight: 'I don't want co-operation with the Lib Dems to crumble away after our body swerve on PR.'

On education, he's worried that our rhetoric is not being matched by reality and that we need to be more radical to improve standards more quickly. Maybe even abolish all LEAs [local education authorities] as Chris Woodhead [chief inspector of schools] would like.

On David Blunkett, TB says, 'He talks a good New Labour game, but is pretty Old Labour in delivery.' The Education Department [DfEE] has lost a bit of momentum since Stephen Byers [who was school standards minister] was promoted to the cabinet. 'Every time I hear something from the DfEE I say yes, but give me five helpings of that.'

Ron's personal statement is distracting attention from Gordon and Peter at the CBI trying to outdo each other on pro-European rhetoric. Peter says we will join the euro when it's in Britain's interests (no mention of 'if' these days). All this makes people very edgy because apparently News International are under the impression we won't make any changes without asking them.

Wednesday, 4 November 1998

Heavily engaged in yet another undercover operation, and one that could prove every bit as successful as our efforts to swing the NEC elections! Two meetings today to see how we can advance Alun Michael in Wales. He scored 5 per cent to Rhodri's 33 per cent in the first opinion poll, so it'll be an uphill struggle. The initial ploy is to call publicly on Rhodri to join a unity ticket, which I predict he'll reject in one second flat. The unions will then be crucial in trying to help Alun win. But the MPs, MEPs, candidates and constituency parties, who are all part of the electoral college, will need a huge effort to win them over. TB makes it increasingly clear that, for reasons nobody quite understands, he won't accept Rhodri. Yesterday, at long last, was my farewell dinner from the BBC. Quite good fun, although John Sergeant [chief political correspondent] got into one of his tedious lecturing modes and I had to move seats to get away from him. Robin Oakley [political editor] made a very nice speech and I think mine went down well – basically a piss-take on Ron Davies – my 'moment of madness' at walking away from the BBC, etc. Slightly bad taste, but what the hell?

Saturday, 7 November 1998

From politics back to sex again very swiftly. As Alun Michael's campaign in Wales gets off to a very shaky start (three to one of Labour's Assembly candidates backing Rhodri in a BBC poll yesterday), we continue to be battered with allegations of a cover-up over Ron Davies, and another 'gay scandal' quite possibly about to break. On Ron, it comes down to AC saying, 'No,' when asked at the lobby if Number Ten had had any contact with the police before TB saw Ron. The truth is that John Stevens, deputy commissioner at Scotland Yard, did come on the line at one point but he didn't add a great deal to what we knew for sure, so when we said we had 'no salient facts' that we didn't give the media I think that was fair enough. The best line that has never emerged was when one of the police officers who went to the scene said to Ron, 'Are you a mini-cab driver, because there have been a lot of attacks on mini-cab drivers?' and Ron replied, 'No, I'm the secretary of state for Wales.' He clearly hoped, and still hopes, that no more details will come out, which shows a quaint naïvety about the Metropolitan Police, which, true to form, has been leaking all over the place ever since it happened.

I had already become the office expert on cruising, cottaging, etc., but I was yet to come into my own. AC's door was shut with something heavy being discussed inside and I knocked and went in, thinking it was more Ron. There was a problem with another cabinet minister, Nick Brown. It appeared that the *News of the World* was about to expose him, that they had tapes and videos, and that other papers – *The Times* and the *Telegraph* – were on to it too. This was all late on Thursday afternoon. TB was on his way to Sedgefield [his constituency in the north of England], Jonathan Powell was about to fly to America in the morning to tell his kids that his new partner was having a baby, and AC was planning a day off on Friday. Nick himself was in Madrid on business and couldn't be contacted. So yesterday, Friday, I was in the thick of it. AC drafted a provisional statement at home and faxed it over to me. Nick was found and asked to come and see Sir Richard Wilson [the cabinet secretary] as soon as he got back from Spain. It was agreed that I should sit in on the interview with Nick because I'd know the right questions to ask, was more likely to spot problems with his account, and might get more out of him as a sympathetic character whom he knew to be gay. The implication was that AC might lead him into the kind of denial mode we'd seen with Ron Davies.

In fact, as it turned out, Nick was as honest as he could be, although Sir Richard certainly felt that I had come up with a lot of questions that wouldn't have occurred to him. [In essence, Nick had had a lengthy relationship with a younger man to whom he'd given gifts occasionally but had not paid. The man had then tried to blackmail him into giving him money, which Nick had refused to do.] After the meeting, Nick went back to his department while we waited for TB to get back from his constituency.

He arrived at seven thirty in the evening and spoke to Sir Richard and me. His attitude was that, while we couldn't be totally sure what was going to come out, we should stick by him. He'd done nothing wrong. No 'serious lapse of judgement' like Ron. If it had been a younger woman and he'd given her gifts or money sometimes, no one would say anything. We had to apply the same tests if it was a gay or straight relationship. We then struggled to find Nick. He turned up twenty minutes later, having been in the Marquis of Granby [a popular Westminster pub] with his regular Friday-night drinking chums. He recounted his story again to TB, though, sadly, a bit less coherently, thanks to a whisky in Sir Richard's office and a couple of pints in the pub. TB made it very clear that the one thing that would destroy him was if he wasn't telling the whole truth. TB was privately a bit disappointed that Nick hadn't told him he was gay when he appointed him chief whip in 1997. TB had asked him if he was part of a Newcastle gay circle [he is MP for Newcastle East]. Rather disingenuously he'd replied no, and if he was part of a Newcastle party circle he'd rather it was a heterosexual one.

Monday, 9 November 1998

Having spent all weekend working to keep Nick in his job, and succeeding, I'm totally knackered but pleased I was entrusted with so much responsibility by TB and AC. In fact, for the first time I know more about the whole story than anyone, except, of course, Nick and even he doesn't know all the comings and goings.

Tuesday, 10 November 1998

Lots more praise today for the way I handled it all, and I do feel as if I've been through the wringer. Though nothing compared to how Nick must feel. I had him with me in Westcroft Square [my London flat] for well over twenty-four hours continuously over the weekend. He arrived about midday on Saturday to discuss what we might say if the *News of the World* did come to us and say they had the story.

When he first arrived I was starting to think we were in the clear. AC had spoken to Phil Hall [editor of the *News of the* World] on Friday night and had been told they were short of a lead story because something about *Coronation Street* stars had fallen down. AC was inclined to believe him and we had heard nothing more. So we started drafting something for Nick just as a precaution, saying he was gay but had never paid for sex. Then AC called on Saturday, after Nick had arrived at my place, to say he'd been rung by a *News of the World* reporter, Neville Thurwell, and would I call Thurwell back? He was very polite but said they had a major story. Nick had had a lengthy relationship with a rent-boy who had been routinely paid £100 to engage in sado-masochistic sex. Nick looked devastated when I told him and said it was bad enough having to deal with the truth, without total lies like that. Could he sue? What about the Press Complaints Commission? I had no choice but to question him pretty firmly to see if there was anything he hadn't told us. He insisted not. He was, and has always been, 100 per cent consistent. I had to make a pretty swift judgement, as AC and TB would clearly take my advice. I decided I believed him. Even then he'd have resigned if I said I didn't think we could go on defending him. But I called AC and told him the whole story and that I believed him. Was I sure? I could never be 100 per cent sure, but I was as certain as I'd ever been since Thursday, perhaps even a little more so. Who knows whether AC wondered if we were two gay guys conspiring to stick to a story we both knew to be a lie? AC had clearly to talk to TB who came back and spoke to both Nick and me. We decided that I should see how late the *News of the World* could wait before we gave them a statement while AC spoke again to Phil Hall.

The answer was 17.00–17.15. So we called Nick's special adviser, Kieran Simpson, and asked him to come over. We knew he might have to do some TV so Nick and I went out to buy him some fresh clothes from M&S. On the way we had to stop and take another call on my mobile from TB and Sir Richard. Very odd standing in M&S while Nick chose his clothes, thinking, 'If only all these shoppers knew what was going on'.

Kieran picked us up outside the shop just in time to get back to the flat and phone over Nick's statement to the *News of the World*. Shortly afterwards AC rang to say that they weren't going to run it in the first edition, but would do it our way, featuring Nick's statement in later editions. AC found himself negotiating the text and, in effect, helping to write the piece. We put out a statement from TB saying, 'Nick Brown has given a full account of his relationship to the prime minister and the prime minister is satisfied with that account' (not exactly warm backing but it did the trick). It hit the wires just as the *NoW* was about to publish its second edition, so the Beeb had it in time for their late bulletin.

So, in the event the news reached the great British people in the most positive light in the circumstances via the BBC. I then had to deal with numerous calls, Nick sitting rather glumly on the sofa or making calls to some of his mates. About a third of the cabinet must have rung over the weekend, with Mo, Gordon and Stephen Byers being particularly supportive. I even called Paddy Ashdown whom I knew was appearing on *Breakfast with Frost* to brief him – treating him almost like a member of the government! He didn't waste the opportunity to lobby me about moving on quickly with the next stage of the 'project' [co-operation between the two parties leading, possibly, to a coalition].

By midnight Kieran had gone and Nick and I had a drink and watched the end of *The Blues Brothers* on TV. We chatted about great movies, etc., and while I was desperate to go to bed, it was obviously doing him good to talk about something else. Eventually he slept on a roll-out bed on the living room floor for a few hours.

In the morning the papers were pretty good all round, with only the *Mail* being a bit snide. Loads more calls from journalists on Sunday, of course, most wanting to know who knew what and when. None of which we answered. There were two questions we did have to address, though. Should Nick go ahead with his regional tour on Monday and Tuesday and should he talk to the media that very day? I was firmly in favour of both, although TB was initially against him speaking. I said he had to or otherwise his tour would be overshadowed by 'If you've done nothing wrong why won't you talk to us, Minister?' My view prevailed in the end and we did an organised doorstep [basically a tip-off to a journalist that if they happen to be in a certain place at a certain time they will catch the minister] with the BBC outside the Agriculture Department. ITN were furious because the BBC had got the interview on the day Ron Davies resigned too. So I had to fib a bit and say that Kieran had organised it.

The *Sun* rang to say they had a tape of Nick talking to a rent-boy. Nick said straight away that this must have been a call that came to him during the election campaign. He'd played it very straight and told the caller to put anything he had to say in writing because he suspected it was being recorded. I spoke to the *Sun*'s night editor and she agreed that the guy didn't seem reliable and they wouldn't be running the story. But they would be linking the Nick and Ron stories. It turned out to be 'Tell us the truth, Tony. Are we being run by a gay Mafia?'

A very interesting sequence of events followed, with the *Sun* very much being put on the back foot and eventually having to say they would never 'out' anybody again, while at the same time sacking Matthew Parris as a columnist for outing Peter!

Peter seems to have survived it all OK. I had dinner with him on Thursday night, when I knew about Nick but couldn't tell him. Martin Dowle [former BBC political correspondent, now representing the British Council in Rio de Janeiro] was there too with his Brazilian partner, Fabricio, during a short visit from Rio. Peter was furious about how the *Express* had behaved with regard to Reinaldo. They had got into his hall of residence in Japan by pretending to be friends of his father, then lied their way into his room by saying they were from the university authorities. He eventually twigged when they asked him if he was a friend of Peter's. In fact he handled himself brilliantly and said nothing he shouldn't have, but what a bunch of shits.

Saturday, 14 November 1998

Having a very nice quiet day after a totally exhausting week. Yet more praise for my work with Nick. AC called it a brilliant job and Anji Hunter and Sally Morgan were very complimentary too. More calls from journalists during the week with unsubstantiated stories about Nick. He said they were being put about by his enemies in Newcastle. So, by getting heavy with the *Mail* and others we ensured nothing appeared. But we still have tomorrow's Sunday papers to look forward to.

TB has been keen to get us all out reminding people about the political record of both Ken Livingstone and Rhodri Morgan.

On Wednesday after PMQs, at which nobody really shone, we put out a joint statement from TB and Paddy agreeing to extend the scope of the Joint Consultation Committee. TB was almost in hysterics in the office, saying there had to be a news blackout on the story in Buenos Aires where John Prescott is attending a climate-change conference. With regard to extending cooperation with the Lib Dems, John had said to him emphatically before he left, 'No way, I'm not going down that road' and TB had replied, 'So can I take that as a tentative yes, then?' He jokes about it all the time, but given the political risk he's taking he obviously thinks it's really important. So we spend our time trying to play it down, while the Lib Dems around Paddy are busy playing it up. It didn't go down at all well with most of our MPs and in the party in the country, but TB clearly thinks it's the right thing to do.

Thursday and Friday we spent in Scotland, which was great for me. My first flight with TB and very close to him throughout. He felt he really had to go for the Nationalists because Donald [Dewar, secretary of state for Scotland and candidate for first minister] wasn't brave enough to. He'd been pathetic at a meeting on Scotland we had in London on Tuesday. A total wimp, with Alex Rowley [general secretary in Scotland] no better and Helen [Liddle] only marginally more convincing. Gordon, on the other hand, was superb as ever. AC is hoping to get Charlie [Whelan] working for the Football Association and out of our hair. Lots of good-humoured banter on the plane on the way home from Scotland. TB said to me, 'I hope you don't mind me asking you this, but when you see a beautiful woman doesn't it do anything for you?' So I explained as best I could!

Sunday, 22 November 1998

Having a fairly quiet weekend after another busy week, and another which involved more attention on the so-called 'gay Mafia'. *Punch* published a long piece alleging that when Peter was in Rio recently on official business he went with Martin and Fabricio to a number of outrageous gay venues, including a bar called Le Boy. It said Martin, as a good friend, 'lent' Fabricio to Peter, who had become obsessed with him. All complete bollocks. But it led the

News of the World and the *Mail on Sunday* to send teams out to Rio to follow it all up, doorstepping poor Martin and Fabricio and forcing them to go into the country for the weekend to avoid the photographers. As it turned out the papers clearly couldn't get anything because not a word has appeared today. But Peter was very worried about it and had AC call Phil Hall on the *News of the World* among others. It all led to some stories about Peter using his power with the media to try to get people sacked over the Reinaldo business. The *Punch* piece also carried a bit on the 'gay Mafia' of Peter's friends who hold key positions in Labour and the government's PR machine. This amounted to me and Mike Craven [former adviser to John Prescott] (who's now left), Mark Bolland (who works for the Prince of Wales) and Howell James (a Tory). So I'm now the sole Mafioso and my violin case is the only one left. Very bizarre.

TB is quite concerned about 'control freakery' and he doesn't want to get into the position of previous Labour prime ministers where the party says it can't trust the government. He says he'll take on the criticisms and answer them, perhaps at some large open meetings of members. There's been more talk of Ken Livingstone and the need to get people out there arguing that it's not control freakery to say his record makes him unsuitable for mayor of London.

We spent much of the week embroiled in a very unfortunate row over closed lists for the European Parliament [a proportional representation system that gives the parties control over who gets elected through 'party lists']. The Tories have used their 4–1 majority based on the hereditaries in the House of Lords to defeat the government on it five times. We did our best to argue that the elected House of Commons had a right to have its way, but the Tories refused to back down and have had some success in suggesting that the unelected Lords are somehow the defenders of true democracy! In fact, I find closed lists quite hard to justify and, besides, most MPs would be delighted if the Bill was lost completely and we went back to first past the post for the European elections. So there's been a lot of tension about and people with very different agendas. Paddy has been putting pressure on TB not to back down on some form of PR for the elections.

Thursday, 26 November 1998

A much quieter week with TB in Ireland for two days and off to Wales tomorrow. The Commons are debating the Queen's Speech, so there's not a lot going on. The House of Lords decided Pinochet did not have diplomatic immunity yesterday and there are riots in Santiago. All a bit difficult for the holiday James and I have planned in Chile after Christmas. The expectation is still that Jack Straw will have Pinochet released eventually on compassionate grounds or something, but I strongly suspect he'll still be under house arrest here when we leave. I just hope it doesn't make a diary story. The Peter/Rio story continues to dribble on – the *Guardian* on Monday and the *Spectator* again today. Martin and Fabricio continue to be harassed by the *Mail on Sunday* and are getting mightily pissed off with it all.

Friday, 27 November 1998

We have been cuffed in the NE Scotland European by-election, coming in third behind the SNP and the Tories. TB in Wales, in what is being portrayed as a 'panic' move to bolster Alun Michael. The Eurosceptic papers back on the rampage over alleged German plans to harmonise taxes across Europe. Yet the polls still show us miles ahead and hugely popular. I met Trevor Phillips yesterday, who is still 100 per cent determined to run for mayor. He'd be very good, I'm sure, but has a woefully low profile and does send his kids to public school. Others say we should go for Tony Banks.

I had a ding-dong with Sian Kevill [editor of *Newsnight*] after Paxman did a totally ludicrous interview with TB on Queen's Speech day. Not a single question on the government's programme and endless questions trying to push TB on Jenkins, the euro and Ken. TB didn't budge on any of them, *Newsnight* didn't get a story and it was a complete waste of everybody's time. I felt a bit let down because I'd argued we should do it when AC had said he saw no point.

Tuesday, 1 December 1998

Similar themes seem to be dominating another week. The mood is very downbeat with everybody rather subdued and worried. The Eurosceptic press are now running endless euro tax scare stories. TB wants to demonstrate that Britain is not isolated on the issue and is winning the arguments by being engaged in Europe. There's a feeling that our efforts to project an increasingly positive vision of Europe are being undermined. Gordon, for example, has been talking about vetoing proposals for tax harmonisation when he could just say that there are no such proposals on the table. AC asked TB, 'Could we find ourselves going into the next election saying that in the next parliament we plan to go into the single currency?' and TB says, 'That's a real possibility, yes.'

There was a hint of things to come when Lord Cranborne [Conservative leader in the House of Lords] snuck in to see AC in his office. It became clear that it was to finalise a deal on Lords reform, allowing ninety-two hereditaries to remain pending stage two, but with stage two following swiftly on, the big advantage for us being the avoidance of endless wrangling in the Lords that holds up other business.

Then Anji asked to see me mid-afternoon to discuss Peter in advance of a meeting with Peter himself. Peter Hyman and Ben Wegg-Prosser were there too. We all agreed that at some point Peter is going to have to come out properly. It's become a live issue because of the continuing stuff about Rio in the papers and the fact that Reinaldo is due to arrive this weekend to stay at Peter's for a month. They want to be left alone and there's an argument that if Peter finally says he's gay and gives the papers what they want he can at least demand privacy for those around him. We concluded that the time to do it was right there and then, so as not to disrupt tomorrow's PMQs and other key announcements.

Ben called Peter who is very hostile, but says he'll do whatever Tony wants. Ben has already passed on to him TB's view, from Anji, that Peter is spending too much time worrying about it and that it could be distracting him from his work. So we then went in to see TB who was pretty undecided but was coming round to the idea before AC came in and said he was totally against it. He thinks Peter should just accept that he can't have an ordinary private life and should behave a bit like Charles and Camilla. He said coming out would be too much like exhibitionism and asked if we were in politics or soap opera. At this, of course, TB backed off and said we shouldn't do anything tonight.

Thursday, 3 December 1998

When we met Peter himself I was expecting him to be hostile and to ask what his friends were trying to do to him. I had drawn up a two-page document basically setting out in black and white why he should come out. To my amazement he's very calm and seems to have decided to go ahead. So we discuss how to do it rather than whether. The preferred option is to do a *Today* programme interview about something serious, then add at the end, 'And all this is far more important than the media's fascination with the fact that I'm gay.' He rejects BBC Five Live on the grounds that if he's coming out it's going to be on a serious programme!

Sunday, 6 December 1998

In the end we did nothing. There were always compelling reasons for not doing it at any particular time. AC remained hostile, the latest edition of *Punch* contained nothing new and everybody was preoccupied with other things. But it does mean we've lost a very logical time to get it out of the way with as little fuss as possible. Although Peter's attitude on the subject until now means it's going to be a huge story if it ever happens. The only result was that at the regular pub quiz that James and I go to every week we won the prize for the best team name: 'I'm Mandy, Fly Me to Rio'. Fortunately nobody in the pub has any idea who I am. Previous efforts, 'Out in the Nick of Time' (Nick Brown) and 'The Clapham Common Wanderers' (Ron Davies) weren't so successful.

Anyway, the main event of the week turned out to be total turmoil in the Tory Party with the sacking of their leader in the Lords, Lord Cranborne, and the resignation of four other frontbenchers. After Cranborne had had a couple of meetings with AC and worked out a deal Hague sacked him on Wednesday after getting wind of it and using PMQs to launch a pre-emptive strike against the plan. Then it turned out that the rest of the Tory peers backed Cranborne and the new leader, Lord Strathclyde, only agreed to take Cranborne's place if he could stick to the deal. So Hague was left having to back the basic deal but having sacked the guy who negotiated it. Cranborne has been totally straight with us throughout. He rang AC's office to apologise during PMQs and later told him he was sorry his judgement was so poor that he thought the Tories were being led by a grown-up.

Alan Clark rang AC to say, 'You've lit the blue touch paper under my party and it's going up in flames around me!' It came out in today's papers that Cranborne met AC. Tom Baldwin in *The Times* was particularly well informed, right down to the fact that Cranborne was wearing red socks, something we all joked about.

Other events of the week, a bit of a row over a report that was drawn up about Ken Livingstone using Excalibur [the Labour Party's computer system that trawls the newspapers for stories]. We've always said we don't use it on our own members. I had almost offered the report to Peter Kellner [*Evening Standard* columnist] the week before and I'm glad now that I didn't. Still unsure about the future of Pinochet, and James and I are starting to wonder about whether to go to Chile. I hope we will.

Meanwhile we're trying to find a new director of communications for the Labour Party. Bill Bush [head of research at the BBC] was interested, which would have been great, but his wife vetoed it.

Tuesday, 8 December 1998

Feeling very weary and looking forward enormously to the holiday over Christmas. I sent Jonathan Powell an email yesterday saying I still planned to go to Chile unless he strongly advised otherwise. He replied saying, 'Fine, look after your personal safety and make sure the consul knows where you are.' Very good news as we were starting to make contingency plans in case we had to cancel. I spoke to the embassy in Santiago today and they didn't underplay the potential for problems, but said so far the difficulties had been confined to the big population areas.

It's been a fairly quiet start to the week here. Peter Mandelson had his announcement on the future of the Post Office, which was panned by the papers and seen as not radical enough and a concession to the unions. The *Daily Mail* quoted 'sources very close to the Chancellor, speaking with Gordon Brown's authority', saying the package of reforms for the Post Office was 'garbage' and how glad they were that the Treasury wasn't in any way involved in this 'rubbish'. AC paged Peter saying, 'Don't retaliate, think of the medium/long term.'

Still trying to find a communications director for the party but without much success.

Wednesday, 9 December 1998

Pinochet decision day. Jack Straw has said the extradition to Spain can go ahead, making him a hero of the Labour movement and an enemy of Thatcher [Baroness Thatcher had been outspoken in support of the general]. So, good news all round. Chile has withdrawn its ambassador to London, so it may not be so great for our travel plans. I had a long chat with Derry Irvine [lord chancellor] and Charlie Falconer [minister at the Cabinet Office] about the legal aspects before helping brief TB for PMQs this morning.

One point that, to my surprise, nobody in the media made much of was that on the day Jack made his announcement, TB was meeting Martin McGuinness at Downing Street. A difference of scale, of course, but it does leave us open to the charge that there are different rules for different conflicts and different processes of reconciliation.

Sunday, 13 December 1998

PMQs on Wednesday was all about Europe in advance of the Vienna summit at the end of this week. James was over there to report on it, so I've been in Brighton on my own this weekend. In fact, I came down on Thursday afternoon for a dental appointment so I've had a rare and very welcome long weekend working from here. On Thursday morning we revealed that we'd reached an agreement with the Tories for the safe passage of the Bill on the European elections. I saw Peter who says Reinaldo is now with him, but they're not going out much and it's a bit of a strain. He's determined to have someone's scalp over the rubbishing of the Post Office deal. Peter and Ian McCartney [minister of state in the Department of Trade and Industry] have had a serious falling out over the Fairness at Work proposals [on workers' rights]. Sally Morgan says we have to keep Ian on board as it's crucial in reassuring the party in the country.

Friday, 18 December 1998

On our way up to Yorkshire to see James's parents for the weekend. The week has been completely dominated by the American and British air strikes on Iraq, which are still going on. They started at ten p.m. on Wednesday night in the middle of the pre-Christmas party season in Whitehall. I was at dinner with the Labour Party press officers and went back into the office for a couple of hours. The Number Ten party last night was cancelled. The military action is one of those events on which TB and AC have been working very closely and in great secrecy together, for obvious reasons, leaving the rest of us pretty much out of the loop. It does seem, though, that Robin Cook may well have tipped off David Yelland [editor of the *Sun*] at the Foreign Office party on Wednesday night. Certainly the *Sun* had it in their first edition somehow. I couldn't help feeling that TB had mixed emotions about sending the boys into action. He said he did it with 'a heavy heart' but at the same time he must have known it would happen sometime and maybe it's part of his coming-of-age as a leader. Although I'm sure he feels Saddam needs to be taught a lesson at last as well. Needless to say, the media has been almost 100 per cent behind him. I'm not sure I can honestly say what I think.

Monday, 21 December 1998

Another truly remarkable day and a very bad one for the New Labour wing of the government. Ben Wegg-Prosser paged me mid-morning to go over to the DTI to discuss Peter and Geoffrey Robinson. It transpired that Geoffrey lent Peter nearly £400,000 to help him buy his very flash house in Notting Hill. This was all kept secret from everyone, including AC and TB, until they got wind that Paul Routledge or the press or both had the story last week. The *Guardian* are now planning a big exposé on it tomorrow. Peter was, as ever, very calm about the whole thing, despite the obvious allegation that he's been compromised because the DTI is investigating Geoffrey for filing false accounts; that he may have fallen foul of the Conduct for Ministers and the Register of Members' Interests; that it will look like Geoffrey bought his place in government and has kept it because Peter, along with Gordon and to a lesser extent TB, are in his debt. Ben and Peter suspect (of course) that Charlie Whelan is behind it and as the day wore on that became increasingly likely in my book. Charlie Falconer and I saw Peter and his team at the DTI, including the permanent secretary, Michael Scholar, at noon. Most of it taken up with whether the department had followed the rules to the letter. This took literally hours. Charlie and I then went over to see Geoffrey at the Treasury at three forty-five. He professed shock, said nobody at the Treasury knew anything about it except him. He was joined by Ed Balls [special adviser to Gordon Brown] and their main concern was over who was going to be fingered for leaking it. Geoffrey said he thought both Peter and himself were in breach of the rules, but he insisted several times that he wasn't 'going to be done over on this one'. But he was generally incoherent and unimpressive. We then saw TB, who said the bottom line was that we were sticking by Peter and that we should simply focus on the fact that there was no conflict of interest for Peter because he wasn't involved in any of the decisions within the DTI concerning Geoffrey. He said later that I should deal with all the media questions so it wouldn't look like one spin doctor, AC, looking after another, Peter. Apparently I'm still Mr Nice Guy.

The additional problem is that it all makes Peter look like this character who has ideas above his station, lives beyond his means and is generally a dodgy individual. AC's view is that he should sell the house. Ben's father, who happens, of course, to be the solicitor who handled the transactions, said the same thing but apparently Peter went white and refused. Already normally supportive people, like Clive Soley [MP, chairman of the Parliamentary Labour Party] have told me they don't think they'll be able to give full support to Peter. Before all this happened we were already facing some difficult questions about what happens now in Iraq. AC was in full bash-the-media mode (especially the BBC) over its Iraq coverage. At least we now have a story that will knock Iraq off the front pages.

Tuesday, 22 December 1998

Peter certainly moved closer to having to resign today and I found myself among the first coming to the conclusion that he would have to go. According to AC, TB said at one point, 'What I ought to do is get rid of both of them,' and that was before the potentially fatal information came to light that Peter had falsified his mortgage application by not referring to the loan. The papers are already asking about it. Today's press could actually have been a great deal worse, but they haven't really got going yet. I told Peter that he would have to be very careful of the flashy lifestyle thing whatever happens.

Wednesday, 23 December 1998

Well, the worst happened. Peter resigned just after noon and Geoffrey Robinson followed this afternoon. I was with Peter in his office as it was all happening and it was a very traumatic and emotional time. I left home late having been discussing with Ben what slim chance there was of wriggling through it. We arranged to meet at the DTI at ten thirty with Peter and also Ben's dad. I got into Number Ten at about nine forty-five and AC arrived about twenty minutes later. He said it was pretty clear Peter would have to resign and that was TB's view too.

In the Private Office, Jonathan Powell was already working on the reshuffle. Jonathan, AC and I were picked up by Peter's driver and taken into the DTI via the back entrance, but even here there were snappers. Ben and Peter were still expecting a meeting to discuss how to get through it. AC said straight away that Peter should talk to TB and the rest of us left the room.

Ben started to talk about the mortgage but I said it had got beyond that. He asked what I meant and I drew a line across my throat. He visibly blanched and tears came into his eyes – the first of several people to react that way. We knew Hague was on TV live at eleven fifteen, presumably to call for resignations, and we didn't want to be seen to be reacting to him, so we started to brief that TB had asked for a report on the situation the night before and was considering it all morning.

It took what seemed like hours for the door to open. Jonathan, Ben and I were just outside the door in the Private Office looking grim and having fairly cryptic conversations. The staff must have been straining to hear what was going on and must have picked up that it was the end, or close to it.

Peter eventually emerged and went off with Ben. AC told me Peter had tried to persuade TB that he should be severely reprimanded instead of resigning. Both Jonathan Powell and I said that would be wrong and he would have to go. We also argued that Geoffrey Robinson and Charlie Whelan should go too. After several minutes I went off to find Peter and Ben in a waiting room. Peter said to me, 'What do you think I should do?' I said, 'I think you have to resign, say you've done nothing wrong but that you're not prepared to see the party or the government damaged.' He said, 'Yes,' and we walked back to his office. I gave his shoulder a squeeze and he had tears in his eyes too. He got on the phone to TB and said, 'You've obviously made up your mind and there's no point trying to change it.'

AC started to draft the resignation letters. There was a fair bit of redrafting and in the meantime I briefed Charles Reiss [*Evening Standard*], and Robin Oakley [BBC], while AC spoke to Michael Brunson [ITN]. The story hit the airwaves at twelve thirty on ITN. We said (quite falsely) that Peter had rung TB last night and said he wanted to resign; that TB had urged him to reflect on it overnight; that Peter had spoken to him again at ten this morning to say he was determined to go for the good of the government and the party. Peter said he didn't want to go at the same time as Geoffrey and Charlie 'like some pack of thieves'. Geoffrey was being difficult anyway, so we briefed that his position was probably untenable and that we'd be making a statement later.

Bizarrely Gordon was on the phone advising Peter. I'm pretty sure he was telling him not to go, knowing full well that if Peter, Geoffrey and Charlie went it would leave him very exposed. As AC said later, Gordon's main concern was what questions were being asked about how Geoffrey had been funding his office. We watched the lunchtime news programmes, ITN good, the BBC pretty hopeless, and arranged a lobby briefing for two p.m. AC, Jonathan and I left about one thirty after more hugs and wet eyes (including AC's). Cameramen chased us down the street as we drove away.

The lobby lasted nearly an hour and was pretty tough. We still didn't acknowledge that Peter had broken the Ministerial Code of Conduct, but pretty much allowed journalists to come to that conclusion if they wanted to. There were some questions about who else Geoffrey had lent money to, but nothing that touched too directly on TB. While it was going on, AC's pager went off and we were able to announce that Stephen Byers was the new secretary of state for Trade and Industry.

Back upstairs after the lobby I learned that TB had decided to make Alan Milburn chief secretary at the Treasury in place of Steve. Promotions too for John Denham and Geoff Hoon. Most of the rest of the afternoon was spent lining up ministers to appear on programmes. Some people in the office, notably Peter Hyman, questioned if the right decision had been made. Clearly it had, and the broadcasters compared this 'swift' resignation with the lingering deaths under the Tories. Everybody in the office felt it was a terrible tragedy but Peter did in the end pay the price of his vanity.

Peter did a very good interview with ITN and a less good one with the BBC. We told him not to do Sky because Adam Boulton [political editor] had repeated on air that AC had said 'fuck off' when asked if TB would do an interview. AC rang Adam and told him he wouldn't be getting an interview and that they no longer had a relationship. I told TB that AC would have to get over it pretty quickly. So what should have been my day off turned into the most tumultuous imaginable.

I feel genuinely sad for Peter, although I think he showed monumentally bad judgement. Ben will be OK. He's already been offered a job by Yelland at the *Sun* and by Tony Bevins [political editor] at the *Express*. I said he should do the job of director of communications for the Labour Party, but Peter says he wants him to stay with him. We've briefed that Peter can expect to return to high office after a reasonable interval. Not much more than a year I would guess. The fall-out over who was responsible for it all will be ghastly and I can't honestly say who I think was to blame. Someone in the Treasury, I'd guess. The government has been severely dented. TB on the other hand remains pretty much unscathed. I go to Chile in two days, partly regretting that I won't be here to watch it all unfold.

1999

Sunday, 17 January 1999

Just back from a fantastic three weeks in Chile, from the Atacama desert in the north to Torres del Paine in Patagonia. We were almost completely cut off during most of the travelling. We never saw an English newspaper and could only rarely pick up the World Service – except on one memorable occasion when I heard that Charlie Whelan had resigned. But it seems that the government has been getting a pretty bad press in my absence. By the third week I was feeling slightly, only slightly, guilty at still being away. It's back to work tomorrow, although I'm feeling very rough tonight having picked up some sort of tummy bug on the plane home of all places.

Monday, 18 January 1999

Apart from AC giving me hell for being off for so long, it's been a good first day back. Actually he's been very good-natured about it, although they've obviously been having a really tough time of it. AC thinks there's been a real shift in the media's tone and attitude that won't be easily reversed. The fall-out from Peter's departure has been massive and damaging. Because it happened over Christmas it was the only story in town. Prescott made some ill-judged remarks about going back to traditional values, which ran and ran. Charlie Whelan was a huge story in itself. AC told me that while TB was on holiday in the Seychelles he told him by phone that he'd 'better get the fucking message' that he wasn't going to work with Charlie any more and if he wasn't sacked then TB 'could find somebody else to go to South Africa' [an official visit that followed the Seychelles holiday]. AC says he was so furious he put the phone down on TB.

It's still not clear who will take over from Charlie, but probably a civil servant. Apparently my name was mentioned as a possible successor in some of the papers and on the *Today* programme! My Chile trip got a mention in the *Sunday Express*. I saw Peter this evening, having first spoken to Ben, who is still obviously very shell-shocked. Peter is thinking of going to South Africa to advise the

ANC. 'Mandy sells the black arts to Africa', as he put it himself. He's going to have to sell the house, which strikes me as a very sensible idea anyway. I said to him he'd be back in government in two years, but he reckons (surprise, surprise) that it'll be sooner than that. Summer reshuffle in 2000, he thinks. In the meantime he'll do some TV and 'raise money where I can'. He says Reinaldo was a tower of strength throughout and now he's back in Japan he really misses him.

Tuesday, 19 January 1999

Scotland discussions this morning with TB, Gordon, Donald Dewar and Douglas Alexander [MP for Paisley South]. Donald was if anything more pathetic than ever, with only Gordon and Douglas showing any mettle. We do seem to be staggering along, still addressing basic strategic issues that we should have sorted out months and months ago. Ben has been offered a job with the *Sun* as some kind of adviser to Yelland. He's very excited about it and I hope it works out for him, but I'm slightly worried he'll get his fingers burned. Peter is concerned that we're not giving enough attention to his ANC offer.

There's a bit of a feeling about the place that TB is losing touch with ordinary people and what matters to them. He seems almost bored with all the ordinary stuff and interested only in all the foreign leaders, Clinton, wars, etc. I get a sense of impending gloom, if not doom. It's all been too easy for too long.

Saturday, 23 January 1999

Got back last night from a two-day foray to Scotland with Prescott, which was quite an experience. Variously charming, growling, witty, incoherent, focused, muddled.

I've always had a lot of time for him, and still do, even though he thinks I'm an unreconstructed Blair/Mandy stooge. John Reid [minister of state in Prescott's Transport Department], who was up too, is obviously finding working with him a real roller-coaster. Prescott was furious about Gordon making a big speech on the same day as his visit to Scotland and initially refused to do a joint photo, but then he relented. Helen [Liddle] was cross about Prescott urging the party in Scotland to pull its socks up (which she obviously saw as a slight to her) and saying, 'We are a national party.' I'm sure he was right to say what he did and so was fairly happy with how things went.

Thursday, 28 January 1999

A huge amount of concern about whether the government is being seen to be delivering on its promises. The feeling is that while a lot of incremental improvements are going ahead across the board, there's not much that will make a big impact on people. Very little they can point to and say, 'Well, at least they did *that*.' TB very alarmed by material David Miliband produced showing among other things that there would be a big increase in the crime figures, according to Home Office projections. He said this would be a total disaster. But the main worry is that improvements on schools and hospitals will be so slow that most people won't notice. Philip Gould said we needed to give some thought to what sort of legacy we wanted. New ideas are being eagerly sought. I did a paper suggesting more rebuttal of inaccurate stories by ourselves and an effort to respond to media trivia. I also added a personal note suggesting I be designated communications director after AC asked if I wanted a proper title. David Miliband and Anji Hunter were both keen on the idea and Anji said TB was too, although I've heard nothing back officially.

Friday, 29 January 1999

On my way to Brighton after another enjoyable week. We've decided to reinstate a TB visit to Scotland next Friday after Philip Gould did focus groups up there showing that the 'London Labour' tag is really hurting us. Not that we have a very clear strategy for fighting it. What he found, however, is that the SNP [Scottish National Party] are very weak on trust, tax and changing their minds over whether to go for independence. Alun Michael in Wales is doing better, although he's got a reputation for concentrating on some things in minute detail, like the precise wording of parliamentary answers and press releases, a fixation with some small issues and refusal to get a grip on some of the much larger ones. Ken Livingstone did a big number in the *Guardian* promising to be loyal if we let him run for mayor, then another piece in the *Evening Standard* condemning the government for hammering Labour councils over the council tax. So in three of our big elections coming up we have either weak leadership or no leadership at all. Meanwhile Alan Donnelly, our party leader in the European Parliament, is about to be outed by the *People* – something he's totally relaxed about.

I had lunch with Alan, Margaret McDonagh and Rosie Boycott [editor of the *Daily Express*] and Tony Bevins [political editor of the *Express*] at the Oxo Tower on Tuesday. They're urging us to come out much more clearly for the euro, something TB is getting ready to do in any case. Peter Mandelson has put his house on the market, which will obviously be a great strain for him, but he'll make a huge profit and will be fine.

Monday, 1 February 1999

Slept really badly again last night for some reason. The same thing happened last Sunday, but at least then I had things on my mind. Last night there was no reason at all. Very annoying as I've been tired all day today, although fortunately it hasn't been too busy. A bit of a controversy over our 'new media strategy', which AC leaked to Patrick Wintour on the *Observer* this weekend. Basically it means doing more interviews with specialist papers, regional media, etc., and relying less on the Westminster lobby, which is obsessed with trivia. Unfortunately TB then went on *Richard and Judy* today where he was asked all sorts of trivial questions. He also managed to overshadow what should have been the main story of the day – a big pay rise for nurses – by adding his name to those calling for Glen Hoddle's removal as England manager over a slight to the disabled in something he said. So for a new strategy it wasn't hugely successful!

Friday, 5 February 1999

Just back from Scotland. A successful end to a rather wobbly week. We did a good bit of Nat-bashing and had no stupid questions about 'London Labour' or anything. By all accounts Donald did well in his televised debate with Alex Salmond [the SNP leader] last night. Helen Liddle is still upset by stories in last Sunday's papers suggesting 'friends of Gordon Brown' were dissatisfied with her performance. But overall we're in much better shape up there.

Nationally the week has been dominated by stories about TB trying to bounce Glen Hoddle into resigning and discussion of our new media strategy. AC seems to think the strategy has to involve publicly taking on the media, even if that does provoke the kind of very negative coverage we've had this week. Others think we should implement the strategy without making such a song and dance about it. Fortunately when the *Richard and Judy* programme invited their own viewers to express an opinion, 87 per cent said TB wasn't hounding Hoddle.

PMQs were a bit odd with Hague asking two questions about Hoddle and then four about genetically modified food. He has a real look about him of a leader on the way out. He seems to have lost a lot of his self-confidence. The trouble is, the last thing we want is for him to be forced out and replaced with somebody better.

Two big events yesterday. I successfully recruited Bill Bush [head of political research at the BBC] to be the new head of research at Number Ten, which will be excellent so long as we can make the job big enough for him. Then last thing in the afternoon we had a heated discussion about how we go about stepping up our support for the euro. The next phase, which may come very soon, is to say that we intend recommending that Britain joins in a referendum just after the next election. There was a row over whether we're ready to deal with the backlash. TB said on the flight back from Scotland that we could get the strategy in place in just a day or two. Others, led by Peter Hyman and supported by Charlie Falconer, said we'd need to spend time getting all the arguments in place and to get businessmen, etc., to support us. It'll certainly be a very dramatic shift. And of course it will raise the question – if you've decided you want to go in, why wait until after the election to hold the referendum? And how do you know it'll work when it's only been going a few weeks? [since 1 January 1999 the exchange rates of all those countries due to join the single currency were fixed against the euro. It would be another three years before euro notes and coins were issued, but the euro now had a real value that could go up and down like any other. The pound was unaffected because it was outside the European Monetary Union following the op-out negotiated by John Major as Prime Minister and maintained by Tony Blair.]

Tuesday, 9 February 1999

Busy weekend in Manchester where TB was speaking to the Local Government and Europe Conference. I annoyed him a little by briefing the papers in advance that he would say, 'Where the Liberal Democrats are wrong you have my permission – go for them.' He said he didn't want the Lib Dems to be the main story, but they were anyway, even with the slightly milder language he used in the end. I thought TB might not even make the conference because King Hussein of Jordan was on a life support machine and it looked as if he might have to go to the funeral instead. In the event the funeral was yesterday and TB went with AC, Ashdown and Hague. Hague was a real embarrassment apparently, and AC says he seems to have lost all confidence. He only managed to get into the shot bowing in front of the coffin because AC grabbed him and pushed him into the line. As it was, he was half out of the picture and the newspapers commented on how he came third after Ashdown.

I had my third Sunday in a row unable to sleep. Up at three thirty a.m. watching a movie.

Sunday, 14 February 1999

Peter Mandelson in hot water in South Africa. Some ANC press officer said they hadn't invited him and didn't need his advice. The guy got the sack but not before embarrassing Peter, who was totally livid and ready to blame anybody, including TB, for the mess. He told me he wouldn't do anything for the government again, as if we were some-how responsible for it all. He's so unstable at the moment, it's quite worrying.

The campaign against Ken is moving up a gear. We have the perennial problem that neither Number Ten nor the party can really get involved, or at least be seen to. But Paul Boateng [junior minister] has written an excellent piece for the *Standard* tomorrow sticking the knife in very artfully.

Thursday, 18 February 1999

Crazy week dominated by media hysteria over GM [geneti-cally modified] food. Alastair is off all week and Godric took Monday to Wednesday off, so I've been dealing with it more or less alone. It's been at times farcical and at times maddening. Jill Sherman wrote a piece in *The Times* today saying that the government was all over the place and pointing out that AC was on holiday. I don't think TB and Jonathan think I've fucked up, but I guess they wonder if things would have been different if AC had been here. GM food is a subject covered variously by MAFF [Agricul-ture Department], DETR [Environment], DTI [Trade] and the Cabinet Office at the centre. Jack Cunningham, the so-called Enforcer, chairs a cabinet committee on it, Misc 6, but far from helping to co-ordinate the govern-ment's presentation he seems to be making it worse. The main allegations are that we are rushing ahead too fast with GM food research and allowing 'Frankenstein foods' to be sold without being sure the technology is safe. It's being claimed, on extremely dubious grounds, that GM foods could cause cancer, kill babies, turn vegetarians and the rest of us into cannibals, while GM crops will help wipe out other forms of life and contaminate non-GM crops. At the same time, the government is said to be too close to the GM industry, too gung-ho about its potential, and that David Sainsbury, the science minister, has a conflict of interest because of his links to the family firm of supermarkets and his known enthusiasm for biotechnology in the past. A pretty fearsome combination of charges.

In the face of a hysterical media we've sought to argue that there is no scientific evidence whatever that GM foods are in any way less safe than their non-GM counterparts, that no GM crops are grown commercially in this country anyway, that those imported foods now on sale were all approved by the Tories, that we're far stricter on labelling than they ever were, that we will evaluate the current small-scale crop trials carefully before any larger trials or commercial production can go ahead.

The week started with TB in a very feisty mood. He both alarmed and depressed David Miliband, whom I like and admire greatly, by suggesting that we should change direction dramatically on both health and education – allowing some treatments like varicose veins and cataracts to be taken out of the NHS and into private treatment, saying the NHS can't be expected to do everything and that people will have to make private provision for some things. David vainly tried to point out that, in both cases, treatment in the NHS was cheaper and more efficient. On education he was talking about closing down the LEAs altogether, while Sally Morgan argued that while some were bad others gave an excellent service to the schools under their control. Anyway, the idea is that it's time to think the unthinkable. On crime as well, and transport on which TB is in despair. John Prescott wouldn't even come out to condemn the Tube strike, which we wanted him to do in order to focus attention on Ken's support for it. He left it instead to John Reid.

Philip Gould is very impressed with TB's mood, saying, 'I don't know what the prime minister is on, but I want some of it.' On GM foods, TB was adamant that we would be mad to slow down on it and totally contemptuous of the environmental groups and others lined up against it. Partly, I think, fired up by Peter, who is a great fan. So, inspired by all this, I took the eleven o'clock lobby on Monday morning and launched a powerful defence of GM, something that personally I'm much more cautious about. During the course of it I was asked if TB ate GM foods. A moment's hesitation or a fudged answer would have been fatal so I said, 'I'm sure he does. He's absolutely confident about its safety and would have no problems at all about eating it.' That led to totally predictable stuff in the media, reminding people of John Gummer [former Conservative agriculture minister during the BSE crisis] feeding a hamburger to his daughter, and asking if TB was making the same mistake. The BSE fiasco is, of course, one reason there's so much unease and such reluctance to believe either politicians or scientists on food safety. The funniest effect of my briefing was the *Mirror* front page, 'The Prime Monster – fury as Tony Blair admits he eats Frankenstein foods', along with a brilliant full-page mock-up of TB as Frankenstein. One for the scrapbook.

TB spoke in public on Tuesday defending both Sainsbury and the need to proceed with trials while putting safety first. So, too, did Sir Robert May, the chief scientist, a very forthright Australian, although he also said he didn't agree with the beef on the bone ban [still in force after the BSE crisis]. Both TB and Sainsbury himself said that Sainsbury absented himself from meetings when decisions were taken on GM foods.

On Wednesday there was a leak of briefing notes relating to a report for the Advisory Committee on the Rural Environment, ACRE, suggesting that it supported the concerns expressed by English Nature about GM and therefore, implicitly, supported the need for a moratorium.

It took DETR ages to get any rebuttal out, or indeed to get Michael Meacher [environment minister] on the *Today* programme. He was then allowed to go off on a visit to Kent where he was too far away from any studios to do further interviews. I wanted him brought back, Prescott overruled it, so I had to persuade John to do clips on the story himself.

TB was a bit reluctant for us to use Meacher on the media at all. He may have been right as Meacher on *Channel 4 News* last night suggested we might extend the current trial period for GM crops, so delaying commercial production. Although this was completely consistent with what we have said all along about being guided by the scientific evidence, it has been written up as the first sign of the government 'softening its stance'. It was all enough to make my head hurt.

As well as all that I was able to have a row with the BBC over its decision to pick up, a whole week after it was written, a mad article by Lord Beloff likening TB's rise to that of Hitler. It was on the BBC website along with pictures of Adolf Hitler and Nazi symbols.

I also tried to co-ordinate a bit of opposition to Ken. TB is moving closer to deciding whom he wants to run as the Labour candidate, as well as getting ready to attack Ken himself.

Monday, 22 February 1998

Alun Michael won the Welsh leadership on Saturday by a margin of 5 per cent. We feebly tried to maintain it hadn't been an old-style Labour stitch-up using union block votes, but of course that was exactly what it was. Messy, but not half so bad as having to deal with a big rebuff to TB and some of the wacky policies Rhodri has already been coming up with.

Then another mess on Saturday night/Sunday as Jack Straw obtained a temporary injunction preventing publication of a leak of the Lawrence Report [the inquiry into the police handling of the murder of the black teenager Stephen Lawrence]. Tom Baldwin [*The Times*], who got the scoop, was ringing me frantically on Saturday night saying, 'You're all going to look so fucking stupid.'

Not far off, but it wasn't all that bad today. TB was in a curiously cautious mood after his hyperactive performance last week. He's against restructuring the press office as a Media and Communications Unit, although he approved all of my note, which I faxed to Chequers, about a twenty-four-hour press office and better rebuttal throughout Whitehall. He's also quite nervous about tomorrow's announcement on the National Changeover Plan [the proposals for how Britain would switch to the euro in the event of a decision to do so]. It doesn't look as if he will now say that he plans to recommend that we join the single currency. He's nervous about taking on the press in a big way. He knows what a huge battle it will be and doesn't seem ready to have it now, although most of the rest of us think he should.

Much talk about how we can be on the right side of the argument over the Lawrence Report and racism, where we deserve to be. The Metropolitan Police commissioner is making it clear he won't resign. But while TB is no racist he thinks some people will see the report [which accused the Metropolitan Police of institutional racism] as political correctness gone mad. More caution, and he's missing the point. It doesn't matter if they do: we have to be unequivocally on the right side. So we'll try to get him to do a big anti-racist speech at the weekend.

Friday, 26 February 1999

The Lawrence Report turned out to be a total fuck-up from start to finish. First it was leaked to *The Times*, then when Stephen Lawrence's memorial was vandalised the police security camera watching it turned out to be a dummy, and then the appendices to the report had to be withdrawn because they included the names and addresses of people who had helped the police investigation. The Home Office had had the report for over a week but apparently hadn't noticed. Its line was that it was Jack Straw's responsibility to publish the report as it was presented to him, but I found that pretty pathetic. It was a terrible oversight that could mean people have been put at very serious risk of attack.

To make matters that bit worse, Jack went on a private visit to France today, leaving Paul Boateng to make the Commons statement on the affair. We should have had a very good story to tell – we set up the Lawrence Inquiry and have at least made a start on trying to tackle racism, but all of that was overshadowed. Speculation continues as to who leaked the report to Tom Baldwin – ministers, spin doctors, the inquiry team, the Met? Meanwhile another document, this time on genetically modified food from a fairly tight meeting of officials, was leaked to the *Guardian*. A proper leak enquiry has been launched into that one.

In the midst of all the Lawrence stuff, TB did the National Changeover Plan with wholly predictable results. The *Sun* went gaga, the *Mail*, *Telegraph* and *Times* were all opposed and, with the exception of the *Express*, the so-called pro-European papers were typically timid. But it was all over very quickly.

Internally, we're pressing ahead with a twenty-four-hour newsroom and a weekly recorded message from the prime minister on the Internet at my suggestion. Philip Gould came back from Scotland to say his focus groups showed we were just not getting our message across. He thinks we need millions of quid's worth of paid advertising, lots more involvement from TB, and a senior spin doctor in place. Somebody like David Hill [former chief spokesman for the Labour Party]. Same old story, really. My hunch is that a strong 'The SNP will hit your pocket' line will bring the voters back when they get into the polling booths.

Sunday, 7 March 1999

Funny sort of a week. It started with the horrible murder of some adventure tourists in Uganda, four of them British, so that took up a lot of media coverage. We didn't have a lot of our own to offer in any case. We're a bit short of good stories at the moment. More money for education to cut class sizes ran well on Wednesday, though.

It's pre-Budget week so that has kept everybody busy. I have deliberately made no effort at all to know what's in it so I couldn't get drawn into any briefing. As a result this weekend has been very quiet.

TB was fairly preoccupied with Scotland this week. His visit on Thursday and Friday was pretty successful. Mind you, we let him down with a cock-up involving the *Daily Record*, by far Scotland's largest-selling paper. I'd seen something put together in preparation for a speech he was making in Scotland that included a section on the Millennium Dome and cheap fares to London for Scots wanting to visit it. Either I must have misread or misremembered it, or the idea was subsequently removed. Anyway, when AC was asked by David Thompson of the *Record* what the Dome story was, he said, 'It's something to do with subsidised fares, isn't that right, Lance?' I said, 'Yes.' In fact it was nothing of the kind. The *Record* did a rubbishing piece saying no Scots would want to go to the Dome anyway. We had to rubbish them back, saying they'd got the story wrong without admitting it was our fault in the first place.

The rest of the visit, though, was very good. We did some off-beat media, including TB virtually co-presenting the Radio Clyde breakfast show on Friday. His speech to the Scottish Labour Conference the same day went well, so he was in a much better mood on the way down than he had been on the way up.

Even so we had a council of war on the plane home. He thinks Dewar simply isn't up to leading a New Labour campaign and that Helen Liddle isn't brave enough. So we'll have to do a lot more ourselves and I'll probably go up again next week.

We continue to debate our media strategy at great length. AC has done a long paper on it. Bill Bush resigned from the BBC on Monday and that caused a huge storm within the Beeb as he's a far bigger loss to them than I ever was. John Birt reaction was apparently 'Oh, fuck.' But Bill will be a huge asset to us.

AC asked me about a piece in the *Sunday Express* 'Crossbencher' column, saying I was unhappy and wanted to be director of communications at the Department of Social Security. He joked that he wouldn't tolerate unhappiness. I said I wouldn't either and told him it wasn't true, which it isn't. But people always assume there's some truth in stories like that.

Monday, 8 March 1999

Yet another discussion of our media strategy. TB is very worried that AC's desire for all-out war on the media could be counter-productive. So it's been agreed that, while we should continue to look for new ways to get our message across and of using TB differently, we won't be so public about a change of strategy. He thinks AC was wrong to be so high-profile about it last time and he'll only be allowed occasional skirmishes. On policy, delivery is the continual worry.

Tuesday, 9 March 1999

Budget day and quite a show. Gordon cut the main rate of income tax from next year and there are a whole lot of goodies before then. On the other side MIRAS [mortgage tax relief] is being abolished, along with the married person's allowance. But the initial reaction has been very favourable indeed.

John Rafferty [Donald Dewar's special adviser] in Scotland threw a wobbly tonight because I hadn't told him I was thinking of going up with Bill Bush on Thursday and because we were having a meeting on Scotland in Number Ten tonight that he got to hear about. He's obviously feeling very threatened. I suppose I could have told him about the trip before now, but it's no big deal. And we can have whatever meetings we like, thank you very much. It was actually to talk about what to do about Donald, how to smarten him up and make him look like a leader. Otherwise we're in big trouble.

I was a bit pissed off this evening because TB wants to cut the number of people he has at his Wednesday PMQs meetings (which are admittedly very large) and both Peter Hyman and I have been asked not to go tomorrow. He only wants AC from the press office. Although Bill, whom I brought in, will of course be there as head of research. Not wildly happy about that.

Wednesday, 10 March 1999

Great headlines for the Budget and TB knocked Hague for six at PMQs. I didn't go to the PMQs meeting this morning, but at AC's suggestion I'll start going again from next week.

Yesterday's mild blues have dissipated. I'm now on my way to Scotland again after a meeting with TB and Gordon on the subject. They basically have to get Helen Liddle out of the way and TB wants to make her secretary of state designate [she would take over as and when Donald Dewar became first minister in the Scottish Parliament after the elections] while Donald concentrates on campaigning around Scotland. Douglas Alexander will then run the campaign, with TB and Gordon's authority. It has to be seen as Helen being promoted rather than sidelined, which will be quite an effort.

I now have to try to find a way of getting some good follow-up coverage to the Budget, starting with a Gordon speech on Friday.

Tuesday, 16 March 1999

Trip to Scotland was OK, if a bit frustrating. John Rafferty getting very tetchy and silly about people jetting in, making suggestions and then jetting out again. But the trouble is that, without us keeping an eye on them all the time, the show never really gets on the road. The idea of changing Helen's role seems to appeal to everyone and that should now happen on Thursday. The problem, as ever, will be getting Dewar to even half-way stick to the script as laid down by Gordon and Douglas.

As I was at Gatwick on Friday evening, about to leave for a short weekend in Lisbon with James, Anji rang to say she was worried about a conversation she'd had with

Peter. He had said we were mad to put Gordon in charge, that we would eventually win, he would take all the credit and we'd be storing up trouble for the future. I said I totally disagreed, that Gordon was the only person capable of doing it and was proving very effective, that it would be seen as further evidence of Tony and Gordon working well together. She said that was her view too and that I was the only person she could think of to talk to about it, and having done so wouldn't now mention it to Tony. She said that after the Budget Gordon had thanked Tony and said that it wouldn't have been such a great success without his advice, something he hadn't said for years.

Peter, I'm afraid, is in danger of becoming embittered and determined to carry on fighting the battles of the past when things have moved on. It must feel to him as if things are moving on without him, which in a sense they are, but he's not going to get himself back on board that way.

Politically the weekend seemed to go well with the SNP under huge pressure on tax.

James and I had a good weekend in Lisbon for our anniversary, although I was rather ill with a killing headache and aches all over, which put a bit of a dampener on it. I was angry with AC for saying, predictably, 'I've never known anybody have as many holidays as you.' I don't call Friday night to Sunday afternoon a holiday, especially when I work eleven hours a day minimum, five days a week, with calls at weekends. I'm already starting to feel as if I want my life back.

The week back in the office started once again with Scotland, Wales, a bit of foreign affairs and the usual discussion of the media. Philip Gould did a big analysis of his polling in Scotland showing Alex Salmond very popular and Dewar losing ground, with us still just a shade ahead of the SNP. His focus groups showed former Tory voters much warmer towards the government than long-standing

Labour supporters, who found us untrustworthy, out of touch and uncaring.

I had a very good lunch with Niall Dickson [social affairs editor at the BBC] at the horribly stuffy Reform Club yesterday, while TB and AC went to lunch at the *Sun* – AC described it as like being at a BNP [British National Party] meeting. Then last night Europe blew up as a story with the entire European Commission resigning over a report on corruption.

Wednesday, 17 March 1999

I started to get a bit low yesterday, partly as a result of total exhaustion, I think. But so much so that by the evening I was lying on my back on the floor at home telling James how I wanted my life back. It's not just tiredness, it's also frustration at AC's reluctance to delegate properly, his taking the piss over time off, and a feeling that he doesn't rate me that highly. In fact, of course, he spends all his time telling people how crap they are and not meaning it at all. So I think I am just a bit thin-skinned because of fatigue. I have to accept that I'm in the kind of job where people don't go around congratulating you all the time, and where the pressure is relentless and you just have to move on to the next problem. The truth is that I can't have a normal life at the moment and I knew that when I took the job on. I was a bit low this morning and at lunchtime, when I sat in the sun in St James's Park, but now it's eight p.m., I'm on my way home and feeling a lot better. And that's because I had a good afternoon actually doing things, making a difference and so feeling I was doing something worthwhile.

We had an excellent meeting on rebuttal, media-monitoring and related issues. Before and after it I was dealing with yet another Scottish problem. Donald Dewar is meeting President Clinton tonight at the White House, but fuck-all had been done about arranging coverage of it. So we had to go into overdrive here to try to get it covered. At one point we were calling it a 'private meeting', which it wasn't. The *Daily Record* then called the White House, who said, 'It's just a handshake,' and we've since had to try to turn it into a proper meeting. One of the benefits of coming to Clinton's defence when he needs it. Sir Christopher Meyer [British ambassador in Washington] says the Clinton people never forget what TB did in public, supporting him at the height of the Monica business.

TB says George Carey [Archbishop of Canterbury] has been talking to 'very senior people' about wanting more religion on millennium night. Much laughter because TB can't talk about his meetings with the Queen and what she says, even to us. Charlie [Falconer, now in charge of Dome planning] horrified because it would wreck all their plans. TB even suggested they might read the Lord's Prayer at midnight.

Monday, 22 March 1999

We are starting to build up to a big phase of 'delivery'. Philip Gould says the focus groups suggest people don't believe what we say because we spin everything and put the best possible gloss on things. Following on from what he said about Scotland last week, he says that while Tory switchers continue to support us, Labour's traditional voters no longer feel instinctively that TB is on their side. He's lost the perception of having a strong mission that he had in opposition. Peter Hyman chipped in to say we were trying to take the sting out of everything and cited Lawrence and race. I agree with him 100 per cent and think we try too hard to be all things to all people.

TB says he knew he'd won the 1997 election when two

young girls saw him outside a pub and said, 'See him, he's *New* Labour' – he knew then that the message had got across. But he was then up against a real opposition, the Tories in power, and was able to engage. He now feels that's much harder to do.

He's very concerned about Kosovo at the moment. We're about to bomb Milosevic and are getting ready to send in ground troops with a high possibility of casualties. But why? What's it got to do with us that makes it worth risking British lives? Do people really expect the UK always to be the European country that takes the lead (or follows America's lead)? What are the actual objectives of our foreign policy? These are the questions we have been airing. TB seems to think it's just obvious that we should lead in order to get our objectives achieved.

Domestically he thinks we should establish very quickly whether we stand any chance at all in the Newark by-election [following the disqualification of the sitting Labour MP, who was later reinstated] and if, as he suspects, we do not, then we should immediately start downplaying it.

Other worries . . . business regulation (always a favourite), A levels (are our changes the right ones?), NHS funding, Longbridge ('We can't let this fail') and the need to rebut false stories. Some discussion, too, about whether we should significantly expand the Number Ten personnel by taking over more space, maybe incorporating Number Eleven, or even moving out of Downing Street and going somewhere else altogether.

Thursday, 25 March 1999

Part of the expansion agenda is a desire to beef up the foreign side of things. Some of us very worried that TB, AC and Jonathan Powell are far too keen on the foreign-policy side already. It's an area where they can get things done. AC sometimes seems more concerned about how things play in the European media than in our own. Anji, Peter Hyman, Philip Gould (and me, of course) far more concerned that we should be focusing on the domestic agenda. We've been trying to build up the message that we're delivering on our promises, but as we went to war with Serbia last night and the situation in Northern Ireland is coming to a head, it won't be easy.

Saturday, 27 March 1999

Slightly bizarre week, with TB and AC at a European summit in Berlin while running our part in the military action, not war, of course, against Serbia [or FRY, the Former Republic of Yugoslavia, as it was known in government]. Public opinion is clearly divided but probably about two to one in favour of the air strikes. TB did a message to the nation yesterday, saying he hoped the whole country would unite behind the action. There have been some curious divisions. Tony Benn against, Livingstone strongly in favour. Hague and the Tory front bench in favour, several Conservative grandees and ex-military commanders opposed. Some unease here about the lack of specific UN backing, but that's impossible with Russia and China against it. My fear is that while we're bombing away and the UN observers and all the journalists are out of the country, God only knows what horrors are being inflicted on the Kosovo Albanians.

I sat in on my first cabinet meeting on Thursday, chaired by Prescott in TB's absence. David Blunkett, who's due to appear on *Question Time* [BBC1] tonight, has been asking what the political objectives are. George Robertson [defence secretary] says it is to avert an impending humanitarian catastrophe. He said that some cynics in other European countries had been saying, 'Let the violence go on until the public is screaming for us to go in,' but that that couldn't be justified.

Some discussion over tactics in Parliament. Derry Irvine [lord chancellor] wonders if we should lock the Tory front bench in by putting down a substantive motion that they would have to vote for [a substantive motion leads to a specific vote, rather than a motion on the adjournment, which allows debate but not a vote]. But Margaret Beckett [leader of the House of Commons] and Ann Taylor [chief whip] say the convention is to have a motion on the adjournment [with no specific issue to vote on] so as not to expose divisions in either party that opponents could exploit. That also avoids subjecting our MPs to pressure to vote against their constituency parties.

I had another big row with the BBC over a TB interview on Kosovo before he left. He had time to do only one interview and the Beeb said it would be Paxman or nobody. We refused on the grounds that it was to be an interview for all programmes and not just a *Newsnight* one. Neither they nor I would back down. So I phoned a friend on BBC World television and he agreed to do the interview without telling the bosses. It ran at length on the *World at One* and *PM* [on Radio 4] and was included on the TV *Six o'Clock News*. So we win again. Anne Sloman [chief political adviser, BBC] was livid. Paxman, according to what was obviously a deliberate BBC leak to the *Daily Express*, was 'incandescent'. Fine by me.

Scotland has taken up the rest of my time this week. The situation has scarcely improved and there's a real danger that the daily lecture Gordon gives Donald on the morning conference call is sapping his confidence further. Donald basically wants to keep his head down and plough on to 6 May [election day for the Scottish Parliament], hoping for the best. Gordon is clearly exasperated. TB managed to get extra European money for the Highlands and Islands at the Berlin summit, which should have been a major turning-point in the campaign, but I'm not sure the Scots have managed to get it up as much as they should have. On Thursday I went to a film première of *Gods and Monsters*, with Ian McKellen. I took Mark Bennett [an assistant in the press office], who's a great film buff and really appreciated it. Apparently Monica Lewinsky was in the audience but we didn't see her. The film was great but the party afterwards was totally ghastly. Real showbizzy horrors and wannabe models. But Ann and Alan Keen [both Labour MPs, married – for Brentford and Isleworth, and Feltham and Heston respectively], Chris Smith and Dorian [his partner] were there, so at least there was some-body to talk to. And I'm off to Paul Gambaccini's fiftieth birthday party tonight.

Sunday, 28 March 1999

Paul's party was quite fun. Usual mix of fading DJs and pretty young things. It's getting on for twenty years now since Paul and I first met [Gambaccini was now a keen New Labour supporter].

The Sunday papers are pretty solidly behind the war, including the *Observer* significantly.

This morning's Scottish conference call was dominated by how Alex Salmond would respond to the conflict. The signs from last Friday's televised debate (at which Donald got a bit of a mauling, by all accounts) were that he'll be very equivocal about it. He said he had doubts about the exit strategy – doubts that Donald then said he shared! Gordon and I said it had to be about leadership at a time when our forces are in action.

Monday, 29 March 1999

TB determined that we must keep on until Milosevic is seen to be losing in Kosovo, then get him to the negotiating table. He seems to have little time for Robin Cook and today suggested we use John Reid (a transport minister!) rather than Robin to attack Salmond over Kosovo. As it happens, though, we did use Robin. Salmond very stupidly used his broadcast in response to TB's to say the action was 'deplorable' and 'misguided'. Tomorrow's papers will annihilate him with a bit of luck.

On the Budget, which has started to unravel, TB is worried that it has left a minefield that will 'detonate all over the bloody place'. In fact, almost everybody I spoke to in Number Ten today, including TB, was unsure whether most people would be better off or not this year. He is still angry with Gordon for forcing the cabinet to forgo their pay rise again this year. We had to reassure him that, despite the rises he's gone without, he still earns (just) more than Hague [who took all the rises], although the rest of the cabinet do not. The question we will have to get asked in the media is, 'Is Hague worth more than Mo?'

TB and AC are now in Northern Ireland, trying to clinch a deal before the end of the week. So delivery, Scotland, etc., tend to fall to me, something I'm more than happy about. It's good to feel I can get on with things without having to refer everything to AC.

Sunday, 4 April 1999

AC, now on holiday in France, wants me to find a back-bencher to attack John Simpson [BBC world affairs editor] and John Humphrys [*Today* programme] for giving succour to Milosevic by their critical reporting and questioning. I'm trying to find one, but this is one occasion where my sympathy is with the BBC. The flood of refugees is making the story more difficult for us, along with the admission by some Foreign Office official that appeared in the media saying NATO had shown 'a failure of imagination'. But the opinion polls continue to show strong support and the Scottish polls have become very good for us since Salmond called the action 'unpardonable folly'. Otherwise I'm enjoying a blissful four-day Easter weekend at home with only the Scottish conference call each morning to burden me. Gordon as ever frustrated with Donald and the lack of thought going into finding a good story for each day.

I helped Gordon do a briefing for both the daily and Sunday lobbies on Thursday. I enjoy working with him and he seems to have a lot more time for me now. All the ridiculous old Blair/Brown rivalries at last seem to be dissipating. I haven't seen AC for days. He was in Northern Ireland trying, with only limited success, to move the all-party talks forward. They're now adjourned until the thirteenth.

Wednesday, 7 April 1999

A farcical day as I tried to get to Chequers to assist TB with some television interviews but we had to turn back because of a big crash and fire on the M40. David Dimbleby [BBC] was also caught up in it, so only Sky and ITN got their interviews and TB had to do them without support. He could have done the *Six o'Clock News* live with Dimbleby on the BBC but wouldn't because he wanted to play tennis. So we'll probably end up doing the *Nine o'Clock News* from Scotland instead, forcing the BBC to send Dimbleby and God knows who else to Inverness so TB can have a decent game of tennis. I don't blame him for a second, but it makes me smile.

Saturday, 10 April 1999

Back from Scotland. I was rather upset on Thursday night in TB's room at the hotel, having a very enjoyable and slightly drunken dinner with everybody, including Anji and Pat McFadden [Policy Unit member responsible for Scotland] when TB was saying how important it was to have a good team. He said to somebody around the table something like, 'There's Lance, masses of experience as a BBC correspondent, and like others, Pat, Anji, etc., he'll get better.' It sounded for all the world like he didn't think I was yet performing at the level he wants. And, if I'm honest, I can see there's some truth in it. I don't feel I always have the quick, accurate judgements they want about how a story is playing or what we should be saying. There are silences when I'm in the car with TB and I can't really think of anything appropriate to say but when I'm sure AC would have plenty to say.

I told James all this over dinner last night and he said I was being too hard on myself and that TB, AC, Anji, etc., have all known each other and worked closely together for a very long time and that I shouldn't be expected to have the same level of intimacy or to be able to second-guess TB in the way they can. And maybe that's the positive interpretation of what TB said. From the way he said it, it clearly wasn't intended to be a put-down or anything. In fact, the trip to Scotland went very well and we got just about everything we could have asked for out of it.

I also set up and looked after a very important twelve-minute interview live on Thursday's *Nine o'Clock News*. He was exceptionally good, despite having serious reservations about the tone of the BBC's coverage from Kosovo. John Simpson's eyewitness account from a deserted Pristina made no mention whatever of the fact that it was

Milosevic's ethnic cleansing that had driven people out to a far larger extent than the bombing. The BBC had said that Simpson has to report subject to Yugoslav restrictions, but that point rarely sinks in with the viewers.

I do enjoy spending time in close proximity to TB, like on the plane or over dinner, although one point of distance comes from me being a gay man with no interest in football. Not that there's much I can do about either of those things. He is, of course, totally preoccupied by Kosovo at the moment, but also very exercised by the decision yesterday to block Sky's bid for Manchester United. No matter what we say publicly, he's very concerned to keep Murdoch on board [Murdoch's News International owns Sky] and he rightly points out that the *Sun* is the one paper to give us unequivocal support over Kosovo. He was furious that the DTI let it be reported that the government had blocked the deal, rather than the Monopolies and Mergers Commission. But the DTI press release did say 'Stephen Byers today blocked . . .'

According to the polls, TB is now far more popular than Thatcher ever was and the Tories are nowhere. So while we continue to agonise over delivery and Scotland and other issues, we're actually in astonishingly good shape.

Monday, 12 April 1999

Spent over an hour discussing internal structures, accommodation, bringing in more foreign-policy advice, building up Bill Bush's research and rebuttal unit (under a different name) and strengthening the Strategic Communications Unit. It makes me wonder if I want to redesign my role as more of a message-briefer and less of an all-round gofer for AC. I'd want to carry on doing the political stuff but that's not inconsistent with what I have in mind. The downside is that it will be my fault if journalists and commentators aren't getting the message.

Sunday, 18 April 1999

I've been working almost non-stop for the past seven days, but it's been very exciting and fulfilling as I've been given a lot of responsibility and have enjoyed it. On Wednesday AC went with TB to Brussels for a mini European Council, so I had to brief the lobby after John Prescott's excruciatingly embarrassing PMQs. [As deputy prime minister, Prescott stands in for Blair at the weekly Prime Minister's Questions if he is away.] He lost his place and paused for literally thirty seconds while he worked out what he was supposed to be saying, then forgot what questions he was being asked, and clearly didn't know what the withholding tax was when he was asked about it. Although, to be honest, I had to find out exactly what it was before doing the lobby because I had only a vague idea myself [it was a European Union proposal for, in effect, a tax on savings] and I knew I'd be asked. When the question came I said, quick as a flash, 'It's a tax on savings and we're against it,' which went down well with the journalists but might have sounded a bit as if I was undermining Prescott.

The expansion plans within Number Ten have been put on hold because Gordon won't give up any space in the flat [he had the original prime minister's flat over Number Ten while Blair took the much larger one over Number Eleven]: he's planning to get married and start a family. I spent much of Thursday drafting answers for questions that readers of the *Independent* had submitted for Peter Mandelson. I did the one on the gay issue, which everybody seemed to like and which Peter looked at seriously, but as ever it was vetoed by AC and TB. So we ended up with 'My personal life is not a secret but it is private.' I honestly hoped he would go further, just to give himself some peace of mind on the issue at last. I thought, in the middle of a war, with the Macintyre book [a biography of Mandelson by the sympathetic journalist Donald Macintyre was about to be published] coming out and talking about his sexuality, there would never be a better time. Failed again.

Since Friday AC has virtually taken over the NATO media machine in Brussels and, of course, it became a story. So I've been doing the Kosovo meetings here as well as the main lobby and the Sunday lobby. The Kosovo stuff with all the top brass was hard to understand at first because it was all expressed in initials and acronyms, but I've been getting the hang of it. There's a problem with the Serb air defences because they're mobile and so hard to hit.

After the Kosovo meeting this morning I was driven up to Chequers to help TB prepare for a *Face the Nation* interview for CBS in America. He invited me to stay for lunch afterwards with the family, which was nice. I then spent almost an hour sitting out on the terrace in the sun with him talking mainly about the conflict. I said my fear was that in three or four weeks we could be in exactly the same position we're in now [bombing from the air but unable to go in on the ground]. He agreed but said that couldn't be allowed to happen. It's pretty clear that he's considering a limited land invasion. I am probably going to Chicago and Washington with him later in the week.

AC will be in Brussels again tomorrow so it will be another busy week. I've had to spend some time trying to get us out of an embarrassing hole over the BBC's coverage, especially that of John Simpson. AC slagged him off to Phil Webster [political editor of *The Times*] and Phil wrote it up, making it pretty clear who his source was. I was named in some of the papers today as having pulled the government back from a row by saying that we understood the difficult situation Simpson was working in. I do agree that some of what he's been saying is questionable – for example, that if the Serbs take him and other journalists to a bomb site they must be confident of their version of the facts – but we have nothing to gain by getting into a spat with Simpson.

Friday, 23 April 1999

In Washington DC with TB for the NATO fifteenth anniversary summit at the end of a very hectic week, dominated again by Kosovo. On Tuesday I went to Brussels and RAF Brueggen with TB for a visit. All part of the UK trying to stiffen NATO's nerve for the conflict. TB was told by SACEUR [Supreme Allied Commander, Europe], General Wesley Clark, that basically NATO can't win this by air power alone. We are now in favour of using ground troops in a 'semi-permissive environment', i.e., when the Serb machine is so damaged it won't put up much of a fight. The Americans are coming round to that point of view and Clinton has pretty much signed up to it. But then when TB saw him here on Wednesday he was less sure. Not helped by the Russians trying to push a peace plan. Their plan is seen to be well short of what's required and so the ground troops debate goes on.

There's been a difficult debate over whether the main Serbian television station is a legitimate target given the propaganda it pumps out. We learned the result last night when Serb TV was indeed bombed.

Our rhetoric is now such that we can hardly get away with negotiating with Milosevic, certainly not in any way that leaves him in any kind of control over Kosovo or indeed able to threaten anybody. One scary aside – Robin Cook told AC last week that he's now more in favour of the use of ground troops after Gaynor took him to see *Saving Private Ryan*.

We were in Chicago yesterday for a visit to a school and a speech to the Chicago Economic Club. Not that I saw anything of Chicago except through the window of the press bus in a painfully slow convoy. TB was quite happy with the speech, although he thinks he desperately needs some better speechwriters. Lots of cracks on the plane down from Chicago, with TB saying that, if Clinton folds and we have to do a deal, we'll soon be saying that we didn't think Milosevic was such a bad guy and we could do business with him.

Wednesday, 28 April 1999

The weekend in DC was fascinating. I had the great experience of being on the conference floor with Clinton, Bill Cohen [US defense secretary], Blair and George Robertson discussing (them not me) the next stage of the campaign. Clinton is somehow different up close. More solid, squat, ruddy, looking exhausted but still very much in command.

On Sunday he chaired a Third Way seminar with TB, Wim Kok [Dutch prime minister], Schröder and Massimo D'Alema [Italian prime minister] in which his grasp of detail was extremely impressive. [The Third Way was the new politics espoused by Clinton, Blair and others who sought to find an alternative to old-style socialism and unrestricted free-market capitalism.] Hillary was in the front row, looking steely and impassive. Cherie thought the whole thing was such a bore that she didn't turn up until the very end. But it was much more interesting than I'd feared: five heads of government genuinely debating the issues and talking without scripts and very directly. Schröder was far and away the least impressive while D'Alema was quite provocative and ready to criticise the others – for example, saying we should invest at least as much in cancelling third-world debt as we spend on fighting the war. The ground troops issue didn't come up much but TB clearly hasn't convinced Clinton 100 per cent of the need to go for it.

The air campaign goes on and while there are some signs that the Serb regime may be starting to crack it seems a long way from collapsing.

The flight back to London was OK but TB was furious that he had to do yet more interviews when we got back on Monday. AC had said to set them up but I got the flak when TB was too tired and couldn't understand why he had to do them. Both TB and AC are a bit irritable at the moment and it affects everybody in the building. So the atmosphere isn't that great.

Monday, 3 May 1999

On my way to London after a very pleasant bank holiday weekend. My first full day off in over three weeks. I've been feeling very tired and stressed of late, but maybe that isn't so surprising. AC has been in Brussels getting NATO into shape so I do my job and more of his, but without the advantage of his total access to TB. As ever it takes me a fair bit longer just to find out what's going on.

On Thursday I accompanied TB to a private lunch at the *Daily Mail* with the new Lord Rothermere, Jonathan Harmsworth (a charming man looking like a young Rory Bremner, but who contributed very little to the conversation), Paul Dacre [editor of the *Daily Mail*], Max Hastings [editor of the *Evening Standard*], potty on the war and all that, but says he'll back anyone in London as mayor who isn't Ken or Jeffrey Archer [the likely Tory candidate] TB said he knew what he wanted on this but wouldn't elaborate and Peter Wright [editor of the *Mail on Sunday*]. TB gave very little away but did say how great a talent Peter Mandelson was, and on the euro said he wouldn't take Britain in if it was going to be bad for the economy but that he expected the single currency to succeed.

On Friday we went to Scotland and Wales in a day. I was convinced it was going to be a total disaster. Anji, who's also at NATO at the moment, hadn't advanced it [Anji Hunter normally checked out all visits beforehand]. We had to change a factory visit in Wales at the last minute after discovering that the owners had just been prosecuted over a death caused by a Japanese employee misusing some heavy equipment because he couldn't understand the instructions on it.

On the plane on the way I learned that TB wanted to do some interviews about the situation in Northern Ireland and nobody had bothered to tell me. So I had to get the BBC and UTV [Ulster Television] reporters up from London as well so they could interview TB at Glasgow airport at lunchtime. A logistical nightmare but I made it.

TB was addressing the Newspaper Press Fund in Glasgow and we discovered only the day before that Alex Salmond was going to be at the top table. It was too late to have Salmond pulled without creating a huge row but we knew he'd do something to distract attention from TB's attacks on the SNP in his speech. Sure enough he pulled out a 'bluff' card from his recent appearance on *Call My Bluff* and showed it to the cameras just as TB was attacking their independence arguments. In the event I think it backfired and made Salmond look like a clown, when most of TB's speech was about Kosovo and the future of Scotland.

Big row before the speech between Gordon Brown and Philip Gould. Gordon wanted TB to attack the Nats over the costs of an independent Scotland. Philip wanted him to be more positive and revitalise the Scottish election campaign campaign with a more upbeat message – all based on a dip in the polls and one focus group he'd done the day before. In the end he did both, but it was the bit that Gordon had wanted that made the news.

Meanwhile the BBC and ITN wanted to doorstep TB about Kosovan refugees and the chaos in the Tory Party. He's very worried indeed about Hague, who seems to be in political freefall. I briefed him on the methods of removing the Conservative leader and electing a new one, which alarmed him further because it raised the prospect of Ken Clarke taking over, something he really fears. I said if I were a right-wing Tory I'd put Clarke in now, let him get our majority down below a hundred and then replace him with Portillo after the election. We joked about how we would have to say any losses we suffer in next Thursday's local elections were a major reverse to try to prop Hague up a bit. But joking apart, TB was really alarmed. We have to save Hague at all costs!

The Welsh leg of the visit wasn't too bad in the end, although it was embarrassingly short for one of our few visits of the campaign.

As I was being driven back to Brighton from RAF Northolt I heard on the car radio about a bomb attack on a gay pub in Soho, the Admiral Duncan. It was a brutal and truly shocking attack with no warning. Three people died and dozens were injured. I urged Jonathan Powell that TB should say something in time for the *Nine o'Clock News*, but it was left to Jack Straw. TB did pieces on it for the *People* and the *Sunday Times* and added a section to his speech at a big Sikh event in Birmingham on Sunday. But at no time did he really address the gay community directly. He was ready to say that 'all the decent people of Britain' would be appalled – happy to talk to the majority but even now terrified of speaking to a minority for whom his precious coalition of support has little sympathy. I was genuinely disappointed and even a little surprised. It doesn't help that I'm currently reading the book by George Stephanopoulos, a liberal who became disillusioned with Clinton's pursuit of the middle ground, so maybe I'm being a bit harsh. I know that I'm significantly on the liberal wing of opinion in Number Ten, which is one reason why I so rarely take a stand on policy. But when we have such power to change Britain for the better why are we being so cautious? The emphasis on education is dead right, and the efforts to tackle poverty and social exclusion through work are admirable (and Gordon-inspired) but will this government be remembered as a great reforming adminis-tration? I hope so.

TB is maddeningly conservative sometimes, though. He says there is no denying the fact that private schools give kids a much better education – almost wistfully. The few, not the many. And on House of Lords reform, he's deter-mined to make the new chamber as undemocratic as possible. Maybe that is in the interests of good, strong government but it's hardly radical. We should be ready to defend our policies in every forum but, not least because we operate in such an adversarial system, every defeat is seen as a setback so we feel we have to win every time. In fact there are a surprising number of liberals and pluralists in Number Ten – Andrew Adonis, Roger Liddle, James Purnell [all in the Policy Unit] and Peter Hyman and I'm sure many others – but the hardliners rule the roost and maybe it's just as well they do. We'd probably throw it all away.

I've been trying to analyse what I actually *do*. I seem to attend a lot of meetings, watch a lot of TV bulletins, skim-read a lot of papers, feed the line to journalists, and that's about it. I sort out a lot of things that AC or some-body else would have to sort out as well, of course. Part of me thinks I should redesign my job to do more considered background briefing. Part of me thinks I should go off and get a university place somewhere and become a pundit. Part of me says why not become special adviser to the next international development secretary, if there is one, and do something useful. Part of me says I should stop being such a wimp and get on with the job.

Thursday, 6 May 1999

Polling Day at last [in Scotland and Wales and local elections in England]. There were some last-minute rows, notably between Gordon and Donald. Gordon apparently hitting the wall – literally – in fury after Donald admitted in an interview yesterday that Labour may not get an overall majority and may do a deal with the Lib Dems. He was right to be angry but it nearly became a big story because he insisted Donald was pulled from the last leaders' debate in the evening. TB was fuming about what he called the crazy electoral system and said we could always change it. It's still not clear who will do what after the election. TB has moved back towards making Helen Liddle secretary of state, although one other possibility would be to make John Reid secretary of state, put Andrew Smith into his old job at Transport and have Helen at Education.

Friday, 7 May 1999

Results day. No overall majority in Scotland but we are comfortably the largest party so no great surprise there. The Tories won around 1400 seats in the locals, which was enough for Hague to live and fight another day. That puts him just where we want him.

The whole building was in a panic over Wales this morning. Pat McFadden was being told we might get as few as twenty-three seats out of sixty, when we were confidently expecting a majority, and there was a strong possibility of Alun Michael not getting elected. TB f-ing and blinding about the whole thing, plus a widespread view that devolution had been a terrible idea. Everyone claimed to have believed all along that it would lead to disaster.

Bill Bush, who is still hiding out in Scotland, phoned to say he though our side was ready to give way on tuition fees even before the coalition negotiations begin [the Liberal Democrats were expected to demand the abolition of tuition fees as a price for joining the devolved executive]. Donald has been refusing to take calls from David Blunkett [education secretary], although TB made it clear to him this morning that he shouldn't concede it. The effect on the higher-education 'market' could be catastrophic. I do a bit of briefing to that effect while stressing that it's up to Donald to get the best deal he can and we're not interfering!

Before we knew Alun's result in Wales [he won] there was much disagreement about who to back for leader in his place if he lost. Sally Morgan says anybody but Ron Davies who would want to work with Plaid Cymru and who has been behaving mischievously during the campaign. She thinks, and I agree, that stopping Rhodri Morgan would be all but impossible anyway. But TB thinks Rhodri would be a slap in the face for him. There was a real sense of panic for a while. We lost a couple of real Labour heartland seats, Islwyn and the Rhonda, to the Nats. But then we held on to some others that we might have expected to lose to the Tories. Meltdown was avoided, after all.

TB also very angry still about the prospect of Clinton selling him down the river to do a deal with Milosevic. 'If he does that, that's it, I'm finished with him.' And this is a guy who's been prime minister just two years. But he's seen in the US media, and by just about everybody else, as the strong man, the hawk of NATO. We discuss the long-term political prospects, which are, of course, excellent, and he always qualifies it with 'unless the war goes badly'. The G7 and Russia have agreed on what needs to happen and Robin Cook has successfully stiffened it up [the G7 was the forerunner of the G8 before Russia became a member]. It's being seen as Serbia losing an important ally, Russia, rather than NATO starting to compromise, which was what TB had feared.

I've been briefing him for his various interviews, etc., while AC has been at home getting his teeth fixed, and he seems to be happy with the way I have handled it. Anji is back from Brussels and Macedonia and has been very supportive.

Tuesday, 11 May 1999

Despite the elections, Scotland and Wales continue to dominate much of my time. Coalition negotiations dragging on in Scotland mainly over tuition fees [after the elections Labour and the Liberal Democrats began negotiations to form a coalition executive to administer the devolved government]. We have to make the UK case without it looking as if TB is pulling the strings from London. He said at the end of last week that the result in Scotland, in which we got around 40 per cent of the vote but couldn't form a majority government, meant 'the death of PR at Westminster' and I'm sure that's the view of much of the PLP [Parliamentary Labour Party].

TB still concerned about the conduct of the war and how he will look at the end of it. He says he's prepared effectively to disown a deal if it's a shabby compromise and doesn't mind being seen as the one who pushed for a hard line but in the end wasn't running the show. 'If I was running the show we wouldn't be where we are now.' I persuaded him today not to lay into Michael Howard [shadow foreign secretary] after he distanced the Tories from the conduct of the war. Anji, who knows Howard, says he always has a good feel for which way the wind is blowing. Derek Fatchett [Foreign Office minister] died very suddenly on Sunday night and people are already hustling for (a) his job and (b) his seat. Best bet for the former seems to be Geoff Hoon, although Charlie Falconer suggested Peter Mandelson, and Denis MacShane lobbied me half-seriously today. Offered me a fiver if I'd put his name in the frame!

Thursday, 13 May 1999

Drunken dinner last night with Matthew Parris and some other friends, including Michael Brown [former Tory MP, now *Independent* journalist]. It set me thinking again about the life of a columnist/commentator. Could be a lot of fun but a bit uncertain.

Meanwhile, at Downing Street we discuss how best to get our message across to the columnists there already are. Phil Bassett [in the Strategic Communications Unit] will be doing a fair bit, which is a good idea. Anji now busy with maps of Numbers Ten, Eleven and Twelve, as well as the Cabinet Office next door, looking where we can send in the tanks to get ourselves some more living space. The war mentality is getting to her. She reminded me of the pictures of Mrs Thatcher surrounded by maps of the Falkland Islands.

Communications with Scotland a little strained as they continue to negotiate with the Lib Dems. But it seems we have forced the Lib Dems to accept some compromise inquiry on tuition fees with, crucially, the proviso that they must be bound by collective responsibility over the Scottish Executive's response to it.

AC has been back in town, but not much in evidence. He is hobnobbing with Hillary Clinton just now. Reshuffle in the Scottish Office [the government department was about to have its workload cut drastically as a result of the election of a devolved administration] tomorrow.

John Reid is clearly not happy that Helen Liddle is to get the secretary of state job. He's feeling the strain of being the eternal deputy, and his relationship with Prescott, his current boss, is not good. I attended my first meeting of the PLP yesterday. TB was paying tribute to John Smith on the fifth anniversary of his death. It was quite encouraging to see that people do seem to speak their minds at it pretty clearly. TB was treating it like any other public meeting and giving them much the same answers he would give to anyone. That is one of his strengths. Fraser Kemp [Labour MP for Houghton and Washington] asked me to help him with a question for PMQs and while I wrote one I then forgot to send it – a bit frustrating as it would have been a lot better than the one he asked.

Friday, 14 May 1999

TB is supposed to be making his Scottish reshuffle now (09.30) but he's still not firmly decided. Gordon very lukewarm on Helen, Pat McFadden dead against. Prescott and I argued that it's not much of a job now anyway, and it would be a disaster to move John Reid from Transport and replace him with Helen. So the reshuffle will now be on Monday.

(*Later*) I explained to the lobby that the delay in the announcement was because of Derek Fatchett's funeral.

The Northern Ireland talks have been going on all day – they have overrun so long that it looks like some sort of a breakthrough or a serious setback.

TB was very vocal today on the subject of ground troops

in Kosovo. He'd spoken to Hillary the night before, who said Clinton was torn between his own feeling that tougher action was needed and the reluctance of others in the administration. Bill Cohen [US defense secretary] is firmly against ground troops, and Clinton thinks the American public are just not ready for it, particularly as it's so far away from their shores. Even so, we were discussing how it could yet be helped to happen. The US could end up supplying less than half the number of troops and the UK could provide as many as half the European contingent, something we could just about manage apparently. But TB as adamant as ever that we cannot fail. News of another NATO error today won't help. Upwards of fifty civilian casualties in a Kosovan village. Still not clear what happened.

Monday, 17 May 1999

The reshuffle finally took place this morning, with TB seemingly in two minds right up to the end. Everyone assumed he was appointing Helen to Scotland but then he caused a lot of raised eyebrows by saying, 'I think it had better be John Reid.' So Gordon clearly won him over during the weekend, arguing that Scotland needed a clever and very political secretary of state to make the case for the Union and that Helen wasn't that person. She was, needless to say, very disappointed and John delighted. Charlie Falconer still pressed 'the case for the Jubilee Line' – that Transport needed a good minister every bit as much as Scotland, a view I shared and expressed. But TB thought Helen would be more than able to push that through. Geoff Hoon, as expected, replaced Derek Fatchett and Keith Vaz got his old job. But TB made that decision at the last minute too, with the alternative being some new guy whom I'd never heard of and whose name I've forgotten already. Otherwise Kosovo still dominates.

TB is in Bulgaria today and Albania tomorrow. He said before he left that the question of ground troops 'will either be resolved this week or it won't', which seems hard to argue with. All the signs from Washington are that Clinton won't go for it, but TB remains very gung-ho and not at all depressed so maybe he knows something we don't. He agrees that we must concentrate more on domestic policy, and Peter Hyman and I have given ourselves the task of finding one big domestic story a week to get him identified with.

Tuesday, 18 May 1999

TB in Albania today as the Germans, Italians and Americans continue to make discouraging noises about ground troops. The debate is getting very difficult indeed, and when he got back he seemed totally exhausted and distracted.

Had a drink tonight with Mike Craven [former aide to John Prescott] and Greg Pope [government whip]. Greg said we had to draw stumps in the debate on welfare reforms on Monday night because we would have lost it [despite an overall Commons majority of 179 after the election in 1997]. People's positions were hardening as the late night wore on, fuelled by a bit of drink and a lot of time spent talking to each other and giving each other courage to rebel. Also a fair number of ministers were absent, so it was more difficult to make up the numbers on our side.

Wednesday, 19 May 1999

Bit of a wobble over the war. AC at this morning's lobby, which I wasn't at, seemed to give credence to the idea that we might back an Italian proposal for a forty-eight-hour pause in the bombing to allow for a Security Council resolution. The deal would be that Milosevic would have to accept all five of NATO's demands during the pause or he'd be hit by the full might afterwards – resumed air strikes plus ground troops. I expressed opposition on the grounds that (a) once you stop the bombing you'll never start it again: Italy, Greece, the US maybe and Germany would all come up with reasons why not; (b) it would be fudged because Milosevic would move a bit but not quite enough during the pause, exacerbating all the problems above; (c) you could never build up enough ground troops in the space of forty-eight hours; and (d) the rest of NATO would be less inclined to use them by that time anyway, not more. Very odd to find myself in a more hawkish position than AC for the first time during the war.

The Irish parties are back at Number Ten tonight after the Unionists rejected last week's deal even though David Trimble [leader of the Ulster Unionists] was supposed to be recommending it.

Wednesday, 26 May 1999

Less talk of peace deals in Kosovo now, more of building up our ground forces. Significant increases, which give the impression that the British position is gaining ground. Yet AC says we could still find ourselves muddling through until the summer.

CNN started reporting today that Milosevic is to be indicted by the UN War Crimes Tribunal. It was all top secret and not due to be announced until tomorrow.

We announced yesterday that Sir Alastair Goodlad [Tory MP for Eddisbury], Hague's nominee to become a European commissioner, is to be made high commissioner in Australia instead. It clears the way for Chris Patten [former Tory Party chairman, governor of Hong Kong and a strong pro-European] to go to Brussels instead. Tories furious and it means a by-election where they have a majority of 1000.

I bumped into Hague [whom I had known well as a BBC correspondent] in Number Ten on Monday morning and we exchanged a slightly awkward hello. He was in for a Kosovo briefing.

TB rather exercised about the party and rightly so. There's a general agreement that we need a strong political figure in Millbank [Labour Party headquarters]. David Miliband suggested Mo and two good deputies (the assumption being, no doubt correctly, that Mo just doesn't have what it takes to actually manage the place). Sally Morgan suggested Ian McCartney and TB agreed he'd be good.

The chaos continues in Scotland along with the in-fighting. There's virtually no press office operation left at all. And nationally there is a general conclusion that our communications strategy isn't working properly with AC away so much. So I wrote a paper proposing some changes and a small revolution has ensued. All very good, with me becoming possibly deputy director of communications or something, but more importantly head of events and planning. I will be doing less day-to-day stuff and more looking ahead and making sure we've got our lines right, have prepared the ground for announcements, etc. It will be more rewarding because I'll be doing a specific job, and I'll have less crap to do and fewer silly meetings, I hope. So all round a good thing. I'll still deputise for AC on political stuff but will have a much more clearly defined role, which suits me. It's a big sidelining of the SCU [Strategic Communications Unit]. It was even suggested that I take it over, which might happen at a later date, I suppose. But I wouldn't want all the management crap. It's not settled yet, but I hope it'll work out well.

Monday, 31 May 1999

Another good bank holiday weekend. I've been musing on the possibility of selling the Brighton house and buying something quite big in Provence, letting it in the summer and living off the income all year. It would open up all kinds of possibilities, like writing, making films, travelling more, who knows? Why are we both working ourselves into the ground? I talked it through with James and he's very keen.

I had to do a bit of work over the weekend but not much. Chris Patten called out of the blue from his place in France to talk about press stories that he wants a better job than Kinnock [Labour's nominee] at the European Commission.

Actually quite looking forward to work tomorrow and making a fresh start with the new set-up. The key thing is to make the change as dramatic and obvious as possible. I dare say others, maybe AC, will want to suggest it's not really that big a change.

Wednesday, 2 June 1999

Trying to get on with the new role of preparing for and developing the big and difficult stories, but finding it very hard to disengage from my normal activities. AC still wants me to deputise for him on the political stuff, which I really want to do, but he also gives me time-consuming on-the-day stuff to do about GM foods, etc. It's not helped by the fact that Parliament is in recess and there's hardly anybody else in the press office. David Miliband, Charlie Falconer and others all keen for me to pursue my new role, but I'll have to be very strict about it or I'll end up not doing either job properly. Tonight we went through the current troublesome issues and discovered that we were talking about the same old subjects.

Meanwhile in the European election campaign [for the European parliament] Hague has been making the running on the euro with some success, helped by the fact that it's now lost 11 per cent of its value since it was first launched. [Although euro notes and coins did not come into circulation until 1 January 2002, it already had a notional value and most European currencies, but not the pound, were tied to it as a prelude to its introduction]. Charlie has become obsessed about it and says it looks like a weak Mickey Mouse currency that we'd be mad to join. Jonathan Powell says he and nobody else seems to understand currencies and it's not about their value. The pound is overvalued and we want to see it lower. The economics of these things have always taxed my brain cells. Politically, TB wants other people, in particular business people, to be out there making the argument for it. We talk, as we have before, about the need for a revitalised European Movement, using younger backbenchers, but nothing is decided. TB seems reluctant to engage on how he wants the debate moved on so we continue to drift.

On GM foods TB refuses to budge but the rest of us think we should be in a different position, holding the ring rather than exposed as advocates of something the vast majority of people are uneasy about. I made a plea today for better communication within Number Ten, which people agreed with but which I will believe when I see.

Sunday, 6 June 1999

We appear to have the prospect of peace in Kosovo after Milosevic backed down in the face of a combined NATO-EU-Russian position. As of now the talks on troop withdrawal are being stalled by the Serbs and the air campaign goes on, but the end must be close.

It happened while TB was at the European Council in

Cologne. AC rang me from there to ask me to investigate the prospects of a prime ministerial broadcast. This I did, sending a shiver down the spine of the BBC suits led by Anne Sloman [chief political adviser]. But it seems AC didn't have TB's say-so for the idea. So by Friday morning I was planning a live press conference timed for the beginning of the *Six o'Clock News*, but in the event it amounted to nothing more than an interview with Robin Oakley [BBC political editor] in Rotterdam where TB was doing a European election event with Wim Kok [Dutch prime minister]. It made us look pretty daft in the eyes of the BBC.

Wednesday, 9 June 1999

The last day of the European election campaign and a feeling that we're starting to get back to normal. Still no final agreement in Kosovo, and Northern Ireland still to sort out. Even so we're looking ahead to other things with me in a more pivotal role.

Big row today between TB and Gordon over third-world debt. DfID [Department for International Development] suggested TB should get involved in an event today at which it would be announced that $100 million of UK aid would be provided to cut debt. I agreed, but the Number Ten Private Office wondered why they didn't know anything about it. Up until late yesterday the Treasury, who were hosting the event, said it wasn't settled and nor was the money. Then, at seven o'clock last night, they finally confirmed everything I'd already been told by DfID last Thursday. Basically Gordon was trying to steal all the glory.

TB was furious because he's been trying to get extra money out of Gordon for Health and can't believe that he can announce this without proper consultation or notice. By all accounts, there were raised voices when they met today. Those who have been around longer than I have seemed to think this was all fairly typical behaviour by the Treasury, albeit a rather extreme example.

TB is meanwhile rather wobbly on the euro message, admitting on the *Today* programme this morning that people wouldn't vote yes to the euro at the moment, and then at a press conference he said that PR was 'more democratic' and meant that your vote wasn't wasted if you wanted to vote Tory in a solidly Labour area. Er . . . the message is supposed to be 'Vote Labour', Tony! A lot of people both surprised and disappointed by his performance.

The Conservative Party treasurer, Michael Ashcroft, has been rejected for a life peerage by the Honours Scrutiny Committee. The Tories think we're trying to undermine him and have briefed the *Telegraph* that his name has been withdrawn. The Working Peers list has been delayed by three weeks because of the row.

News has just come through that an agreement has been reached in Kosovo, so I've been putting out statements and taking loads of calls. Very good news.

Sunday, 13 June 1999

European election results later today. The pundits are saying we could come in behind the Tories, which is certainly TB's view. He bet Philip Gould as much. Even if we come out on top it will mean very little. The Tories fought a very effective single-issue campaign on the euro, and we were pretty crap all round. But, then, we were handicapped by not being able to campaign effectively on the euro, either for or against. Mind you, does it really matter? So what if we do badly today? Victory at the next general election is all but certain and, you never know, we may decide we don't want to go into the euro in two or three years after all. We do at least have the advantage of flexibility, and a poll today in the *Sunday Telegraph*, while showing a very clear margin against the euro now, suggested that if it was clear the euro was in Britain's economic interests there would be a solid majority in favour.

Very interesting discussions on Friday. A political away-day that should have been at Chequers but was at Number Ten instead. Interrupted by a potential crisis in Kosovo where the Russians dashed across Serbia and entered Kosovo ahead of NATO. But it was essentially a day for free thinking. TB a little distracted, as ever these days. He really came alive only while we were discussing GM foods: he wants us to change position to become honest brokers, but insists that scientists and others must make the arguments strongly in favour if we don't – which, of course, they won't.

We talked about the lack of a clear message during the European elections and this spread to a discussion about the reluctance of much of the cabinet to think and act politically. Only TB, Gordon, Blunkett and sometimes Jack Straw ever really act politically. Margaret McDonagh [general secretary of the Labour Party] said too many of them had become administrators and not politicians. I pointed out that some ministers saw their way to the top as to keep their heads down and not fuck up, to which Margaret said, in front of everyone, 'My God, and I thought I was blunt!'

TB said he was crying out for interesting speeches from ministers and I said I was trying to organise some.

He said I should tell him if some ministers were refusing to do programmes like *Question Time* (which they undoubtedly are) and he will write to them.

There was the usual inconclusive discussion about getting someone in place in the reshuffle as a sort of party chair, speaking up across the board but also organising the party better.

We talked about the core vote, who are generally

perceived not to have come out in the European elections just as they stayed at home in Wales and, to a lesser extent, in Scotland. It was agreed that we shouldn't differentiate our message but that we did need to find some better ways of connecting all the same. As ever it comes down to delivery. Bill Bush [head of Research] said we should mount a strategy based on TB 'coming home' with more soft and regional interviews. Perhaps a summer campaign on 'Britain's Getting Better'.

David Miliband talked about what the government's legacies would be – independence for the Bank of England, the national minimum wage, devolution, a settlement in Northern Ireland (hopefully) and the Dome. It was agreed that dealing with education was also crucial, along with the issues of community and social inclusion. It was pointed out that it was difficult for a government that is perceived to be so close to the monarchy, wealthy business people and the military to be seen as meritocratic. Also that, despite our rhetoric, the extra investment in health and education was nothing spectacular and (in the case of the NHS) was largely being eaten up by wages. Far more money was going into supporting families and the less well-off through the Working Families Tax Credit and Child Benefit.

On transport, the generally woeful state of things was the main conclusion. But it was felt that the new Jubilee Line and improvements to the Northern Line would look to some like a significant step. Otherwise crappy initiatives, like the M4 bus lane, should go. It was pointed out, though, that much of the problem was that we had been *too* successful in getting people back on to public transport.

On GM, the feeling was that the public argument might only be turned round when we had genetically modified chips or chocolate cake that didn't make you fat.

Later, TB signed up to our new communications structure, although I'm not sure it will amount to all that much, especially as there is a real reluctance about announcing it in any way. Still, I feel very fulfilled and happy about the way things are going. I felt better, too, when TB said, in very general terms, that when new staff joined, after a year or so 'they get a lot better', suggesting that his comment about me in Scotland [see 10 April 1999] really wasn't meant personally.

Monday, 14 June 1999

The European election results were absolutely chronic. We finished 7–8 per cent behind the Tories, and overall the Socialist Group lost its majority in the European Parliament. So, on the face of it, we should have had a gloomy day today. In fact, while there was lots of 'bloody awful' and 'really bad news' about the place, it wasn't exactly seen as the end of the world. Not good news for the European project, of course. A more mixed result for the PR project. It could be argued that the fact that it was an election under proportional representation put people off because the constituency link was lost – except that nobody ever had the first idea who their European MEP was anyway. As for the party itself, they have to face up to the fact that we'd have had far *fewer* MEPs if the elections had been fought under first-past-the-post as before. The basic conclusion is that we do need to connect with our heartland/core vote, that we do need a party chairman-type figure and that our stance on the euro isn't doing us a lot of good.

AC and I advised against a proposed dinner with Rupert Murdoch tonight on the grounds that it would leak and that it would look like we were pandering to him in a panic over the elections. I made the mistake of entering the morning meeting and saying to Philip Gould, 'Where's the bottle of wine, then?' [he had bet TB a bottle of wine we would come out on top] only to be told, 'Oh, fuck off.' He promised lots of polling and focus groups and said, 'We can fix it. We will fix it.'

In fact the results are not such a disaster. Hague stays, much strengthened. Good. The party and ministers realise that even though the government is popular Labour can still lose elections and they have to go out and fight. Very good. And MPs and others might just think, 'I wish we had Mandelson back.' Good for Peter.

Sunday, 20 June 1999

Interesting week. The discussions post European elections go on, although nothing like as dramatically as the newspapers would have you believe. Even so, lots of comment from the likes of John Monks [general secretary of the TUC] that New Labour is treating its traditional supporters like embarrassing elderly relatives at a party (quite a good image, really!).

I'm not at all sure what the plan is with Peter, although I'm picking up increasing vibes that he might be returning with a job at Millbank that's short of being party chairman. TB said on Tuesday that he wasn't happy with all the speculation about Peter because 'It makes it more difficult for me to do it.' That was on a trip to Northern Ireland, my first with TB, that I really enjoyed. We flew by army helicopter from Aldergrove airport to Stranmillis where he was making a speech, then went by car to Castle Buildings for talks, and back to the airport by chopper. TB made a very powerful and direct speech, making it clear he's getting pretty exasperated but saying the 30 June deadline [for an agreement on a devolved administration] was very real.

On the plane over, TB was working with Jonathan on a paper entitled 'Europe', but I didn't get to see it. In a way it's frustrating, but I don't mind that much. It's interesting, reading Donald Macintyre's book [*Mandelson*], that in Peter's days with Kinnock [when Mandelson was the party's director of communications] he often briefed journalists based on guesswork and intuition because he didn't get to talk to Kinnock as much as he wanted to and often felt in the dark. So I'm not the first!

On Wednesday I went up to Scotland to talk to them about setting up a Strategic Communications Unit and a decent press office for the Scottish Executive. Their big problem is that, unlike at Number Ten, there's no clear political direction. They don't know if they are supposed to be New Labour or something different. Are they supposed to be selling Labour or the Lib-Lab partnership administration? Some partnership, though, when the Lib Dems apparently feel they can vote against the government whenever they feel like it. And Donald Dewar is not cracking the whip. As if.

I was spotted in the street by Ian McWhirter and Peter McMahon [of the *Scotsman*] so there was a bitchy piece in the paper the following day about London telling the Scots how to do it. Yawn.

Went out on Thursday to the Oxo Tower with Peter Hyman to celebrate his wedding.

Monday, 21 June 1999

Papers still full of 'Labour in turmoil' stories. This morning John Edmonds [general secretary of the GMB Union] added to John Monks's comments about elderly relatives at a party in typically unhelpful fashion by saying we should adjust our policies to please our core supporters. It wasn't helped by some briefing from Millbank to the effect that TB would be using a speech to the PLP to tell people to calm down. AC was furious, and there's a feeling that the party people are far too keen to brief on what TB thinks or says without any reference to AC, me or anybody else.

Our line is to say that the European election results were about Europe and not about the government's ability to deliver on its promises. There's a problem with people's perception of Europe, with apathy, with turnout, but that's it. After all, the Tories got 8 per cent of the population to vote for them and we got 6 per cent to vote for us. TB's view is that while there might be a problem with the heartlands it isn't going to be solved by targeting some special message at them. It's a general reconnection problem. The answer is to take the New Labour message outwards and downwards and get it across. On the euro he says, 'I must sit down with Gordon and sort out the problems.' He thinks our present position is fine and in an interview over the weekend during the G8 in Cologne he said it would be 'daft' for Britain to go in now. Ken Clarke [former Tory chancellor and strong pro-European] said as much a week or so ago, but it wasn't much reported. In the general election TB says we should stress the referendum, which would come early in the next parliament. The optimum time to go in would be three or four years from now when the rest of Europe would be desperate for us to go in and we could get the terms we wanted, rather than in ten years when we'd be desperate to join and would get a far worse deal.

Talking about the putative launch of Britain in Europe, TB says it must not be just a pro-euro campaign. [Britain in Europe was an all-party campaigning organisation set up to argue for a more positive attitude to the European Union. It was launched on 14 October 1999 by the Prime Minister and the Chancellor, with former Conservative cabinet ministers Kenneth Clarke and Michael Heseltine and the Liberal Democrat leader Charles Kennedy also on the platform. There were tensions between those who wanted it to campaign actively for the UK to join the single currency and those, like Tony Blair, who insisted that it support the government position of recommending membership of the euro only if the economic conditions were right. Campaign Director Lucy Powell announced that it would be wound up in the summer of 2005 after it became clear there would be no referendum on the European Constitution.] It should have an overarching message of Britain engaging constructively in Europe, with the underlying message on the euro that you shouldn't rule out any options. Ken Clarke, Michael Heseltine and the business leaders involved with Britain in Europe 'must come into line with me' and all pro-Europeans should be making the same case. Charlie Falconer says it would be absurd for TB to go on a Britain in Europe platform and refuse to speak about the euro. That would be like going to an anti-abortion meeting and saying, 'I'm not prepared to talk about abortion, just childbirth in general.'

This evening I told TB that *Newsnight* were doing a report saying he could be leaving it too late to convince people of the merits of the euro if he didn't start soon. But he said, rather exasperated, 'They just don't understand. You could mount a campaign on that in just a couple of months.' He wants more attack lines on the Tory positions on the New Deal, the Working Families Tax Credit and their membership in the [pro-Europe] European People's Party group in the European Parliament. He wants a tougher anti-crime message from Jack Straw, and says that while Ann Widdecombe [shadow home secretary] is 'ghastly' she would still be able to get up a tough message. It's been an exhausting day. I'm supposed to be getting a campaign up to refocus what we're saying about welfare reform, but I just don't have time to do it.

Two Gurkhas were killed in Kosovo today. So far the media think they were trying to deal with a Serb arms dump, but it now seems it may have been unexploded NATO bombs. Unfortunately TB did a news clip before the latter information emerged and clearly implied they were Serb weapons.

Wednesday, 14 July 1999

First week back after a fantastic fortnight's holiday in Iceland. Work has been crazy since I got back. No great crisis, although the Northern Ireland peace process is in big trouble again. The Ulster Unionists are refusing to join an executive until the IRA disarms. It was all going on while we were away and has continued this week with legislation going through the House of Commons to allow for devolution. That will now be put on ice.

I've been more involved with planning a series of big speeches. It started today with a Jack Straw speech that hasn't made much of a splash. I coined the phrase 'New Labour Working' to cover them all. It was much liked by AC and Philip Gould and was used twice by TB at Prime Minister's Questions today. It will probably be our slogan for the summer campaign too, although we have to be very diplomatic and bring Gordon, Prescott, Margaret Beckett *et al.* along too – something I had to be reminded of.

Quite a lot of paranoia about Gordon around at the moment with some people thinking he's been behind various stories leaking out – although it's clear Peter has been doing his usual trick of talking to a lot of journalists and letting them think he knows TB's mind. He's been talking on the summer reshuffle in particular, which everyone is paranoid about and on which there's been loads of bad stuff in the papers already. So there's now a ban on any reshuffle speculation.

TB and Prescott had a big row about the public services while I was away. TB said off the cuff to a meeting of venture capitalists that he 'bore the scars' on his back of trying to reform the public services. Prescott, who's been very sensitive of late and thinks we're all briefing against him on transport, hit back the following day saying how much the public services had contributed, etc. He finished by saying, 'I'm glad I got that off my chest.' He said faceless wonders had been briefing against him and *The Times* did a typically inaccurate cuttings job on special advisers, including me.

TB is concerned about how the cooling off in enthusiasm for the government, which he thinks is inevitable, is manifesting itself. He thinks a rejuvenated Tory Party gives us a good opportunity to get some better definition ourselves. Widdecombe will be heading the Tories' summer campaign but she agrees with us about fox-hunting, an issue TB revived largely unintentionally on *Question Time* last week. There's been a lot of debate about whether we should do something about hunting and run the wrath of the countryside lobby or not. We've raised so many expectations with our own backbenchers that I think we must. TB is convinced the Tories will come at us on crime soon and wants to make sure that Jack doesn't buy the view of those officials who think crime is bound to go up because of demographic trends, etc.

Tuesday, 20 July 1999

Just about adjusted to being back now and much more fulfilled with my new role. I'm currently planning for August and it looks as if things are far better organised than last year. A much more political campaign is in the offing, which is just as well as the Tories will be really motoring. TB has asked for a lot of planning. For some reason he didn't think it was a good idea for Prescott and me to just busk it! We've got lots of plans for TB to get re-engaged on the domestic front, on health, education, crime and welfare. But Bill Bush and I have discussed the risk of spreading him too thinly. One plan, now fairly well advanced, is for him to do a three-day visit to the North West. A kind of foreign visit but at home. I'm a bit worried it will look gimmicky, but if it means him being seen in schools and hospitals, etc., in a concentrated way then I'm for it. Cherie isn't keen, even down to saying that TB shouldn't go into an A&E ward because he's a bit squeamish and that he doesn't like staying in hotels. We decided today that TB should go up to the Eddisbury by-election [caused by the Tory MP, Sir Alastair Goodlad, being made high commissioner in Australia]. I was against, as was AC for a long time, on the grounds that it would suggest we thought we could win the seat when it ought to be an easy one for the Tories. It will just set Hague up for a bigger victory. But the team up there say they've got real momentum and the Tory candidate isn't popular. Fox-hunting is working well for us there too because there's a really unpopular local hunt.

We did a forty-five-minute *Newsnight* special on education yesterday. I set it up and was very nervous as it could all have gone horribly wrong but everyone, including TB, thought it was good. Although some people who saw it only on TV rather than in the room where it was recorded thought he looked uncomfortable and didn't come out of it well. But we said we wanted definition through conflict, TB taking on his critics, etc., and that's what we got.

The 'vision' speeches have been working pretty well. Straw flopped but Frank Dobson [health secretary], Alistair Darling [social security], Blunkett and Prescott have gone OK. So it's good to feel I'm making a difference.

Reshuffle speculation continues unabated. Peter making

a very unsubtle bid through the media to be Northern Ireland secretary. Mo got fed up and finally said yesterday that she hadn't had her fill of Northern Ireland and wanted to stay. Dobbo similarly made clear he didn't want to move from Health. It's all incredibly destabilising. We're all totally banned from commenting. Not that I know anything anyway. TB has asked his political team to give him views on ministers privately.

Sunday, 25 July 1999

The end of a baking hot weekend. The papers full of ill-informed stories about the reshuffle and the usual rubbish. I'm still busy preparing for August and it seems we should have quite a decent campaign running. The attack on the Tories will be a combination of drawing attention to a forty-seven-billion-pound black hole in their finances and an attempt to brand them as extremists using a theme from *The X-Files*. X for Xtremism, etc. A Phil Bassett idea that seemed good.

I had my first meeting with Prescott about the summer on Thursday. He doesn't really want to work this August and would rather go on holiday but he will, he says, because he's told Tony he will. He looked totally shattered and was very frank. He said he had another couple of years' campaigning in him and he didn't need to be rushing around the country. He was very proud to be DPM but implied he had no other ambitions, so he should be fairly easy to work with over the summer, provided he doesn't feel he's being undermined. His first question was, 'What's Charlie Falconer going to be doing?' Truthful answer: taking a lot of decisions and keeping in touch with TB. Answer I gave (true in so far as it went), he'll be chairing an afternoon campaigning meeting and making sure ministers do their bit. I'm quite looking forward to the summer recess, mainly I guess because I'll have a lot more authority than usual.

Thursday night was the Number Ten barbecue in the garden, the first that partners have been allowed to attend. James came and he was a bit nervous at first but relaxed after a few drinks. He met TB, who didn't say a lot because he was also talking to a couple of women from Switch. Cherie was a bit more chatty. She gave me a kiss and said if I wanted to stay over at Chequers in a couple of weeks when TB is seeing some newspaper editors up there then I'd be very welcome.

Anji told James that she and some of the other women had been looking out of one of the upstairs windows and had decided that he was definitely the best-looking man there and had been disappointed when they saw him coming up to me.

The Tories have held on in Eddisbury, although they only added a few hundred votes to their general-election total. It has been widely written up as a very bad result for them. Hague had said he was going to give us a good kicking and Peter Kellner wrote in the *Standard* that he didn't even give us a slap on the wrist.

I'm seeing a lot more of Philip Gould these days as Peter Hyman is away. His analysis is that people no longer think of TB as being 'on their side'. Which is why we're doing lots of reconnection efforts, like the *Newsnight* education programme and phone-ins. Another farce with the BBC. Anne Sloman vetoed the phone-in on Nicky Campbell's show on Five Live because we were insisting on choosing the location and including an audience of local people. So we did it on *BBC Breakfast TV* instead and she allowed it under exactly the same terms. Probably because I said to *Breakfast*, 'You've got two hours to decide or I'm offering him to GMTV or Talk Radio.'

On Wednesday we'll know if Peter is back in the cabinet.

Monday, 26 July 1999

TB launched the government's annual report this morning at a hospital and it got far better coverage than last year, mainly because it wasn't so much of a PR job but admitted that there were areas where we can do better. He did the phone-in and got some tricky questions on health at the Q&A session at the hospital. But it showed him engaged in issues that really matter to people. He came back and asked if the strategy had been right to admit that not everything was hunky-dory. We all did our best to convince him that it was. He complained that he was the only person in the government trying to put over a 'big picture' message. In fact others, well, some of them, do try but only he has much success in getting coverage.

John Prescott has been on the warpath because of Sunday newspaper stories saying that Frank Dobson would be our summer hitman against the Tories and that Charlie Falconer would be monitoring his Transport brief. He's hugely sensitive at the moment. Plenty of other cabinet ministers are reading unflattering pre-reshuffle stories and they don't spend their whole time complaining about it.

I went to the Dome for the first time today with Charlie and all the Labour Party staff. Very impressive, though at the moment it's just a huge building site.

Monday, 2 August 1999

Well, August has officially begun, although TB is still in the country. He's at Chequers and I went all the way up there to attend a meeting between him and Gordon today. Partly about summer campaigning but also some policy issues. Gordon is still obsessed by the Working Families Tax Credit.

Last week's planned reshuffle turned out to be a disaster.

We were forced to announce on Wednesday that there wouldn't be a cabinet reshuffle beyond appointing a new Welsh secretary to replace Alun Michael. AC tried to turn it on the media, pointing out that we had said all along that their stories about the reshuffle were garbage and that we had done nothing to encourage them. All true. But neither had we sought to discourage them when it was perfectly clear that the whole government was being destabilised by the speculation. Mo, Dobson *et al.* saying they didn't want to move. So when it didn't happen it was written up as Weak Blair unable to wield the axe, pushed around by his ministers, etc. He was pretty depressed about it. And, of course, the Tories had great fun with it. He carried out a pretty major reshuffle of middle and junior ranks on Thursday although even that brought in only five new faces. The number of casualties was small too, though they were generally well deserved: Alan Meale, Tony Lloyd, Doug Henderson, Glenda Jackson, Tony Banks. John Morris went as attorney general and there were a couple of other resignations by people nobody had much heard of anyway. It does seem that TB found himself unable to do what he'd wanted.

Then it emerged over the weekend that George Robertson [defence secretary] is to become the next secretary general of NATO. In fact TB had wanted Robin Cook to do it and then make Jack Straw foreign secretary and David Blunkett home secretary. There were ructions all weekend about the party too. Prescott said on *The World This Weekend* that he was stepping down from his party campaigning role. Ian McCartney has been given a badly defined party role as well as being minister of state at the Cabinet Office. But TB doesn't want him to be the main front man for the party and wants him out and about in the country instead. We've already been accused of having a party chairman at public expense, but we haven't actually got the benefits of a proper one.

Peter has agreed to go in to Millbank from September to plan for the election, but keeps changing his mind about whether to announce it now. He agreed with TB at Chequers last night that he would, but phoned me this morning to say that he'd changed his mind again.

Sunday, 8 August 1999

I feel as if I'm truly in charge now, with TB, AC, Godric Smith [Civil Service deputy to AC in the press office] and just about everybody else away. It's quite an odd feeling, although AC did call from France at eight thirty this morning to ask what was in the Sunday papers. Not a lot, as it happened, except some stuff about Geoffrey Robinson's forthcoming book – including the fact that Anji has been trying to talk him out of writing it.

Pictures of TB and Cherie in Tuscany, although he nearly didn't get there. There was so much publicity about the over-zealous Italian authorities having closed off the beaches for five kilometres around his villa that he was insisting furiously on Friday morning that if they weren't reopened by lunchtime he wasn't going. We managed to get that done and put out a statement saying that while he thanked the Italians for their careful concern for his security he didn't want anybody to be stopped from visiting the beaches. It did the trick and he became Hero Blair riding to the rescue of the locals. But we added a plea to the media to let him enjoy his holiday in peace.

The *Sun* had great fun on Thursday after I'd rowed with them about some very old modelling pictures of Kate Hoey [the new sports minister] in a bikini. I had a ridiculous row with David Yelland over it in which I completely over-reacted after Kate had pleaded with me to stop them and he put the phone down on me. So the paper called me a 'receptionist' who 'in an unnecessary outburst of political correctness' had said they shouldn't use the pictures because they wouldn't have wanted to print pictures of Tony Banks [her predecessor] in his trunks. So I took the brunt but the pictures weren't used.

TB took to calling me most days last week to discuss his holiday coverage and other stories. Actually our first week has gone very well with lots of government activity and some success in getting the 'extremist' tag running against the Tories. I've written two letters to William Hague this week, one from Ian McCartney and one from Robin Cook, just to keep the pressure up. Needless to say, he hasn't replied to either.

The papers alluded this morning to Robin having been the first choice for NATO secretary general, but didn't go on to say that he'd seriously considered taking it.

Much argument internally during the week about how quickly we can have a by-election in Hamilton [the seat George Robertson would have to vacate to take up the job at NATO]. Margaret McDonagh wants it as soon as possible but TB told her not to rush. Apparently it's very hard to call one during the parliamentary recess anyway – but not impossible.

Wednesday, 11 August 1999

The day of the big solar eclipse, which was a bit of an anticlimax. There was cloud all over Devon and Cornwall, where the view should have been best, and here in London too. But we all went into the Downing Street garden at Prescott's invitation and had a drink to watch it. It was about 95 per cent in London. Everyone was ignoring the official guidance and squinting at it, or looking through plastic 'eclipse glasses'. So we put out something saying Prescott had looked at it through a pinhole camera. Not worth the hassle of telling the truth.

There have been pictures of TB and family at the Leaning Tower of Pisa. Not good. It was opened especially for him, having been closed to the general public for nine years. It really is a holiday for the few not the many. But as he was in a public place, knowing there would be cameras, we can hardly complain.

Otherwise the news has been OK. John Major attacking Thatcher. Jeffrey Archer and Prince Philip making allegedly racist comments. Some good unemployment figures and other useful announcements. There are still worries over the economy, though. The Treasury think things could still turn bad and were pissed off with Blunkett and the DfEE [Department for Education and Employment] for talking it up too much. Blunkett said today he hoped we could make more progress towards our aim of achieving full employment, when nobody thought it was our explicit goal – and when the Treasury thinks unemployment could go up again [Treasury policy was to achieve the highest possible levels of employment rather than 'full' employment].

Things seem to be going well with Prescott. Perfectly amicable meetings – much better than last year. I saw Mo today, back from her holiday and as curt as ever. She's keen to do party stuff but says she hasn't been asked, so we'll have to find something for her to do. AC has been calling every day. He's in a perfectly good mood and seems happy enough with what we're doing.

Saturday, 14 August 1999

As Philip Gould, Charlie Falconer and others all ring to say how well things seem to be going, we are in the middle of Project Hague. It has proved a total disaster for the Tories. A leaked memo appeared from Ffion [Hague's wife] and Amanda Platell [Conservative Party director of communications] saying they wanted to relaunch Hague again as a cross between a family man and Action Man. They wanted to distribute a mixture of romantic shots of him on the beach with action pics of him abseiling and doing judo. All the papers took the piss mercilessly while we said, with some success, that it wasn't Hague who was unpopular but Tory policies.

The *Sun* have been trying to run a story about renovations to the Blair's private bathroom at Downing Street. I struggled a bit to find the facts with everybody away on holiday and must have given away my uncertainty because the *Sun* described me as 'a politically correct receptionist' again and said I had been behaving like a schoolboy caught with a pocketful of Curly Wurlys who couldn't get his story right!

In the meantime we have been trying to stir up trouble for the Tories after Thatcher was quoted in *The Times* this morning saying Britain should pull out of the EU.

I had lunch with David Hughes [political editor] of the *Daily Mail* on Tuesday. I was determined not to give him a story but made the mistake of more or less agreeing with him when he said towards the end of the meal that he thought other sources of funding should be looked at for the NHS, like charging for certain extra hotel-style facilities. I was very vague because I hadn't really given it much thought, but it then appeared in the paper as TB's view! I've never been caught out like that before but fortunately I also made clear that universal health services should still be free at the point of use and he put that in too.

Ben Wegg-Prosser rang to say that one of the papers would be running the story that Peter had avoided the higher rate of stamp duty by buying his new flat for £249,995 while paying more to cover the cost of repairs.

Monday, 16 August 1999

We managed to get the Tory Europe story up in lights again by writing a joint statement from Robin Cook and Menzies Campbell [Liberal Democrat foreign affairs spokesman]. One of my few bright ideas. So the rare event of a two-party statement was in all the papers, the *Today* programme and ITN. The Tories tried to do a tax-cutting story but it was a rather vague statement from Hague that they might do something about the higher rate of tax. We did a little number about us standing for the many not the few and held them to a draw. So we're still well ahead of the game.

TB is at the Palio today [the controversial horse race in Siena] which won't be good. He rang this morning and effectively gave me the chance to tell him not to go after some animal rights campaigners made an issue of cruelty to the horses involved, but he said the Siena authorities would be very upset if he didn't go. I figured it would probably look worse if he pulled out so I just told him to keep a low profile(!). It will certainly be a story tomorrow.

John Reid and others are still strongly urging an early by-election in Hamilton. John probably hopes to become defence secretary but everybody seems to think we'll do better if it's earlier rather than later.

Sunday, 22 August 1999

There's no point denying it, I rather like this being in charge bit. Making decisions, setting stories up, not having to consult dozens of other people all the time. I can see why AC puts up with the massive disruption to his life. A lot of discussion this weekend about the by-election situation. TB and Gordon decided on Wednesday to go for both Hamilton and Wigan [where the sitting Labour

MP had died] on 23 September, making George Robertson a peer in the process. Everything was being put in place to make an announcement next Tuesday when it appeared in the *Glasgow Herald* on Friday morning. Word for word. Every element of what we'd been discussing with almost total accuracy. Who knows who leaked it? Although we have some favourite suspects. In any event, it stopped us being able to take the SNP by surprise. They have been able to spend the weekend accusing us of underhand tactics and trying to undermine their conference (which will be on at the same time) while we've been unable to make our case at all as no official announcement has been made. But as we didn't confirm anything the story died on Saturday and there was barely a line in the Sundays. In fact it was the most harmless pile of Sunday papers I think I've ever seen. Apart from a nasty piece on Peter saying the service chiefs had said he couldn't be defence secretary unless the ban on gays in the military was lifted first.

In the meantime Ian McCartney seems to have managed to get the Wigan by-election delayed by convincing TB that the party in the area just wasn't ready and that we risked another big heartland collapse just before Party Conference. Probably the right decision but it makes it harder for us to justify calling Hamilton as planned on the grounds that the seat shouldn't be left unrepresented for too long.

Wednesday, 25 August 1999

We made George Robertson a lord yesterday and called both Hamilton and Wigan by-elections with the predictable howls of protest from the other parties. On the whole the media thought we were pulling a fast one but it wasn't a huge story. Even the Scottish media didn't go over the top. The people most miffed were Prescott and Ian

McCartney, who were eventually overruled on whether to have Wigan on the same day. TB was getting a lot of conflicting advice but obviously wanted to go for both of them together so eventually, with the clock ticking towards the deadline for an announcement, I called him on holiday and said, 'I think you've made up your mind, haven't you?' He said basically yes, so I offered to call Ian back and tell him the bad news. It undermines his authority at Millbank and shows what a botched appointment it was at the reshuffle with him having no official role as party chairman.

I made a sneak visit to Scotland on Monday afternoon to help plan the by-election. Because I didn't want to be seen in Delta House [Scottish Labour Party headquarters], John Reid, Donald Dewar, Douglas Alexander, Lesley Quinn [Scottish general secretary] *et al.* all came out for a meeting at the airport. Of the politicians, Douglas as ever was the only one with a really decisive grip on things.

In London, Anji is now back from holiday and we had a good chat. Should Peter come back as defence secretary? Was his being gay a problem? I said no. Was it too early for him? She thought so and I more or less agreed. I said it would be a huge story and would make it very difficult for him to do the job effectively.

Saturday, 28 August 1999

AC now back in the country but not yet fully engaged. He popped in on Thursday and seemed very relaxed. Said of the five years since he's been doing the job he was disturbed least this summer. So I took that as a kind of compliment. It looks as if Alastair himself may be the biggest problem in tomorrow's papers. The first stuff to emerge from the biography that's about to come out on him [by Peter Oborne] says he wrote a spoof Queen's Speech just after the election in New Labour-speak and that he had a meeting with officials in which he went through the personal lives of all the cabinet. Neither story too serious but the *Mail* will make the most of it.

We've had a bit of a Prescott problem too, on a couple of fronts. The papers have started asking where he is. His press office were telling people he was on holiday from this weekend when he's supposed to be still running the country. I then made matters worse by writing a speech for him and putting it out saying he'd made it in London – simply because I didn't want to give away his whereabouts so as to give him a bit of peace. He's actually in Cornwall with friends. So then we had to say that he'd intended to give the speech to a Young Labour meeting but had been delayed and couldn't deliver it. If it hadn't been for the 'Where's Prescott?' hunt it wouldn't have mattered at all. But it makes me look a bit like the boy with the Curly Wurlys again. Then Prescott rang me yesterday to say he'd done a newspaper interview with Andy McSmith [of the *Observer*] in which he'd been rude about Philip Gould and had said he didn't think much of focus groups. He also said some vaguely half-hearted things about the single currency. Andy wanted to do a big number on it – Prescott says he can't rule out being on the opposite side to Blair in a euro referendum, etc. I managed to kill that one by giving Andy an unequivocal statement from John saying he'd support whatever collective judgement the cabinet makes on the euro. The Philip Gould story will still run, but that's nothing like as damaging. So I've spent most of today dealing with things like that.

Saturday, 11 September 1999

A long gap in writing but funnily enough it hasn't been all that eventful. TB now back in the saddle but in a rather odd mood. He is, quite rightly, being very strict about his time but it means he's cut out some of the things we wanted him to do to be seen to be engaging with people. His planned three-day tour of the North West became one day and has now been cancelled altogether. Likewise a proposed tour of the South West. Sometimes it seems that he doesn't really want to meet ordinary people. He doesn't exactly have the Clinton touch when it comes to ploughing into crowds and engaging with people. He sometimes looks rather uncomfortable and doesn't really know what to say. And he'll often ask us, 'Why am I doing this?' And yet the conventional wisdom, of course, is that he's brilliant at it.

The same is true of programmes like *Richard and Judy*, which he did again this week – alongside Gordon to launch the Working Families Tax Credit [WFTC]. It was Gordon who looked the most comfortable and was on top of the facts, when it always used to be TB who shone at those sorts of things and Gordon was uncomfortable. Gordon has a very clever and successful de-spin strategy these days, ever since Charlie Whelan left: keeping a low profile and letting others say how brilliant he is. Yesterday he was made top banana chancellor of the IMF [International Monetary Fund] as chair of the Interim Committee, which sounds dull but is apparently a great accolade. He still has a huge influence over TB.

Much to Alistair Darling [social security secretary]'s fury, Gordon has got the launch of the WFTC separated from the government's forthcoming anti-poverty strategy and TB is not taking part in the announcement of the latter at all. I think Gordon wants to be seen as this government's champion of the poor and the dispossessed and wants no other rivals for that crown.

Very funny scene on Monday when a member of the Chinese Politburo was in Number Ten to see TB. Chris

Patten was in the Cabinet Room doing a briefing on the RUC [he had been commissioned to produce a report on the future of the Royal Ulster Constabulary]. Jonathan Powell had to lurch for the door to make sure the Chinese didn't catch sight of the man they loathed so much when he was governor of Hong Kong.

The main political event of the past fortnight has been the death of Alan Clark [Conservative MP for Kensington and Chelsea] and Michael Portillo's announcement that he was going for the seat, preceded a day earlier by his admission that he'd had gay relationships as a young man. Mainly at Cambridge he implied, and not since he's been in public life. Says he's been faithful to his wife for the past seventeen years. But a close textual analysis of what he said (which the *Daily Mail* did yesterday) leaves all sorts of questions about the ten years after he left university and before he became an MP. Huge speculation about his motives and what it means for his chances of replacing Hague. Portillo said that before returning to public life he wanted to deal with the rumours that had been circulating about him before, and that meant denying the lies and admitting the truth. Peter Lilley [a former Conservative minister] meanwhile supported what Portillo had done but said he found the idea of homosexuality about as appetising as eating cardboard. I'm inclined to take Portillo at his word about wanting to clear the air, although I'm not sure about his judgement as it will inevitably leave all sorts of unanswered questions unless he's willing to go into far more detail (which he won't). He's been broadly supported so far for his honesty, but it's bound to narrow his base of support within the Conservative Party. If he becomes leader (which AC thinks will happen very quickly, but I disagree) it will probably leave the public a bit unsure about him too. It adds to the sense that there's something fishy about him. Not the fact that he's had gay affairs, but that he seems to be trying to box them off as some sort of youth-ful exuberance in order to rehabilitate himself. TB is fascinated by it all.

Peter Mandelson, whom I saw yesterday, has said noth-ing to me about it, but I haven't been alone with him to talk about it properly. We still haven't announced what role Peter will have at Millbank, although TB and Gordon discussed it all this week. Basically, Gordon wants two parallel committees, one in the party and one in govern-ment, preparing for the election, with Peter just on the former but him on both. He seems happy for Peter to play a big role at Millbank but wants to stay in overall charge himself, although TB would chair the government commit-tee and be the final arbiter throughout. I'm sure it won't work out like that. But I certainly want to get on the party committee [in the end I was on both].

The other big surprise has been the departure of Bill Clare, the very likeable Foreign Office secondee to the Number Ten press office, to go and work at Conservative Central Office. He's an old mate of Liam Fox [former Tory Foreign Office minister] whose private secretary he used to be. Unfortunately he's got a lot of inside information about how we work and God knows what he's heard us discussing in the past few months. So far we've laughed it off, but I think it could be quite serious. AC said as a result that 'life is on the record', so I guess it will now be OK for me to publish my full and frank account of life at Number Ten!

Last weekend, in an *Observer* interview, TB called for a new 'moral purpose' in Britain. It was totally vacuous and was made up just to give us a good story after two twelve-year-old girls were found to have got themselves pregnant. But it worked and gave us a good talking-point for several days until Alan Clark's death.

Monday, 13 September 1999

This afternoon we had a meeting with the heads of information from the various government departments to try to encourage them to put across a common government line that underpins all that they do. Modernising Britain to put power, wealth and opportunity into the hands of the many not the few. All that sort of stuff.

Michael Portillo continues to be big news after his ex-lover told the *Mail on Sunday* that they continued to have a gay affair on and off for about eight years until well into his late twenties. They first met when Portillo was eighteen and had sex when he was twenty – so under the age of consent that applied then. It's added to the charge of hypocrisy and the feeling that he still isn't coming clean properly. I meant to call Peter and see what he made of it over the weekend but I was enjoying my work-free life too much. The general feeling about the place is that it's doing Portillo more harm than good.

Sunday, 19 September 1999

Last week remained rather quiet at work with TB at Chequers most of the time. Nick Brown [agriculture minister] has a bit of a farming crisis on his hands and came up with the best line of the week – his policies are 'for the many not the ewe'. Peter Kilfoyle [defence minister] is unhappy, thinks he's being sidelined at the MoD. He says TB is hopeless at looking after his own loyal supporters, like himself and Fraser Kemp [Labour MP for Houghton and Washington]. While Gordon works incredibly hard on building up his support (he wrote personally to every new minister in the last reshuffle apparently), TB does nothing. He doesn't even use his most powerful tool – patronage. Kilfoyle has something of a point. There's no loyal army ready to defend TB when the going gets tough. But I guess he thinks the whole party should and would do that if the opposition comes from outside. If it comes from inside he probably thinks he can go at a time of his own choosing so won't face an internal challenge. If he's got any sense that's what he'll do. But power can be pretty addictive and there's no doubt he loves it. There's the vanity factor too. He's started wearing glasses for reading, but doesn't want ever to be seen in them! So we are devising a glasses strategy – some friendly profile writer 'spotting' them on his desk by chance. The trouble is that TB thinks it's cool that they are made by Calvin Klein and AC wants to get him a pair on the NHS.

Friday, 24 September 1999

Speech-writing and pre-Conference interviews by TB continue to dominate everyone's time. The speech [Blair's speech to the annual Labour Party Conference was always 'the speech'] is causing an unusual amount of grief this year with everyone searching around for inspiration. No decisions yet on what policy announcements to make, although as usual there is a broad range of options. There's everything from a new DNA database to new national parks, including the South Downs. James Purnell [Policy Unit] is urging that TB announce the abolition of the eleven p.m. closing time for pubs, which I strongly support. TB doesn't seem too keen, though.

Meanwhile big row between Gordon and Robin Cook – us siding with Gordon – over comments Robin wants to make on Europe at a fringe meeting on Sunday. He wants to move the argument on by saying that while the economic conditions must be met there are significant political advantages to us joining the euro. It took some heavy pressure from here to get him to take it out, but then it seems he said as much off the record in comments to *The Times*, which appeared today. Some of the papers have got to hear about the row and there's now lots of finger-pointing about who is responsible. It all happened just as I was telling the media last night that all the old bad blood was behind us.

Charlie Whelan has been putting it about that TB has at last apologised to Gordon over the remark attributed to AC that he's 'psychologically flawed'. We continue to maintain, of course, that AC wasn't responsible for the remark in the first place. [The remark first appeared in a newspaper column by Andrew Rawnsley of the *Observer* in January 1998].

It's been an unusually busy day today, compared to recent weeks at least. We did really badly in yesterday's Hamilton by-election where the SNP came within 550 votes of beating us. Nobody on the ground had picked up how things were going so we were all taken by surprise. If the Nats had realised how close they were they would have pulled out all the stops in the last few days and would probably have won. But our people should have detected it too.

Then the head of the Oratory [where TB's sons were at school in London] sprang a story on us this morning saying that he was asking all parents to fork out thirty pounds a month to help meet a funding shortage, with fifteen pounds for a second child. Blaming it on the government's misguided education policies. It's not the first time he's pissed everybody off like this. So we unleashed the dogs of war (without telling TB, who would have urged caution), mainly in the form of an article by Bridget Prentice [Labour MP for Lewisham East], who used to teach at the Oratory, saying it was outrageous of him to use his position in this way with no regard for the well-being of the children in his charge. AC would have had him taken out and shot.

Peter Oborne's biography of AC has been serialised in the *Express* all this week, but it has been pretty complimentary on the whole. It played up his role in Kosovo, saying he was negotiating directly with Clinton, but otherwise there were no real problems.

We will almost certainly have a problem on Monday, though, when the ECHR [European Court of Human Rights] judgement on gays in the military comes out. The MoD will lose but are being incredibly conservative and are refusing to accept that the policy [of banning homosexuality] will be dead. I've been trying to get a line that Michael Cashman [MEP], Stephen Twigg and Ben Bradshaw [both gay MPs] can support, but I don't think I've succeeded. Of course, people probably think I've been lobbying for the Stonewall [gay rights organisation] agenda, whereas I just think we are going to be left in an illogical and indefensible position. I actually have some gut sympathy for the view that it's hard to force the army to accept out gays in combat roles, etc. But the policy is going to have to change and we should bite the bullet now in my view.

Saturday, 25 September 1999

In Bournemouth for Party Conference. Trying to damp down a story about a sting operation the *Observer* carried out on John Reid's son who has been working for us in Glasgow. It doesn't sound too serious to me but it will play big in Scotland, I'm sure. John Reid is blaming Donald Dewar for overreacting and calling for enquiries [into whether there was any impropriety in the way he was paid] even before he's seen what evidence the *Observer* has. It seems it's not much at all.

I travelled down to Bournemouth from Brighton by train with Anji – as usual, talking to her is a great way of finding out what's going on. The big question is, who do we make defence secretary when George Robertson goes – which is by 15 October? Too early for Peter, Mo would be a disaster, George is opposing John Reid for some reason probably buried deep in Scottish Labour politics. Anji says, what about Jack Cunningham? TB wants Mo to go for mayor of London but she's resisting hard. She thinks she's due for a major promotion. If we said it's mayor or nothing, she might well opt for nothing, and the risk of having her on the backbenches is too great. So then it's step forward Nick Raynsford [local government minister] for London. Ken Livingstone said today in the clearest possible terms that he wouldn't run as an independent if he doesn't get the Labour nomination and it's clear we won't let him be our candidate. We talk about making Peter Kilfoyle deputy chief whip. But he may be just too factional, albeit on our side.

On Peter, Anji says he's blaming all of us around TB for keeping him from coming back because he can't bring himself to blame TB personally. She says he needs to be patient and if we do a proper reshuffle next spring he can come back then.

Sunday, 26 September 1999

The Sunday papers are full of 'TB tells GB: You'll never be PM'. It's all based solely on AC saying, 'Yes', when pressed three times by the lobby about whether TB would stand at the next election with the intention of serving a full five years as prime minister if he won. What else was he supposed to say? The Sunday hacks obviously got together and decided that that meant he would fight the election after next as PM and seek to emulate Thatcher by going on and on. TB was on *Breakfast with Frost* and tried to laugh it off, although he also said that Gordon had the qualities to make a great prime minister. But our aim has been to knock the story out by coming up with a better one. So, with half an hour to go before TB's appearance we decided to launch a war on drugs. I suggested TB say that he would fight drugs with the same vigour he fought Milosevic, although somebody pointed out that Milosevic is still there! But we decided to announce that the Queen's Speech would include a Bill that could bring in mandatory testing after arrest for suspected criminals, and new drug treatment schemes. Not a bad story, but not enough in itself to keep all the rest of the soap opera stuff off the front pages.

We had an hysterical scene of everybody running around trying to ring Jack Straw and Keith Hellawell [the 'drugs tsar'] to warn them of what was coming in a few minutes. Jack was OK about it, although he says the lawyers have warned that it might be ruled against at the European Court of Human Rights. Margaret Beckett [leader of the House of Commons] was pretty pissed off that she hadn't been warned as she was doing another interview shortly after Tony. Still, it could have been worse.

Gordon, who's in Washington, has been on the phone concerned about all the coverage of him and TB.

Thursday, 30 September 1999

Almost at the end of the week. It's gone pretty well, although we haven't had a total grip on the media. Some froth today about Prescott driving 250 yards from the hotel to the conference centre to make a speech in which he encouraged people to use their cars less. It was a stupid thing to do and then he compounded the error by saying on ITN that he'd only used the car because his wife didn't like getting her hair blown about. He's been absolutely furious about it. His staff say they are often paralysed by lengthy discussions about how he gets about – just because he's transport secretary.

TB's speech on Tuesday went down well, although some columnists thought it was a bit too preachy and personal. I didn't think it was his best, but it did set out a detailed political argument about the 'forces of conservatism' holding back progress and reform. Then, because they were worried about it being misinterpreted, TB and AC decided it needed a bit of recalibrating yesterday so TB did interviews in which he said he wasn't attacking all Conservatives and there were many One-Nation Tories who'd be a lot happier in the Labour Party. Some of us thought this was a mistake, but fortunately not too many people in the media saw it as backtracking on the speech.

Before the speech there had been the usual last-minute panic, despite the fact that huge amounts of time had been set aside for it at the beginning of the week. They were up most of Monday night doing almost complete rewrites. The call went out for jokes both on Monday night and even Tuesday morning. I did a few that AC quite liked. I spoke to Tony Robinson [the actor who played Baldrick in *Blackadder* is a committed Labour supporter] but he didn't come up with much. Afterwards AC claimed to have trounced TB again in the scoring for who got most soundbites on the evening news. The coverage was pretty good, although the *Sun* managed to turn some rather unremarkable words about Europe into a front-page pic headlined 'Surrender!'.

Europe is still a bit of a problem, with Gordon and Robin sending out different messages. Journalist friends tell me that Ed Balls [chief adviser to Gordon Brown] has been briefing quite heavily against the idea that an early referendum is inevitable.

The week got off to a potentially difficult start with the long-awaited ECHR [European Court of Human Rights] judgment on gays in the military. Even as news of the judgment was coming through it wasn't clear how we would react. It ended up with George Robertson [still defence secretary until he took up his post at NATO], John Spellar [armed forces minister], Alasdair McGowan [Robertson's special adviser] and me in a closed room here at the conference hotel. We were picking up the judgment from the radio, Ceefax and phone calls Alasdair was making to London. The MoD came to the conclusion that it wasn't as harsh a judgment as they had been expecting. If we had gone along with the contingency lines drawn up by the MoD at that point we would have announced that we would look at the policy in the light of what the ECHR had said but that it wouldn't be changed quickly. Parliament might be expected to vote on it in 2001. I argued that this simply wouldn't wash and George could clearly see that. Spellar spent most of the time cracking jokes but didn't put up any real resistance. So even before we knew the full judgment, George had drafted a response saying that, like all governments, we would have to accept the judgment and that ministers would make a decision in a timely fashion. The only question was what would happen to cases of gays facing dismissal still in the pipeline. Could this present problems? What, I was asked, would happen if someone turned up on the parade-ground tomorrow in a pink tutu? I realised that we had just a few minutes in which it could go either way and argued strongly that the only possible way forward was to say that all current investigations would be put on hold. It was a matter of policy not law so we weren't constrained. How could we justify the next discharge that happened on the grounds of sexuality alone? And how would George deal with being asked about becoming secretary general of NATO when Britain was so out of line with almost every other member? I also argued that it was better to bite the bullet now in the wake of the judgment rather than stalling for nearly two years and doing it just before an election. We would then get the worst of all worlds.

George spoke to Sir Charles Guthrie, the chief of the defence staff, on the phone. Guthrie said he had told the other defence chiefs that they just had to be grown-up about it and that change was inevitable. He also approved suspending further discharges. George said we would probably need a vote in the next session of Parliament. So we ended up with a much better position than the MoD had wanted or thought we could get away with.

After the meeting I phoned Angela Mason of Stonewall and she thought it was brilliant. At the Stonewall party that night I was treated like a hero, although I urged everyone to play down my role. But I got a big wet kiss from Chris Smith and it was a rather drunken night. I was feeling a bit rough afterwards but had a quick afternoon nap to recover.

Friday, 1 October 1999

Last day of Conference with a round of early interviews for TB, marred by the fact that we hadn't cooked up a story. AC wanted to attack the BMA [British Medical Association] but was warned off by Robert Hill in the Policy Unit. He also wanted TB to say that he hated fund-raising and wanted to get to a situation with a mass membership of the Labour Party so that it wouldn't be necessary. But I said no. TB would be fund-raising big-time for the rest of his time as prime minister so there was no point creating problems for ourselves later. So it was a slightly scrappy end to the week. But I think it was largely successful overall.

AC paged me tonight to say thanks for all my help and to give his love to Asmara [the capital of Eritrea, where we had a holiday booked immediately after Conference]. It seems he was in Eritrea when he was a journalist a few years ago at the height of the war and really loved the place. We talked about the reshuffle today, and what to do with Mo, who should be defence secretary, could Dobbo [Frank Dobson] be persuaded to go for mayor, etc.

Sunday, 17 October 1999

Back from two weeks' holiday. Eritrea was a beautiful country but the trip was hard work. Our luggage didn't arrive for three days, then I got dreadful food poisoning after drinking some fruit juice with ice in it. I'd been lulled into a false sense of security by the very European feel of Asmara. As a former Italian colony the country retains a bizarre mix of black Africa, Europe and Arab North Africa.

While I was away the Tories had a very Eurosceptic conference dominated by Thatcher. Dobbo has announced he's running for mayor and left the government. So there's been a reshuffle, putting Peter back in at the Northern Ireland Office, Mo to the Cabinet Office, Geoff Hoon to the MoD, Alan Milburn to Health and Jack Cunningham out. A really good reshuffle all round. Very good for Peter. I don't know about the knock-on changes lower down the ranks. I'll have a lot to catch up on when I get back to work tomorrow.

Tuesday, 19 October 1999

I wasn't particularly looking forward to going back to work and slept really badly on Sunday night, but it's actually been rather fun. Needless to say, nothing has been resolved about how we do things about the place. TB had a real go at AC yesterday about how he should stand back more from the day-to-day stuff and give himself more time for strategic thinking. AC was very reluctant and said afterwards that he'd had three days of it from TB while they were in Finland for the Tampere European summit and had a lot of time on their hands. TB obviously misses having Gordon and Peter's long-term thinking and needs AC to fill the gap, but AC clearly doesn't think he can take his eye off the ball in terms of all the daily stuff. I've tried to encourage him to delegate (genuinely) a bit more. He says he will but he won't. TB says that ministers will have to take things from me and not just from AC. But I've given up pushing too hard for changes and don't really expect much to happen.

Lots more discussion on Europe. TB says we don't know where we'll want to be in a year's time so we can't say anything more specific now. He says the debate has to be about Europe itself – the Eurosceptics know that the only way to attack us is to attack Europe so we can only win the debate on the euro by winning the wider debate about Europe. He says Britain in Europe must be kept in line.

The other main worry is about whether our promises are being seen to unravel. Jack Straw has been in a bit of hot water over appearing to claim that we were providing five thousand extra police officers when all we're actually doing is stabilising police numbers.

We had almost continuous meetings yesterday about whether we over-claim, over-spin and try too hard to get stories. Worries too that TB is backtracking on his 'forces of conservatism' speech, which apparently Peter thought was a big mistake. I compared us to Thatcher who chose her enemies and attacked them relentlessly. We choose enemies and run away as soon as they react. Philip Gould analysed our problem very clearly. We don't know what we are. Gordon wants us to be a radical, progressive government but thinks we should keep our heads down on

Europe. Peter thinks we are a quasi-Conservative Party but that we should stick our necks out on Europe. Philip didn't say this, but I think TB either can't make up his mind or wants to be both at the same time. Increasingly I'm in the Gordon camp emotionally and intellectually, despite being seen as an arch-Mandyite. Bizarre.

Dobson, it seems, went all of his own accord although his mayoral campaign isn't exactly going well so far. Trevor Phillips will pull out as a candidate tonight in return for being deputy mayor and chair of the London Police Authority. Glenda [Jackson] may well pull out soon too.

Friday, 22 October 1999

AC now says he wants me to look after planning and the grid [the schedule of government business produced by the Strategic Communications Unit] when Alun Evans [head of the SCU] leaves to work for Prescott. But another civil servant will need to be in charge of the SCU for management reasons.

At the tail end of the week allegations emerged that Geoffrey Robinson would say in his forthcoming book that he helped fund TB's office in opposition to the tune of £250,000 after being asked for the dosh by Jonathan Powell. So far as I can tell it's bollocks. Margaret Jay, who chaired the trustees of the blind trust that paid for TB's office, did a search and put out a statement saying Geoffrey never contributed to it [a blind trust is a fund designed to hide the names of those who donate to it from the beneficiaries]. Jonathan and AC, whom the Tory MP Julian Lewis accused in the Commons of trying to solicit cash, both flatly deny it. Geoffrey seems less than sure what he gave, when or to whom. He did sign a cheque for £50K (though it seems he remembers it as having been more) and gave it to Jonathan. But it was made out to the

Labour Party and the party has declared him as a donor so there's no problem there. The cash would have just gone into general party funds. It all gets very complicated but the media seem to be accepting our denials. In fact it wouldn't even matter if he had contributed to the blind trust so long as it was genuinely blind and not linked in any way to the DTI inquiry into Geoffrey's finances.

The other story the hacks are chasing is who was responsible for leaking the story so that it might be in Geoffrey's book. The obvious suspicion falls on Charlie [Whelan] in order to build up the book as a potential blockbuster. But Geoffrey has told Anji and AC that he thinks it was Peter. The theory is that Peter wants Geoffrey to be labelled 'embittered' and a 'pariah' now so as to undermine his credibility before the book comes out – embittered because Peter is back in government and he's not. It's credible. Just. Peter should really be concentrating on Northern Ireland where things are looking pretty bleak.

I was mentioned in the *Daily Telegraph* as one of Number Ten's 'chief image benders' who as 'a friend of Peter's' turned up in the Commons along with Waheed Alli to watch Peter's first appearance at Northern Ireland Questions. *Punch* magazine this week has me as one of the 'rat pack' of Peter's allies. And I've barely spoken to Peter for months! He certainly doesn't treat me like a friend.

Friday, 29 October 1999

Another week of angst and deliberations about how we're perceived and how we're getting our message across. It seems to be a permanent part of our lives these days. Our headline poll ratings continue to be stratospheric, but our polling suggests TB is starting to be seen as increasingly arrogant and out of touch, which leads to more discussions about events to show him 'on your side', etc. This week he travelled on the Tube after getting stuck in a traffic jam on his way back from doing an Internet interview with the *Sun*'s new online thing *bun.com*. AC had to give him twenty quid to buy tickets for all the party but it got quite good coverage. He obviously never carries money. I had to give him a tenner so he could buy himself and Prescott lunch on the train up to Hull yesterday.

The *Sun* event nearly descended into farce when the person transcribing the interview for the website decided to cut it about in bizarre ways so it looked like TB was answering questions he hadn't been asked or was giving anwers that didn't match the questions. So it appeared on the website for a while that he supported a referendum on the monarchy in Britain (he was talking about Australia), that he wanted to cut doctors' pay and that we were about to enter the euro. Much rushing around to get it all corrected.

We seem to be in a dire state over London. Have been discussing whether it would be better to have Ken as Labour mayor or as an independent mayor. TB thinks that if he has to win, it would be better as an independent. What we can't allow is to have an alternative Old Labour power base set up in London around Ken. Dobbo's campaign [for the Labour nomination] doesn't seem to be making much headway. He doesn't have a proper campaign manager, except Nick Raynsford, and as Nick is still a minister that just makes Frank look like the candidate of the party leadership, which is bad for him even if it's true. TB did a Q&A session on London on Wednesday night in which he said Frank had the right policies for London whereas Ken would just take us back to the 1980s. But nobody is really taking the gloves off and destroying Ken. Part of my task in going up to Hull yesterday was to persuade Prescott to do Ken in over transport and I think he'll do that on Monday.

The idea of New Labour as some ruthless election-winning machine seems pretty wide of the mark at the moment. We're hoping that the Pre-Budget Report and the Queen's Speech will be seen as effective step-changes in radicalism. Lots of talk of tough messages being delivered, although there doesn't seem to be much in the Queen's Speech to set pulses racing. We have agreed once again that we must improve our 'top line' message and push it more effectively – help for hard-working families running underneath the attack on the forces of conservatism. I wrote a new narrative on our agenda, which seemed to go down well. It gives our discussions a bit more bite. I then adapted it as a script for Mo to use at Cabinet in her new role. It was an almost entirely political cabinet this week [when the cabinet goes into a 'political' session the career civil servants all withdraw] with some quite interesting contributions. Clare [Short] and Blunkett the most radical, not surprisingly. I sat in on Cabinet and will try to do so as a matter of course from now on. It fits in with my new role [which included preparing a weekly briefing for the cabinet on the week ahead]. I'll have an excuse next week anyway because the political cabinet is continuing. I might then make a habit of it. Nobody seems to mind! Not that it has revealed a lot so far other than how little real influence it has as an institution. TB said at the beginning that he hoped they would be able to have a good discussion and when somebody made an aside about making a decision he said, 'Oh, I don't think we should go that far.' His disarming manner allows him to get away with murder like that. More generally, things are slowly getting geared up for the election. Gordon will chair the election strategy committee and Douglas [Alexander] will be in Millbank almost full time.

Sunday, 7 November 1999

There are some signs that we're making progress on improving communications. Cabinet this week was a political one again. Mo did a little spiel, prompted by me, arguing for better political communication, and the result was that ministers seem keen to get some proper briefings from us at weekends. Some of them are looking for media training too. Mo is happy to work from the scripts I give her for Cabinet so she will be very useful in that respect. We have received a review copy of the Denis Kavanagh/ Anthony Seldon book [*The Powers Behind the Prime Minister*], which has some pretty unhelpful stuff in it about the death of cabinet government (which has to be true) and some quotes – we think from Jonathan Powell – about TB being a Maoist! Everyone saying, 'We should never co-operate with something like this again', but of course we all did because we want our place in history.

More discussions this week about London and Europe. On the latter, TB says, 'We're miles away from public opinion on this.' Philip Gould wonders if we should be more sceptical in the run-up to the election. He suggested a 'forces of conservatism' speech but this time about Europe, to help identify us further with the reform agenda in the EU. The implication is that public opinion isn't going to be shifted in the next eighteen months so we will have to move instead. I wrote a note arguing the opposite case – that TB would massively lose credibility if we shifted our stance and that instead we should try to reinforce the referendum to give us a defence at the election, accepting that we might lose it but that the public would be given the final say on the euro.

TB says the problem is that we don't appear to be speaking for Britain. People like Chris Patten are saying the right things, but others are foolishly saying publicly that we are not European enough. TB wants a crude appeal on the basis of jobs plus an intellectual argument on the question of influence. The problem is that we don't have a clear script for everybody to read from, unlike the Tories who are being much more political about it. Overall they are hardening up their support in the country at around 33 per cent, which is not enough to win but is enough to make considerable progress. So we've been thrashing out some possible new slogans and messages, which Philip is supposed to go away and test. It feels like good politics, provided it translates into something.

There's a sense of depression about London. Frank is performing worse than we feared and it looks like Ken will win one way or another. Frank's campaign is getting bogged down by questions of process. Right now it's whether he's had improper access to party membership lists. TB was around number ten on Friday, always a problem because he doesn't have enough to do and starts getting restless. He was fuming about Cardinal Winning [Glasgow], attacking him over a letter TB had written saying there was no urgency in reviewing the Act of Succession. He said the one thing that made him mad was 'fucking prelates getting involved in politics and pretending it was nothing to do with politics'. He said that as the Royal Family were all Protestants it clearly wasn't an urgent issue. Pat [McFadden] and I had to explain that they couldn't marry Catholics either and he said he didn't realise that. Why had he been allowed to write a letter without this being made clear to him? All very tetchy.

Sunday, 14 November 1999

Fairly momentous week in which TB finally decided that Ken should be allowed to stand for the Labour nomination in London. The decision was taken on Wednesday and was supposed to be a big secret (not least in case TB changes his mind again) but by Saturday it was all over *The Times* and the *Guardian*. Basically, the fear of splitting the party and endangering a few good seats in London at the next election was the deciding factor. If he's asked, TB will say that Londoners obviously wanted him on the ballot and so did Dobson. The hope is still that Frank can beat him but nobody is at all confident. We will have a long campaign [before the party in London chooses its candidate], with the result not until January or February, in the hope that Frank can overtake Ken. If Ken wins we box him in with a very New Labour manifesto. But neither plan can be sure of success. The mayor was always envisaged to be a very powerful post with its own mandate. So in all probability Ken has outfoxed us. Margaret McDonagh [general secretary] was very keen that he should be allowed to stand and be beaten. She doesn't want party membership in London to drain away.

On the national level, I have been asked to be on the General Election Planning Committee, chaired by Peter, which is great news. The first meeting will be next week. It's what I'd hoped for. My first weekly political briefing was faxed to cabinet ministers this weekend. I'm making a lot of work for myself, but I prefer it that way. It means working quite closely with Mo, which is a variable experience. I'm sure AC is grateful, though. She had her first appearance as Cabinet Office minister on *Breakfast with Frost* today and was actually very good. She's dying to say that she smoked pot in the sixties but didn't like it and is now wholly anti-drugs. She says it happened only once. But it's very self-indulgent of her to want to make a splash about it now. Her husband, who was something in the City, a 'banker wanker', she called him, has lost his job. She wants to sign a contract for a book about her time in

Northern Ireland now, although she's not allowed to profit while she's still in government.

Big discussions about how much to use TB these days. Peter Hyman wants him out and about, doing one big event a week that really connects with people. Philip Gould says privately that the polling shows people are starting to feel a bit bored with him, or even irritated by him, and he thinks we should rest him for a while. AC's view, which I broadly share, is that we should be seen to take a few hits at the moment while continuing to batter away at the Tories. We're probably suffering the nearest we are going to get to a mid-term low and it's better just to weather it.

Everyone agrees that TB should have been more high profile on the Welfare Reform Bill. We got it through this week (just) but we lost the argument hopelessly. We also got Lords reform through. The hereditaries are gone, but for the ninety-two agreed under the deal with the Tories. So the deal delivered the goods.

The Pre-Budget Report was a big hit on Tuesday and there don't seem to be too many hidden taxes for people to spot later on this occasion. Francis Maude [shadow chancellor] was totally useless in response, so Gordon is on a high. He and TB did the Nicky Campbell phone-in on Five Live on Wednesday, which went well, Gordon the better-sounding interviewee as usual.

Driving back from the studio we were passing some horses in the Mall just as someone said something about the forces of conservatism. AC thought they had said 'horses of conservatism' so we now have a new slogan for our fight against fox-hunting. We announced a bit of a fudge on that on Thursday, but one that could eventually lead to it being banned.

TB is still obsessed with having somebody shadow Britain in Europe full time but nobody really wants to do it. But he's in a pretty confident mood about the Tories.

He says our side needs better ammunition but that while Hague has some good lines he's let his economic policy 'go crap'. We have to keep hitting them on all the things they opposed – Bank of England independence, the New Deal, the Working Families Tax Credit, etc. Also their double standards in saying they will cut taxes while voting for spending increases.

Thursday, 18 November 1999

Cherie is pregnant. In this job you never know what is coming next. She's already thirteen weeks gone but they've been keeping it very close and didn't intend to make an announcement until next week. The *Mirror* have got hold of it via Max Clifford of all people. Fiona [Millar, AC's partner] had also told her friend Rebekah Wade on the *Sun*. Cherie had been spotted at the hospital and the *Sun* were asking if she was ill. I heard about it after AC had been on the phone to Piers Morgan [editor of the *Mirror*]. TB appeared in AC's office shortly afterwards. He is most concerned that nobody should think the news came out as some sort of spin operation. The papers and the cartoonists will have a field day. Cherie came down and looked genuinely happy and I gave her a kiss and a hug.

We're off to Florence this weekend for a Third Way conference. It'll be a total nightmare. No serious politics for a while. It has been all London this week. Ken was at a party selection interview on Tuesday, along with Frank and Glenda. He said that if he was chosen but didn't like the manifesto, and especially the bit about the financing of the Tube, he would withdraw as the candidate. He also said the candidate selection would be in part a referendum on the Tube. It sounded to me as if he was being deliberately provocative so they would block him and leave him clear to run as an independent. Since then, however, he has withdrawn his threat to pull out and leave us without a candidate if he disagrees with the manifesto. But he still maintains that if people vote for him they will be voting against the public–private partnership plans for the Tube. There have been endless meetings at Number Ten about it all. Some people, Sally [Morgan] and Margaret [McDonagh], still say Frank can win, but nobody else really believes it. I've always thought there were ample grounds for blocking Ken's candidacy and he gave us more on Tuesday. He's clearly desperate for martyrdom. It was what made him when Mrs T abolished the GLC [Greater London Council] and he believes being made a martyr again will propel him into the mayor's job as an independent now. So we have no choice but to beat him in the selection contest and TB did a whole series of hard-hitting interviews tonight, designed to show him as someone who would just take us back to the days when Labour was perceived to be extreme and unelectable. Fortunately, because of the way he's been behaving, Ken has infuriated both John Prescott and Ian McCartney who will both now speak out against him. As will Gordon and Blunkett.

Mo is playing a ridiculous game, more concerned with her own popularity. She really is useless. She went on the *Today* programme to discuss the Queen's Speech this week and not only failed to talk about either fairness or enterprise, our chosen themes, but failed to deny that taxes were going up or that class sizes were rising and waiting lists getting longer. She is supposed to be in charge of improving our message delivery.

The good news this week is that the Northern Ireland peace process seems to be back on track, with a carefully choreographed sequence of events now in train that should lead to a new all-party executive and the decommissioning of weapons.

Sunday, 21 November 1999

Florence turned out to be a very enjoyable trip. Although the Third Way conference – except Lionel Jospin [French prime minister] wouldn't let it be called that for his own domestic political reasons, so it became Progressive Governance for the Twenty-first Century – was an almost total waste of time. Too big and too public for any serious discussion and with no side seminars to give the policy wonks a chance to exchange views properly. So it was just the leaders expounding on some well-rehearsed views. TB's heart clearly wasn't in it. Clinton on the other hand told AC he really loved that kind of stuff and AC told him he was sick. All the media were interested in, of course, was Cherie who barely appeared in public.

Back in the UK Lord Archer was forced to quit from the mayoral race after admitting getting a friend to lie in court for him [the offence for which he was later jailed]. That has done us some short-term good, but it means the Tory candidate will now be Steve Norris, who will be a much more formidable opponent. Clinton infuriated the other leaders by not turning up for a breakfast today that he'd wanted and they had all been against. It could have been something to do with the fact that he, Hillary and Chelsea were up talking and drinking with TB and Cherie until one forty-five this morning. TB not in a good mood because last night's dinner was badly organised and a waste of time. My main function over the weekend was to organise a kind of European *Meet The Press* programme with TB last night, hosted by Andrew Rawnsley with journalists from France, Germany and Italy as well. It'll go out on Radio 4 tonight and I'm quite pleased because it was my idea.

Saturday, 4 December 1999

I've just left Downing Street after a meeting that could
lead to a pretty momentous development. Present in TB's
flat were the prime minister, Peter Mandelson and I, as
well as Shaun Woodward who, until Thursday night, was
the Tories' front-bench spokesman on London. AC joined
us for the first half an hour on the speakerphone. It was
the third meeting Shaun has had at Number Ten since he
was sacked from his job at six thirty p.m. on Thursday,
and it was the one that finally clinched his decision to cross
the floor of the House [of Commons and so become a
Labour MP] before Christmas.

The saga started last Sunday night when I was at the
Stonewall Equality Show at the Albert Hall. It was a
controversial evening, with the tabloids anyway, because
of an Elton John set that featured strippers dressed as Boy
Scouts. Cherie and her mum were in the box next to ours.
With us were Hilary Armstrong [Labour local government
minister], Alan Keen [Labour MP], Simon Hughes [Liberal
Democrat MP for Bermondsey and home affairs spokes-
man], Angela Mason [head of Stonewall] and Shaun and
his wife, Camilla. Shaun was going on at inordinate length
about Section 28 [the controversial clause introduced by
the Conservatives under Margaret Thatcher banning the
'promotion' of homosexuality by local authorities. Labour
wanted to abolish it.] The Tories have decided to have a
three-line whip [forcing all Tory MPs to vote with the party
line] against its repeal. He was clearly totally obsessed by
it. I joked with Shaun that he should follow the example
of a former adviser of his, Brendan May, and come over to
New Labour. He looked uncomfortable at the suggestion
and didn't say anything more.

I didn't think much more about it until Thursday when
Ann Keen [Alan's wife, and also a Labour MP] rang me

and said she was with Shaun. They were about to go off and meet the new Metropolitan Police commissioner, John Stevens, to talk about the issue. It had to be a big secret because Shaun said he'd been told by the Conservative whips office that he shouldn't discuss his views on Section 28 with anybody in public or in private. Ann said she thought he was so worked up that he might even leave the Tory Party over the issue.

When the meeting at Scotland Yard was over Ann called again from Shaun's house nearby, said he was getting increasingly emotional and that she really thought he might do it. So I spoke to him myself and we agreed that in total privacy he should come and talk to Cherie about it (he knows her and trusts her) and to AC and myself. He seemed very agitated but Ann said he was relatively composed and sober. We agreed that he should come to the Cabinet Office entrance [which leads through to Number Ten via a connecting door] at seven fifteen p.m.

I brought him through to AC's office and we talked for about an hour. By this time the Tories had sacked him because he had refused to sign a bit of paper saying that he agreed with the party line on Section 28 that their chief whip, James Arbuthnott, had given him. He's convinced that it was part of a plot by his boss, John Redwood [Tory shadow cabinet member], to force him to resign. Shaun had asked Arbuthnot for some time to try to work something out and says they had agreed that he could have until the end of the evening. He says he left his pager in his jacket pocket while he talked to a lawyer about trying to draft an alternative clause and when he looked at it again at six forty p.m. there were three messages on it from Arbuthnott. The first two demanded that he call immediately. The third said that if he didn't get in touch by six thirty p.m. he would be sacked. So by the time Shaun came in to see us he was very red-eyed and would talk about nothing else but Section 28. We tried to talk about the possibility of him crossing the floor over it but he was in no state to talk about it with any clarity. AC said that if he was to make the break it would have to be on a much wider platform than just Section 28. Shaun asked repeatedly to see Cherie 'as a human being', saying he knew her through charity work they had done together. We had been very reluctant to drag her into anything too political but eventually agreed. I phoned her and she popped down and spent twenty minutes alone with him. While this was going on AC and I chatted and tried to work out if there might be something bigger behind it all.

When Cherie went back up to the flat, Shaun asked me if I'd go for a drink with him. We were spotted by Nigel Warner and Andrew Lapping, Mo's two special advisers, on the way out of the Cabinet Office. I spoke to them after and said I'd cut their balls off if they told anyone. Shaun and I ended up in a little pub called the Two Chairmen near Trafalgar Square. We stood out a bit among the drunks and the blowsy barmaids, but fortunately the place was fairly empty and we could talk privately enough. After a couple of pints, talking mostly about decency in politics and the extent of his dissatisfaction with Tory policy on Europe, tax and the right-wing take-over of the party, we went back to his house.

Ann [Keen] was still there, talking to a very good-looking guy – Ben, a friend of the family, said Shaun, who works for him. We drank more, white wine this time, and carried on talking. Much of it was a rather self-indulgent monologue from Shaun. It was evident that he had an exceptionally high opinion of himself, that he could be (or could have been) a future leader of the Conservative Party. He was making it very clear he would need to be confident of a good seat and a good career if he jumped ship. I said I was certain we would do everything possible to find him a seat, that there was a very good chance of success, and if not there was always the House of Lords. I said my reading was that TB would want to make him a minister quickly, not least because it would then be easier to find him a seat.

We were joined by Tom Chandos, a Labour hereditary peer who'd lost his seat after the abolition but will be coming back soon as a life peer. He's an old friend of Shaun's – in fact, Shaun kept referring to him as his best friend. Tom joined Labour from the SDP [the short-lived Social Democratic Party] in 1994 when TB became leader. He says he urged Shaun to do the same and that Shaun thought seriously about it back then. Tom's judgement was that Shaun was very definitely in the wrong party but that he needed to be cautious about the timing of any move.

Ann and I eventually got away at about one in the morning after I'd promised to arrange for TB to talk to Shaun on the phone the next day. Shaun had asked for a meeting at Chequers, where TB was, but I warned him not to be seen to be demanding too much or doing too much to try to feather his own nest.

On Friday morning, after five hours' sleep, I went to Downing Street and called Tom Chandos, who said he thought Shaun was serious but that after we'd left the night before they had been to see an unnamed third party who had urged Shaun not to rush but to wait until maybe the New Year. My fear all along has been that he would get cold feet if we didn't land him quickly. There were then a difficult few hours with Shaun refusing to answer my calls, while TB rang me several times from Chequers to see what was going on. TB had agreed to speak to him and maybe see him later in the weekend. I tried to get messages to him via Ann and Tom, but still he didn't call. It turned out he was doing a whole round of interviews about his sacking and about Section 28 and doing them very well. Eventually, later in the afternoon, he did call and said he'd been talking to Sidney Blumenthal [leading Democrat adviser in the US] and to Jonathan Powell. We agreed that he should come in and see TB at Downing Street at ten p.m. last night. TB then said that was too late so I rang him back and eventually Shaun came back in via the Cabinet Office at eight fifteen.

Sunday, 5 December 1999

I'm now on a train back up to London with time to complete the story so far. Shaun turned up at the Cabinet Office but TB was running late. We started to head off to find somewhere for a coffee when my pager went off with a message from TB to take him up to the flat for a drink with Cherie before he got back. Further evidence, of which much more would follow, that TB is very keen indeed to clinch this one. So up we went. A bottle of wine was produced and TB arrived not long after. Shaun was obviously nervous but much more together than he had been the night before.

The three of us went into the sitting room for what TB and I hoped would be a relatively short conversation, but it wasn't. TB was swigging a Beck's by the neck and topping up our glasses of wine every few minutes. Shaun talked at length about Section 28 and decency, etc., and TB was very patient. Shaun at one point apologised for going on so long. TB would try to steer it back to practicalities but it was difficult. TB talked about Europe and the right-wing of the Tory Party and tax and so on. He said once or twice, 'Well, it seems to me you're obviously in the wrong home.' Shaun talked himself up and said others had been kind enough to talk about him as a future leader of the Conservative Party one day. TB talked about

Hague's misjudgements, of how when Michael Foot was leader of the Labour Party the policies had been mad but at least he was trying to pull the party back from the brink and fought hard to limit defections to the SDP, etc. Hague, by contrast, seemed intent on driving the moderates out. TB said that when he had fought the Beaconsfield by-election [TB was selected as the Labour candidate in 1982 aged twenty-eight; he came third, Labour's share of the vote was halved and he lost his deposit], Foot had said he was just the sort of candidate the party needed, so he felt it was worth staying and fighting. Shaun said that if he hadn't been at Harvard at the time that TB was elected leader he'd have joined New Labour. They talked enough about the timing of his defection for me to conclude that he had gone too far, with me there as a witness as TB wanted, to be able to pull back now. TB, who clearly wanted to go to bed by this time (ten thirty), said AC and Peter would be best at judging what would look credible in the media and he suggested another meeting yesterday morning. So I went home and arranged a meeting for nine a.m. and agreed to meet Shaun at his house first.

I was there for eight forty-five although he left me standing on the doorstep for ten minutes. TB rang to say that AC didn't seem to be ready (he hadn't read my pager message rearranging the meeting for nine a.m.), so we decided to go ahead but with AC on the speakerphone from home.

Shaun and I walked across the park and into Downing Street via the back entrance. Peter was already there, with his beautiful little dog, which he's had the audacity to call Bobby. ['Bobby' was Peter's secret name during TB's leadership campaign when it was thought politic to keep his public involvement to a minumum.] TB was in the bath. I made coffee and we went back into the sitting room.

Shaun was on a high because of the very favourable press he'd got all round for taking a stand against Tory policy and the fact that all of his constituents [he was MP for Witney in Oxfordshire] interviewed by the TV had supported him. Peter was draped over one sofa with Shaun and I facing him on the other. AC was on the speakerphone apart from one interlude when the dog knocked it off the coffee-table and cut him off. We talked about how to make his defection appear as credible as possible. AC and Peter, having agreed it beforehand, were arguing for sooner rather than later. Shaun talked about February when the Commons would be debating Section 28. He said his friends, like Chris Patten with whom he would be spending Christmas, would say it was totally out of character for him to do anything too quickly without talking it all through. But after a lengthy discussion, by which time TB had joined us, Shaun agreed that before Christmas would be best. Peter said Shaun would have a happier Christmas that way. Shaun said emotionally perhaps, but not socially with all the Christmas parties, etc. However, he was persuaded in part by the argument that if he left it too long it would look as though he was being totally calculating and there was a big risk of something leaking out. He was alarmed that Jonathan Powell had been speaking to Sidney Blumenthal about it, and I told him that we had been seen by Mo's special advisers. He must know that he's taking a risk coming to Downing Street so often, but then he's obviously a risk-taker.

Then we got down to the real nitty-gritty about seats, etc. There were always a few seats when people went to the Lords. We weren't spoilt for talent and there was no reason why he shouldn't become a minister. Shaun said his defection would be a huge event. We said it would be akin to Peter going the other way. Except it wouldn't, of course. Shaun then upped the stakes by saying his wife, Camilla, was very worried about his future, giving up a safe seat with such uncertainty. He said he needed 'for Camilla's sake' (oh, yeah!) a guarantee of a job in government. TB said he never guaranteed that to anybody, not even to Peter, and that there was a propriety thing about it. He just couldn't make a guarantee. But the sooner Shaun came across, the easier it would be. Still Shaun pushed and eventually TB said something like 'I can promise you it is my intention to do it' and Shaun accepted that. So it was as good as settled that he would come. The question of when wasn't resolved but the working assumption is now that it will be before Christmas. Shaun said he would have to talk to Camilla. He went off for a walk in the park with Peter and I dashed for the train to Brighton.

TB rang me while I was on the train to thank me and to say that he liked Shaun and to ask me how good I thought he was. I said he was a good communicator and good in the House, and that some of our people said he ran rings round them in debate. TB said he still didn't feel the deal had been clinched but I said it would be impossible for him to back out now. I also spoke to Charlie Falconer and said to him that, while we're all decent people and all that, somebody might have to point out to Shaun that he would have to be mad if he thought we would let him go on to become Tory leader or even a cabinet minister, given what we now know. I said to Charlie, and separately to Ann Keen, that people on our side of the House should say spontaneously to Shaun how impressed they had been by the way he'd handled himself.

There's a worry about the reaction of Prescott, who hates all Tories, and the likes of Ian McCartney. To be honest I'm not sure myself that I want any more Tories in our ranks, but I'm only here to serve. I just hate their pretensions and their arrogance and their belief that they have some sort of divine right to run things. Anyway, the whole thing has already damaged Hague, with both Steve Norris and Ivan Massow [a gay businessman], who are running to be the Tory candidate for mayor of London, saying they agree with Shaun about Section 28. If he does come over I think he might bring a number of like-minded people with him. Not those two, but others like them.

Generally I am doing more work in the SCU. I'm sitting in on Cabinet on a regular basis now in place of Alun [the Strategic Communications Unit's former head, Alun Evans, had left to become John Prescott's communications director], which is great.

We've had the first meeting of Gordon's Election Strategy Group, which was very funny. It was quite short, very disciplined (unlike the endless meetings we have at Downing Street). Gordon said what he thought, asked everyone for their view, then tasked them to take forward what he had clearly already decided were the conclusions. None of his ideas were exceptional or a problem, but his style was something to behold.

Tuesday, 7 December 1999

Yesterday was the culmination of an extraordinary example of communications driving the government machine. A week ago we were discussing TB's trip to the North West yesterday and today and how to make an event of it so it would generate some publicity. AC suggested we should commission a report on regional variations in unemployment, house prices, etc., and the impact of government policy in different parts of the country. It should take on the idea of a north–south divide and show that the situation was actually a lot more complicated than that. We had done something similar on AIDS internationally before the last Commonwealth heads of government meeting and it had been a great success. So, just half an hour later, during the eleven a.m. lobby, AC talked about this report that the prime minister had asked for. There then followed five days' mad scramble to get it researched and written in time for the trip, involving several departments as well as people here and at the Cabinet Office. Almost everybody was sceptical about the idea but it was too late. Gordon was furious and argued strongly that it would reopen the funding debate about public expenditure in Scotland and elsewhere. TB was uneasy too, to say the least. But the report turned out to be very good, and while it didn't and couldn't deny the north–south divide, it did help focus on government policies like the New Deal, the Working Families Tax Credit, the minimum wage, etc. The stuff we trailed in advance was very good but the coverage of the report itself today has been a lot more critical, picking out those statistics that show the north is indeed worse off in many ways.

In fact, the story was blown off the front pages by Jack Straw's announcement of a big increase in the fees for passports to twenty-nine pounds. He insisted on making a full statement, although we repeatedly urged him not to lead with his chin quite so dramatically.

Mo has been announced as the person to oversee the government's new Social Exclusion Unit, although there are real doubts about her ability to grasp all the detail. She's proved pretty hopeless at delivering a message so far and the problem is that people are being made far more aware of her deficiencies in this job than they were when she was in Northern Ireland.

Wednesday, 8 December 1999

Just left Shaun after yet another secret meeting, this time at the Meridien Hotel in Piccadilly. We are definitely in business. The only question is whether it happens next

Friday or the following Monday. So, while TB worries that it still might not happen, I'm 100 per cent sure that it will. We've started discussing a speech Shaun will make to the Social Market Foundation on 'values, people and politics'. If he makes the jump on Friday, he may ask to see his constituency party that evening and say to them that the Conservative Party has left him and not vice versa. That would give us the weekend to manage the media, which I'm sure we could do well. He said Esther Rantzen [former presenter of *That's Life*, on which Woodward worked as a producer], David Puttnam, Corin Redgrave's son and others had all tried to persuade him in the past that he was in the wrong party. Esther called him last Thursday night to suggest he should consider crossing the floor. He said she was against him leaving the BBC to go into politics on the grounds that he was clever enough 'to be DG' [director general]. He's clearly very much more at home with the idea now and is talking about doing some work on the Race Relations Bill and going around the CLPs [Constituency Labour Parties], including some of the difficult ones. Tony Banks [Labour MP for West Ham] is a friend of his, apparently, and he thinks he will be helpful. I even started to like him a bit more tonight, although I had to listen to another monologue on the speech he wants to make.

Thursday, 9 December 1999

Phoned TB last night to bring him up to date on Woodward and spoke to him again today about it. He sets enormous store by it and said on both occasions what a good job I was doing. So we're now in business for next Friday, I think, even though it will mess up my pre-Christmas weekend with Mum and Dad. Peter Mandelson held the first of his General Election Planning Group meetings at noon today. Rather more open than Gordon's strategy meeting last week. Impressive presentations on 'Operation Turnout' and the use of new technology. The simple aim is to hold on to as many of the 146 gains of the 1997 election as possible. And that means motivating both our switchers [those who switched to Labour from the Tories in 1997] and our core voters [traditional Labour supporters] to come out, with the latter group being the biggest problem. There's no attempt to pretend there's any question about when the election will be – May or June 2001.

Beef came back to hit us as an issue today with the French cabinet voting to continue the ban [on British beef following the BSE or 'mad cow disease' crisis: the European Union had ordered France to lift the ban]. TB furious and worried. He said Jospin was having difficulty with his coalition partners and that it showed the difficulty with coalitions.

Tuesday, 14 December 1999

Another hour and a half with Shaun this lunchtime, this time at Paul Gambaccini's flat. We needed somewhere safe to meet near Westminster and I knew Paul would be happy to help if it was to do with Section 28. AC and I went there separately and Shaun arrived twenty minutes late, in part, no doubt, because Paul's place is so hard to find. Everything is pretty much in place for Friday/Saturday. Shaun showed us his big speech, which is fine if a bit too wide-ranging. He still has a phenomenally high opinion of himself. He thinks TB should sack Keith Vaz and make him Europe minister in his place. He wants to see TB again but I'm not sure that's such a great idea for either of them.

TB went to see the Dome today and was suitably

impressed. He was very pleased with the dark blue shirt and tie he was wearing. He said he'd seen me wear the same combination and thought how smart it looked!

There was much hysteria in the office on Monday. I had been to recce the Dome visit and Anji Hunter said she'd had to veto my idea for a photo of TB up in the top of the canopy because it involved him being trussed up with a leather harness round his crotch and being suspended hundreds of feet in the air. AC said he thought I was just trying to get some private kicks and TB seemed to think it was all very funny. He's not good with heights apparently.

TB has been tearing his hair out about various ministers this week. No wonder having Shaun Woodward in the government looks attractive.

Prescott totally fucked up the launch of the ten-year strategy for transport by telling the *Sunday Times* he would be handing over a lot of day-to-day control of transport to Gus MacDonald [his deputy].

It has emerged that Mo has already signed a deal, said to be worth £350K, to write a book even though she says she has no plans to leave the government. She's also been writing to ministers advocating the legalisation of cannabis.

Donald Dewar is in trouble for having sacked his talented chief of staff, John Rafferty, allegedly for speaking out of turn to the press, a decision that has caused uproar in Scotland. Meanwhile AC is to be questioned by the police investigating the murder of [*Crimewatch* presenter] Jill Dando. He bears a remarkable likeness to the photo-fit of the main suspect, but apparently that's not the reason. He was a friend of hers. He thinks the story will leak but it hasn't so far.

After the French decision on beef and a very difficult summit in Helsinki, TB says that Britain's problem outside the single currency is that 'It's like trying to tell a club you're not happy with the way they're doing things without being willing to pay the membership fee.' So politics is as lively as ever and I'm playing a very full role in it all.

Still not quite sure how Prescott will react to Shaun's defection. AC plans to speak to him.

Wednesday, 15 December 1999

I wrote the official history of Shaun Woodward's defection today so that we all have a script to stick to when it happens. TB told me this one was for me to deliver and he still doesn't seem to be certain it will happen. It was odd sitting through planning meetings, including Gordon's Election Strategy Committee, discussing where we will be politically over the Christmas period and not being able to refer to it. I spoke to Ann Keen today and she was desperate for news and delighted to hear from me. I told her she would have a key role in the official history.

Gordon's meeting was interesting. Peter turned up for the first time and there was quite a fruitful discussion about how we should play the economic card in the New Year. Gordon sees it as building on solid foundations. Peter said we should be stressing productivity and the modern economy, something he said the DTI seemed to have gone quiet on. Douglas Alexander favoured jobs and Gordon seemed happy with both. The body language between Gordon and Peter was actually very positive, so that bodes well. Mind you, Peter did look a bit of a prat on the front of the *Sun* today with his dog, so maybe that cheered Gordon up. Gordon has a curious way of descending from fairly lofty discussions of economics (e.g., 'The Americans have won their productivity battle, we haven't') to extolling the virtues of remarkably unsophisticated political slogans. Today's was 'The Tories are worse than ever'. But at least he recognises the need for pithy slogans and can formulate them.

TB has been doing an initiative on rough sleepers today, something I was closely involved in setting up. It has gone very well indeed so far.

Sunday, 19 December 1999

Well, the deed is now done and it went almost entirely according to plan. Shaun Woodward is now the *Labour* MP for Witney, the Tories are struggling to undermine him and the left of the Conservative Party is in turmoil.

On Thursday after Cabinet I arranged to meet him at Paul Gambaccini's flat for a second time. He had a revised version of his speech and drafts of his letters to Hague and his local Conservative Association chairman. All of them were pretty well word-perfect from our point of view, so there was no tinkering to be done at all. We discussed timing again, agreeing to stick to Saturday if possible for his actual announcement. Shaun was worried that the Tories would respond to his speech on Friday by just taking the whip away [so he would no longer be a Tory MP]. My view was that even Hague wouldn't be stupid enough to sack him for calling for tolerance and an end to discrimination. The question was whether his criticism of the Tory stance on Europe and their tax proposals would be enough to justify kicking him out. I said I thought they would want to play it down but Shaun wasn't convinced. He thought they might want to play it tough again. Paul came home and met Shaun for the first time.

As we walked back across Westminster Bridge, AC asked me how I knew Paul. I told him I'd met him in a gay pub over twenty years ago but that I hadn't recognised him because I was much more interested in the guy he was with. AC and I agreed that Shaun and Camilla should come in and see TB that night [Thursday]. They were due to come at eight and I arranged for our party press officer in the South East, Phil Dilkes, to be there so they could meet each other before rendezvousing as agreed in Oxford on Saturday. All was going to plan until I was at the door to the Cabinet Office at eight p.m. to meet Shaun, and who should come out but Donald Dewar and Charles Kennedy, who had been having a secret meeting of their own at Number Ten about tuition fees in Scotland. I was terrified that Shaun was going to bump into them but fortunately one of his kids had been playing up and he was five minutes late. So I took him up to the flat, which was empty, and into the sitting room.

Cherie came in as I was making tea. She gave Shaun and me a beer and then when TB returned from making a short speech to the Labour Party Christmas dinner for staff in Victoria, he insisted on champagne as it was Camilla's birthday. It was mainly a social chat but TB read Shaun's speech and was very impressed with it. We had already arranged for the meeting to be broken up at nine by a fictitious call from Bertie Aherne so it wouldn't go on for hours like the last one. Shaun left, saying how good it all felt to him.

I went off to the Labour Party dinner and proceeded to get horribly drunk, fall asleep on the Tube, miss my stop and have to get a cab home from Acton Town. The party wasn't even very good. Despite all my efforts I could get nothing out of Alan Donnelly about why he'd just resigned as Labour leader in the European Parliament.

On Friday morning, feeling decidedly rough, I went in late. Most of the day was spent on Shaun. Two visits to his house near St James's Park to see him and his researcher, Matthew Johnson, who now knew what was going on and had decided to leave the Tories too. So he can now help us.

Shaun delivered his speech as planned at lunchtime. There weren't hordes of media, however, and by evening it wasn't even running on PA. No reaction from the Tories at all. Our big worry was that Tony Bevins [political editor of the *Express*] kept trying to get hold of AC. He had been closely in touch with AC at the time of Alan Howarth's defection [another Tory MP who had switched to Labour in 1995]. Sarah Womack, also on the *Express*, managed to talk to Shaun and ask him if he was thinking of defecting and Shaun told her such talk was 'dotty' and that he just wanted to talk about the issues in his speech. Just in case it leaked out early I had letters to Hague signed by Shaun and dated both Friday and Saturday so we could deploy them at any time, along with TB's words in response welcoming him to the Labour Party.

Friday night was quite a nervous one, but Moray Borthwick in our Media Monitoring Unit told me that the *Express* story, although it was on page one, was quite speculative. The other papers must have thought it was a bit of a flyer and didn't follow it up.

On Saturday morning there was nothing on the radio or TV bulletins but Sky quickly started running as their lead story that 'senior Labour sources' were saying something would happen that weekend. It was either AC, nervous that Shaun might bottle out at the last minute, or Phil Murphy [Labour's recently appointed director of communications], who tends to talk too much and might have felt he'd been left out of the loop. Both denied it. The only effect was to generate a few calls from other journalists that we had to avoid. It also meant Shaun had to finish his constituency surgery earlier than he had planned. His local chairman had come to see him, rather than meeting him at the Randolph Hotel as had been arranged. So, just before noon Shaun's staff started faxing out his letter of resignation to Hague. I followed immediately afterwards with TB's words. Sky managed to get it on their midday bulletin, but the BBC flunked it for their news programme ten minutes later.

Then it was a question of talking the Sunday papers through the agreed script, which was almost entirely accurate apart from omitting Shaun's visit to Downing Street on the night he was sacked by pager. I spoke to all the broadcasters, arranged for Shaun to go on *Breakfast with Frost* in the morning, and tried to monitor how the story was playing. The Tories took ages to respond and then a very pissed-off-looking Michael Ancram [Tory Party chairman] showed up on TV to say he had never been able to take Shaun at face value (shrewd guy!) and that he should call a by-election. We were able to point out that six Labour MPs had defected to the Tories since the second world war and not one of them had called a by-election.

I was in constant touch with Shaun and Ann Keen, who was minding him. She did a number of interviews and as everybody thinks she's a good thing that will help our people take to him. Jack Straw did some clips to welcome him as well. The TRG [Tory Reform Group, left-wing Conservative pressure group] put out a statement saying it was 'a significant blow to the current Conservative Party leadership' and their 'increasingly worrying attempts to take the party further to the right'. So it all went well and the Sunday papers have been fine, apart from an evil little piece by Simon Walters in the *Mail on Sunday* under the headline 'Tory Defector Slams Gay Slur', reporting that Shaun had condemned anonymous Conservative sources who had said he'd been blackmailed into leaving the party by militant gay campaigners who'd been threatening to 'out' him. The *Sun* tomorrow are doing a piece on Shaun's transsexual brother–sister, Lesley, something the *Mirror* reported on way back in 1992 anyway.

Shaun has been excellent on the broadcasts. I just spoke

to him as he was driving through the snow back to Oxford-shire. It may be about to get very ugly for him.

Wednesday, 22 December 1999

On my way down to Brighton for what I hope will be quite a long period off over Christmas and the New Year. I've just been rung by Margaret McDonagh, though, to see if I can find out what Ken said at a lunch with the *New Statesman*. She's heard that after a few drinks he said he would run as an independent if he lost the contest for the Labour nomination overall but won in the members section [of the electoral college]. She thinks he even told them the form of words he would use to get out of his promise not to run as an independent. There's been a bit of Shaun Woodward stuff in the past few days and the tabloids are clearly looking into his private life with a vengeance. It must be very tough on Camilla. Shaun has had to spend hours on the phone to his sister, Lesley, who feels like she's being treated by the press as some kind of freak. Shaun has been to a meeting of the south-eastern group of Labour MPs and has been in to Downing Street. TB suggested he take on some kind of campaigning role but obviously hasn't given much thought to what that might be. As for seats, TB said Brian Sedgemore [Labour MP for Hackney South and Shoreditch] was standing down but he didn't think his would be a very suitable seat for Shaun. Not a word of thanks from TB for pulling it off, despite him telling me last week he was relying on me.

2000

Monday, 10 January 2000

First day back after a long Christmas and New Year break. Christmas in Paris was lovely apart from a very heavy cold that I started to develop on Christmas Day. We only just got back to London on Boxing Day after a massive storm closed the airports. A bit of work between Christmas and New Year but not too much. New Year's Eve, Millennium Eve, we spent in the Dome with the great and the good. There was a major cock-up over ticketing and very long queues to get through Security on the night. This led to a long period of media criticism about the whole Dome project, not least because so many newspaper editors had to wait for up to three hours to get in. But once we were there the show was great. Getting back home afterwards was a struggle, though, with half the Tube stations closed.

On New Year's Day we flew off to Florida for a week of sunshine and total indolence. I feel exhausted after just one day back at work! It wasn't even particularly busy. There seems to be no real strategy for the coming weeks. TB has written a twenty-seven-page note for us all that doesn't seem to say anything very new, so far as I can see. So on we go.

Mo is very unhappy about a *New Statesman* article by Steve Richards last week that said Downing Street had lost confidence in her. I read it and noted a couple of anonymous quotes from me, which is a bit worrying, although to be fair to Steve the piece was pretty accurate overall.

Robin Cook caused a bit of concern by going out on a very strong pro-euro and pro-PR line on *Breakfast with Frost* yesterday – neither position in line with what TB wants at the moment. On the euro he has been seen by the newspapers as trying to take on Gordon.

Frank Dobson's campaign in London seems as good as finished. He'd made no progress at all, his relaunch last week flopped and he got slammed for sneering at 'toffee-nosed people' having to queue for the Dome. So Ken looks set for an easy win. I get a sense that AC feels a bit guilty that he got all the praise for the Shaun Woodward operation when it was really mainly my work.

Sunday, 16 January 2000

TB was on *Breakfast with Frost* this morning, trying to deflect some of the current criticism about the NHS. Promising more money in the future, etc., and it seems to have done some good. We weren't helped by an interview with Lord Winston [prominent doctor, TV personality and Labour peer] in which he was very critical of the government. AC rang him and got him to put out a statement rowing back from much of what he'd said but that, inevitably, led to yet more 'spin doctors out of control' type stories. We had hoped the media would be distracted by his other gaffe in which he said Cherie was planning a Caesarean (she was very angry) but that didn't really happen. It's not even true. She was in the papers herself after having to pay a penalty fare for travelling on the train without a ticket. But it actually played quite well for her in the sense that people seemed to think it could happen to anyone and that at least she travels by train.

The first week back felt like a long one and I've had quite a lot of work to do this weekend too. Not that I mind now that I'm back in the swing of it. Mo has managed to stir up more controversy after admitting to smoking dope and inhaling while at university. But the Tories haven't gone mad over it and I don't think it will be a huge story.

Peter is pretty gloomy about the chances of decommissioning in Northern Ireland but the Patten reforms to the RUC [which was changed to the Northern Ireland Police Service] are going ahead.

Thursday, 20 January 2000

Another difficult week on the NHS. TB's promise of extra money on *Breakfast with Frost* (which I thought was a good move and well planned) was, it turned out, not agreed with Gordon in advance. And TB was fairly specific, talking about bringing UK spending up to the EU average in five years, which means some £11 billion a year or something. The figure hadn't featured in any of the discussions with Gordon so he was in orbit about the whole thing, saying it gives the impression that money is the answer to everything and that the NHS is a bottomless pit and you can't just throw money at it. It undermines the CSR [Comprehensive Spending Review] negotiations that are now under way. The Department of Health, of course, is delighted. Education and other departments are circling for their slice of the cake. I'm not too sure if TB did it because of his frustration at his inability to get Gordon to commit to significantly more NHS spending or whether it just slipped out somehow because he had this figure somewhere in the back of his mind. We know from the fox-hunting débâcle that he's quite capable of saying things without thinking about it, but to be so specific this time suggests to me that he knew what he was doing.

Mo's drugs comments didn't really go anywhere. She is now the beneficiary of a huge *Daily Mirror* campaign to get her as mayor of London, despite AC's best efforts with Piers [Morgan, *Mirror* editor] to get him to drop it. They have been conducting a phone poll of readers today and I'm told the results are: Mo 11,000, Ken 4,000, Glenda 700 and Frank 300. It really knocked Frank back at a time when Ken had at last been on the back foot after giving an interview to *Face* magazine praising the anti-capitalism rioters in Seattle and London. The *Guardian* also did a big anti-Ken piece at last and had a story about him trying to get some independent candidates for the GLA [Greater London Assembly] so he wouldn't be shackled by the Labour Group if/when he's mayor. I actually believed for a day that Frank could do it after all when a few, admittedly very loyalist, MPs said their phone canvassing was picking up a big shift. But I fear he is well and truly lost, despite a very powerful public meeting with TB and Gordon last night.

The crime figures this week were pretty bad, going up for the first time in six years, but we managed to sell it as a mixed picture across the country with some areas doing very well and others – the Met and the West Midlands in particular – doing badly. We had one mad meeting in advance in which somebody helpfully pointed out that if you took out the areas where crime was going up then crime was going down! It occurred to me that we could apply the same principle to hospital waiting lists. The whole meeting dissolved into unreality until AC told us he had to leave because we sounded like we were at an *EastEnders* script conference.

Friday, 21 January 2000

Pretty extraordinary day yesterday. A very secret attempt to get Frank to pull out on the eve of the ballot papers going out so that Mo could enter the race. She was up for it, although she refused to run against him. If she had she would almost certainly have beaten Ken and Frank together. AC talked about 'letting it be known' to a couple of papers that Mo was interested in the hope of building up such demand for her to run that Frank would have to pull out. Would Glenda pull out for another woman with a real chance of winning? I suggested a write-in campaign for Mo, but Sally Morgan asked who would organise it and said it was against the rules anyway. I said I was certain Ken would run as an independent, no matter what we did, but TB said he didn't think he would. He said it was absolutely ridiculous that we had someone who wanted to run, whom people wanted and who could win but we couldn't get into a position where she could. The only option was for TB to meet Frank and his wife, Janet, whom Sally thought was more persuadable, and to tell him the hard facts. Anji said later it was essential that we avoid the huge damage that Ken winning would do to TB and that Frank could have whatever he wanted if he agreed – the Lords, an ambassadorship, whatever.

At six p.m. we left for Southall and a meeting of mainly Asian party members. All a bit surreal. John Prescott, who supports Glenda, said he would only go if Frank wasn't there, so John was on the platform and Frank wasn't. TB praised Frank, but not with a passion, and most of the questions weren't about him anyway. The audience was very pro-Frank, as most Asian groups are, and there were no pro-Ken questions at all. We left via a back entrance so John could avoid the Channel 4 comedian Mark Thomas, who had eight Jags lined up outside so he could have a go at Prescott [who had been labelled 'Two Jags' by the tabloids because he had an official one and one of his own]. I went straight home and TB went to Number Ten to see Frank and Janet. Apparently he told them that Mo could win but Frank couldn't. Frank and Janet, however, said that Frank had been humiliated enough already and this was too much to ask. Frank argued, though not convincingly, that things were going well and he *could* win. So this morning when I went to meet Frank and TB for a photocall outside the

National Theatre Frank was very frosty towards me at first. But when TB arrived nobody would have known anything was wrong and Frank warmed up a bit later.

Friday, 28 January 2000

Fairly quiet day with TB at the Economic Forum in Davos making a speech on economic reform. We have briefed the Sunday papers on what could be a very difficult visit by TB to the South West next week, with farming in severe crisis, etc.

More worrying signs of briefing and counter-briefing by the Treasury and the Foreign Office on Europe. Not sure what to do about it. Even if Gordon and Robin were called in by TB and told to stop it they would only deny it. We heard that Ed Balls had been telling French officials that there would have to be evidence of 'sustained public support' before Britain would join the euro – i.e., not just a quick, narrow win in a referendum. Does that amount to a sixth condition? [The government had set out five economic tests for membership.]

TB and AC are concerned, as ever, about the media. Do we need somebody like Norman Tebbit [former Tory Party chairman] to attack the media systematically? It seems to work. AC suggests Gerald Kaufman [Labour MP, and minister in the 1970s]. TB complains that, apart from David Blunkett, nobody in the cabinet is capable of carrying a good cross-government message.

We've got problems in the Commons because some of our Bills are growing in length and will have to be cut back if we're to get them all through. On Section 28 we've been sending out very mixed messages as to whether repeal would be a free vote or whipped. It's now been agreed that it's a government measure so it will be treated as such – i.e., whipped. Our backbenchers are livid at any suggestion to the contrary and have been getting very excited about it. So Ann Taylor [chief whip]'s silly suggestion of a free vote has been killed off. Everybody remembers her voting against lowering the age of consent in the past so she has no credibility on the issue. People are suspicious of Blunkett's new guidelines on sex education in schools for the same reason.

There was an all-night sitting in the Commons on Tuesday, provoked by the Tories. A truly inept bit of party management by Hague. So that led to Prime Minister's Questions being cancelled on Wednesday.

More problems in Scotland with the resignation of another senior special adviser. Bill [Bush] and I had been planning for some time to go up this week but we cancelled the trip. Otherwise it would have been 'Blair aides fly in to tackle crisis'.

Thursday, 3 February 2000

Section 28 still getting far too much attention for anyone's liking. We are facing almost certain defeat in the Lords next Monday. I have been encouraging Blunkett to give a statement on his planned sex education guidelines on the same day, which he's ready to do and that will help the Scots too. [The Scottish Executive had committed itself to pushing on with abolition of Section 28 faster than the Commons.] But the Churches are now weighing in and saying the guidelines should be statutory, which we clearly don't want. TB to his credit is standing firm on this so far, but the antis (Taylor, Blunkett, John Reid, etc.) are doing their best to shift the debate from one that rejects all prejudice to one where we would come close to saying that heterosexuality and marriage were the best way.

What worries TB is that while a debate like this rages on we are not seen to be addressing the core issues, which matter more. He's concerned that we don't have a good script for the next few months, although AC keeps telling him it's OK. We had another long chat yesterday about the inability of most cabinet ministers to talk the big picture. Gordon can, but he's very silent at the moment. Blunkett can and does. [Stephen] Byers can on a good day, and that's about it.

Mo is fuming again thinking people are briefing against her after a really shoddy piece in the *Independent on Sunday* saying people were alleging that her brain tumour had left her unable to do her job properly. I've never heard anyone, however little they think of her, suggest that. I'm sure she thinks someone below AC is at it at Number Ten and may even suspect me. But apart from one careless conversation with Steve Richards I haven't said a word.

Gordon is still diddling around. We discovered, via the *Telegraph*, that he's planning a tour of 'heartland' areas. He's also doing a speech on Britishness, trying to argue that despite devolution, etc., being British still means something. It also helps portray New Labour as 'patriotic' and defends us a bit from the European arguments we'll face at the election. But AC believes it's really about stopping people arguing that a Scot can't be prime minister of the United Kingdom.

Meanwhile Robin Cook seems to be kite-flying about the possibility of running to be first minister in Scotland. AC remarked when the Indonesian president, Wahid, who's blind, turned up for a visit that he might try to start a debate about having a blind PM. Stocks in Blunkett are very high at the moment.

TB is in the South West for a couple of days, and we're trying to say that while farming is in crisis, the rural economy as a whole is not.

Meanwhile Northern Ireland is in a very bleak period with the IRA refusing to decommission and the Assembly about to be suspended (or 'paused', as the Irish government want us to call it). It seems pretty clear the IRA never will disarm. It's part of their theology not to. But how can you ask people to go into a democratic executive with others who have a private army at their backs?

Sunday, 6 February 2000

Not much in the Sunday papers to worry us. More Mo stuff, almost certainly inspired by her, about how she's being frozen out. She's doing herself no favours at all and I honestly don't believe anybody at Number Ten is seriously trying to undermine her.

Still trying to finesse things on Section 28. Yvette Cooper, who's now public health minister, says she doesn't want too much emphasis on marriage on the grounds that if too many teenage girls got romantic ideas about marriage they might get themselves pregnant into the bargain. That provoked a typically dismissive response from AC and I can't see it getting very far with TB or Blunkett. But at the moment we're probably still heading for defeat in the Lords tomorrow.

Wednesday, 9 February 2000

Pretty catastrophic day but a mood of bizarre levity about the place. Alun Michael has resigned as first secretary and Labour leader in Wales, rather than be defeated in a no-confidence vote in the Assembly, with his own group unwilling to give him full backing. So despite all our efforts last year Rhodri [Morgan] will now become first minister after all and probably form a coalition with the Lib Dems [Labour had been governing until then as a minority administration]. TB says he has no choice but to admit he was wrong and accept that Rhodri has shown himself to be both loyal and a good minister. All very bad news for Frank. If TB was wrong then, isn't he wrong now? Answer: in truth, no. I've never understood why he was so anti-Rhodri, although I don't know the guy well enough to make an independent assessment. However, one immediate effect is almost certain to be a rise in Labour's support in Wales. We have to learn lessons and TB accepts that he must too.

He's very worried at the moment that the Tories will be able to coalesce around a powerful right-wing populist agenda, including anti-gay sentiment, racism, xenophobia, asylum, drugs. In fact, he was wonderfully robust on Section 28 at PMQs today. But he's tearing his hair out on the rest, especially the home-affairs stuff. After all, he built his agenda on 'tough on crime, tough on the causes of crime', etc. I lightened the mood at the weekly meeting saying I had personally vetoed a message of support from him to 'Gay Day' at the Dome on Saturday. For some reason everybody found that incredibly funny. So we've agreed that a tough new statement from him on hard drugs will help seize the initiative.

I also suggested talking openly about the possibility of splitting up the Home Office and creating a Justice Department as well as maybe moving Jack to be foreign secretary and making Blunkett home secretary. TB wants to be seen to be firm but fair. Peter [Hyman] and I remain the great liberals in all this, insisting he must remain robust against all forms of discrimination. We have to find a tough response on bogus asylum-seekers without being accused with any justification of being racist.

The cry has been going up with increasing frequency, 'Where's Gordon?' Nowhere, when it comes to defending the government's overall position but very public when he wants to highlight his generosity on good issues like debt relief or helping charities.

Friday, 11 February 2000

In Scotland to try to get their general-election planning in shape and make sure there are no turf wars between the Executive, Scottish Office and Number Ten. It has all been pretty harmonious, apart from a spat I inadvertently set off about TB addressing the Scottish Parliament. Donald [Dewar] had agreed with David Steel [the new speaker of the Scottish Parliament] that he should talk to MSPs [Members of the Scottish Parliament] in the chamber without it being a formal session. [Because TB wasn't a member of the Scottish Parliament he couldn't speak there during a normal debate.] I had had only a rather garbled account of this beforehand so, without really thinking about it, I said, 'What's all this crap about him speaking in some side room and not addressing the Parliament?' That riled Donald enough but then Douglas [Alexander], whom he apparently can't stand, weighed in with all guns blazing, saying it was outrageous that the British prime minister shouldn't be able to address a parliament in the UK and was being treated like a visiting foreign leader. Nobody else could quite see what all the fuss was about and we've settled that he should do it as agreed. It will look no different to most people than if he was speaking in the parliament itself. Otherwise the plans for a joint general-election planning committee sound fun. It will mean me coming up with Bill [Bush] every few weeks but that's fine by me.

The situation in Wales has produced some discussion about devolution in general. We should be proud of having decentralised more than any Western government ever has in modern times.

Prescott is concerned about the Barnett Formula [which fixes the amount of UK public spending devoted to Scotland at a higher *per capita* level than elsewhere] as well as regional government for England, which he clearly doesn't intend to give up on. There's a bit of a worry, too, about mayoral races destabilising Labour politics all over the country.

Peter is very sombre about the situation in Northern Ireland. I had a long chat with him on the way back from the General Election Strategy Group meeting at Millbank. Mainly about Mo and how badly she is behaving, telling people she hasn't spoken to Peter since he took over the job from her. We also talked about Shaun Woodward, who he says is very unhappy.

The election meeting was very good, the best of the kind so far. Gordon very focused and things seem to be getting under way. Labour's website was relaunched yesterday, except that TB's first web-cast was badly recorded and had to be done again, which was a bit embarrassing.

There's been a hijacked plane from Afghanistan at Stansted airport. Most of the passengers are asking for asylum and it looks as if it might all have been a big scam. TB wanted Jack to be very tough on it and he duly was in a statement to the House.

On Section 28, TB wants to go hard on the principle, as he did at PMQs, while trying to reach a sensible accommodation with the bishops.

Thursday, 17 February 2000

Busy week that got off to a bad start. I set my alarm in Brighton an hour late on Monday morning by mistake, missed breakfast and made the morning meeting ten minutes late. Not that I need have bothered: it was the usual rather depressing discussion about the hostility of the press, how we weren't getting our message across, how we needed better stories, better strategy, etc. AC has now decided to agree with TB, maybe to stop him going on about it so much and giving AC such a hard time. In fact AC says (and he's right) the press could be a hell of a lot worse.

Philip [Gould] is very worried about the responses he's getting from his focus groups. He says people are as hard on us now as they ever were about Major's government. He can exaggerate a bit at times, but I'm sure there is a fundamental problem. People do feel let down that more hasn't been done and they're not ready to accept any more excuses. The problem is there is no evidence that Gordon is willing to find the money for health and education. I'm told by people who used to work for him that he's never been very interested in public services, believing them to be inefficient and a drain on resources.

AC has decided not to replace Alun Evans as head of the SCU. Instead Phil Bassett will do long-term planning, I'll do medium-term, and Godric will take over at the two-week point. It's a pretty daft system, a sort of mad relay race. But there we are, who am I to argue?

The good thing from my point of view is that I can continue to attend Cabinet every week, which is great. I was a bit depressed about it at first, though. Not because I wanted to head the SCU. Better to keep my flexibility and ability to do increasingly political stuff. But I just felt we were having the same weary discussions and nothing was changing at all. I had an overflowing in-tray, dozens of emails to answer and no secretarial support. I was frantically organising a drugs event that, under the new system, should have had nothing to do with me. I didn't mind much because it was a story that interested me and the event went well. We announced a likely extension of 'drugs courts' and a proposal to have anonymous drugs hotlines advertised in schools. We appointed Shaun Woodward to take the latter forward because I thought it was a good idea [he had helped set up ChildLine with Esther Rantzen] without telling anybody in advance, apart from Keith Hellawell [the drugs czar]. Mo and Ian McCartney were very pissed off at not even being consulted.

Mo is as much of a loose cannon as ever. She now really wants to run as London mayor, having refused to do so when she might have been able to. She's even talked about running as an independent, although that would mean expelling her from the Labour Party. We will know soon enough. Some people still hope Frank might pull out if he wins the nomination by only one of his many whiskers, but I can't see there's the slightest prospect of him agreeing to that. We will get murdered in London whatever happens, and coming on the back of Rhodri that will be tough.

Meanwhile we have no strategy or leadership in place for the local elections in May when we could suffer some very serious reverses. Gordon continues to contribute very little but he has come up with what he thinks should be the narrative we use to talk about ourselves, along with dividing lines from the Tories. Needless to say, it's almost all about his policies – making work pay, a strong and stable economy, cutting unemployment. Next to nothing on investment in health and education.

I had a couple of sessions chewing the cud with Charlie [Falconer] this week, which provided some respite. I said I thought Portillo would be making the same calculation as us – a Labour majority of over a hundred at the next election would make it all but impossible to beat us in the one after that. Therefore, I said, Portillo would try to seize the leadership before the election. I said as much to a rather sceptical-looking TB. But Charlie agreed and said he thought he would move in the next month. My money is on the autumn.

Monday, 21 February 2000

Just had a wonderful weekend in Scotland with James's parents. No TV or radio and even the mobile was out of range. The nearest paper shop was ten miles away.

Back in London in time to deal with the fact that Frank beat Ken for the Labour nomination by about 3 per cent and is now the official candidate. Ken is playing games and looks about ready to announce that he will run for mayor anyway as an independent, although no significant union or political figure has come out to support him as yet. We're hitting him quite hard on his promise not to run. AC thinks we should go a lot further but TB, who's at Chequers, seems to be reining him in. Ken has certainly been telling his supporters in the media (the *Guardian* especially) that he will run. If he runs, will we try to push Frank aside and let Mo in?

Wednesday, 23 February 2000

Well, the answer to the question above is, probably not, although Mo clearly hopes we will. There have been stories about in the media of a plot to run Mo. I've been at the forefront of knocking them down. We think they were put about by Ken himself to try to undermine Frank, but there's little doubt Mo will have been giving some private encouragement to them. I did both lobbies [morning and afternoon] yesterday, saying that we had a candidate and weren't looking for another. I said all the stuff about Mo was a smokescreen to help Ken avoid saying whether he'll keep his promise to support Frank. That did some good, but today Ken has decided to challenge us to change policy on the financing of the Tube or face an election that is a referendum on the subject. There are now two camps: those who want Ken to stand so we can take him on, and those (fewer in number) who think it will do us too much damage and we must keep him to his promise, if at all possible, even if it means offering him something. The fact is, in my view, he's going to run anyway so there's no point in us trying to do any deals to stop him. He'd make them all public anyway. TB said to me that he doesn't think Ken has made up his mind, but I'm not so sure. He'll just keep us dancing to his tune day after day, so that he is permanently the story, and then he'll go for it. But I'm sure a lot of people on the left will be urging him not to. He might end up with the job he wants but having done a huge amount of damage to them in the process. In one lovely irony, TB wrote a note to Frank telling him to distance himself from TB. He even told him to wear an open-neck shirt and suggested what he should be campaigning on. We tell the puppet to insist there is no way he's going to be our puppet!

Monday, 28 February 2000

On my way home from a couple of evening events to mark the Labour Party's centenary, attended by a very reluctant leader of the Labour Party. I thought it looked very rude at the end of the last one when he disappeared as fast as he could and didn't wait to hear Callaghan, Foot and Kinnock [previous Labour leaders] speak. To be fair, he did attend the whole of the main celebration yesterday, on a Sunday, but his body language has hardly expressed his deep love of the party and pride in its history! For all that, his speech yesterday was very good and did, for once, acknowledge that previous Labour governments, and not just the Attlee one [1945–51], achieved a great deal.

Today was almost as depressing as most Mondays, with the usual downhearted morning meeting. And that despite a pretty good press this morning. AC was a bit cross that he had allowed the centenary to be overshadowed by some TB repositioning on GM food. It was an article for the *Independent on Sunday* in TB's name that brought his personal position into line with that of the government [i.e., more of an 'honest broker' than an advocate]. It was portrayed as a huge U-turn. My mind went straight back to my famous pro-GM lobby briefing [see 18 February 1999] that had led to the *Daily Mirror* front page 'The Prime Monster'.

I spent too long at the end of last week talking to Janet Street-Porter [the new editor of the *Independent on Sunday*] about providing something for her big relaunch of the paper. In the end we gave her the article, but we should have known that she would over-hype it.

Sunday, 5 March 2000

A major row at Cabinet on Thursday found its way into the media. Clare Short [international development secretary] really ripped into Geoff Hoon [defence secretary] over the amount the MoD had been trying to charge for four Puma helicopters to fly emergency aid to Mozambique [where there had been disastrous flooding]. Clare was trying to get the very best value for money, quite rightly, whereas the MoD was offering a Rolls-Royce standard service at Rolls-Royce prices. Unfortunately, given that the UK really does have an excellent record on Mozambique aid, Clare made her feelings pretty clear on Friday morning on the *Today* programme. Really stupid, as it achieved absolutely nothing and just got us bad headlines. TB had had them both behind after Cabinet to sort it out. Unfortunately, however, it still appeared that at least a day was lost in getting some aid to the region. And when the helicopters finally arrived today (after a disagreement with the

South Africans over landing rights) there were no longer any significant numbers of people in the trees needing help.

TB's ex-nanny has offered a book to publishers and foolishly spoke to the *Mail on Sunday* about it. They were about to run what read like excerpts in their first edition before TB got an injunction to stop them.

The Frank and Ken show goes on. Ken hasn't yet declared his intentions and Frank got the better of him on *Question Time* over it. He went on the programme very reluctantly after TB insisted. He was sure he would get done over, but actually he was OK although he missed every opportunity to get across any policy message or any sense of why he wants the job.

I'm trying again to get some decent drugs stories up, as part of my new planning role. I met Keith Hellawell again on Friday and we might be making some progress. I'm a bit disillusioned by our inability to get a sensible communications structure in place. AC's fault really. I get the feeling that he's trying to keep me down. Some meetings have been cut in size and people like me, Pat [McFadden] and Bill [Bush] have been excluded. I have asked firmly that this be changed, but no reply yet. AC also said I couldn't go to Scotland or St Petersburg [where TB was meeting the newly elected President Putin] this coming weekend. So I haven't been in the best of moods.

Monday, 6 March 2000

Feeling a bit better today despite a really crap night's sleep. Anji rang me last night to say AC wanted me to attend the meetings on 'message' again. It was cancelled today anyway, because of Ken declaring that he would run as an independent. Totally inevitable in my view. TB was actually in quite a good mood about it. Glad to have it out in the open, I think. I travelled with him to the launch of the government's heart-disease strategy and said I was convinced Ken would win. He wasn't so sure, but accepted that I was probably right. In fact, Frank was on very good form today and it may have been a mistake to have TB intervene so quickly to attack Ken as we did. But he [TB] is still quite fired up about it and really does think Ken would be a disaster.

I spent this evening at Mike Brunson's farewell at ITN [he was retiring as political editor], which was a good party. It was fun to chat to a few Tories for a change and to Menzies Campbell [Liberal Democrat foreign affairs spokesman], who clearly has little time for Charles Kennedy. He said, 'We're still waiting to hear from Charlie what the strategy is,' and we agreed that it would be a good thing if Robin Cook threw in his lot with Scotland and left the cabinet. Tony Benn told me Ken's decision would mean the death of New Labour, but he's certainly wrong about that. He clearly thought I still worked at the BBC!

Friday, 10 March 2000

TB now in Scotland and heading off to St Petersburg tonight, hoping to get in with Putin before the French and Germans do, but also hoping to avoid accusations of running after a man with civilian blood on his hands from Chechnya [where Putin had previously been responsible for security]. It means the past twenty-four hours have been fairly quiet at Number Ten. The week has gone as fast as ever with Ken and Frank still the main political issue. TB called me into AC's room on Tuesday to discuss where we are over it. He concluded that 'Ken has us over a barrel.' Nobody seriously doubts now that Ken will win. But TB has had two objectives throughout – that Ken shouldn't be the official Labour candidate, and that if he were to run as an independent he shouldn't take half the Labour Party with him. Both of these have been achived and, arguably, Ken becoming mayor is something that was so likely from the outset that nothing was going to change it. Except maybe Mo, but she decided too late. So control freakery doesn't always work.

TB thinks Ken can still be checked by talking about crime and the cost of his plans for the Tube. That is what Frank will do, and I've been urging him not to talk about everything in terms of Ken. It just builds Ken up as the story. We've been told to stop calling him Ken from now on. It's Frank versus Livingstone. I've floated the idea of doing a deal with the Lib Dems to run a joint ticket with Susan Kramer [the Lib Dem candidate] as deputy mayor if Frank wins. It hasn't been completely ruled out. The main problem is that she probably wouldn't accept it.

Philip Gould and Peter Hyman are spending quite a lot of time with Frank and doing a lot of good, but closing the 55 per cent lead Ken has in the latest *Evening Standard* poll may be a struggle. There's concern about some of the briefing that is coming out of the party press office – that TB had said Ken should no longer be branded a liar and that party members wouldn't be disciplined for campaigning for him.

I made a huge fuck-up at Cabinet this week. AC had been talking about using the phrase 'working hard for hard-working families'. If he said it shouldn't be used until after the Budget then I missed it. So I put it in the spiel Margaret Beckett read out in Cabinet in Mo's place [she was away] on the week ahead. Gordon rolled his eyes to the skies and shook his head. TB sent a note to me asking where the phrase had come from and I couldn't even remember at the time. Gordon stomped into TB's study after the meeting. It was obviously the product of some high-level strategy meeting. But it was such an unexceptional phrase and completely consistent with the sort of thing I've been saying for ages that I thought it was fine to urge people to use it around the Budget. I told Jonathan to tell Gordon it was all my fault, but he thought that would only make matters worse. What we did agree on was that, so long as it wasn't repeated elsewhere, it wouldn't do any harm as none of them takes a blind bit of notice of what they're told about message at Cabinet!

On Thursday Gordon slipped out the update of the National Changeover Plan [for the euro] at Treasury Questions. I thought he'd face a huge row about how it had been announced but he pretty well got away with it. He certainly is a master of news management. He got a big splash this week on a crackdown on the black economy. If only the rest of the cabinet had a fraction of his media skills.

Thursday, 16 March 2000

Plenty of controversy this week on several fronts. Most of them public too. AC, when asked how he could remain anonymous when he's having the cameras into his lobby briefings, said there was nothing he could do about it if the papers chose to refer to him by name. [AC was normally referred to as 'the prime minister's official spokesman', in reports of his lobby briefings. This was a step towards greater openness as the Tories had insisted on 'sources close to the prime minister'. AC was now planning to allow BBC cameras to film some lobby briefings for a Michael Cockerell documentary on the press office.] He gave the distinct impression, although he's tried to deny it since, that he was perfectly relaxed about it. So the papers and the BBC promptly did just that and the *Guardian* printed a whole lobby briefing verbatim. AC then tried to back off, wrote a letter to the *Telegraph* saying he thought 'the prime minister's official spokesman' was quite sufficient. But he didn't say that people couldn't refer to him as Alastair Campbell so the matter was left as unclear as ever.

Yesterday AC really goofed when he acknowledged that the tax burden will be higher at the end of this parliament than at the beginning, something TB and Gordon have bent over backwards to avoid doing. He was pretty chastened about it, implying that it was because he was tired. Some of the journos saw it as a deliberate strategy to convince our heartlands that we are actually delivering for them. But it was cock-up rather than conspiracy.

Gordon was strangely calm but was muttering darkly about having to change the Budget strategy as a result. The fear was that he would now go back on his agreement to provide a big cash injection for the NHS so that he could be seen to be reducing the tax burden. Just as well Cockerell wasn't filming throughout that episode.

Most people inside Number Ten think the whole Cockerell thing is a big mistake and a bit of an ego trip for AC. I'm all for greater openness but this is a pretty artificial sort of openness. I think he genuinely believes it will get across the idea that we are 'more spinned against than spinning'. But if Cockerell were to see and report how we really work it would be hugely damaging.

Communications driving policy has been evident again this week, over asylum in particular. TB determined to have something tough to counter tabloid stories about professional beggars, mainly from Romania, who are claiming asylum. Barbara Roche [Home Office minister] and I came up with some strong measures, which, under pressure from us, the Home Office said TB could use at PMQs. Fortunately he didn't because most of them have collapsed under further scrutiny. What's left we may use for the Sundays, I think.

Meanwhile, on drugs Mo has been fighting a lone battle to decriminalise cannabis, hoping to use a Police Federation report in a couple of weeks as cover. A coalition of TB, Jack Straw and Keith Hellawell have prevented that. She was already furious about an announcement made to the *Sunday Express* last week about having a Drugs Bill next year and reappointing Hellawell for another stint as drugs tsar. I should have called her to warn her it was coming but I forgot. Not that she would have been in any position to do anything about it. She now says she doesn't want to be used for any lengthy interviews about cannabis, which is ridiculous as she's supposed to be the minister in charge of drugs policy. The real fear is that she will brief her mates in the media about her reservations anyway. She's already strongly suspected of telling Piers Morgan on the *Mirror* that TB still wants Frank to stand aside for her, even though it's no longer the case. It would never work now as a wheeze anyway.

Ken's lead has been cut from 55 per cent to 45 per cent so there's all to play for! He took a serious knock yesterday when the parliamentary commissioner ruled that he had to apologise for not declaring £200K of income from journalism and after-dinner speaking. However, he was back in his favourite role as victim in no time when it emerged that the guy who is supposed to have made the complaint against him in the first place knew nothing about it. Very mysterious and Ken was able to suggest dirty tricks.

Meanwhile a huge row over Section 28 with loads of ministers, including Alan Milburn, Mo, Margaret Jay, Chris Smith and Angela Eagle all furious with the wording agreed by Blunkett with the Church of England bishops on the teaching guidance on marriage and personal relationships. Angela Mason [of Stonewall] said she thought it was worth swallowing to get rid of Section 28, but I'm not sure it will achieve that. I think the Lords will pocket it and vote against Section 28 anyway. So is the row over the guidance worth the candle? We had the worst of all worlds today. The *Daily Mail*, *Telegraph*, etc., saw the guidance as allowing the promotion of homosexuality because of a gender neutral reference to 'stable relation-ships' while most of the rest of the media see it as a fairly cynical attempt to buy off the Lords. In Scotland, Donald Dewar has refused to go as far as Blunkett on the wording, so we've shafted them on the day of the Ayr by-election [for the Scottish Parliament] into the bargain.

Sunday, 19 March 2000

Glorious weekend in Cornwall, almost entirely untroubled by work. There's not much going on at the moment. The government is gearing up intensively for the Budget and the CSR [Comprehensive Spending Review]. Surprisingly little pre-Budget speculation in the papers, largely because Ian Austin [Gordon Brown's press officer] isn't behaving the way Charlie [Whelan] used to. There's been a bit of 'a Budget for hard-working families' type stuff, but that's hardly a surprise and Ian has to give them something.

Wednesday, 22 March 2000

Yesterday's Budget operation went very well, with a mass-ive boost to NHS spending. It seems that all Gordon's threats about shifting from spending to cutting the tax burden came to nothing. It was all done in a pretty straight way for once, although that has led to the predictable questions about whether we have dropped the double counting methods that produced £21 billion for health and £19 billion for education [Gordon Brown's decision to produce a cumulative figure for spending increases over three years in the previous Comprehensive Spending Review had been widely derided as misleading spin]. The honest answer is, yes, we have, but of course we don't want to admit as much. Not least because if we had done it this time (and no doubt the papers will do it for us) it would add up to squillions of quid.

TB did a very rare statement in the Commons on a domestic issue today, on health. The Tories have been left exposed and they've been going on in a very statistical way about the tax burden, etc. Stephen Twigg [Labour MP for Enfield, Southgate], whom I bumped into, says people in his archetypal switcher constituency were more than happy to forgo tax cuts in favour of better hospitals, etc. The key, therefore, is that the NHS should be seen to have visibly improved before the election next year. God help us if we end up delaying the election while waiting for more evidence of delivery. I've spent much of the week running a little unit to co-ordinate a regional roll-out of the Budget, sending ministers all over the country to do local TV and radio interviews, etc. I had to cope with a few clashing egos yesterday. I had the great pleasure of saying we wouldn't use Mo at all as she was refusing to go to any of the places we wanted. So, lo and behold, she changed her tune and went where I'd wanted her in the first place. Alistair Darling threw a strop because we shifted him from Newcastle to Plymouth, even though he'd said earlier he wasn't the ideal person for our 'heartlands'. He did as we asked in the end, but it was a real effort. I went to see [Hollywood actor] Michael Douglas speak at the Commons on Monday evening. It was virtually a CND rally, but it's as well I went because he called on TB to go to an arms-control meeting in New York next month and I ended up having to draft a response explaining why he couldn't.

Saturday, 25 March 2000

Difficulties in Northern Ireland with David Trimble only narrowly winning his leadership election [of the Ulster Unionist Party] against Martin Smyth [who opposed the Good Friday Agreement]. TB back from a European summit in Lisbon, where the media seemed interested only in whether he was going to take paternity leave, and in the fact that TB, Gordon and Robin had all used separate planes to get there. Strategy note fron Stan Greenberg [American political consultant brought in to advise in advance of the general election] suggests serious disconnection from the public. It was one of the reasons TB has decided to do a big speech on 'Britishness' next week.

Tuesday, 28 March 2000

TB in a complete state over his 'Britishness' speech this lunchtime. It was Gordon's idea, but by mid-morning TB still wasn't clear what he wanted to say. Michael Wills [DTI minister] was asked to produce a draft but at noon TB was sitting in his study, ashen-faced, working at it. Just imagine if it had been a Brown speech: a huge amount of work would have gone into it and it would have been properly briefed and launched. This has been an object lesson in how not to do it. I had to do the eleven o'clock lobby on it, which wasn't easy when I knew it was still being agonised over.

Gordon has been manic ever since the Budget, demanding stories on health, etc., every day and TB has echoed him. I've made it clear that I disagree and that we should have a smaller number of stronger stories. There is so much cynicism about everything we say and do that we have to be very careful not to be seen to be over-spinning stories that aren't very strong in their own right.

Mo and Ian McCartney [her deputy in the Cabinet Office] are unhappy about how little they are being used and how Keith Hellawell and (even worse) Shaun Woodward have been built up on the drugs issue. Ian threatens to resign on a regular basis. By all accounts Mo is often hysterical when out and about on visits, as she was in the North East on Friday – hammering against windows in frustration. There are far too many signs of chaos and barmy behaviour all over the place at the moment. Too many individuals losing their grip and it could yet infect the whole government.

Friday, 31 March 2000

Philip Gould's fiftieth birthday party at County Hall last night. Free ride on the Millennium Wheel [the London Eye], loads of champagne but not enough to eat so I got a little bit pissed. Then spent most of today at Chequers for a political cabinet. TB and Gordon setting out the path towards the election. Gordon very impressive and Alan [Milburn] pretty good on the NHS. Jack Straw hopeless and Mo rather embarrassing. It's finally been agreed that David Blunkett will head up the local election campaign [ahead of the elections in May], God help him. I travelled up with Peter Mandelson and the dog, which has now doubled in size and is incredibly friendly. Peter says his job is awful, going over the same number of points with all the parties time and time again. Michael Ashcroft [Tory Party treasurer] finally got his peerage today, but in circumstances that were totally humiliating for Hague. The Honours Scrutiny Committee said Ashcroft had to give up being the UN ambassador for Belize, where he lives much of the time, and promise to move back to Britain.

Tuesday, 4 April 2000

More of the same pointless, circular discussions about how we need better message lines, etc., etc. Same stuff that we've been saying ever since I came here. We should have a proper agenda for our meetings and report-backs, however brief, with roles clearly assigned to people. But evidently that isn't the way that TB or AC want to work. God knows why not, because so much time and effort is wasted doing things the way we do them at the moment. And far too much hasty reaction to events. TB called me in on Monday because he wanted me to take a special look at the West Midlands media. It was because he'd got a bad press there after an article in his name in the *Sunday Business* that said we no longer intervene to prop up ailing businesses. Because of the Rover crisis [the car company based at Longbridge in Birmingham was looking for a new buyer], we will now do a special piece for the local paper to-morrow. [Stephen] Byers is still on the rack over Rover, rather unfairly. [Byers had been trying to find a buyer that would continue mass car production.] But he's making the big mistake of launching a huge self-justification exercise so that it looks as if he's more interested in defending himself against criticism than he is in defending jobs in Birmingham. He's not doing himself any favours either in the media or with TB. I try to forget my unsuccessful efforts to get him to go on programmes like *Question Time* and do wider government-message stuff and remember that he's one of our few reliably New Labour ministers. Except he's shown worrying tendencies to play Citizen Steve of late (perhaps anticipating a leadership battle against Gordon one day) and he doesn't show any real signs of understanding business.

Had a big row with Ian Austin over whether to put Andrew Smith [chief secretary to the Treasury] on *On the*

Record [BBC1, Sunday political interview programme] last weekend. He was plain wrong to refuse and he has this infuriating habit of ringing me up and telling me what I should be doing (prompted by an instruction from Gordon about what needs to be done, I have no doubt).

Tuesday, 11 April 2000

Home from a great weekend away in Oporto. I'm enjoying the job as much as I have ever done and things have settled down into a generally good working arrangement. This week has been odd because Michael Cockerell has been in filming his documentary. Most people still think it's a huge ego-trip for AC but it hasn't stopped some of them playing up a bit for the cameras. Monday's lobby meeting was a disaster because they managed to film a ding-dong on asylum where we were clearly on the defensive, and it was rather political with AC talking about the Tory and Lib Dem manifestos. Enough for there to be a row when it is aired. [Strictly speaking, AC was supposed to comment only on Labour policies, not those of the opposition parties.] AC said he thought it was fine, but he looked a bit uncomfortable afterwards.

The cameras were in again today but the lobby was a bit more run-of-the-mill. So far there has been nothing to show the lobby journalists as a bunch of wankers interested only in trivia and personalities, which was the idea of doing it.

Quite a constructive discussion in the office today (not filmed!) about how the public doesn't understand New Labour phraseology. There's a language barrier with things like 'enterprise and fairness', 'opportunity and security', etc. Thatcher managed to get her messages across instinctively with a sort of kitchen-sink language that people understood immediately. We do now have some good lines

– like 'a lot done, a lot still to do', which we will use for the local elections. The challenge is in getting people to use them. I have yet to hear 'working hard for hard-working families' on the airwaves or to read it more than once (and that was by TB) in the papers. They all think they're too intellectual or something to go in for sloganising. Having said that, I used to hate being at the receiving end of all the sloganising Labour used in opposition when I was at the BBC.

The hacks continue to have it in for Byers at the moment, as well as looking for a row over asylum. TB and Gordon still want us to get more stories up about health, but it's proving very difficult. Gordon has started trying to get involved in other stories very late in the day, which pisses everybody off. Today he was rewriting the press release for tomorrow's story on tackling social exclusion, and when I left the office at eight tonight it still hadn't been settled. He also tried to change the venue for TB's first proper London campaign visit with Frank Dobson tomorrow. Everyone disagreed with him (he wanted it to be on social exclusion too despite the fact that it would have clouded the story rather than making it clearer). We are now sticking to the original plan.

Thursday, 13 April 2000

Alan Milburn is getting exhausted and fed up with Gordon constantly demanding more stories on health so as to get value for money from the Budget spending.

Pretty grim news for Frank today. He's third in an *Evening Standard* poll, 1 per cent behind Steve Norris [the Tory candidate]. Livingstone has dropped by about 12 per cent since the campaign began but Frank is failing to pick up his votes. He said yesterday he was actually enjoying being seen as a martyr. Gallows humour, I fear.

Wednesday, 19 April 2000

Fairly quiet week in the run-up to Easter. Godric is on holiday so, with TB and AC in Northern Ireland, I did both lobbies yesterday. It was both tricky and fun because Hague was launching a big attack on asylum-seekers to help boost his local election campaign. He was suggesting that all asylum-seekers should be put in detention centres and those found to be bogus quickly booted out. It was certainly illiberal and some people might say racist. We attacked it for being both impractical and hugely expensive, all of which successfully took the shine off his speech. But it will still be working well for him on the doorsteps and our campaign has no big salient issue to match it. Our election broadcasts on TV have been lamentable, all statistics and no flair.

Thursday, 20 April 2000

This morning TB did a press conference with Frank, who was fairly impressive on the platform. He has a good, well-thought-out case now as to why he should be mayor, but it's clearly too late. He was less confident in private and must have felt a bit deflated when TB made the obvious point that they should go on and attack Ken first, then move on to Norris, so it wouldn't look as if the real battle was for second place. That, however, is the truth of it, although I still find it hard to believe that Frank won't come second. TB asked me how bad I thought it would be when Frank loses and I said it would be seen as a snub to his leadership but that most people by now expected a Ken victory. Ken has said he wants a deputy from the Green Party so if that means better cycle routes then maybe some good will come of it.

Glenys Kinnock [MEP] was in last night talking about

the importance of education in Africa. She's just been in Zambia where 40 per cent of kids are now AIDS orphans and more teachers are dying of AIDS than new ones entering the profession. It convinced me yet again that this is an area I'd like to work in. The Tories aren't making much mischief, except on asylum. And even on that Hague failed to raise it at PMQs but was duffed up by TB over the running costs of government instead. He never recovered once TB pointed out that the amount of public money going to the Tory Party in opposition had just been increased three-fold. AC deliberately started talking about a reshuffle story in the *Sun* at the lobby today just so that Cockerell could get some film of him attacking the media for inaccuracy and trivia.

Thursday, 27 April 2000

Reasonably quiet week with both TB and AC away. The only real excitement has been taking on Hague over Tony Martin [the Norfolk farmer jailed after shooting an unarmed intruder in the back] and the right to self-defence. TB very unsure how to respond. Torn between accusing him of opportunism and jumping on any media bandwagon, and acknowledging that there's a problem over self-defence. We need to appear more in touch with public opinion than Hague. Having the right to take on burglars is a good populist issue and is probably the kind of thing TB would have tapped into in opposition – as he did over Jamie Bulger [TB was Labour's home affairs spokesman at the time of the murder of two-year-old Jamie Bulger by two ten-year-old boys in 1993]. I said as much to TB but he said he would have had a much better-thought-through policy than Hague. Most legal and police opinion has come out against Hague, but the *Sun* and the *Mail* loved it, of course. It will play well for him in the locals.

Ken had a big boost in an *Evening Standard* poll today showing his ratings going up again: he now has a 34 per cent lead over Norris in second place, with Frank falling back to 12 per cent. So there's now every chance that Frank will come third, if not fourth.

As for our local election campaign in the rest of the country, it seems to be virtually non-existent. At Gordon's strategy meetings today and yesterday there seemed to be no good ideas at all for how to get up a real story and give people a reason to vote Labour. Gordon seemed to think the final weekend before the poll should be Alistair Darling repeating a pledge Gordon himself has already made on pensions, and Blunkett saying that the latest figures for the New Deal show that Labour's policies are working. And he's supposed to be our best strategic brain. We have never yet worked out how to fight campaigns while in government.

Poor Ann Keen [who helped run Frank's campaign] sounded pretty desperate on the phone today. Still looking for any little thing to help Frank. She has shown great stamina and grit and keeps on even though everybody but everybody knows the game is up.

Tuesday, 2 May 2000

Not too busy. Mainly rubbishing a number of contradictory stories about Frank that appeared in the Sunday papers – that he's going to quit as an MP, that he's going back into the cabinet, that he's going to write a book and blame Number Ten for it all. I still think he could come fourth on Thursday. TB now says Frank has been a disastrous candidate and we'd have done better with Nick Raynsford. But that's not how it looked last September. I went to Slough with TB this morning for a local election campaign visit and he was in pretty good form, considering that he's getting a bit of a pounding just now.

The *Sun* did a big 'Mayday, Mayday' attack on TB yesterday, talking up Hague. TB wrote a response to it at Chequers yesterday and AC sent the *Sun* part of his handwritten note, but today's *Sun* just had the headline 'Rattled' and poked fun at the '395 words Tony Blair has written in answer to the *Sun*'s criticisms'.

There were big anti-capitalism demos in London yesterday with, shock, horror, graffiti sprayed on the Cenotaph and Winston Churchill's statue, so that has kept the media busy today. TB went a bit over the top saying, 'This sort of thing must never be allowed to happen again,' and suggesting that such demonstrations should be kept out of London. I asked him what that would mean in practice and he talked about how the miners had been kept away from big demos during the miners' strike in 1984. But when you're dealing with demonstrators of whom most look like ordinary members of the public, it's quite hard to say how you would segregate them and keep them out.

Meanwhile, Longbridge is looking pretty grim and TB has been getting more of a pasting in the West Midlands media.

Friday, 5 May 2000

Local and London elections yesterday and we took a hit, though not as bad as it could have been. Ken failed to win on the first ballot [but was still overwhelmingly elected under the proportional representation system] and Frank at least managed not to come fourth. The turnout was so low that Ken can't claim to have a massive mandate. But we did much less well on the GLA [Greater London Assembly] than we'd hoped and were beaten by the Tories for constituency seats, only matching them nine–nine when the top-up seats were included. But the Tories didn't do as well as they needed to do in the locals and, thank God, the Lib

Dems took Romsey off them in the parliamentary by-election there. So TB, who's in Ireland, did a bit of humility, governing for the long term, stuff that he delivered very well. Frank looked pretty forlorn and nobody really knows what he will do. He won't be back in government but we'll find something for him, if he wants it. There's a question mark over whether our GLA members will take jobs if Ken offers them, which he will. They probably should. If we had got ourselves a candidate to take on Ken much sooner he could perhaps have been beaten, and my small claim to a bit of judgement is that I did raise London at various meetings in the middle of last year and was told that we didn't need to address it yet.

Thursday, 11 May 2000

There's a general sense that we need to sharpen up our act in the wake of the local elections. Fortunately TB hinted at PMQs that the general election wasn't far off so the speculation that it may be delayed [from the spring of 2001] seems unfounded.

There have been lots of meetings going on of the main players (TB, Jonathan Powell, AC, etc.) about internal structures and the rest of us have been trying to divine what's going on as best we can. It's all fairly familiar. AC doing fewer lobby meetings and more strategy, so Godric and I will do more. Charlie [Falconer] has been given a rather ill-defined new role in getting the grid in shape and making it more political.

Friday, 12 May 2000

AC announced the changes this afternoon and I'm perfectly happy with them. He said I was to become 'basically my deputy' on the strategic side, with Godric taking over as the main government spokesman in all but name. Godric will have a deputy of his own, probably Anne Shevas [currently with the Scottish Office]. It all makes good sense if it means we really do sharpen up our act as a result. Phil Murphy will go from the party job [director of communications]. He'll be found a job in government somewhere. Conor Ryan [David Blunkett's special adviser] may well get his job. AC says he will be writing a lot more notes and things that should be very useful and he wants me to be less involved in the day-to-day stuff. It looks like all systems go for the election, although we don't want to have any stories to that effect.

Margaret McDonagh did what I thought was a very useful interview for the *New Statesman*, basically saying that ministers should get up off their arses and go out campaigning on the government's record. She's right. They were, in the main, pretty hopeless during the local elections and seem to be far happier just getting on with being ministers. Straw and Blunkett were the main exceptions.

TB is now to tell the cabinet about upcoming business rather than Mo. AC prepared him a note yesterday but he only half delivered it, so it had to be sent round to them all afterwards. What made it worse is that I had squared it with Mo's office that TB would be doing this but he must not have read the note about it or something because he then said, 'Right, Mo.' She said, 'It was agreed yesterday that I wouldn't do this.' Given that we were trying not to let it look like she was being shafted again it had exactly the opposite effect.

The Tories have managed to get a bit of a bounce out of the local elections, but all the commentators still see them as being miles away from a serious challenge at the next election. But the press generally, and the Tory press in particular, are being extremely nice to them at the moment and giving them a very easy ride.

Otherwise the news is dominated by Ford ending car production at Dagenham, plus British troops going into Sierra Leone, ostensibly to secure the airport and help to evacuate British nationals, but in reality to do all they can to keep the rebels back from the capital. Clare Short was the strongest voice in favour of action at Cabinet, describing the rebel leader as a cocaine addict and a madman who must never be allowed to win over the UN.

Jonathan [Powell] is very aggrieved at being described as 'the Downing Street poisoner' by Julia Langdon in last Sunday's *Mail*. He was considering suing after the article suggested he had shafted Mo over Northern Ireland and forced Frank to run for mayor. It's very harsh. He and Sally [Morgan] swear blind, and there's no reason to disbelieve them, that Frank made up his own mind to run and we were never that keen, having already settled on Raynsford.

There's been much to-ing and fro-ing between Ken and the Labour Group, which has resulted in him agreeing to the idea of an independent panel to examine Tube financing (which was in Labour's manifesto) and in Nicky Gavron [Labour member of the GLA] becoming deputy mayor.

I went to the opening of the fantastic new Tate Modern last night with TB, mainly to prevent or handle any chance meeting with Ken, but their paths didn't cross. It was a great party and I stayed late with James Purnell [who covered the arts in the Policy Unit], being introduced to all sorts of presumably famous arty people that I'd never heard of. One of them (Stephen Daldry, I think his name was) was clearly gay and may well run the Royal Court Theatre. He kissed my cheek when he left, though there had been nothing at all gay about our conversation, and there was some half-serious suggestion that I should join the board of the Royal Court. The Tate is in a great building with fantastic art and great views out over London from the top.

Sunday, 14 May 2000

Splendid weekend, but as ever too short. Lots of discussions with James about buying a house in France, which we're both excited about. It suddenly dawned on me yesterday that maybe I should take over Phil Murphy's job at Millbank [as director of communications for the Labour Party]. I didn't want it before because it was too far away from the centre of the action, but the dynamics have changed now the election is getting closer. I'd be nearer to the top table, involved in Gordon's morning meetings, and would probably have as much serious engagement with TB as I do at Downing Street, if not more. It would be harder work, but I'd have a proper job with real responsibilities and be more of a player than I am now.

So, after taking ages to get to sleep last night thinking about it and then mulling it over a bit more today, I mentioned it to AC. He was surprised, but seemed to think it was a good idea. He said he'd think about it and see how far Margaret [McDonagh] has got in talking to Conor Ryan. That was probably no more than a perfectly reasonable stalling tactic while he talks to TB. They may feel that I haven't shown much flair or contributed much so far, although I would argue that that has been more to do with being in AC's shadow the whole time. It would be good to get some management experience and to have people working to me. And I would be able to stay pretty well plugged into Number Ten and everybody. So, on balance, I hope the idea gets the thumbs-up.

The big news of the weekend is that Robin Oakley has been made to retire early [as BBC political editor], to be replaced by Andrew Marr, who was variously described in the Sundays as 'Blairite' and 'New Labour'. So it has to be good news for us, although I know what it's like being a Labour-supporting BBC journalist – you tend to be even harder on the party you support just to make sure you can't be accused of bias.

TB's political note to everybody today was quite funny. They never seem to produce any real action because of our ludicrous lack of an effective command structure and absence of discipline. He has obviously spotted this and says, 'I don't write them for fun!'

Friday, 19 May 2000

An expectant nation awaits news from an expectant Cherie, who is now at the hospital about to give birth. It looks like we may have a development later today. Our policy is to be as unhelpful to everybody in the media as possible so we can't be accused of spinning the birth. In fact down-spin all round remains the order of the day on every kind of story, and I've been telling the departmental special advisers to play everything very straight.

Things are actually sharpening up significantly already, now that AC is looking closely at the grid and forthcoming stories. Byers, Milburn and Straw all gave good cross-government message interviews after AC spoke to them. Mo, on the other hand, was dreadful on the media on Tuesday, telling people she might like to be party chairman and failing to get any real message across at all other than thanking 'everybody who supported me' in an opinion poll that said she was the most popular member of the cabinet! But overall AC is able to get things reordered and get ministers to put over a decent message in a way that I was never able to do. TB has said again that he wants a twenty-four-hour press office at Number Ten, but that's really a battle for Godric to fight.

No word from AC about whether I should go to Mill-bank, beyond him saying that he thought it was probably a good idea but he hadn't had a chance to talk to TB about it yet. There are advantages to me either way, so I'm not losing sleep over it. If I went to the Labour Party job I'd miss out on attending Cabinet, but that would be OK now that I've seen it operate for some time.

I had my health screening today, which concluded I was extremely fit and healthy. Low cholesterol, low blood pressure, no liver problems. The computer seemed to think I should drink a bit less but the nurse, who looked as if she probably enjoyed a drink or two, seemed to think I was all right.

In news terms it's been a mixed bag. TB's big speech to the CBI on Tuesday was knocked off the front pages by Peter making a speech to the GMB in Belfast. 'As a well-known boilermaker,' said AC [the GMB was formerly known as the General Municipal and Boilermakers Union]. Peter extolled the virtues of the euro for providing exchange-rate stability. Gordon was livid and Ian Austin has been out briefing that Gordon makes economic policy while Peter was 'a very good Northern Ireland secretary'. The fact is that Peter didn't tell anybody he was doing it, so far as I am aware, and that became part of the story.

Meanwhile Trimble has been slow to capitalise on the IRA's offer to decommission some arms and has put off a meeting of the UUC [Ulster Unionist Council] until next weekend, meaning that devolution can't be restored on 22 May as we had hoped. Peter says it looks pretty bad with Trimble having a less than 50 per cent chance of getting his party to back it.

Jack Straw has ignited a devolution row by agreeing to let Mike Tyson [the US boxing champion who had been accused of rape] fight in Glasgow. Some members of the Scottish Executive expressed their 'private' view that he shouldn't be allowed in and it became a Scotland v. England row.

The papers have been going a bit potty about some GM seed that got mixed up with some ordinary rape seed by mistake and was planted all over the place. The fault lay with the seed company and no harm was done to anybody or anything, but there was a bit of a flurry.

Sunday, 21 May 2000

Baby Leo was born at twelve thirty-five on Saturday morning and the nation rejoiced. It really was like a royal birth – seven pages in the *Mail on Sunday* this morning. TB came out looking very casual and hunky-dad-like on Saturday and was so Tonyish that it was funny. It could have been Rory Bremner. No one's allowed to ask the question, of course, but you can't help wondering what the effect on the polls will be. It certainly puts us back as a family-friendly government. The media has been going nuts because we wouldn't tell them anything, but they seem to have got over it now. The press office was overwhelmed with calls.

Tuesday, 23 May 2000

TB called me up to the flat at three this afternoon. Stepping over the presents (*Pretenders' Greatest Hits* from Geoff Hoon – why? Kid?), and with little Leo crying upstairs, I went into TB's study. I assumed he wanted to ask me to go to Millbank and he did. Fortunately I could say I'd suggested it in the first place. He said I should continue to attend meetings with him at Number Ten and that it was essential that Millbank was properly locked in. He wants me to work with the papers, thinks the *Sun* will come round and that even the *Mail* can be persuaded to be fair. Doesn't think we should continue to be at war with the media – says he's said to AC that you either do it all out, and now is not the time, or you pull back. He thinks we need to have Hague positioned by conference time as somebody who may have jumped on a few bandwagons but hasn't got a coherent programme. Someone who tried a softer brand of Conservatism but the right-wing wouldn't have it. Then he had tried a return to Thatcherism at his conference last year but that didn't work with the public. So now he's gone for total opportunism, which can be exposed easily. So I'm very pleased as the new job gives me a seat at the top table. I can also produce notes, write papers and contribute ideas in a way that I haven't really been able to until now. The other good news is that Pat [McFadden] is coming down to Millbank with me as a policy supremo of some sort.

Friday, 2 June 2000

Had a very successful weekend off in France. Loads of driving but we got a good sense of the kinds of properties available and have both fallen in love with one – La Micoc-oule in the Cèze Valley [we eventually bought it]. I've got a very good feeling about it.

While I was away Gordon launched what's become known as our 'class war' by attacking Oxford University for failing to give a place to a Newcastle girl from a state school who wants to be a medical student, Laura Spence. She ended up going to Harvard. It's been highly contro-versial and is still running, with Oxbridge accusing us of setting back rather than helping their efforts to get in more state pupils. Prescott, Margaret Jay and others have weighed in to support Gordon. TB, of course, is still off looking after Leo, and I don't know what he makes of it all. But so far we haven't backed off in the way we did over the 'forces of conservatism'. Anji is very against it all, saying we seem to be against excellence and success and that 'It's not Tony.'

Blunkett is pissed off because Gordon strayed into his territory as education secretary without even warning him. Poor old Godric only found out about it from George Pascoe-Watson [of the *Sun*] on his way to do the four o'clock lobby last Thursday. If he hadn't been tipped off it would have looked as though he, and therefore Number Ten, knew nothing about Gordon's speech. Which, it seems, we didn't. Even so, AC has been right behind Gordon keeping up the pressure on the grounds that it gives us good definition and puts us on the side of the many not the few, opportunity for all, etc. So we've split our liberal supporters, half of whom are still pining for their Oxbridge days. I'm all for it as long as the wording is right, but I've always been instinctively a class warrior on education. Certainly a lot of people have been saying that it feels good to be working for a Labour government again.

One small personal irony. While I was working on a weekend briefing paper on it all, I got a call from some woman who said I'd been at Hertford [College, Oxford] with her and would I give some money for a new graduate centre? I said there were many good causes in the world, some of which I give to, but Oxford colleges were not among them.

More generally, there has been a lot of discussion, mainly in the form of political notes, about how we should position ourselves for the election and the second term. I've been supporting a radical programme that builds on the 'reassurance' we've achieved so far. There are real divisions opening up between the radicals and the big-tenters [people who wanted the Labour Party to be a 'big tent' so anybody, even former Tories, would be welcome to join], which can only be healthy . . . so long as the radicals win!

In Northern Ireland the Ulster unionists have voted to go back into government with Sinn Féin, so Stormont [the devolved Assembly] is back in business this week, despite all Peter's pessimism – which, as I told him, was partly downplaying expectations. He clearly wants to take as much credit for it all as he can, and the polls suggest he's getting it. Northern Ireland certainly has that effect on ministers.

No mention of when I might move to Millbank. I was going to go and see Margaret [McDonagh] about it this week but she's been in Spain. I'm keen to get on with it now.

Tuesday, 6 June 2000

Office in turmoil in a way I've never seen before. TB is due to make a very important speech to the Women's Institute tomorrow and everybody is in a panic over it. TB wrote it himself while tending Leo at Chequers and everybody agrees it's total drivel. It's an apparent effort at some repositioning – blending the new with the old – but it's a total mish-mash of New Labour jargon mixed up with John Major-style pleas for old-fashioned values. If he makes it as it is now, he'll be laughed out of court and everybody but him can see it. AC says he's been trying to tell him this for days. [David] Bradshaw [former *Mirror* journalist working in the Strategic Communications Unit] says he's never seen such a bad speech. Hyman is trying to rebuild it with scraps of paper containing stuff TB has agreed to add. Anji is going round saying, 'Why is a speech to be delivered to ten thousand women being written by all these men?' They won't have a clue what it's all about.

At the four o'clock lobby the journos were almost laughing as AC briefed it. 'An orgy of abstractions,' Donald

Macintyre called it. Many of them will write it up as a retreat from both the 'forces of conservatism' and Gordon's speech about Laura Spence ten days ago. TB seems to be suffering something of a mid-life crisis.

Hague has been making the headlines with some success on education and sin bins in schools today. And we look like falling flat on our faces tomorrow. The General Election Planning Group met yesterday, although Peter couldn't be there to chair it. Margaret [McDonagh] ran through the election structure, but I wasn't on it. I spoke to her afterwards and she said AC hadn't spoken to Phil Murphy yet to tell him. She agreed with me that it was fairly typical of a reluctance at Number Ten to take the difficult decisions quickly enough.

Friday, 9 June 2000

The speech turned out to be a total disaster and was all blamed on the spin doctors. 'PR disaster', 'WI savages Blair', etc. There was slow handclapping, a small walkout and lots of complaints about him making an inappropriately political speech. All a bit ironic as AC was in the forefront of those telling him the speech was crap. In fact, the advance headlines were a lot better than we'd feared, but maybe that just pissed the women off because they thought they were being used. I'm sure he should have done a Q&A session and a much shorter speech, but that's easy to say with hindsight. There has been a lot of argument, too, about whether he was invited to go and make the speech or whether he invited himself. In fact, it seems he was invited to go to the same event two years ago but couldn't go then, so decided to do it this year instead. Anji has been in the firing line a bit, although not very fairly, and there has been lots of running around trying to find the original letters of invitation. TB was very funny when he went to Millbank yesterday to speak to Labour Party organisers. They gave him a standing ovation before he even started, presumably out of sympathy, and he said, 'Come on, it wasn't that bad,' and then promised not to make another political speech.

News of a government Bill on fox-hunting slipped out overnight, prompting the obvious allegation that we'd done it to move the news agenda on and put the WI behind us. But the papers have all been saying that the WI will be remembered as one of those disasters that politicians are for ever associated with. It has certainly woken our people out of any complacency. But it makes it trickier to announce changes, like Godric taking over the lobby briefings, although a story to that effect appeared in the *Times* Diary today.

Wednesday, 14 June 2000

Huge fuss over AC pulling back from doing so many lobby briefings. Big stories on all the TV and radio bulletins and in the papers, and there will be loads more tomorrow. It became obvious, or at least more obvious, because AC decided not to do the Monday-morning lobby this week, which is the biggest and most important of the week. The fact that it was the first Monday after the WI speech, and after the leak of a very embarrassing Philip Gould memo in the *Sunday Times* [copies of several of Philip's memos to the prime minister had fallen into the hands of News International, apparently having been stolen from his dust-bins at home] made it far worse. The latest spin is that there is no more spin, is how the *Guardian* put it. It's being seen as short-term panic after the WI or evidence that we're gearing up for the election, or sometimes both at once.

Poor old Godric, who did the lobby, was described as very good but 'boring' by Peter Oborne on Sky. At the post-PMQs lobby this afternoon, which AC did do, they were all at him, complaining that however good Godric was he couldn't have the same closeness to TB, that we had given up on the media, and that we were blaming the messengers for our own problems, etc. And in the middle of all this I'm trying to negotiate my exit to Millbank. I met the key guy down there, Jonathan Upton, who's being very hard-line about not matching the government's redundancy package and only meeting what I am being paid now – so less than Phil Murphy who I'm replacing. And on top of all that I put the house in Brighton on the market today and made an offer on the one in France.

Politically we're still a bit in the doldrums after the WI but AC and Charlie [Falconer] are taking a keen interest in the grid that Paul Brown [SCU] and I put so much effort into and are trying to get departments to raise their game.

TB seems strangely off form at internal meetings although he still looks strong in public. We had a very private meeting on fox-hunting yesterday at which he said he didn't think banning it was the right thing to do and he wanted to retain the option of shifting his position to some sort of partial ban. Sally [Morgan] and I both said we didn't think that was credible and that the PLP would vote for a total ban whatever. TB says he expected the Burns Inquiry [into the impact of a ban on the rural economy] to make life easier for him, and still thought he might be able to bring enough MPs round to avoid a total ban.

He still seems to be under the illusion that he can move political mountains, despite all the evidence from London, etc. I don't know just how good his political antennae are at the moment. He certainly seems to be misjudging the party badly. The papers are running stories about a cabinet split on the euro because Byers, Peter and Robin seem to be more vocal in its support, and allegedly with TB's backing. I don't know if that's true, but it may well be.

Certainly TB's confidence with me a year or so ago that he could win a referendum campaign in a relatively short period strikes me as highly questionable now, not that I really believed it at the time. So it's politically the most fascinating time, even if you don't believe the *Mail on Sunday* poll that put us only 3 per cent ahead of the Tories.

Thursday, 15 June 2000

Amazing news – our offer on the place in France has been accepted. So, things are moving ahead on that front terrifyingly fast. I'm now travelling down to Brighton to get the house ready for viewing and do some hasty decorating.

Meanwhile negotiations are still going on for my change of job to Millbank. It hasn't leaked out yet but I'm sure it will soon as so many people now know. Alistair Darling said to me on the way to Cabinet that he had heard I was moving. It will obviously be a bit of a story as the papers are still full of AC and Godric, although not quite on the scale that we had feared.

We are getting into more euro problems. Gordon will restate the current position very firmly in his Mansion House speech this evening. We made Robin take some of the warm words about the euro out of a speech he was about to deliver in the Commons, but the Foreign Office had already handed out copies of the original, marked 'Check Against Delivery'. So we faced all the predictable questions. Who told him to tone it down? Was he muzzled? Who is in charge of the policy? The media are determined that we should have the same divisions as the Tories over Europe, when the truth is that the disagreements on our side are far less profound.

Monday, 19 June 2000

Great weekend in Yorkshire after Jonathan [James's brother] and Cathy's wedding. A few relatives found out about James and me for the first time, as ever at weddings, but there were no adverse reactions.

Today was more or less my first day in the new job, and already Margaret has been winding me up. First she all but accused me of briefing the changes so it looked as if Pat [McFadden] and I were having to fly in to boost a sagging Millbank, whereas I didn't speak to a single journalist and just got the Number Ten press office to announce it straight. In fact the coverage could have been a great deal worse. There was no real 'Labour Gears Up For Election' and very little suggestion, which we'd feared, that AC should be paid by the party too. It was pretty low key. Then when I had further discussions with Jonathan Upton it seemed Margaret was still trying to revisit our wage negotiations. I'm going to stand my ground but not make a huge issue of it. I need to help improve relations down there not add to the problems. She and I then went up to the BBC to meet Tony Hall [chief executive, BBC News], Mark Damazer [head of political programmes] and Anne Sloman [chief political adviser] and have a go at them about bias on *Panorama*, party political broadcasts, etc. Always slightly strange for me, but I have to stick to the party line. I reserved my comments to the growth of journalism on the BBC with an agenda attached, sloppy pieces that reinforce political clichés, and the fact that some producers feel that because the Tories are so crap they have to provide the opposition.

Wednesday, 21 June 2000

Spent the day recruiting assistant press officers to work both at Millbank and in the regional offices. Great fun and it feels good to have a clear managerial role for the first time in my life. My secretary, Rebecca [Goff], is brilliant and has been helping me enormously in getting settled in. I think she'll be a huge asset, given my total lack of management experience so far and the fact that I've never had to look after a large budget before. *PR Week* want to do a big profile on me because they say I've just taken over the most important political PR job in the country.

I missed PMQs for the first time in ages today because I was doing the interviews. I'm feeling slightly cut off from Number Ten and have to make sure I remain 100 per cent plugged in, otherwise the same old problems in the Millbank–government relationship will only creep back in. But TB and AC have been in Portugal for an EU summit anyway.

Thursday, 22 June 2000

I feel like I'm really doing the job now. Planning a major assault on the Tories over health policy, starting tomorrow and ploughing through next week when we expect them to launch their own health initiative. Had a meeting with Peter, who asked why I wasn't at his meeting with TB this morning, which is a good sign, Philip Gould and TBWA [the party's advertising agency]. I'm also trying to get a handle on this summer's campaign, which will now be signed off next Thursday. I'll be away then, which seems a shame, but I really need a holiday right now.

I'm getting the hang of the Millbank dynamics a bit better. I've been advised to get Margaret on side as general secretary in case she sees the arrival of Pat and me as weakening her position rather than strengthening it, and that she'll use some of the existing staff to do that. It won't work because the combined strength of me, Pat, Douglas [Alexander], Philip Gould and Spencer [Livermore, head of the Attack Unit] will make it impossible. Spencer is clearly excellent and I'm really looking forward to working with him. So, too, as far as I can tell, are the TBWA team.

I was interviewed by *PR Week* today. At first I thought it might be a bit self-indulgent but then I decided it could be an opportunity to say something about media cynicism, etc., which is what I tried to do. We'll just have to see how it comes out.

Thursday, 29 June 2000

On a ferry between Hvar and Split, almost half-way through an idyllic holiday in Croatia. We're on our way to Graz to see Helmut and Sandra [Austrian friends] before coming back to Hvar for another few days of sunshine. I haven't picked up a paper and we don't have a radio with us. The feeling of being cut off from the daily cut-and-thrust is fantastic. The truth is that I can happily get engaged in it all when I'm there, and I genuinely want the good guys to stay on top, but in the great scheme of things it's not that important at all. My mind is full of France and the only people who know how to contact us out here are the estate agents in Brighton.

Sunday, 9 July 2000

On the plane heading back to London. I managed not to think much about work at all, apart from a few musings about how to staff the press office and some vague thoughts about the election. The thought of getting to Gatwick and buying all the Sunday papers is pretty depressing. But it's only for another few months. Neal Dalgleish [friend and BBC producer] rang yesterday to say that Euan Blair was arrested on Wednesday night drunk and incapable in Leicester Square, taken off to a police station where he gave a false name and address until they emptied his pockets, found out who he really was and called Special Branch. Poor kid. I've accepted a very good offer on the house. A hell of a lot to do in the coming weeks.

Tuesday, 11 July 2000

I've only been back two days and I'm knackered already. Mainly through lack of sleep and too much on my mind. I am currently on call every evening and was rung very late last night about the Tories shifting their ground on their 'tax guarantee' [at the Tory Party Conference in 1999, the then shadow chancellor, Francis Maude, had announced the 'tax guarantee' saying 'at the end of the next Conservative Government the state will take a smaller share of the nation's income in taxes than at the beginning.' The new shadow chancellor, Michael Portillo, wanted to drop the guarantee to give him more room for manoeuvre in opposing the government] and just couldn't get back to sleep again.

As usual when I got back from holiday on Sunday I read that the government had just had its worst week ever, and for once it seems it may have been true. Philip says that on all the key questions our ratings are massively down, by up to 35 per cent and well into negatives for the first time. TB is clearly very tired and the baby is both wearing him out and distracting him. Although, to be fair, he was more alert at the Monday meeting than I had expected. We are in pre-CSR [Comprehensive Spending Review] mode, which is why our main aim today was to insist that the Tory tax guarantee was still in place and, if anything, more specific and more extreme. It would have been easier to say that abandoning the guarantee had been a humiliation for Hague, leaving Portillo running the show, but that would have been to concede that they had shifted policy.

There's a lot of work to be done getting Millbank in shape and the right people in place, not helped by Margaret constantly saying that we don't have any money. It's not hard to see why morale is so low. But I've made a start.

Friday, 14 July 2000

I'm hoping to start today on a detailed report on how I want to reorganise things at Millbank. I hope Jim Godfrey will be joining us from the IPPR [Institute of Public Policy Research, a New Labour think tank] and he's excellent. I spoke to him today and I think he'll come. I feel very good about the new job and I'm sure I'm doing the right thing.

Peter is being very supportive, but telling me that while he was director of communications he started at seven a.m. and worked all evening.

It's been a mixed week. TB was very good on Wednesday, with a news conference at Number Ten and then PMQs in which he knocked Hague all over the place. He was far less good in the House yesterday, launching the government's Annual Report, which had some serious inaccuracies in it. The whole thing has been an embarrassment every single year.

Peter Hain [Foreign Office minister] managed to make things worse with an article in the *Independent* in which he called some ministers 'automatons'. He had sent it to me saying it was for *Progress* [New Labour magazine], which doesn't come out for a week or two. I passed it on to Matthew Doyle to read. I should have read it myself straight away, but I didn't think it was an immediate priority.

He then had the cheek to use the fact that he'd sent it to me to help claim he had got authorisation for it. Sally [Morgan] had seen it a while ago and TB had seen it and demanded some changes. I don't know whether the offending bits, and there were several, were from the original or the amended versions. In fact his argument was right that ministers should be more political and get out in the country making our case, it just shouldn't have been made so publicly or with such injudicious language.

We saw, as did the media, an advance screening of Michael Cockerell's documentary on the Number Ten press office yesterday and it wasn't half as bad as I had feared. I still think it was a mistake to do it because we don't want all this focus on spin again, but AC gets his case across against the media. I'd say 8–2 to him over the journalists. The biggest problem was the scenes with AC and TB in which they look, at best, to be equals. AC allows himself some little asides that play straight into the Rory Bremner image of the pair of them, and while AC is very articulate throughout, TB is rather hesitant and unfocused. Not really his fault: AC had plenty of time to think about what he was going to say whereas TB was effectively ambushed when he simply walked into AC's office while they were filming. I feel a bit sorry for Godric who is portrayed as the civil-service deputy whom everybody likes and respects but whom the hacks don't think is any substitute for AC. I managed to keep my own appearances down to a couple of cut-aways, thank God.

Friday, 21 July 2000

Another good week, making some real progress. I have secured the money for an editorial assistant and have all but agreed Jim Godfrey's move to the party – subject to one more call with Peter, who is keen to use Matthew

Doyle more because he's so good. My paper on restructuring the office seems to have gone down well. No substantive responses but I shall take the absence of any objections as approval.

The CSR [Comprehensive Spending Review] went down well but was badly sidelined by yet another leaked memo from Philip [Gould] about how the New Labour brand has been contaminated and how TB appears out of touch, etc. We have had to respond by saying that Philip is there to write challenging memos, and while the media may get terribly excited about them, the government knows what the real priorities are and we are getting on with them. The CSR is proof of that.

Meanwhile the Tories acknowledge that the spending gap (i.e., their cuts) amounts to £16 billion and the dividing lines are drawn [Labour and the Conservatives argued right up to and throughout the 2001 election campaign about how big the difference in their projected spending plans was and what the consequences would be for cuts in the public services].

TBWA have been coming up with some good creative ideas for the summer and Conference, along the lines of 'Done that; doing this'. So we go all out on Tory cuts.

Peter had to be reined in from rocking the boat on the euro last night. His original speech would have provided plenty of ammunition for those who wanted a Labour-split story, and a combined operation involving me, AC, Jonathan Powell and Gordon made him change it. I told him very directly what I thought in front of Jonathan, including reminding him that he didn't always know best, especially when it came to his own speeches and his own career. Peter Hyman, who watched it all, congratulated me warmly afterwards. Eventually during a meeting with TBWA at Millbank Peter said archly, 'I've made your silly changes.' This was after I had given him a handwritten note on what he needed to change during an earlier meeting, ending with the words, 'You know all this. Up to you whether you take any notice.'

We seem to be having problems with the guy who made an offer on the house in Brighton. It may have to go back on the market.

Sunday, 23 July 2000

Weekend papers not too bad for once. The *Mail on Sunday* ran a long profile on Reinaldo, which was very intrusive but not unflattering. Peter told me he was surprised to learn that Reinaldo had come from a slum as he'd been there and the house was good enough for him.

The *Mail* also led on a guy who sells stuff he collects from dustbins, implying that he had got hold of Philip's leaked memos that way. It didn't have a lot of substance to it but Peter says we should quietly encourage the idea as it counters all the talk of a traitor in our midst who's been leaking. I got Denis MacShane to write to the News International editors to ask what links if any they have had with the guy.

Peter still won't give a firm yes to taking on Jim Godfrey, which is a bit hard on Jim because it keeps him holding on. Post-CSR the worst anybody can throw at this government is that it's too obsessed with spin and hasn't delivered as much as it could. Set against the achievements, that isn't a lot to worry about. I actually think we should be downplaying expectations of any major breakthroughs in delivery this side of the election. We can say we had two tough years sorting out the public finances and the debt and that we were then able to invest, but that nobody sensibly expects that investment to produce immediate effects. But TB will still cry out for things we can point to as real change.

Tuesday, 25 July 2000

Fun and games continue. I had dinner last night with Ivan Massow [a wealthy young gay businessman] who appears ready to leave the Tories and join us. It would be a major embarrassment for Hague as he's about the only face left of social liberalism in the Tory Party. According to Ivan, Hague asked him to stand as their London mayoral candidate and often calls him for advice. Ivan says they had lunch after the New Year and Hague was on the point of resignation. Shaun Woodward, who knows him well, is very keen for it to happen and when I told TB and Sally they were both quite excited at the prospect. Peter sounded horrified at the mention of his name, saying he didn't trust him, but also that it's a free country and he can join us if he wants to. Peter also wants me to write a no-holds-barred assessment of Millbank for him, which is really for TB who is very worried about the situation. I said things weren't as black as he might have heard.

TB did a public Q&A session in Hammersmith last night where he got a pretty rough ride but performed well.

Thursday, 27 July 2000

The Massow defection is limping along to what we hope will be a fairly low-key conclusion next week. AC, Anji and Peter are very nervous, to say the least. AC doesn't want another gay story and is uneasy about Ivan's motives. Ivan himself is very nervous too, but for different reasons. And Shaun is totally obsessed with it. He spent four hours helping prepare Ivan on Tuesday night and has produced an article that's 100 per cent Shaun, reads like his own defection statement and is all about tolerance, diversity and non-discrimination. I will have to turn it into something about health cuts and economic competence with a bit of tolerance thrown in. I told Ivan tonight when he came in to Number Ten that it would greatly improve his chances of political advancement within Labour if he broadened his attack on the Tories. He was hoping to meet TB but Sally thought it would be unwise, given AC's reservations, so it was almost a French farce as I steered Ivan towards the front door when I heard TB's voice approaching and saw Sally shaking her head at me. Ivan clearly thinks it's going to be a huge story, but I think it will be a bit middling. Pat, Margaret and Sally all think AC is being too cautious and that it will be good for us.

I wrote Peter a very hard-hitting note about Millbank yesterday, especially relations between Douglas and Margaret. He'd asked for it to be no-holds-barred and it is. He said he would show it straight to TB. I just hope it never comes out.

We had another leak, a TB memo this time partly on the euro, that appeared in the *Sun* and *The Times* this morning. All designed to take the gloss off the launch of the NHS plan that came out today and otherwise went very well.

It's been a very busy day all round with a General Election Planning Group, an agency meeting with TBWA about the summer and Conference, a separate meeting with TB on the same issues, the early Gordon meeting and a meeting with TB about Millbank. Sir Richard Wilson has objected to me attending Cabinet now as I'm not on the Downing Street staff any more, but I could barely have fitted it in anyway.

I had less sleep than I would have liked, thanks to the leak and some pretty unsuccessful efforts to influence the *Today* programme against going overboard on it.

Barbecue at Number Ten tonight, which was quite enjoyable, although I cried off going boozing with Anji, etc., to celebrate her birthday. Just too tired.

Thursday, 3 August 2000

I'm sitting in a grotty pub in Wiltshire with Ivan Massow and Jonathan Freedland, who's interviewing him for the *Guardian*. The defection went just about as well as could have been hoped. It was the splash in the *Independent* yesterday after they agreed to go big with it in return for an exclusive. So the story took everyone by surprise. Stupidly Ivan had let Channel 4 know and we had to get very heavy with *Channel 4 News* not to break the story on Tuesday night. In the end Ivan rang Michael Jackson, the controller, and told him his staff were breaking their promise to keep it confidential. Eventually Jim Gray [editor of *Channel 4 News*] agreed and backed off. Andy Grice [political editor, *Independent*] was paranoid about losing his scoop but we managed to preserve it. Great to see all the other papers running around trying to catch up. Alan Milburn who had come down to London earlier in the day to launch our summer campaign agreed to put out a few words about Ivan but flatly refused to do any interviews. It's amazing how unpopular ex-Tories can be. But John Reid, as ever the hero, agreed on the spot to do a round of interviews welcoming him. And I'm pleased to say that AC, who was initially so cautious, was suddenly well up for it. He was nervous about Mo doing a photocall with Ivan yesterday but in the end she was fine.

Ivan and I had a very odd meeting in her office before doing the pictures. She was typically playing up her 'I'm the most popular politician in the Labour Party because I dare to be different' act and suggesting to Ivan that he shouldn't let AC and me push him around too much. But fortunately Ivan has been very sensible about it all. He even agreed to do the interview in this pub rather than in his rather nice house down the road. I didn't want lots of millionaire-lifestyle stuff or references to all the fox-hunting pictures on his walls.

I've been doing my best to de-gay the story, partly at AC's insistence. I banned Stephen Twigg, Ben Bradshaw and Chris Smith [all gay ministers] from doing any reaction interviews and I've been trying to keep Shaun out of the way too. The *Telegraph* have managed to piece together most of the story today, naming both Shaun and me, but they haven't really done it as a gay Mafia thing. I had a bizarre phone call from Shaun, who's in Mustique following it all on the Internet. The Tories have tried to dismiss Ivan as a nobody whose defection will be forgotten in twenty-four hours, so I'm now in the business of keeping it going as best I can.

In a quiet period politically we've been doing pretty well. A surprise story has broken overnight to derail us a bit. Gordon announced at eight thirty last night that he's marrying Sarah Macaulay today. The first I heard about it was when the *Sun* rang me for a comment. I flannelled just in case it was a hoax, but I didn't want to appear as if I hadn't been told even though I hadn't. In fact it seems TB was only told a few days ago.

Friday, 4 August 2000

It turns out TB heard about Gordon's wedding only the day before. They had a long discussion about some policy or another and then at the end of the conversation Gordon said, 'Oh, and I'm getting married tomorrow.' Anji told me this and she thinks the whole thing is hysterical. She's now helping me turn another defector, Bernie Jordan, the former leader of Hove Council. TB has just rung me to congratulate me on the Massow stuff. So he's going off on his holidays relatively happy and it was nice of him to call.

Thursday, 10 August 2000

It's been a bitty and rather busy week. Trying to keep in touch with more potential defectors from the Tory Party, including a woman Cherie rang to tell me about from Tuscany. She is talking about a group of pro-European Tories, including some MPs, perhaps coming across, but it all sounds very vague to me. I've seen Ivan a couple of times by chance. He continues to crave the limelight as interest in him fades.

Yesterday the estate agents rang to say Julian Clary was looking for a house in Brighton and wanted to view mine. I made a point of being in Brighton today so I could meet him. His main worry seemed to be whether his cat might turn on the halogen hob by mistake if it walked on it.

Prescott has been on the road this week pushing cheap transport for pensioners. It went pretty well, although *The Times* did an interview with him and tried to turn it into 'Prescott says the spin must stop'. It pissed me off a lot because even the reporter who wrote it acknowledged that he hadn't said that. He blamed the sub-editors, as they always do.

Hague made a total prick of himself by telling *GQ* magazine that he used to drink fourteen pints a day as a teenager, which absolutely nobody believed. But on our side we have avoided any cock-ups so far and have won the first two weeks of the summer hands down. But there's not much news about at the moment, apart from an on–off campaign by the *News of the World* about paedophiles, so it's a dangerous atmosphere. Anything could come out of a clear blue sky.

John Bercow [Tory MP] got himself some coverage, but also a bit of a hammering, because he likened Cherie to Lady Macbeth after she wrote an article about the ECHR [European Court of Human Rights]. Even so there were doubts about the place as to whether she had been wise to do it and we didn't even know about it until it appeared.

Wednesday, 16 August 2000

This week has been a continuation of the John Prescott Show, with a big speech yesterday, most of which I wrote. It was very well received by the *Guardian* and quite well by *The Times*, but Nigel Morris on the *Mirror* took the piss mercilessly about Prescott's grammar when he delivered it. The same theme was picked up in the later editions of the *Sun* and the *Independent*. Really shoddy reporting.

I had a bit of a horror on Tuesday morning while briefing Prescott before the speech – he was in his boxer shorts and I inadvertently caught him naked while he was changing. He's been in a pretty good mood since getting back from his holiday. He takes the bad press well, although he does insist on ringing journalists personally, as he did with Nigel today.

I had a call from Charlie Falconer's office to say that Geoffrey Robinson had been in touch to ask the date that Charlie and I had been to see him prior to Peter and his resignation in December 1998. Clearly he is now writing his book. I must ring Anji and tell her.

There was a very funny moment on Sunday when the likely defector from the Tory Party in Hove, Bernie Jordan, rang the London flat looking for me and spoke to James. James thought he was a plumber and said, 'Are you going to help us with our watery problem?' Bernie said it would take a while to dry out the Labour Party and the phone call ended without either of them having a clue what the other was talking about. Had to ring Bernie back to apologise.

We are still winning hands down in the summer battle

with the Tories. An ICM poll in today's *Guardian* shows us widening our lead to ten points again. Written up by everybody as the Tories' populist gestures failing to dent our lead. Another poll yesterday showed that only 8 per cent of voters thought the Tories had the best policies for the family. I keep expecting the Tories to come out fighting but they haven't.

Friday, 25 August 2000

Brief holiday in St Petersburg. Fabulous city with wide open streets and canals and dramatic architecture. But it's still Russia, so there's the noise of trucks and ancient cars, and the smell of diesel and leaded fuel in the air everywhere. The Hermitage was excellent and much less stuffy than I'd expected.

The day we arrived, Wednesday, was a day of mourning for the crew of the *Kursk*, the Russian submarine that British divers were belatedly allowed in to try to save. It was the big story at home when we left. I was, as ever, a bit nervous about leaving work, but the Tories seem to be nowhere at the moment and there's no sense of trouble.

Tuesday, 29 August 2000

My first day back after what felt like a lot more than a week off, but wasn't. Not at all nice to be back, although all the returnees acknowledge that we've had a very good summer. Prescott had his final meeting at Number Ten this morning and was very pleased with himself and, I think, impressed by the effort everybody had put in to help him. The truth is that it was made a lot easier because the Tories were nowhere to be seen. We expect that to change with the launch of their pre-election policy document next week and we're starting to gear ourselves up for it. Peter

Hain wanted to do another dig at ministers 'lacking passion' in a piece for the *Observer* last week but it was vetoed.

Friday, 1 September 2000

Very funny day. Last night the Tories got hold of our party political broadcast that was due to be shown in Scotland next Monday. They passed it on to the *Daily Mail* as another 'leak'. My initial reaction was to say, quite truthfully, that I had never seen a video that fitted the description I was given: I don't routinely check Scottish broadcasts. But then I realised we could use it to our advantage and accuse the Tories of a massive own goal, thanking them for getting much more publicity for our party political than we could ever have dreamed of. So we did that today to huge effect. The Tories ended up cancelling their planned news conference when they had been going to show it. They had egg all over their faces. Some people even thought we had leaked the broadcast ourselves! We had a press conference of our own organised by ten thirty, before theirs was due to start. We had VHS copies of the broadcast to hand out to the journalists, along with a statement from Prescott about 'the real Tory manifesto'. I said at the press conference that it was a very serious matter that a broadcast which we wanted as many people as possible to see had been leaked in this way and that if I ever found out who had done it I would give them a pay rise. I didn't expect half as much coverage as we got. Parts of the broadcast were shown on the *Six o'Clock News* on the BBC, on ITN and on Sky. Some of the papers will probably try to do it as a 'Labour mole embarrassment' but most won't. In fact, of course, it is a worry as to how it got out, but I hope we've minimised the damage.

Monday, 4 September 2000

Great weekend, including a nice birthday yesterday. Very busy today, though. I heard on Friday that there were rumours in Redcar [Mo Mowlam's constituency] that Mo was about to announce she was standing down. The press picked it up very quickly and today she was forced into confirming it. She's been very good, not blaming anybody for briefing against her, but a lot of the papers will write about how we've thrown away our greatest asset. It's not all bad. She has successfully knocked the Tories off the front pages, despite their big policy launch tomorrow. And it means we won't run the risk of her storming out after some row. Nor do we have the problem of having her on the backbenches after resigning from the government because she'll continue as a minister up to the election. We just have to hope she can remain disciplined between now and then. We had lots of meetings about Party Conference, including what to do about Mo. Hopefully she will do a big conference opening and then we can have a big finale with TB and Nelson Mandela [who had been invited as the party's international speaker]. We've been looking around for conference music, partly as a dry run for songs for the general election campaign. Canned Heat's 'Let's Work Together' is an early favourite. 'Ain't No Stopping Us Now' is a maybe, although perhaps a bit too triumphalist.

Wednesday, 6 September 2000

Another very good day yesterday, with a lot of praise for the way we handled the Tories' policy document launch, 'Believing in Britain'. It was actually pretty thin but we did a massive demolition job, and it certainly fitted in with the media's instinct to condemn it as an inadequate effort for the Tories so close to the election. Steve [Bates, Labour's chief press and broadcasting officer] came up with a good stunt, handing out calculators outside their press conference with a statement saying, 'The Tories' sums don't add up so this might help.' John Reid gave them out and got a bit of stick from the Scottish media who thought it was demeaning for a cabinet minister to be doing something like that. We got some pictures on the main news bulletins as a result, though.

Gordon came round Millbank today to thank people. Everybody's mood seems to have lifted considerably and I sense that morale in Millbank is a lot better. Bill Bush, who has good Tory contacts, tells me that a lot of people at Conservative Central Office are very unhappy with Hague, not least over the fourteen pints fiasco. There are obviously some serious tensions over there. The good thing is that everybody at Number Ten seems very happy with what we're doing at Millbank. I'm very pleased I made the move.

Thursday, 7 September 2000

More conference planning, this time with Peter. He seems broadly happy with the plans so far, although some people worry there's not much excitement in what we have planned. I said it would all hinge on the strength of the policy announcements we get from ministers. TBWA have put forward quite a dramatic proposal for a PPB [party political broadcast] on the Tuesday of Conference based on 'Tory Time'. Don't go back to the way we were, etc., complete with Barbra Streisand music. It involves old film of the Tories and there's some rule about not using footage of your opponents in a PPB. But I said I was quite happy to have a row with the broadcasters over it if it helped us get more coverage.

Peter called me last night to discuss Millbank again and

to ask if we should replace Margaret as general secretary before the election. He said he'd heard that morale was very low and that some good people would leave if we didn't get rid of her. I disagreed. I said I thought morale was improving dramatically, that people felt there was a real buzz about the place again, that Prescott and Gordon had both been in – and that Peter himself should be about the place more too – that we were working well together, and that now would be a very odd time for anybody to resign. I said it would be a disaster to get rid of Margaret, short of a total crisis, and that wasn't where we were. I think he accepted that.

I've been trying to tone down a speech Peter is making to Progress [a New Labour activists' group] on Saturday. He insists on having a passage about Europe, which we don't want, and he has a bizarre line about the tax burden going up, which will have to come out. I've shown it to Ian Austin [Gordon Brown's press officer], which I dare say Peter would regard as an act of betrayal.

I have had to call Ivan Massow after his picture appeared on page two of the *Sun* as a Eurosceptic businessman who signed an ad for BFS [Business for Sterling, an anti-euro pressure group]. He needs to know he's going nowhere in the Labour Party if he remains high profile on the euro and fox-hunting, which he's also passionate about.

Thursday, 14 September 2000

Bizarre week in which from nowhere we suddenly found that the country was being held to ransom by fuel block-ades. France was suffering the same last week, but while the French government made concessions to the lorry drivers we have decidedly not done so. The way in which it hit us was extraordinary. On Monday I was at a party away-day at the AEEU [Amalgamated Engineering and

Electrical Union] retreat in Esher, discussing our much improved poll position and the prospects for the election, and got back into central London to find there were blockades at most of the fuel depots and the country was just a day or two from shutdown as a result. TB was forced to pull out of a dinner for Prescott's thirtieth anniversary as an MP in Hull on Monday night because of demos. Then on Tuesday he cancelled the rest of his regional tour and his visit to the TUC conference dinner in Glasgow to fly back and sort it out. It meant demanding that the fuel companies take action to get their tankers moving, which they had been strangely reluctant to do, getting the unions to tell their members to stop colluding with a bunch of militant farmers and Poujadist small businessmen and get driving, and getting the police to stop standing back and doing nothing. It took a while but it seems to be working. Unfortunately on Tuesday TB said things would be 'on the road back to normality' within twenty-four hours, which was a major hostage to fortune. Twenty-four hour later, a very small number of tankers had left the depots but the shortages were still getting worse. Number Ten were fighting to get any ministers to go on and defend the government. As ever John Reid showed himself to be the only one with the necessary balls. Byers did one *Today* programme interview and was pretty dreadful, having been talked into it at midnight.

Gordon has been in denial all week, virtually refusing to discuss it at our morning meetings and saying it shouldn't be allowed to become a tax issue. It was a battle to get him to do any interviews, although he eventually did yesterday lunchtime. Where would we have been if Gordon had been in charge of the crisis?

TB on the other hand has been very determined, although at times infuriated at his inability to pull the necessary levers and get things moving quickly enough. He was up against this bizarre coalition but there was substantial public support for the protests and we will probably take a big hit in the next polls. Even, so I think it's a test he had to face as a Labour prime minister and in the long run there will be big benefits.

Friday, 15 September 2000

Ian Austin thought we were slow to pick up on the fuel crisis last weekend because we were all so focused on the Rawnsley book. [The journalist Andrew Rawnsley's book, *Servants of the People*, was being serialised. It was a detailed assessment of the first Labour term and seen to favour Blair over Brown.] Actually, no, Ian. Some of us were more concerned about the fate of British hostages in Sierra Leone (freed in an SAS rescue on Sunday). Gordon is concerned to know who has been briefing the papers about the Rawnsley book and doesn't seem to accept that nobody has. Because, of course, his people do lots of briefing whenever Routledge's books come out [Paul Routledge was seen to be very pro-Brown]. Gordon is reluctant to do any interviews at the moment, it turns out, because he's afraid of being asked about what's in Rawnsley.

There are worrying signs that Gordon's people at Millbank are becoming difficult. I'm really desperate not to have Blair-Brown rivalries at Millbank. Jim Godfrey [recruited from the IPPR think tank to become senior press officer] has really pissed off both Steve [Bates] and Matthew [Doyle, broadcasting officer] because of a piece on him in *PR Week*. It talked about the previous siege mentality at Millbank and said both Steve and Matthew can be abrasive and difficult. I had to pacify them and tell Jim how annoyed I was.

Meeting today with TB today about Conference although it turned out to be a session on the fuel crisis. He seems positively revitalised by the battle he's had. But he says he hasn't yet written a word of his conference speech. I think both he and AC are in denial over it. But I have a feeling it may well be better as a result. We're trying to dissuade the T&G [Transport and General Workers' Union] from putting down an emergency conference motion calling for the abolition of food vouchers for asylum seekers. John Edmonds [GMB Union] and Rodney Bickerstaffe [public service union, UNISON] are both determined to cause problems over pensions. It is mad that the unions can still force things on to the agenda at Conference, even if they are clearly out of order, because they have a majority on the Conference Arrangements Committee so can bend the rules to their hearts' content. The 'Tory Time' party political broadcast has been re-edited but nobody is sure whether to go with it or how big a campaign to mount round it. AC says today, not for the first time, 'Sell Byers, buy Milburns.'

Monday, 18 September 2000

The second instalment of the Rawnsley serialisation yesterday was pretty low-key. It included an episode in which Gordon was driving down the motorway listening to a TB conference speech, which listed the WFTC [Working Families Tax Credit], New Deal, etc., and saying out loud, 'He opposed that, he fought that,' etc. Fuel is still dominating the news, although Paula Yates's suicide led all the tabloids yesterday. Our strategy is to separate the hauliers and farmers from the rest of the public, acknowledging that they are going through difficult times, but denying the Tory claim that there is a general 'taxpayers' revolt'. That would be hugely damaging in the run-up to Conference. TB says we have to take on the wider tax agenda. If you don't have taxes on fuel then you have to have them somewhere else. And if you just injected billions into the economy to help the truckers and farmers then interest rates would go up and everyone would suffer. For all that, TB doesn't seem to be focusing on his conference speech and is wandering around wondering why nobody loves him any more. There is a sense of rabbits caught in the headlights. I've got a real feeling of foreboding about Conference.

Tuesday, 19 September 2000

Gordon said yesterday that we were 'attacking each other when we should be attacking the Tories'. A bit rich coming from him in the first place, but little did he know what was to come today. It was the third part of Rawnsley in today's *Daily Mail*. Most of it was a rehash of old Bernie Ecclestone stuff. [The Formula One boss had donated a million pounds to the Labour Party, which was returned soon after the 1997 election after allegations that he had bought influence to exempt motor-racing from a ban on tobacco sponsorship.] I was able to answer all the questions about TB easily enough by saying there was nothing new from three years ago. But Gordon was in a total tizzy about what it said about him. Basically that he'd lied when he went on the *Today* programme and said he knew nothing about the loan because he'd already discussed it with TB. Rawnsley says that he went back to his office in a fit saying that 'I lied. If this gets out I'll be destroyed.'

At first Ian [Austin] had no lines for the media, and when he did, he refused to tell me what they were. Clearly Gordon wouldn't let him [Brown said the allegations were completely untrue, based on unsubstantiated gossip]. Interestingly, I was one of the few people not invited to his post-wedding party yesterday. But it's not just Gordon.

Everybody is a bit exercised about it. It's the return of Labour's worst story since the election and they hoped it was all behind them. Today's *Guardian* poll had the Tories four points ahead of us. The *News of the World* on Sunday had it at two points.

Thursday, 21 September 2000

Big rows with Ian Austin on Tuesday night and again today. He phoned me well after midnight on Tuesday to say he was sorry he'd put me in a difficult position and hoped it was OK. I said it wasn't OK and refused to give any ground. I said he couldn't leave the party press office out of the loop like that. I couldn't go round the press gallery [the newspaper and broadcasters' offices in the House of Commons] without a line on Gordon. It made me look as if I was washing my hands of him. I might have added that it was ridiculous for me to have to wait until I was handed a copy of what PA were saying before I knew what the line was. Apparently it was OK for Gavin Cordon of the Press Association to know what his thoughts were but not me. Not easy when I was then immediately asked to explain a line of which I'd had no notice.

Then today we had a meeting of the party's Economic Policy Commission [part of the party's policy-making structure], which agreed a statement on pensions ahead of Conference. Ian said he would call me to give me the line. He didn't. I paged him twice. He eventually came back and said he'd been too busy and that he was now accompanying Gordon to do a *Channel 4 News* interview. He'd already briefed the broadcasters but the papers were now phoning me to get a steer. Ian said he would get somebody else to call me back but nobody did. I eventually had to page him again and say it was totally unacceptable. This was a party document going to Party Conference and he hadn't even told the party press office what the line was. I'll ring him tonight and tell him exactly what I think.

In fact, the Economic Policy Commission went better than we thought, and the unions and the left agreed to the statement Gordon wanted without a vote. We still don't know if the unions will insist on sticking to their own motions [linking pensions to average earnings] but even if they do the Commission document will also go through so Conference may well end up voting for both, which is better than a straight defeat for the leadership. In any case Gordon is prepared to be defeated rather than lose the government's reputation for strength. There's no way he'll restore the earnings link and nor should he. He argues that it would wreck our credibility and lead to higher interest rates. The papers today were full of how the 'Downing Street poisoners', principally AC and Anji this time, had given extensive help to Rawnsley.

Friday, 29 September 2000

It's been a pretty extraordinary conference week here in Brighton. Far from what we had planned. We went into the week clearly behind in the polls. But it was a long way from being a failure either. Blair's speech was superb. For once I really would say that it was his best conference speech that I can remember. He was a bit concerned when all the papers carried headlines like 'Blair Sweats It Out' when his dark blue shirt was visibly dripping with sweat at the end of it. We tried to say it was because he had put so much energy into it, etc., and I don't suppose any ordinary viewers will have had any trouble with it at all. They may even be happy that he had to work so hard to convince them that he was still there for them. I felt ever so slightly responsible, but only in so far as I played a small part in winning him over to wearing dark blue shirts. He usually wears white but has remarked in the past how good my blue ones look. But maybe I'm claiming far more influence over his dress taste than I really have!

There was much agonising before the speech over how far he should go in apologising for mistakes like the Dome, the 75p increase in the basic pension and the fuel crisis. In the end neither the word 'sorry' nor 'apologise' appeared. But he did make it clear that if he had his time over again he'd have concluded that the Dome was too ambitious for a government to do. And on pensions and the 75p, he said, 'We get the message.' There was a terrific ad-libbed bit at the end (which, of course, he'd practised beforehand) about his 'irreducible core' and how he would never use race as a weapon in the asylum argument, and that he would never attack foreigners for political reasons or cut overseas aid or give in to prejudice. Superb. A few good jokes. One about how good a deputy Prescott was because he'd never once mentioned that over the summer when he was in charge we were twenty points ahead in the polls. And another about Hague's fourteen pints boast: that after fourteen pints John Redwood appears sane, Michael Portillo appears loyal, and even Hague could appear like a prime minister. We wanted to include an extra line that 'after fourteen pints Ann Widdecombe looks like . . . Ann Widdecombe', which we were all in stitches about, but TB decided against. The absolute highlight of the week was when Nelson Mandela spoke so magnificently. I shook his hand twice and even found myself left alone with him for a few minutes. I had no idea what to say so we just talked about how beautiful the countryside was in Sussex, which he'd seen on his drive down. And how nice Brighton was. Hardly the most meaningful exchange, but he started it by saying how much he liked the area.

His visit helped distract attention from the previous day,

which appeared for all the world like a return to the days of the Labour Party in the seventies or eighties. Rodney Bickerstaffe and John Edmonds refusing to withdraw a motion that all but demanded a link between pensions and earnings. Gordon was adamant that it couldn't be accepted and had flown back from the IMF in Prague to argue his case forcefully. Behind closed doors, of course. TB had to cancel some meetings and interviews to argue the toss with the old dinosaurs. It was utterly preposterous. Everyone working themselves silly trying to twist arms to prevent it coming to a vote on the conference floor. Rodney looked positively shaken to the core by all the pressure, but Edmonds was full of bluster and wouldn't let him back down. Rodney wants to be the next president of the Pensioners Forum, or whatever it's called, and that was what was making him so stubborn, it seems. So their motion was carried, and Gordon made it absolutely clear he had no intention of changing the policy so it made for a bad day's headlines.

I've had more run-ins with Ian Austin all week for not telling me what he's doing. AC had a go at him and told him if he wanted to go the same way as Charlie [Whelan] he could. He really looked under pressure, though, and I don't entirely blame him as he's only doing what Gordon tells him to do. I saw Geoffrey Robinson at a reception and he said, 'I've mentioned you in my book . . . I think I've been a bit naughty.'

Monday, 2 October 2000

Tory Party Conference gets under way today, with continuing tensions over Europe and whether they still represent One Nation. We, of course, insist they don't and are ever more right wing. We went into overdrive yesterday because we were worried they would try to trump us by offering more on pensions. TB rang me to see how it was going and was frustrated that the broadcasters weren't leading on how the Tories' figures didn't add up.

Ian Austin is very twitchy about the Geoffrey Robinson book, which means Gordon is too. Prescott fired a warning shot in his end-of-conference speech on Thursday saying everybody, 'from top to bottom' – which he repeated twice – should not fuel the froth in books and the media. Quite right too.

Friday, 6 October 2000

It's been a distinctly fractious week, during which poor relationships at the top of the party have spread deep into Millbank. Douglas Alexander and I seem to have had a major falling-out, which was certainly not planned by me but apparently is a consequence of things I have said and done (or not done). At yesterday's General Election Planning Group I did a presentation on behalf of the Media Task Force [the party organisation was divided into a series of task forces ahead of the election]. I ended by saying that we needed better communication between ourselves at Millbank and also a much better sense of where we are going and what we want to be saying at key points between now and the New Year. I'd said as much already to TB, Peter and Anji. My main argument is the lack of a War Book, a grid, any clear messages or any really firm direction within Millbank.

Things have got pretty bad with Douglas and his friends off in little huddles the whole time and big decisions not being discussed openly. It's probably a product of the fact that Gordon is like a bear with a sore paw at the moment. We did a couple of things during Tory Conference just to try to keep him happy. An advertising van in Bournemouth [where the Conservative Party Conference was being held] and a £20K ad in the *Evening Standard*. Both a complete waste of money. Anyway, Douglas took everything I said as some kind of personal attack on him, when actually I had meant it as a plea to Peter to get a grip on things. A number of people congratulated me afterwards for having said things that badly needed saying. And most people around the table had certainly been nodding in agreement. Maybe other people have been having a go at Douglas – well, I know some people have – and what I said was just the last straw. He called me into a side room after the meeting and was almost white with anger. He said he'd never kept anything from me and it was rather the other way round. He cited as an example the bandwagon we had, complete with a live band on the back, going round Bournemouth. His big mate Spencer [Livermore, head of the Attack Unit] certainly knew about it because he called it 'fucking ridiculous'. But it was the only stunt that got us any coverage at all, including pictures on *Newsnight* and something in the *Mirror*. Then when we put out words that AC wanted from Prescott and Beckett after Hague's rather vacuous leader's speech, I asked Spencer if he thought they were OK and he said yes, but I didn't actually call Douglas. He seems to think he has some kind of veto over AC's instructions. AC's attitude is 'Just do it.' And while AC may not always be right, he's right more often than anybody else I know. And, in any case, he's TB's spokesman and speaks with TB's authority so that trumps everybody else, so far as I'm concerned. I'm very sure of my ground and I will stick to it. Douglas's idea that the Attack Unit produce the bullets and we just fire them isn't on either. I'm not the sort of person to pick fights for the sake of them, but if others want one they can have one.

Wednesday, 11 October 2000

Donald Dewar died today after suffering a brain haemorrhage last night. Genuinely sad for everyone and it was very unpleasant that even before his life support was switched off at lunchtime we were getting calls from journalists about the process for electing his successor. Gordon and TB are determined that Henry McLeish should take over in as smooth a way as possible, although Jack McConnell [like McLeish, a minister in the Scottish Executive] is making it clear that he may force a contest, which would mean a long campaign, electoral college, etc. I've been referring almost all calls up to Scotland.

Gordon's morning meetings have been reduced to a rather pointless daily grid session at the moment unfortunately. But it does seem that my timely intervention last week is already having an effect. A proper diary is being produced, more meetings are being held and there seems to be a much greater sense of urgency. I hope Douglas may have realised by now that he overreacted.

Thursday, 12 October 2000

Every day that goes past reveals yet more absurdities in the camp warfare we are currently enjoying. Rows involving Gordon, Peter, etc., over who should be writing strategy notes and who shouldn't, who should be chairing which meetings. AC has been telling people (not me) that they're acting like children and if that's what they wanted to do then he didn't want anything to do with them. He's considering resigning from Number Ten himself and coming down to sort things out. The problem with that is that it would signal as clear as day that the election will be in May, and we need to keep some flexibility. When the main players are behaving so stupidly it's the job of the rest of us to get on better and pull them back to a more sensible position. But I worry that Gordon's allies just goad him on and feed him conspiracy stories galore. On the other hand, on the rare occasions that I get engaged in really political discussions with Peter (whose man they think I am), I try to draw him back from confrontation, tell him to take stuff out of speeches if they are obviously provocative and, for Christ's sake, show his speeches to Gordon's office. For which I'm sure I get not the slightest bit of credit from either side. The truth is that TB and Peter don't have teams of loyal followers engaging in anything to undermine Gordon, but he clearly believes that they do. He wouldn't understand that they don't behave like he does.

I'm worried that after London and Wales we are now playing games in Scotland too. It's absolutely crucial that we shouldn't be seen to be trying to influence the result or play around with the election process in any way. That would be fatal. For now we're holding the line that there will be no decision or anything until after Donald's funeral on Wednesday. The latest idea is for the party's Scottish Executive to meet on Saturday, along with the MSPs, and elect an acting leader.

Douglas is back, in a very frosty mood today after I tried to break the ice a bit earlier in the week. Apparently he's on a promise of a minister of state's job after the election.

Meeting on Europe this week with Keith Vaz [Europe minister], MPs and special advisers. A lot of complaining that our line isn't clear, doesn't address the issue of the euro and isn't convincing against the Tory slogan of 'In Europe, Not Run By Europe'. I said TB and Gordon had been completely consistent for the past three years so nobody could claim not to know what the line is. And if they didn't like our response to the Tories – that they would take us out of Europe if they could – they had better just accept that that's what the line is and get on with it. They all want their purist little intellectual arguments over it all, but they just can't have the luxury.

In the midst of all this James and I edge closer to moving most of our stuff over to the house in France.

Monday, 16 October 2000

Horribly stressful weekend trying to pack up stuff in Brighton, keep Miles and Joe [nephews] entertained and handle hassle from France in various forms. I had to have a second medical that the building society had forgotten to tell us about. Lots of tests. Fortunately all the results were excellent apart from the bizarre news that I have Gilbert's disease. Apparently it means nothing more than that I have an abnormally high level of bilirubin in my blood. It's the stuff that makes you go yellow when you've got jaundice. Except if, like me, you've always had it (the bilirubin, not jaundice), you don't go yellow and it has no effect on you whatsoever. So the insurance company had better not make anything of it.

The main political news is now full of Geoffrey Robinson's book, which says that Peter asked him for the house loan rather than him having offered it. Incidentally, it also accuses me of being very rude and obsessed with Charlie Whelan when Charlie Falconer and I went to interrogate him [see 21 December 1998]. Not my recollection at all, although I do remember being very firm just to get him to remember what had happened. He was all over the place. So how he now claims to have such a good recollection of the dinner with Peter when the loan was first discussed is bizarre.

At this morning's strategy meeting, Gordon descended into the room looking a total mess, hair all over the place, a deep gash in his chin from shaving, and announcing, 'Right, we're going to talk about the Conservatives.' There followed an hour's worth of how to get the argument right over the economy and the £16 billion black hole in the Tories' figures, and how not to repeat the mistake of the Democrats in the US and allow the issue to be simply how to spend the budget surplus. It was barnstorming stuff and undoubtedly right. He is a brilliant strategist in that respect. But he was totally avoiding the main political news of the day, which AC finally mentioned at the end of the hour: 'What are we going to say about Geoffrey?' He got the mumbled answer, 'Nothing. If we descend into the gutter it does nothing to help.' Geoffrey, meanwhile, goes on TV and radio calling Peter destabilising and saying that without him, TB and Gordon would get on much better. Which, frankly, is almost certainly true. Even so, I didn't really enjoy the day as all this sort of rubbish just depresses me.

Wednesday, 18 October 2000

Donald Dewar's funeral. A huge and very dignified occasion in Glasgow Cathedral. Fortunately his impish personality and his lack of religious faith were more than adequately reflected in the service. It was conducted by Douglas Alexander's father, also Douglas, who was excellent. Very moving tributes from Gordon Brown, David Whitton [who had been Donald Dewar's special adviser] and Ruth Wishart [journalist and broadcaster]. Almost the entire cabinet was there.

I chatted afterwards to Sir Richard Wilson [cabinet secretary]. He said Geoffrey should have shown him his book in advance but hadn't. He's had to read a lot of them – Major's, Hezza's [Michael Heseltine], etc. – and insisted on only minor changes. But he's making Stella Rimington [former head of MI5] completely rewrite hers because he doesn't want to open the floodgates to officials revealing all. Apparently Sir Robin Butler [former cabinet secretary] had been presented with Alan Clark's diaries on the day before they were due to go to the printers with a demand for early clearance, but he had insisted on substantial changes.

Peter has been behaving very stupidly about Geoffrey's book. Yesterday's *Daily Mirror* contained quotes about what Peter had 'told friends'. Including that it was all an effort to destroy him as a pro-European minister and that the people behind Geoffrey had allies in parts of the media who were both anti-European and homophobic.

By coincidence I had breakfast with Piers Morgan, the other Mirror Group editors and Victor Blank [chairman of the Mirror Group]. Piers mentioned that he had spoken to Peter the night before so that explains where the quotes had come from. Peter told me later that he'd rung Piers to tell him he wouldn't do an interview and that his trust had been abused when Piers turned what he did say on the phone into a virtual interview. But then, later in the day, he very stupidly went on the *PM* programme [Radio 4] and said that what the *Mirror* had printed 'didn't neces-sarily' reflect his views. Piers was furious and paged me to ask if I could find out what Peter was contesting. When Peter told me that he didn't want to start denying part of what they printed and so confirming the rest, Piers went to PA and said how surprised he was by what Peter was saying as he'd spoken to him personally the night before. So then today's papers were able to run 'Mandelson in War of Words' stories. Peter just never knows when to shut up. We'll have 'Labour in Funding Confusion' stories tomorrow, too, after Margaret McDonagh told the Neill Committee [into Standards in Public Life] that the Labour Party had never funded the Leader's Office in its history [another story that sprang from the Geoffrey Robinson book]. That contradicts what we've been saying for the past few days. God knows why she said it. She says he was talking only about the principal sources of income for the Leader's Office. But the fact is that 'the Labour Party and its affiliates' had appeared in TB's Register of Members' Interests [where MPs must declare their sources of income] since 1996.

Sunday, 22 October 2000

Well, the removal men left on Friday and the Brighton house is now completely empty, though as yet unsold and with no tenants in it. It feels weird but not exactly unpleasant to be reduced to a very simple life in a one-bedroom flat in west London. It's quite liberating in a way. But it's madness that the house in France has never been properly surveyed or checked over, yet we're forking out a hell of a lot of money on it. I don't normally take risks like that so I'm trying to convince myself that it's not really such a risk at all.

Monday, 23 October 2000

Another mad day. Douglas utterly paranoid about a diary item in the *Express* saying Millbank was divided into two camps, with him, Spencer and one or two others as the Brownites and me, Pat and Margaret the Blairites, with some Prescottites stuck in the middle. I just shrugged, but Douglas said he had been cold with anger when he saw it.

Thursday, 26 October 2000

AC has decided that we should go ahead with a stunt this weekend when the clocks go back: 'Don't Let the Tories Turn the Clock Back.' Spencer has already said he thinks the idea is 'facile'. It's actually a good way of getting a simple message across. I was prepared to let it drop but AC wants us to go ahead.

TB has been at the PLP [Parliamentary Labour Party] and a political session of the cabinet today, giving them a clear message about our dividing lines with the Tories. We are starting to get our arguments in place, although there's a real danger that polls like the one in *The Times* today, which puts us back up at 43 per cent, will renew the old fears of complacency. Some journalists, like Steve Richards whom I spoke to today, are already saying that we are on course for another huge majority.

Friday, 27 October 2000

Small triumph. The 'Don't Let the Tories Turn the Clock Back' stunt is in place. We've done a picture, which the *Mirror* say they'll run on Sunday, as will the *Independent* – on their front page. Mo is going on *Breakfast with Frost* to talk it up. Great free publicity.

Sunday, 29 October 2000

Fantastic weekend in France. We finally signed the final papers for the house at a little ceremony at the *notaire*'s. James reckons he understood most of it, while I managed 60 per cent at best. So the place appears to be ours. It's not insured yet, but the power is on and the phones work and a lot of boxes are already unpacked. There's a huge amount of work to be done still. It seems that in my absence our little stunt with the clock went off OK without backfiring. In the *Independent on Sunday*, *Mirror* and *Telegraph*.

Monday, 30 October 2000

Storms batter Britain. It was hell getting back into London from Stansted yesterday. Our internal Millbank storms seem to have abated, though. Douglas has been much more mellow so far this week and things have been going well. We have had our first news conference in the refurbished Media Centre, which was fine except for a rather over-complicated economic message that the journalists struggled with and which even I didn't understand fully. It's designed to prevent Portillo [shadow chancellor] claiming that by promising to match our public spending in the first year he can somehow reduce the £16 billion's worth of cuts their plans would mean.

Sunday, 5 November 2000

I'm writing this in flight between Washington DC and Nashville, two days before a US presidential election that is too close to call. [George W.] Bush seems to have the edge, but it's so tight and the electoral college is so unpredictable that [Al] Gore [vice-president and the Democrat candidate to succeed Bill Clinton] could yet do it. If he doesn't then Nashville [where Gore's campaign was based] won't be a lot of fun on Tuesday and Wednesday. I left James in DC. He's broadcasting from there tonight before going down to cover the particularly tight race in Florida. Trust him to get sent where there are sunshine and beaches.

I'm trying to compile as intelligent a report as I can on the media lessons for us, but it's a fun trip too. In fact, I've been working quite hard on a Media Campaign for our own election. Peter asked me to prepare it during a strategy meeting with TB last week. He wants it by this Thursday. At first it seemed a bit of a chore, and tricky, given the absence so far of an agreed Campaign Plan (we're not supposed to call it a War Book). But I've managed to get hold of Peter's draft plan and the 1997 War Book so I'm basing it on those. And I can use this process to get agreement at last on a wider media strategy. Peter, I guess deliberately, has given me a tool with which to broaden the scope of Millbank's attack and to shape the campaign more to his and my liking. Useful in all sorts of ways.

Peter was, as ever, scathing about the Brownites. We had a chat in Number Ten after he made a point of catching up with me even though there were just a few minutes before Cabinet. He thinks Gordon has been very preoccupied with Scotland since Donald's death. Some deal has been hatched with Dennis Canavan [left-wing MP expelled from the Labour Party after a row when he was prevented from standing as a Labour candidate for the Scottish Parliament]. The aim is to readmit him to the party and so to prevent a by-election in Falkirk [Canavan's seat] that we'd probably lose. Unfortunately, after London and Wales, it could look like another good old Labour fix. It doesn't help us counter cynicism with politics at a time when we desperately need to do so.

Next Wednesday's PBR [Pre-Budget Report] will vie for attention with the US presidentials, which seems a bit odd but Gordon says he has good reasons for that. There's to be something for the pensioners but not much on fuel taxes.

One of the main tasks last week, before I left, was to continue trying to separate the fuel protesters from public opinion more widely. After the threat to block food supplies we had some success in that. AC masterminded quite an effective little operation to put the protesters very much on the defensive. It's been a stressful week and a lot of people are saying that the early meetings and long days are starting to wear them down. I keep thinking it's only for six months and we should enjoy it as best we can, but it will be exhausting. I seem to be surviving on less sleep than I used to need and rarely feel crushingly tired. James says he doesn't know how I keep it up, but I seem to have got used to it.

Meanwhile, back in the real world, we have decided to accept a lower offer on the Brighton house so we can get rid of the mortgage on the French one.

Thursday, 9 November 2000

At Dulles airport, after an amazing few days. [The election was neck and neck and Al Gore still had not conceded that he'd lost.] We still don't know who the next president will be. Florida (where James has been working) is still recounting its votes, with Bush currently 600 ahead. Election night in Nashville was extraordinary. At first it seemed Gore had won Florida, Michigan and Pennsylvania and the networks were calling the election for him. Then CNN, followed shortly by the others, took Florida away from him and put it in the 'too close to call' column and it started to slip away. The election was then declared for Bush, Gore rang him to concede, and we all went out into the rain to hear his concession speech. We waited and waited, until the big screens told us, via CNN, that Gore had phoned Bush to take back his concession and there was going to be a recount in Florida. So it was great fun and I had good access to all the top Democrat strategists – Bob Schrum, Stan Greenberg, etc. I had meetings today at the embassy here in DC, while James has been broadcasting non-stop from Florida. It's very hard to give much thought to proper work.

Wednesday, 15 November 2000

Our own election seems rather mundane after being in the US. Just back from a very good visit to St Albans with TB to launch our huge 'Thank You' poster campaign, which is costing over £600K. He thought at first that it was a bit naff to be saying thank you to the voters [the posters, which were very well received, carried slogans like 'If You Voted for Extra Teachers – Thank You'], but we persuaded him and in the end he delivered it very well. There may still be a healthy dose of scepticism about the campaign in the papers tomorrow.

TB seems in pretty good form. Anji is protecting him from us a bit – she thinks we would have him working every spare hour doing visits and interviews, etc. She says Clinton's people always protected him very well in the same way, although given his love of staying up half the night chewing the cud you'd wonder why they bothered. She tells me TB and Murdoch had a very good meeting recently. Murdoch won't back the Tories, doesn't rate Hague and wants to back a winner. He's still a sceptic on Europe, of course, but has good business interests of his own for being less hostile to Europe generally.

Gordon is in a bit of a grumpy mood because TB and Cook are doing speeches on Europe on Monday and he thinks we should still be campaigning on public investment. He complains that government departments aren't capable of getting decent coverage out of spending/investment announcements, etc.

Sunday, 19 November 2000

The week carried on pretty much as it started. Peter got himself into hot water by saying to a Britain In Europe dinner on Wednesday night that pro-Europeans had to talk about the political as well as the economic case for the euro. There was the predictable outcry from Gordon, etc., not least because the story was in Thursday's *FT* [*Financial Times*], which could only have happened if they'd been briefed about it in advance. TB must have spoken to him because he was pretty shaken by the reaction and had to put out a statement saying there was no case for a political discussion at all. As ever it just came straight out of the blue, as Peter's stuff always does.

At Friday's political cabinet at Chequers, Prescott made a point of raising it and several people, including Cook, Milburn, Blunkett and others, made a plea for greater unity. When Robin said they should all be publicly nice to each other, Blunkett said, 'At least I won't be able to see who's kissing me!' Peter said nothing on the subject, other than that his speech had been intended to get 'zero coverage'. But it was, for once, a very good discussion with lots of useful contributions. Jack [Straw] was a bit disappointing, as usual, as were Byers and Hoon. TB said he wanted to be sure that everybody had a chance to contribute, but then he didn't call Mo. She turned round at the end of the meeting and said, 'It's nice to be included,' before packing up her bag and leaving.

There was much hilarity earlier in the day at a truly embarrassing piece in the *Sun* about AC paying a lone visit to a showbiz party for Britney Spears, whom he never stops going on about. In fact he'd gone with Douglas ('a bit of bonding') and they had left at about one thirty in the morning without ever meeting her. Some flirtatious woman AC had been chatting to announced she was from the *Sun* and another was from the *Telegraph* and then when he approached Ms Spears he saw there were photographers all round her. What made it worse was the dreadful picture the *Sun* printed of him, looking very disreputable and apparently doing up his flies. But he had asked for it and, as somebody said, 'Why doesn't he just go out and buy himself a sports car like everybody else?' We had good coverage from AC's briefing after Cabinet, though, about how the economy will win the election for us and how the Tories know they can't get Hague into Downing Street through the front door so they're trying to do it through the back door.

Tuesday, 21 November 2000

James is in France buying a car and an answerphone and doing some decorating. I really wish I was there. It's not that exciting here at the moment. Gordon was in a rather negative frame of mind this morning. There have been a lot of stories in the papers recently about how all his cabinet colleagues hate him, so that may be playing on his mind. He's still in a grump about all the European coverage, but there's not much we can do about that.

There were stories about a possible European army today, which Hague promptly jumped on. Bill Newton-Dunn [Tory Member of the European Parliament] has defected to the Lib Dems, which has spiked Hague's guns a bit. Gordon says he wants our speeches next week to carry a common theme, but he didn't seem to have any better idea than the rest of us what that should be. Something about investment under Labour versus cuts under the Tories probably. Meanwhile Dennis Canavan has done the dirty on us and withdrawn his application to rejoin the party, so we'll have a tricky by-election in Falkirk in the New Year.

Thursday, 23 November 2000

Waiting for by-election results tonight from West Bromwich, Preston and Anniesland. We had a narrow squeak in the election for the chair of the PLP [Parliamentary Labour Party], when Clive Soley [MP, and the leadership's preferred candidate] won by just six votes after it went to a second ballot. My strategy of getting minimum coverage for it seems to have worked. Clive did virtually no interviews before the election, which may or may not have helped him, but I wanted to minimise 'Labour divisions' stories. Gordon very angry about a couple of stories in the *Independent* by Andy Grice [political editor], which included comments from his strategy meeting yesterday and about his speech to the PLP last week. He said it gave away our tactics to the Tories. It was actually a perfectly good piece and AC said to him that he thought Gordon had given it to Andy himself. Gordon said, 'No – (a) I don't leak, and (b) it was Andy Grice.' [Grice was perceived as being closer to Mandelson and Blair than to Brown and his allies.] We all smiled but I don't think he realised what he had said. It was so funny that I couldn't resist telling Andy, which was a mistake because he repeated it in Ian Austin's hearing. I was furious with Andy and told him so in no uncertain terms. Fortunately, when the original story about the PLP came out I could point out quite truthfully that Andy had seen the minutes of the meeting that were sent to all Labour MPs, complete with what Gordon had said. But all in all the episode clearly won't do anything to raise Gordon's no doubt already low opinion of me!

Monday, 27 November 2000

Fairly quiet weekend apart from a story the *Sunday Times* had wanted to run, alleging that TB had privately promised Mandela loads of dosh for his AIDS charity during Party Conference, implying that it was a reward for coming and giving us such a lift. In the end all our rebuttals and denials seemed to work because nothing appeared, although they may be holding back, trying to get more material, so they can do it next week.

The Tories were put on the back foot after a MORI poll in the *Mail on Sunday* showed the public backed us on the establishment of a European rapid-reaction force. It forced the *Mail*, who had obviously hoped for a different response, to bury their own story. Our robust attitude to Europe seems to be paying off at the moment, which is very heartening. I worry a bit about our dual strategy of trying to depict Hague as a bit of a tosser but as a threat at the same time.

Tuesday, 28 November 2000

Gordon is a real grump yet again this morning, presumably because we're not up in the media talking about public investment or getting up any big economic dividing lines. AC is in Brussels briefing journalists there before the Nice summit. In fact, the Europe argument seems to be going very well for us today and most journalists I've been speaking to think the Tories are in a really bad way. The *Sun* had another go at Portillo this morning, mainly over him telling *El Pais* (whether in Spanish or not we don't know) that his gay past won't hold him back. The *Sun* basically said he should stick to his current job and start making an impact there, which so far he'd failed to do, rather than worrying about the future leadership of the Tories.

I had coffee today with the director Peter Kosminsky, who's making a TV play about New Labour [*The Project*, eventually broadcast to mixed reviews in November 2003]. He's pissed off because everybody of any note has refused to co-operate with him and he was threatening to write an article saying we're a bunch of crazed control freaks. I think I mollified him a bit. My aim was to prevent a public spat with him and to find out as much as I could about what he's planning. The good news is that it certainly won't be aired before the election. Part of me wanted to kill off the idea with an appearance of kindness, and I think I did enough to stop him writing an article at least, but part of me is also attracted to the idea of writing drama for TV or radio myself one day. I'll see how I feel after the election.

Monday, 4 December 2000

Just had a fantastic weekend in Berlin, which is developing into a really great city. It was for a long and, at times, very dull conference of centre-left parties. But I also found time to walk miles around all the main sites, looking at the new architecture, etc. We were given a tour of the Reichstag Dome, and I slipped away to visit the haunting new Jewish Museum. Actually, a lot of the conference was quite interesting, although the star turn, Dick Morris [American political consultant], was utterly ghastly. And he was no better at seven thirty on Saturday morning when Margaret organised a breakfast meeting with him. Hectic day back at work today with all the usual tensions. Trying to get up a pre-emptive strike on an economic speech that Hague is making tomorrow. We didn't get any lines cleared until six p.m. and we then discovered that Peter was making another speech on Europe that we knew nothing about.

Tuesday, 5 December 2000

Much to my surprise, our efforts to undermine the Tories' latest attempt to make their economic policy look more credible were a great success. Alistair Darling did a good, intelligent demolition job on it all and we organised an ad van that got good pictures on TV – not least because the Tories were mad enough to try to block pictures of it with a moving car and so gave the cameras some great Keystone Cops type shots. The Tories were on a hiding to nothing anyway. There have been lots of stories appearing about how Portillo isn't sure he wants to carry on and is having inner doubts – all fuelled, according to our sources, by Amanda Platell [Conservative Party communications director]. So for them it's all just about who's going to be leader after the election. Peter's speech on Europe didn't get much coverage and, surprisingly, Gordon didn't erupt about it.

Sunday, 10 December 2000

TB has been in Nice at a very tricky European summit. AC has been enjoying his new-found freedom to slag off the Eurosceptic press left, right and centre. There's a great new self-confidence about the place, born of a long-overdue realisation that no sensible European policy is ever going to satisfy the *Sun* and the *Mail*.

TB himself is on great form and very robust. He knocked Hague about during the Queen's Speech debate and finally used the line we've been pushing on him after Hague said he wanted policies that could be summed up in six words – 'I'll give you six words: "You are the weakest link, goodbye."'

Mark Lucas [Labour Party adviser on party political broadcasts, etc.] did a very good PPB on the night of the Queen's Speech all about crime.

Peter is being as controversial as ever. He said at a drinks party in his office on Thursday that Bush shouldn't be president because he's more pro-IRA than Gore. Peter Kilfoyle [who had resigned as defence minister some time before] had a go at Peter in a letter to the *Telegraph*. Peter said Gordon was behind it and when I pointed out that Kilfoyle had always been rabidly anti-Gordon, he said that used to be true but that not long after Kilfoyle had resigned

Geoffrey Robinson had moved in on him, on Gordon's behalf, with lots of hospitality, etc., which was now paying off.

Tuesday, 12 December 2000

Quiet at work, which is just as well as I have a lot of hassle to sort out for the sale of the house, etc. The Nice summit ('Blair triumph'), the US elections (probable Bush triumph in the next few hours) and Clinton's visit to Ireland have all taken care of the main news agenda. My main tasks today were to chat to some visiting Zambian journalists, and talk to David Butler as he prepares for his latest general election book [*The British General Election of 2001*].

James has now resigned from the BBC and is delighted. He'll be more or less full time in France from Christmas.

TB has put himself, Cherie and Leo on his official Christmas card, which makes a bit of a mockery of our efforts up to now to stop people using pictures of the baby.

Wednesday, 13 December 2000

TB had a bit of a grilling on TV last night. It was an *Ask the Prime Minister* programme, with a big audience. Jan [a Danish friend] said afterwards, 'Why does he want to be prime minister when everybody in Britain is such a whinger?' He actually performed very well. And there's a very authentic-sounding Q&A with him in the *Independent* this morning, done with the help of the SCU [Strategic Communications Unit]. It makes him sound like a real regular guy who listens to Oasis, has to get up for Leo in the night, and likes nothing better than watching a good video with the kids.

The latest Tory infighting has them turning on Francis

Maude [shadow foreign secretary] for going soft on Europe and not pushing for a referendum on the Nice treaty. It seems Hague's lot are willing to undermine any potential rival, whatever the cost. It really does make ours seem like bosom buddies. I'm feeling very bullish these days. I just want to crush and humiliate the Tories for their petty, narrow intolerance and overall ghastliness.

Friday, 15 December 2000

Philip Gould now strongly advocating an election in early April. What a fantastic idea! The polls are looking very good for us, with two today in *The Times* and the *Telegraph* showing us in the high forties and the Tories in the low thirties. Hague has been branded a racist by the parents of Stephen Lawrence and by the more liberal press for saying that the Macpherson Report [which recommended changes to police procedures after the murder of Stephen Lawrence] has led to higher crime.

AC has been very funny about what it was like at the Nice summit. Imitating Chirac calling haggis 'shit' and saying, 'When you eat it you wish you had shit because it tastes worse than shit', calling the Luxembourg foreign minister a wanker and saying the Finnish foreign minister wasn't worth listening to. No wonder everybody has hated the French presidency [of the EU, which rotates every six months] so much.

AC was asked by Eban Black on the *News of the World* for a bit of colour for his piece. What had TB had for lunch, what was his room number at the hotel, etc.? AC told him he couldn't remember the room number but it was on the eighth floor – he wanted to see if Eban would check that the hotel only had six floors. His piece on Sunday duly started, 'Looking out from his eighth-floor window, Tony Blair . . .'

We still don't feel ready for an early campaign. All our documents and speech preparations seem to slip further and further away with people complaining that the departments can't provide all the stuff needed in time, etc. Despite the looming election Byers and Milburn still refuse to go on *Question Time*, which is in danger of becoming a trial of strength between us. Bad boys.

Wednesday, 20 December 2000

Winding down for Christmas. TB was a bit crap at PMQs on crime but mercifully he managed to get in a couple of good one-liners at the end. Hague has been in hot water for suggesting that the death of little Damilola Taylor [the ten-year-old black schoolboy murdered on a south London estate in November, 2000] was thanks to cuts in police numbers. Some people in the media have been accusing him of being a racist, but TB said he wasn't accusing him of racism but opportunism. And that while he hoped the police would continue to use stop-and-search procedures he hoped Hague would use 'stop and think'.

TB is not at all convinced by the early election option, so it looks like 3 May still.

My Christmas card from Gordon seems to have got lost in the post again this year. Peter's, with a picture of himself and two dogs on the front, is generally thought to be ill-judged and ghastly. I got two from TB for some reason – one just from him and one from him and Cherie. I've been trying to avoid Christmas parties as best I can with so much sorting out to do at home for the post-election move.

Thursday, 21 December 2000

OK. Well, I went for a Christmas drink with some of the Millbank crew. One of the guys who works in the call centre tells me I'm a bit of a hit with several of the women and some of the gay guys in the office because they think I'm a real person and not some political careerist. So that's nice. Today has been my last day at work before heading off to France for the holiday. We've had worries over John Reid. The final report by Elizabeth Filkin [parliamentary commissioner, see 25 September 1999] into his son comes out tomorrow. But fortunately the Select Committee that looked into it and which includes the Tories, Lib Dems and Martin Bell [independent MP for Tatton and anti-sleaze campaigner] unanimously rejected her findings. [John Reid was investigated and found by Ms Filkin to have used money provided by the House of Commons for office expenses to fund political campaigning. Among those employed was Mr Reid's son. The standards and privileges committee of the House of Commons did not accept the report.] The Tories are out to get her as much as we are, not least because she's planning to go after John Major next. But I persuaded AC not to launch an all-out assault on her on the day she strongly criticises a cabinet minister. He tells me he went up to Alan Duncan [Conservative MP for Rutland and Melton] last night at some party and said to him, 'Ah, the Peter Mandelson of the Tory Party', which is how Alan fancies himself. He then saw Nicholas Soames [Conservative MP for Mid-Sussex] and said he had to go and talk to a real Tory instead. He asked Soames what he thought of Duncan, and in Alan's hearing got the reply, 'Ghastly little cunt.' AC loves arch Tories like Soames, which is why he got on so well with Alan Clark. I had lunch with Ben [Wegg-Prosser, former adviser to Mandelson, now employed by the *Guardian*], whom I really like. He says he hates Westminster these days, with which I have some sympathy. I don't mind working there so long as it's on my own terms, but I feel a mixture of sorrow and contempt for those who make it their entire life.

2001

Thursday, 4 January 2001

Back after a great ten-day break in France at the new house. Constant stream of visitors, both family and friends, and an excellent party on New Year's Eve. I had a few work calls but not too many. One tricky moment last Sunday when the *Telegraph* printed a story saying we had a party donor who had given two million pounds but whom we wouldn't name. We didn't have to name him, of course [under the rules then covering political donations], and we didn't for two days until TB and AC decided we should. So we then revealed that it was Lord Hamlyn, an all-round squeaky clean good guy who's abroad and quite ill so couldn't be contacted earlier. It now seems that we have two other donors of the same amount, and TB has decided we should name them too: Lord Sainsbury and Christopher Ondaatje. The story had gone away but we're about to reopen it and will also have to explain why we're naming the two-million-quid donors but nobody else. I think we're probably making a mistake and should name all our donors over five thousand pounds, even if it means handing some money back to people who don't want to be revealed. Lord Levy [the party's principal fund-raiser], however, has said we mustn't go any further. He's not very happy about what we're doing anyway. Margaret, who's on holiday in Portugal, is equally unhappy. The problem is that we're sort of sticking to the existing rules but being more open where it suits us.

Later the same day. I did the briefing on donors at three p.m. It went okay but, as I expected, the questions soon turned to how many one-million-pound donors we had and why we wouldn't say who they were. We've tried to turn it on the Tories, who are far more secretive than us, but the journos would rather run 'Labour's Hidden Millions' stories. Having said that, the coverage on TV has been fine so far. *The Economist* has been trying to claim that we only revealed Sainsbury and Ondaatje because they were about to break the story. Completely untrue. It may be that they only heard of the story today from Christopher Ondaatje himself because one of their arts correspondents was doing a piece on him and he let slip that the announcement was coming. I had a long chat with TB about it this afternoon, putting my argument that we should contact all our donors over £5K and publish a full list, even if we have to give back a few donations. He readily agreed but the problem is in getting Levy to do it.

Dealing with all this kept me away from much of a meeting with TB in the flat about the manifesto, pledge cards, the set-up at Millbank, etc. The bit that I did get to was good, and TB clearly wants to get some serious politicians into Millbank. I said that our Attack Unit was too focused on economic arguments, too dependent on Gordon's directives, and nothing like proactive or imaginative enough. He agreed and is considering bringing in someone like Ben Bradshaw or Fraser Kemp [backbench Labour MPs for Exeter and Houghton and Washington respectively] to sharpen up our attack. We seem to have agreed to have an election pledge card with five achievements on one side and five pledges/ambitions for the future on the other. We also had a talk about message lines, etc., which was terribly familiar and should really have been resolved a year ago. But TB was in pretty good form.

Tuesday, 9 January 2001

There's a real sense of momentum developing. TB gave a storming performance on *Breakfast with Frost* on Sunday, saying that the economy would be the key battleground and that we've made real progress through choices we've made and not by chance. We're now on our way to Bristol where he will reinforce that message in a speech and Q&A session.

The funding story rumbled on into Sunday, but it wasn't as bad as I'd feared. The *Sunday Times* seems to have got hold of bank records showing where our donations have originated from – including Ondaatje's from Bermuda where he has a house. They tried to make it into a 'Labour Hypocrisy Over Tax Havens' story [the government had been closing tax loopholes including those affecting tax havens] but nobody else picked it up. It all meant I had a very busy weekend.

TB called us all into a two-hour meeting at Number Ten on Sunday afternoon, focusing on message and getting the right narrative for the government's achievements, etc. All the usual stuff but at least we all felt more engaged. Gordon's meetings have sharpened up too. Yesterday's was an interesting session with Stan Greenberg on the American elections, although I suppose inevitably it was all about how they had given all the right advice despite the fact that the Democrats lost. His conclusion was that their positioning was right but that the American people took a dislike to Gore, thought he was boastful and arrogant and that you couldn't trust what he said, that they didn't want him in their living rooms on TV for four years, etc.

Later the same day. The Bristol visit was pretty successful, marred only by a tomato hitting TB squarely on the back, thrown by a student protesting against Iraqi sanctions. The car had stopped right in the middle of the protesters for some reason. There were no barriers keeping them back and very few police. As I walked up to the place where TB was about to make his speech I passed an ad van with a Tory poster on it – 'You've paid the taxes so where are the police?' The first time I've agreed with a Tory poster in a long while. I offered to let TB use my suit for the speech but he thought it would be wrong to change it, so we just cleaned his up. Some discussion about whether to refer to the tomato-throwing in the speech. TB wanted to in case people thought it had been a protest over education or something. I thought not as nobody in the hall would have known anything about it as they were already sitting down when it happened. Anyway, it would just do what the protesters wanted and give more publicity to their cause. AC seemed to agree with TB but in the end nothing was said about it. At the very last minute, though, TB decided to refer to the fact that we are about to publish long-term plans for crime, welfare and education. So we had to brief the journalists very hurriedly on all that.

Thursday, 11 January 2000

Amazingly positive poll and focus-group findings presented to the General Election Planning Group by Philip. We are way, way ahead on most, if not all, issues and have a huge overall poll lead. It worries me that we have almost certainly peaked too early and that we can't maintain it. It's already impossible to make anyone in the media or the party believe that we will do anything other than win big. A hell of a lot could still go wrong, but all the humility we showed after the fuel crisis and the investment in public services seem to have had a dramatic effect. I think people are just focusing more on a real decision they will soon have to make and can't contemplate Hague or the Tories.

TB is still very engaged. He floored Hague again at PMQs yesterday, thanks to some quotes from a Tory candidate, Nigel Hastilow, that Adam Bowen in the Attack Unit pulled out. All about how confusion reigns throughout the

Tory Party and how people would be mad to nail their colours to the Conservative mast at such a time of crisis within the party. TB has asked Fraser [Kemp] to take on a big attack role for the campaign. It feels good that things are moving my way and that I seem to have won all my Millbank battles by standing my ground and not giving way. TB and Gordon want us to rise above all the pre-election frenzy and start looking like a government concentrating on the long term, etc. But the media just aren't going to let us do it.

Very funny day in Number Ten when the official cabinet photo was put on show. Gordon, Nick Brown and John Reid hadn't been able to make the photo session so they'd had to be electronically imposed. It was all very well done but Gordon did look slightly smaller than he should have done.

Paul Routledge has taken to calling me Lance 'cheap at half the' Price in the *New Statesman*. He swallowed the line that I had hastily arranged a press conference on the Ondaatje donation because of *The Economist*, which just isn't true. David Sainsbury is in angry correspondence with *The Economist* about it and I'm now trying to calm it down.

The media have latched on to the fact that we aren't going to meet all five pledges on the 1997 pledge card, especially the youth justice one [the card had promised 'fast-track punishment for persistent young offenders by halving the time from arrest to sentencing']. A ridiculous position for us to be in, especially as Jack Straw had chosen that pledge specifically as something that could be easily achieved. It's not even about reducing crime. We haven't quite met the one on class sizes yet either ['cut class sizes to 30 or under for five-, six- and seven-year-olds'] but we probably will before the election is called. We will just have to say that the pledges were for a five-year parliament and that we've achieved a hell of a lot more in other areas that we never said we would.

Friday, 12 January 2001

On my way to Glasgow for a meeting of the Scottish General Election Planning Group. The papers are reporting that TB will vote for a total ban on hunting when it comes before the Commons next week and that we've reassured Murdoch there won't be an immediate euro referendum after the election. Both sensible. Murdoch clearly wanted to back us anyway, and we haven't offered much to secure it.

The *Sun* has shifted dramatically since Christmas and has been very nice about us, while continuing to have a grudging respect for Hague. TB was quite funny yesterday. He said the *Sun* were calling Hague 'a man of stature' and Portillo 'useless' while the truth was the other way round.

Monday, 15 January 2001

The Scottish meeting went okay although John Reid [Scottish secretary] and Henry McLeish [new first minister] are already having a difficult relationship. Henry wants to talk about a Scottish government [officially it was a Scottish Executive] and wants to offer the teachers there a 23 per cent pay rise.

Hague was useless on *Breakfast with Frost* yesterday. His only story was a challenge to TB to debate him on TV during the election. The BBC and ITV have put forward a joint proposal that Hague has accepted. It puts us in a bit of a difficult position, hedging our bets for now but determined not to do it in the end. There's really nothing in it for us at all. So we're just saying it's all very complicated and that we don't want there to be a legal challenge from the Nationalists, etc., for not getting equal time. But we need to find a way to get ourselves off the hook once and for all.

Tuesday, 16 January 2001

Very grumpy Gordon again because the rise in the figures for violent crime today overshadowed a small fall in crime overall. He believes, quite correctly, that it's becoming a given that crime is rising, that schools are on a four-day week all over the country (not a single one is) and that our hospitals are failing (because of one incident in Bedford where bodies were left piled in a storeroom). He believes that we're not fighting back strongly enough – which is true – and that we're not getting up big positive messages – also true. And so he thinks the Tory ad campaign ('You've paid the taxes so where are the . . . ?') is therefore having some effect and wants us to run some counter-ads. That is, until he was told it would mean fewer ads nearer the date of the election itself. So, after last week's optimism, everybody is a bit down in the dumps again. We're looking to kill the TV debate issue fairly quickly by rejecting the BBC/ITV proposal. Fortunately the SNP came out yesterday, saying that if the debates were broadcast UK-wide they would insist on being included. Most people are against us doing a debate, including TB, but some think we should do one and win it. One good line we can use is that Hague only wants it so he can remind people who the leader is and keep Portillo, Maude and Widdecombe out of the limelight.

Wednesday, 17 January 2001

The day started with a lengthy discussion about whether we should stick to the £16 billion figure [for cuts in spending under the Tories] or accept that the Tories have changed their policy and revise it. [The Conservatives insisted that their planned spending was only £8 billion lower than Labour's]. Everybody acknowledges that the £16 billion figure isn't accepted by any serious commentators. But, then, they didn't accept the figures attached to the Tories' 'Tax Bombshell' campaign in 1992 or, indeed, the fairly spurious '22 Tory Tax Rises' that Labour used over and over before the '97 election. The argument for those wanting to stick to our guns over the £16 billion, which was most of us, was that if we have a big public row over whether it's £16 billion or some other figure it still tags the Tories with big cuts. Philip [Gould], whose latest polling remains very good, says £16 billion works very well for us in the focus groups and he thinks the Tories must be getting the same results from theirs. Just at the end of the meeting Ed Balls walked in and said, 'Yeah, it's a great figure, let's have a row over it,' which, amid great laughter, was seen as the definitive answer from the chancellor's chief economic adviser.

The next discussion, over at Number Ten, was about whether TB should go to Northern Ireland rather than vote in the hunting debate tonight. While there is probably good reason for him to go at some point soon, there was no particular reason for him to go today. I strongly argued for him not to go, but TB and AC wanted to show that fox-hunting wasn't high on his list of priorities so he went. The headline in the *Evening Standard* was 'Foxy Blair Runs for Cover' and I think he looked really weak and cowardly.

The Tories made the same charge of cowardice when, out of the blue, AC told the lobby after PMQs that we were saying no to a TV debate. He messaged me just as he was going in and I had to scrabble round to Number Ten to get his letter to the broadcasters confirming this. Shortly afterwards Sir Richard Wilson said it was too party political to go out in AC's name so it went out in mine.

So I've earned my footnote in the book of the campaign. We're taking a hit on it but I think it's right.

Big row with the editor of *The Economist* over the Ondaatje business. Very boring and I rang Adam Raphael [political editor] and said we must have lunch to kiss and make up. I'm pushing 'Keep On Moving' as our campaign song. AC wants a supergroup to record something new for us.

Thursday, 18 January 2001

We seem to have got out of the debates row with relatively minor damage. The coverage on the TV contained more weary resignation than anything else. It's not on many front pages and while some of the commentators aren't too impressed with my letter – which they say includes arguments we could have made at any time so why did we sound quite warm to the idea last year? – they still think the outcome was pretty well inevitable. If I'd had time I might have tried to rewrite it a bit.

But hunting is a bigger story. Some criticism of TB for scuttling off to Belfast, mainly in the *Mail* and the *Telegraph* not surprisingly, but not as much as he probably deserved. The news broke last night that the Tories have landed a £5 million donation so that's the issue of the morning.

Monday, 22 January 2001

Long meeting with TB first thing at which he said we didn't have the structures right to deliver on our objectives (hear, hear!) but then did nothing to improve on them, beyond saying that we all needed more 'quality time' together. We had a canter through polling, media plans and advertising. The main task is to make ministers realise that it all matters and that they have to fit in with our communications plans, etc. TB plans to talk to the cabinet about it in the next two weeks – far too late, really.

The £16 billion question still isn't properly resolved. I asked Margaret McDonagh to stop talking off the record to Tom Baldwin [of *The Times*] and she accused me of being disrespectful. I had said exactly the same to everyone else after he had a piece in the paper on Saturday showing exactly where everybody sat at Millbank, etc., but she can be very sensitive.

Tuesday, 23 January 2001

It should have been a good day today – but it wasn't. Hague was on *News at Ten* last night talking about his spending plans. We had known for hours that he was going on but we really had to fight to get a decent response from us. Ian Austin said it would be absurd to use Gordon because it was 'opportunist' – what bollocks. Who can imagine Ken Clarke when he was chancellor refusing to go on and attack the opposition before an election? So we agreed hurriedly this morning to do a rebuttal press conference and launch our own advertising campaign. The same ad campaign that yesterday was unresolved, and which included the £16 billion figure that people have been getting cold feet over. We didn't want it to look like what it was, a hasty response to Hague, so we got an ad van pasted up in a hurry and did a big production number, as if we'd been planning it for weeks. Alistair Darling, our regular Gordon surrogate, did a fantastic job and finessed the £16 billion figure brilliantly. But it soon became clear that it was going to be largely a waste of time because Number Ten was being forced to admit that they had misled the lobby yesterday. [A story had appeared in the *Observer* the Sunday before – 'Mandelson Helped Dome Backer's

Passport Bid' – accusing Peter Mandelson of using his influence as a minister to ask the Home Office to look at a passport application by S. P. Hinduja who, along with his brother, had been a big financial backer of the Dome.] Number Ten had said Peter had had no direct contact with the Home Office over the Hinduja passport application. Peter said over the weekend that he had asked his private secretary to deal with it and hadn't become personally involved. But yesterday he had to be 'reminded' that he had phoned Mike O'Brien [Home Office minister] himself. The original offence was negligible – calling to enquire on behalf of a big Dome donor who wasn't a constituent of his – but add to that a perceived cover-up and you've got a huge story that has been leading all the bulletins and which will be awful in tomorrow's papers. Every headline Peter gets is a bad one for him or the party or both. He may, I guess, have genuinely forgotten. I haven't asked him. But he may have given an incomplete or misleading answer in the hope it would all go away. [A report into the affair by Sir Anthony Hammond was published in mid-March and cleared Peter of any wrongdoing. The media called it a 'Whitehall Whitewash'.] So our ad campaign and attack on the Tories will go just about nowhere. Time for a relaunch, I feel.

Philip was very funny today, given all the 'Gould' memos *The Times* got hold of. He was desperately searching around the office for our entire advertising campaign. He couldn't remember if he'd left it in his car or brought it in to Millbank. I don't know if he ever found it.

Wednesday, 24 January 2001

Peter's second resignation. Almost like Groundhog Day. Less painful, less dramatic than the first, but more despairing because it was so unnecessary. Last time I was sure he had to go from the night before. This time I thought he should stay. But it was lying again that did it. Peter went because he lied to AC over the weekend when he said he'd played no direct role in the passport affair. This is like lying to TB. AC then gave what Peter had told him as the official line to the media and subsequently had to correct it. TB said to me, 'If I wasn't convinced he'd fibbed over the weekend then I'd have kept him, whatever the shit I'd have taken, but I was convinced he had fibbed.' He was making two points: that it wasn't the media clamour that had forced Peter out, and that he stood by people whenever he could. The last point, curiously, was in reference to Alun Michael, whom he was thinking of bringing back into government in the forced reshuffle. I was against: I said it would be a story, albeit a small one, in itself and would look as if he was bringing him back for political reasons, because he felt bad about how things had turned out in Wales, and not because it was the right thing for the government.

Peter will go as chair of the GEPG [General Election Planning Group] too, which is a real blow, even if he had been only semi-engaged so far. I lose a key ally, the party loses a great brain, and Gordon strengthens his position. AC may be the only person able to stand up to that. John Reid [who replaced Mandelson as Northern Ireland secretary] could perhaps? Gordon couldn't disguise his good mood at this morning's meeting, even before anything was announced. Suddenly all our stories were strong ones and everything was looking good. Pathetic. Helen Liddle gets Scotland [as secretary of state to replace Reid].

Thursday, 25 January 2001

Predictably vile papers this morning, with the *Sun* and the *Mail* being particularly vicious and homophobic. Peter is lucky to be out of it. He said today he would stand again at the election in Hartlepool, but obviously didn't come in to chair the GEPG. Much to my delight Prescott appeared to chair it. If he hadn't it would have been Douglas. It might be a bit chaotic if John chaired it regularly. Charlie Falconer is a possibility.

This morning's meeting in Gordon's room was horrible and I wish I'd followed my initial instinct, which was to boycott it. Hardly anyone there and it was very short, with everyone avoiding eye-contact. Gordon does that in any event, but today everybody else was too. AC refused to go. Nobody is sure even now if it was stupidity, mendacity or arrogance that led Peter to say what he did over the weekend. I felt a lot worse this morning about it all than I did last night. I haven't spoken to Peter. I just paged him saying, 'Let's talk properly when you're ready. Take good care.' Meanwhile there are worries developing about Keith Vaz [Europe minister] over money and the Asian community, possibly including the Hinduja brothers.

Saturday, 27 January 2001

Good trip to Scotland for a GEPG, chaired by Helen [Liddle] and with George Foulkes, her new deputy, and Henry [McLeish]. Helen promised a new beginning in relations between the government and the Executive – so that should last about three weeks.

Everyone in London livid with Henry for apparently agreeing to free long-term care for the elderly [which it was considered too expensive to offer in England]. Others think he can wriggle out of it because he's only offered to 'bring forward proposals' in August. It was all to stop the Lib Dems walking out of the coalition on the Executive. My suggestion, that we should have let them resign and gone into a minority to teach them a lesson, didn't get a lot of support.

The political world remains gripped by Peter fall-out and particularly the involvement of Vaz, and to a lesser extent Byers, with the Hindujas. Vaz is remarkably relaxed and jovial about it all, although I'm more worried what else the hacks will turn up if they go sniffing around Leicester [where Vaz is MP] or Asian politics. There is, of course, a healthy dose of racism at work, which is why I'm wary of taking all the rumours too seriously without any proof.

Tuesday, 30 January 2001

Madder and madder. Peter turned up at AC's house on Saturday night, on the eve of a self-justifying piece he'd written appearing in the *Sunday Times*. It was Fiona [AC's partner]'s mum's birthday party. He behaved as if he was the guest of honour, pushing himself into pole position for the group photo. When Audrey, Fiona's mum, started playing the piano he asked her if she knew, 'Who's Sorry Now?' and proceeded to sing along to it. We're all perplexed as to why he wrote the article, which has made things worse for him, rather than better. But while I still think that his resignation could and should have been avoided, not many people agree with me. Most politicians seem glad to see the back of him and, once again, he's paying the price for not keeping his friends and so openly working against colleagues.

Yesterday was a strangely quiet day with the media moving on to Keith Vaz – who is also a bit lacking in the political-friends department. So far he's surviving. Despite his many enemies, nobody has delivered a killer blow.

There was a political cabinet this morning that was singularly uninspiring. TB went through his strategy note, which he's very proud of but which doesn't seem to say all that much. Fairly predictable contributions from everyone. Clare [Short] said everybody should be nice to each other and stop briefing against colleagues. And it was Clare who went on *TW2* [*The World This Weekend* on Radio 4] on Sunday and said, 'Peter Mandelson is over.'

Gordon very concerned that the Tories are changing strategy, trying to close down the policy debate by saying they agree with us on targeted rather than across-the-board tax cuts and on the need for top-quality public services. He went through the morning headlines and said that 'Hague' and 'Labour' could be virtually interchangeable in most of them. It can be quite funny watching Gordon work. He is always there with a new sheet of paper that gets covered with his scrawl of capital letters as the latest strategy is mapped out. It sometimes feels like there's a new one every day.

At the end of the cabinet I got TB to say that Tony Benn would be the Labour representative on *Question Time* this week because they had all refused to go on. Byers went red but Milburn had already left.

Thursday, 1 February 2001

Philip's polling shows us holding up well under last week's onslaught. No measurable shift in voting intentions, with a 14 per cent lead, but some slippage on the more detailed stuff. The headline figure is always the last to move. We've lost a few points on the NHS, mainly because of the pictures of bodies piled up in a hospital chapel, also on overall trust (Peter) and a bit on crime and asylum-seekers, which are the big Tory campaign issues. Philip found him-self doing a focus group made up only of Tory supporters by mistake – and they all despised Hague. So it was fairly encouraging and there's still no suggestion of any other date than 3 May. Eight weeks to go to the start of the campaign. TB wants a whole series of strong 'next steps' speeches with good policy ideas, which seems improbable.

I had an entertaining meeting about election broadcasts with the BBC and other broadcasters yesterday morning, chaired by Anne Sloman. [BBC chief political adviser]. All the parties were there, except the BNP [British National Party] who didn't turn up – even Arthur Scargill [who had set up his own Socialist Labour Party]. Andrew Scadding from the Tories, David Walter from the Lib Dems and I were able to make common cause on most issues – mainly on scheduling and trying to get some sort of broadcasts on Radio 1 so we can reach younger voters.

The main problem is the allocation of broadcasts in Scotland where the broadcasters says all four parties, including the SNP, should have four PEBs [party election broadcasts] during the campaign. At the last election it was 5–5–4–3 with the Libs and SNP getting fewer respectively. Gordon and Douglas are very exercised about this and say we should take legal action. Unfortunately we wouldn't win and wouldn't have the support of any of the other parties. The Tories say they couldn't justify having five broadcasts to the SNP's three when there are no Conservative MPs in Scotland at all at the moment. All they would do is say that we had 'raised some valid points' if we took action. So I honestly don't think it's worth the candle, but Gordon is adamant and I don't really want to be seen to be opposing him for obvious reasons. I get the impression that TB doesn't much care but, then, he wants Gordon to run Scotland anyway. I went from the BBC to see Ivan Massow, who's got a mad idea that he should run as an independent candidate in Tatton and says Martin Bell [who was standing down in the seat] would support him.

I expressed some doubts that the Lib Dems, never mind us, would stand down for him [as they had for Bell in 1997]. Anji said he should go to the Lords. But it's really absurd to put him there when he's got no political talents whatever that I can see, just to stop him doing something stupid, but there you go. He'll probably end up there and I guess I should be pleased if it means more young gay people in there. [Massow eventually rejoined the Conservative Party in 2003 when Michael Howard became leader.]

Tuesday, 6 February 2001

I had lunch with Ivan Massow yesterday. He claims *Newsnight* had been on the phone because they had heard he might run for Tatton and a small piece appeared in *The Times* today saying Number Ten had already approved the idea. I persuaded him not to pursue it in return for some very vague hints about the Lords.

Douglas and Margaret are very exercised about a few pieces in the papers taking the piss out of a trendy new logo that's appearing on our merchandise. We did brief it to the *People* but the real damage was done by the *Mail*, who picked it up for themselves. Maybe we should be more careful about that kind of story, but Douglas gave the game away when he said that MPs were laughing about it, that it didn't reflect well on Millbank (i.e., him) and that people would say we were falling apart now that Peter has gone. Unfortunately we had to change the logo because nobody wants to buy anything with the trademark rose or 'New Labour' on it any more!

Still more calls about Keith Vaz but I've looked into it all very carefully now and nothing has appeared in anything I've seen, or in the media, that justifies sacking him. Anyway, we can't lose another pro-European minister and we could suffer among Asian voters if we weren't seen to have defended him properly.

It seems that if we want to we can get Westlife to say some nice things about TB and Labour during our conference in Glasgow next week. They're playing in the same venue. But it makes me very nervous as these things almost always come back to bite us. But maybe if you thought like that all the time you would never do anything.

Friday, 9 February 2001

Fairly mad few days. Peter is badly misbehaving, talking to the papers as 'friends of Peter Mandelson', saying he wants to come back as a European commissioner. He then went on the radio in Hartlepool and said it was all speculation and that speculation is by definition untrue. He'll just find himself accused of lying again. He can't stop himself using the media in the naïve belief that by putting stories in the press about something he can just make it happen. He makes it worse for himself every time. What little chance there ever was of him getting an EU job will now have disappeared altogether. [Mandelson was eventually appointed as Britain's European commissioner in July 2004.] AC wants me to get a backbencher to go on the radio to say he should keep quiet and allow Hammond to do his work and report. I ran it past Ben [Bradshaw, Labour MP], who wouldn't do it. Then AC messaged me again to say TB didn't want us to stir it. But Clive Soley has already done something off his own bat. So there will be acres of all that tomorrow. It's such massive self-indulgence. Peter is losing friends by the hour. The other very big event has been on the euro.

Hague asked TB at PMQs if 'early in the next Parliament' meant there would be a judgement on whether we should join in the first two years after the election. To the surprise of everybody (possibly including himself), TB said, 'Yes.' In a way it's just a statement of the obvious, but it caused quite a stir.

Gordon did a good job of sitting next to him in the Commons looking impassive but he was furious. He hadn't been consulted – nobody had. Then yesterday morning he said we absolutely mustn't go any further. By saying two years, he thinks we have turned it into a political decision as to when to make the assessment, whereas the vaguer 'early in the next Parliament' allowed us to say we would decide at the appropriate time, etc. If it's going to be within two years, how will you decide when exactly? Why not eighteen months? Why not now? And it allows the Tories to run a 'Two Years to Save the Pound' campaign.

Monday, 12 February 2001

Just off the phone from Peter. He was livid that I had asked Ben Bradshaw to put some words out urging him to keep quiet. It followed a ridiculous couple of days in which it turned out that Peter had gone in person to the *Mail* and the *Telegraph* and had briefed them that he would clear his name and wanted to come back as a European commissioner. He was demanding that I tell him whose idea it had been. He was full of conspiracy theories about who had been briefing against him, giving quotes to the papers criticising him, including one that he 'should go off and have a nice life with Reinaldo'. He said people thought you could control a story like this with just a tweak on the tiller but you couldn't. Hence the deluge of bad headlines for him on Saturday, including one in the *Guardian* saying he was being branded a traitor. I said he'd been around long enough to know that not every headline was a reflection of something anybody had said and that the whole thing was being flamed up by the media. I tried to tell him that not everyone was out to get him, but he is literally paranoid. He says he will fight Hammond if he finds against him on the evidence he's been given. He thinks he won't win Hartlepool otherwise. I tried to urge him to moderate his response and not unleash the dogs of war against the party, because he would never be forgiven and would never be able to achieve anything afterwards as he would be totally without friends. But he kept saying he would have no choice unless everybody was offered a way out. I don't know quite what he means by that but I assume he's got some idea. So, do we kill him as cleanly as possible or do we do a deal? If it's the latter I may end up as some sort of go-between. But he uses every phone call to try to gather information about those he suspects of being his enemies. I told him if he wants a way out he should talk to TB and Charlie [Falconer]. Serious stuff.

Wednesday, 14 February 2001

Spent half an hour with Peter this afternoon in his tiny backbencher's room somewhere up a tiny staircase behind the Speaker's chair. When he sat down and stretched his legs out they almost touched the opposite wall. But he was much, much more relaxed than he seemed on Monday. We had a perfectly sensible, grown-up conversation. He's still looking for betrayal everywhere and recounting snippets of gossip he's picked up about who is supposed to have said what. But at least he knows last week's events played badly for him – always somebody else's fault, of course – and that it can't be allowed to go on. He wants the outcome to be that he resigned through 'muddle not malice', that he didn't do anything wrong but contributed to a very confused situation in which everybody must take a share of the blame. He now says his visits to the *Mail* and the *Telegraph* – which he'd discussed with TB as part of the need for him to talk to those papers that were accusing him most viciously of being a liar – took place on the strict understanding that the conversation was 100 per cent off the record on the matters of his resignation and Hammond. He says the papers broke the agreement, probably colluding with each other. His main target at the moment, however, is the Home Office, whom he accuses of coming together to establish a version of events that just doesn't accord with his memory.

Had a long session with a lawyer, Charlie [Falconer] and Douglas on whether we should mount a legal challenge to the allocation of PEBs. I also had a bizarre meeting at Number Ten with AC and the rest of the Group of Six [AC, Peter Hyman, Philip Gould, Douglas Alexander, Pat McFadden and myself] which was almost all about whether TB should be pictured with Westlife. This conference [the party's annual spring conference] has more potential disasters built into it with every day that passes. The Scots are demanding some sort of parallel conference. Jack McConnell says it's outrageous that ministers in the Scottish Executive don't have a central role.

Stories have been appearing in the press quite a lot about unhappiness at Millbank, criticising various people including Margaret.

Saturday, 17 February 2001

In Glasgow. What should have been a great pre-election rallying conference is getting knocked sideways a bit. Yesterday Gordon's speech was relegated by news that the US and Britain had bombed sites near Baghdad. I can just hear the Brownites asking how far Number Ten is prepared to go to keep Gordon off the front pages! Today we should have been concentrating on good speeches from Blunkett, Straw, Prescott and Milburn, but both Blunkett and Prescott decided to insert bits in their speeches criticising the phrase 'bog-standard comprehensives', which AC had used last week when he was briefing a TB speech on education. It was controversial at the time. The teachers and lots of MPs hated it. For whatever reason AC briefed that TB wanted 'an end to the bog-standard comprehensive' even though TB didn't use the words himself. So AC sees Prescott and Blunkett's words as a direct attack on him. He thinks of David as a friend and ally and has pulled Prescott out of so many scrapes, so thank you very much. I can't understand why they were both so self-indulgent while distracting attention from the stories in their own speeches at the same time. So, when I tried to talk to AC this evening about limiting the publicity around the meeting with Westlife he really wasn't interested and said he was past caring.

Sunday, 18 February 2001

At the last minute last night I agreed to go and see Westlife perform with John Watts [from the Events Unit at Millbank] and Rebecca [Goff, my secretary]. They loved it but I couldn't get round the fact that they don't seem able to sing or dance. I was more convinced than ever that we shouldn't make a big thing of TB meeting them.

This morning's papers weren't too bad. The *Sunday Telegraph* led on Blunkett and Prescott rounding on AC. The *Sunday Times* ran a story about Derry Irvine [lord chancellor] inviting lawyers to a Labour Party fund-raising dinner when he has power over their careers, which I thought might be a bit of a problem. The *Sun* are splashing with it tomorrow – 'Cash for Wigs'.

TB arrived at Conference earlier today, rather tense but with a very good speech. New policy announcements on paternity leave, a register of class-A drug-dealers, and new literacy and numeracy tests for job-seekers, so that went down pretty well. Some of the journalists were a bit fed up that some of the advance lines I gave them yesterday didn't appear in the speech. I'd made some up because I didn't have a text to brief from, although I had a good idea what he was planning to say. I decided a while ago that you can brief one message from a speech in advance and get a good initial story up, and it doesn't matter much if you then get a very different story up with the speech itself. Two bites at the cherry and you can always say the speech was redrafted.

I then had to choreograph TB's long-awaited meeting with Westlife. He saw them in his room and they talked mainly about pop music, so far as I could tell. He then went on to do a photo with Helen Liddle and Henry McLeish before returning to do a reception for young members. I didn't want Westlife to appear on camera so I had all the cameras cleared from the room before the guys came in, stood rather sheepishly at the back while TB made a speech and then left. So the only pictures are those on our own stills camera, and hopefully we remain in control.

Thursday, 22 February 2001

Well, the Westlife story never did appear, except on ITN Online's entertainment page. Weird. I can't quite believe I wasted so much time and effort worrying about it. It has been a funny week with no big stories hanging over from the conference. To listen to Gordon on Monday morning you would have thought that the whole conference had been an utter disaster. He asked why we had got into confusion over whether it was a pre-election rally or not. The confusion only arose because of his great rallying call at the opening – just hours after we had decided it wasn't to be that kind of event. He said we didn't have enough policy to announce when we had loads. What he meant was that he didn't like all the policy, especially on paternity leave. There was obviously some kind of Gordon eruption after TB's speech. I was called almost immediately by Ed Miliband and Ian Austin asking various questions and it was pretty obvious that Gordon wasn't happy with it. He said the paternity stuff should have been made as part of a much bigger argument about the importance of the family, etc. But I suspect he'd really wanted to announce it himself. He's against TB announcing the rise in the minimum wage at the Welsh party conference next week on the ground that it's 'budget related'. The interesting thing about his daily meetings is that they do force him to show his hand on all these things. Derry [Irvine] has been in hot water all week over Cash for Wigs. It was raised in the House by Michael Fabricant [Tory MP widely believed to wear a wig] – so wigs for cash in his case – and less than expertly handled by Derry. At one point he was trying to blame Millbank. He probably thinks, as I do, that it was unwise of him to sign the invitation letters.

Monday, 26 February 2001

Lovely three-day break at the French house. It was pretty quiet at home. TB was in the US with GWB [George W. Bush], who, AC says, is not as stupid as he looks. Shame. Much hilarity as it seems that AC had to persuade TB not to wear some dodgy casual gear Cherie had bought for him during the interviews – all in front of Bush. It was the Battle of the Dress-down Leaders, with GWB naturally much better at it. TB wore a ghastly jumper that looked like something you'd been given for Christmas and had to wear once. The *Sun* today called it 'naff'.

Tuesday, 6 March 2001

We now have a proper election grid and are looking seriously at the micro-detail, so it's all starting to feel real. We were due to have a full afternoon meeting on it at Philip's house on Sunday but it was cancelled at the last minute – I'd already left and was stuck in traffic jams caused by a bomb outside the BBC the night before. Anji tells me TB was quite serious for a time about an April election, which would have meant calling it this Friday. That's now off but the May option is still live.

The FMD [foot-and-mouth disease] outbreak seems to be under control now [cases of foot-and-mouth in cattle and sheep had been spreading since mid-February] and there's no serious disruption to people's movements in the vast majority of the country. I was in Gloucestershire and Wales with TB on Thursday and Friday and the farmers there were happy on the whole with what the government is doing.

For some reason Nick Brown [agriculture minister], who's been doing well so far during the crisis, has suddenly started talking publicly about how difficult it would be to campaign in the present circumstances and how we were considering legislation to move the local elections [fixed for 3 May, which was widely assumed to be the date for the general election too]. TB was furious. But the visit, including the party's Welsh conference, was fine. TB went away from his speech and ad libbed for half an hour – I think he was trying out his stump speech [a speech made over and over again 'on the stump' during a campaign] for the election.

Hammond has now been postponed, probably until this Friday. Peter is still trying to hold everyone to ransom, demanding that the report be seen as a complete vindication of himself. He's written a long question-and-answer sheet on all the issues. AC is struggling to produce a line for when it comes out – he says it's the hardest he's ever had to write. Last week when it looked like it was going to be bad for Peter I had lunch with Ben [Wegg-Prosser] and we discussed little else. I said Peter should say that he disagreed with Hammond's findings if he came out of it badly but that he would give his reasons after the election. I just wanted to minimise any collateral damage to the party right now. Ben wrote him a note to that effect but Peter rejected it out of hand. However, he now seems to have persuaded Hammond to exonerate him – and has widely briefed the papers to that effect. There has been no counter-briefing from us at all, so that is becoming the accepted expectation in the media. The problem now is how to say that nobody handled the situation well – but without calling TB's judgement into question. Ben, probably reflecting something Peter will have said, even suggested that Jack [Straw] would have to resign but I said that was ridiculous. Clearly that is what Peter would prefer – the idea that the wrong man took the rap.

Friday, 9 March 2001

Hammond came out today and so far the coverage has been as good as we could have hoped for. Peter was cleared of any wrongdoing. He did a very good doorstep interview in which he said he was grateful for the outcome but accepted his part in the 'muddle' and didn't want to go back into government. TB did an interview up here in Inverness [where Labour's Scottish conference was being held] saying Peter could start to rebuild his life 'without a stain on his character' but that, as both he and Peter had already said, he wouldn't be coming back into government. It was obviously the main story on all the bulletins but didn't wreck the conference, where TB made a very good speech.

It was actually the Scottish Executive that managed to fuck things up. They lost their first vote in the Scottish Parliament because too many of their MSPs were on the way up here. Very stupid. So it was that vote, on fishing, and Henry [McLeish] refusal to accept the result that was the main story in Scotland. The overall mood is very good, though.

The Budget on Wednesday got some awesome coverage yesterday and at the same time the *Sun* came out big to say that they were going to support us at the election. That's a great relief because I didn't relish having to be part of some charm offensive to win them over.

No Gordon meetings this week because of the Budget, which is a blessing. He's looking very pleased with himself. [Alistair] Darling and Andrew Smith [Treasury chief secretary] did a post-Budget attack on the Tories yesterday that was totally incomprehensible but was designed to establish that they had to find at least £10 billion of spending cuts to fund their plans. I just hope nobody asks me to explain why!

Monday, 12 March 2001

I've just had tea with another likely defector from the Tory Party, their former candidate in Dewsbury, Paul McCormick, who is appalled by Hague's stand on race and immigration issues. He seems a terribly decent guy and, for once, not on some great ego kick. I'm hopeful we can do something with him soon.

Otherwise the immediate future is looking a bit bleak. Three weeks or so before the election can be called and not much to fill it. We've got a great 'Economic Disaster II' poster to launch later this week, based on an old movie poster and warning of what would happen if the Tories came back, but Douglas is balking at doing it in a cinema with a bit of wit. He and Gordon want some straight economic argument that's in danger of getting little coverage. A briefing that the Treasury lot organised today, without consulting me at all, featuring Alistair Darling in a Commons committee room, was thinly attended and generated approximately zero coverage. A lot of 'Tony's people' are saying to me that they think the Brownites feel they're now in control at Millbank and that the campaign will be pretty miserable as a result. TB certainly seems to have handed the election over to Gordon, although I hope he'll reassert himself during the campaign simply by making the right kind of news when he's on the campaign trail. Fortunately it will all be over soon, so either way it doesn't matter that much. Well, it matters a lot, but it won't matter for long.

We had a meeting today to look at pledge cards, but they had far too much information on them, and in particular far too many figures.

Tuesday, 13 March 2001

The day started badly – five minutes alone with Gordon in his office because I turned up early for the meeting. He was in a really bad mood over something and was pretty curt but also totally socially inept. He seemed almost embarrassed and said virtually nothing. He does come across as a pretty ghastly human being sometimes, but his friends seem to like him! The meeting was the usual diatribe about stories that weren't strong enough and the usual obsession about trying to convince journalists that the Tories' figures don't add up. Not much fun. Mercifully Gordon doesn't get involved in the detailed campaign planning, although Douglas does his best to bring Gordon's brand of wet blanket to the table as much as possible.

We spent over three hours at TBWA this afternoon,

going through the grid of events, concentrating to a large extent on TB's stuff. We are desperately short of opportunities to use women well in the campaign. We will have to try to get Margaret [Beckett] chairing as many news conferences as possible, as well as using Clare [Short], Estelle [Morris], Yvette [Cooper], etc.

Anji was very funny during the meeting when I said we should take Yvette on a health visit and she thought I'd said 'a vet'. She thought foot-and-mouth was worse than we feared. It doesn't look like it's going to scupper the campaign, although the journos are starting to suggest that it might.

Thursday, 15 March 2001

Yesterday AC did his best to kill off speculation that we would delay the election. It was starting to build up steam in the media as foot-and-mouth refuses to subside, so we felt we had to do something. TB refused to answer questions on it at a news conference to mark unemployment falling below one million, and Hague didn't ask about it at PMQs. So AC told the afternoon lobby that there were no logistical reasons why the local elections shouldn't go ahead on 3 May. Everybody knew he was really talking about the general election [general elections are often held on the day fixed for local elections and this was widely expected to happen in 2001]. He said postponing the elections would send out the wrong signal. The tourist industry is worried that if we said we can't have elections and suspended the democratic process, people would think the UK was too dangerous to visit.

There's a lot of commentary accusing us of arrogance, etc., this morning, but the Tories can't criticise us openly for fear of looking scared of an election, and fortunately most of the public just seem to want to get it over with.

They cancelled their latest tax-cutting announcement yesterday because it would have been buried by all the foot-and-mouth stuff, so we cancelled our own poster launch too, much to the disappointment of many of us. So it continues to be a rather frustrating and not very enjoyable time.

Friday, 16 March 2001

The Labour Party gala dinner last night. Pretty ghastly as usual. Actually, it was more boring than anything else. I was hanging around in the lobby for the first forty-five minutes, making the odd call just so I wouldn't have to go in and make small-talk. My table was full of managers from Dixons plus Kate Hoey so it wasn't too bad. Lesley Smith [Dixons' communications director and former Labour Party press officer], who's going to come back and work for us during the campaign, had organised it. I did have to chat about computers and retailing for a bit, but not for too long. I also met Christopher Ondaatje for the first time, having spoken to him on the phone several times during his donation period, and that was a real pleasure. The day had consisted of sorting out some internal stuff in the office and starting to make a list of exactly who will do what in my team. Rebecca [my secretary] and Jo Murray [press officer] were fantastically good at helping me get on top of it all as usual. Inevitably there was a bit of lobbying from people to see if they could attend all the best meetings, etc.

On Wednesday I got my first proper look at the manifesto in the Cabinet Room for an hour. I did a note on it for David Miliband [who wrote it] and AC.

The Electoral Commission are starting to cause us real grief. Not just by refusing to intervene with the BBC in our dispute over broadcasts but also ruling that we can't use any printed materials that were produced before 16 February because they don't comply with the new rule that says they must all say whose campaign they are supporting. We (and the Tories) have got millions of leaflets and posters and things that were printed before that date but are still in use and it would be mad to have to pulp them all and reprint. Margaret has written a stroppy letter to Jack Straw about it [the Home Office was the department responsible for overseeing the independent Electoral Commission].

I've also written a line to use in the media if we're asked about lobbyists and other people coming in to Millbank to volunteer during the campaign. My line all along has been that we shouldn't take people who have a financial or professional interest in joining us, but Margaret overruled that. In fact, however, just about everybody who's coming has a good track record with the party and isn't coming for either financial or professional advantage. We had a bit of a scary moment when Jim [Godfrey, senior press officer] accidentally sent Mike Prescott, of the *Sunday Times*, the wrong version of a highly negative video we've made to help promote our 'Economic Disaster II' posters. It's a very, very good video but it does use the music from *The Omen* and it does, albeit indirectly, suggest that Hague is the Antichrist. It makes me a bit nervous, but everyone seems to love it and we'll have to hope we don't get attacked too vigorously for going negative. Better to get those accusations out of the way now in any case.

Monday, 19 March 2001

Gordon, and therefore Douglas, very pissed off about 'Son of Satan', as the video has become known. [It had been given a press launch over the weekend]. The story got a bit out of hand, but not as badly as I feared. Both the

Sunday Times and the *Mirror* wrote it up as us depicting Hague as 'the son of Satan', although they said it was funny rather than nasty. At first Douglas was cross because we used Ross Kemp [*EastEnders* actor] to launch the video – it was Margaret's idea because she was having lunch with him on Saturday. Douglas thought using him devalued our economic attack – yawn. If they had their way we would do nothing that actually got into the papers. Gordon raised it with TB today. It sounds like he was fine about it. AC isn't concerned.

Amazingly the Tories refused to condemn the video – they obviously thought we were setting them up and that we wanted a row. In truth, if they had set a bishop on us as we did over their Demon Eyes poster before '97 it would have caused havoc. [The Conservatives used a poster in the run-up to the '97 campaign depicting Blair with 'demon eyes'. It was widely condemned and Labour got the Bishop of Oxford to condemn it so that it rebounded badly on the Tories.] So they rise to our bait when they shouldn't and don't when they should.

The bigger Sunday stories were more Vaz allegations about him frustrating Filkin [Elizabeth Filkin, the Parliamentary Standards commissioner was carrying out an investigation into allegations that he hadn't declared a financial relationship with a man he recommended for an honour]. And an *Observer* piece on Mike Craven [former adviser to John Prescott, now a lobbyist] planning to work for Prescott again in the election. Mike has decided not to do it after all, but I spent part of today trying to stop it appearing like a climb-down because that would just turn up the heat on other good people we want, like David Hill. The *Mail* ran something on Steve Byers and Geoffrey Robinson, which Steve has threatened to sue over, encouraged by AC's desire to take the war to the *Mail*. We're getting into a serious battle of wills over sleaze stories, etc., and we just have to show the media that we're tougher than they are.

It still seems to be full steam ahead for 3 May and we've been encouraging the unions, etc., to say that there shouldn't be a delay because of the impact on tourism, etc. We had a fairly chaotic meeting this afternoon on the grid with AC getting visibly annoyed with Margaret as she tried to rearrange things. So there's a lot more tension in the air. I'll get on and sell the story when they've all decided what it is, but I'm not going to join in the scrapping.

Tuesday, 20 March 2001

I had a bizarre encounter with Steve Norris [former Conservative candidate for London mayor], walking back from Millbank to Number Ten this morning. He may have thought I still worked for the BBC, although I kept saying 'we' in reference to the Labour Party but maybe he didn't catch the significance. He said it was definitely the Tory strategy to hold their vote at 32/33 per cent and see Labour's vote tumble – apathy and indifference, they hope. He clearly disagreed with the strategy but said Hague was very bright and knew what he was doing. Likewise he disapproved of the 'foreign land' speech [on 4 March Hague had made a speech in which he said a Labour victory would turn Britain into 'a foreign land']. He said Hague was clever enough to make sure there was nothing in the text itself that could leave him open to the charge of racism, but once it was left to the spin doctors everybody knew which way the story would go. He said 'some of us' try to keep their integrity throughout it all, but he regretted what was happening.

Our morning meeting was a bit tetchy. Phil Webster had a splash in *The Times* this morning saying we were going to fight a tough campaign because nobody would pay any attention to the Tory threat unless we did. Gordon's team wanted to know where he'd got it from. It looked to me like a clever bit of inoculation. AC just shrugged his shoulders and looked a bit downcast when challenged about it but said he didn't know where it had come from. So Gordon is twitchy, TB is twitchy – he can't decide if he wants AC with him on the campaign bus or at Millbank – and we're twenty points ahead in the polls. Just imagine what it would be like if we were twenty points behind.

The polling remains astonishingly good. We continue to go up and Hague gets further into the toilet with every day that goes by. He looked dreadful on TV today and didn't know whether he was saying we shouldn't have an election because of foot-and-mouth or not. Charles Kennedy looked far worse, literally as if he'd been up all night boozing. Apparently when he came in to see TB recently he looked the same. But he didn't cut up rough about PR.

Wednesday, 21 March 2001

First real evidence that the election might be put off. TB apparently very twitchy, angry that money has been committed to the poster campaign without him knowing about it, worried about the Tories' ability to stir up farmers and say that some of their candidates can't take part properly.

There was an hour-long meeting at the Treasury this morning which was dominated totally by foot-and-mouth. More and more people convinced that it's very difficult for us to call the election and Gordon is obviously very worried. I don't think I could face a delay until the autumn or next year.

Friday, 23 March 2001

After I wrote the above, TB had a pretty good PMQs and then did a series of interviews in which he said that when it comes to the local elections – the only ones set for 3 May – he would listen to all the representations he received, but people had to remember that there was another argument about the cost to tourism and the impact more widely if we said we had to suspend democracy.

There seems to have been a bit of calming down today, although Gordon was still a bit mad. He wouldn't do interviews about the tourism issue because he said it wasn't a big enough sector of the economy. It makes you wonder if he has the courage ever to become leader. But he does at least seem to be working on the basis of 3 May again. TB is wavering between that and June but there doesn't seem to be any suggestion that he'll put it off beyond then. TB made the point in his interviews that if you put elections off, how long do you put them off for when people are saying the crisis could last for months?

Meanwhile the wobbles in the US economy are already starting to have an effect here, with share prices falling quite sharply. Another good reason for us to go now, before it gets worse. People forget, too, what it would be like if we didn't have foot-and-mouth: the Tories would be landing punches on us on all kinds of populist issues like asylum, crime, etc. They've been forced to go quiet on the main political stuff and that's probably working to our advantage. They have very little profile right now and the polling, up until two nights ago, remains very strong.

I spent much of today briefing on the deal TB has done with Charles Kennedy over PR. Basically a classic TB fudge saying we will review the situation in the next parliament, after the next Scottish and Welsh elections, and if we do decide to recommend a change then a referendum would be the way to do it. The Lib Dems, amazingly, have bought it and are saying how pleased they are, when it's a significant watering down of the 1997 position, doesn't guarantee a referendum at all and doesn't even say that any referendum would be on the basis of the Jenkins Report. Most of our lot, including the AEEU [the engineering union, which was traditionally very anti-PR], seem happy, although there may well be ructions to come.

James wants me to go out and see him in France this weekend and I'm very tempted, but I don't think I can risk it.

Saturday, 24 March 2001

Margaret tells me TB is now more exercised about 'Son of Satan' than he was at first and about any talk of negative campaigning. He's been blaming all and sundry (no doubt including me). I keep saying to anybody who will listen that I'm more than ready to take responsibility. But because nobody else ever says that, the more I say it the more nobody who matters thinks it can have been my fault! I've been feeling a bit depressed today because I'm increasingly convinced that the election is going to be delayed. TB was caught by a cameraman in Stockholm at a summit telling Romano Prodi [president of the European Commission] that he had to make up his mind in ten days. We have been saying that he's only concerned about foot-and-mouth and not election dates!

The foot-and-mouth situation goes from bad to worse at the moment, with some estimates suggesting it could get ten times worse before it gets better. So, delaying until June looks pretty pointless as things probably won't seen any better in a month's time. And delaying to October is just far too awful to contemplate. I jokingly told everyone yesterday that if that happened I would resign or take four months' unpaid leave. Margaret laughed nervously but then began to think I might mean it so she said I couldn't leave others in the lurch and, anyway, I had to give three months' notice, etc.

I met my latest little Tory defector from Dewsbury on Friday at Shaun Woodward's house. Shaun thinks his allegations of Tory racism are pretty explosive and that we should get a journalist to investigate them independently. Shaun still doesn't know if he's going to have a seat to fight. We're not willing to impose him [in the past some candidates had been imposed on constituency parties, leaving them with no choice but to accept them] so he will have to fight a selection contest. He's reluctant to do that so may end up empty-handed.

Ivan Massow is trying to use campaign ads in the gay press to promote himself and his company. I wrote him a stinging email saying as much. He gives the impression sometimes that he's only interested in self-promotion. Oh, and fox-hunting. He texted me only last week, asking me to get TB to soften our stand on fox-hunting so as to buy us some peace and quiet in the countryside.

Sunday, 25 March 2001

I've just had a long chat with Peter who thinks May is no longer possible. He says the 'umbilical cord' between us and 3 May has snapped. He says he's spoken to TB every day this week about election timing and thinks he should postpone it until June. But he also says TB is resolute about not holding off until the autumn. So that's just about manageable in personal terms. I told Peter how much we missed him and how wearing it can be dealing with Gordon and Douglas. Needless to say, he sympathised.

Monday, 26 March 2001

June 7 is now looking marginally the most likely election date, although Clive Soley [MP for Ealing, Acton and Shepherd's Bush and chairman of the Parliamentary Labour Party] has been out on his own bat today widely arguing for 3 May and saying that's what 70 per cent of MPs want. TB will probably decide by the end of this week. If he's going to postpone the local elections he'll announce it on Friday. A lot of opinion is shifting to June, including Philip Gould. Financially, delaying to June will cost us half a million quid and October much more, quite apart from poster sites we'd have to cancel but still pay something for.

Monday, 2 April 2001

It's one in the morning. It's now all but official: 7 June it is. I've been coming to terms with it for several days. It was pretty clear on Friday that TB had made up his mind, confirmed by AC on Saturday. The media have generally supported it with everyone, except the *Mirror*, discovering they were in favour of it all along. They're pissed off because the *Sun* splashed on it authoritatively on Saturday morning. [I caused controversy after the election by confirming at a conference that Labour had tipped off the *Sun* because it was more important to keep them supportive. The *Mirror*'s support could be taken for granted.] We're all a bit deflated but resigned to it and at least 7 June does seem to be an absolute. So, the election grid has been extended by another five weeks with very little idea of how to fill it. Foot-and-mouth will continue to soak up the news for the next week or so, I expect.

[Former Serbian leader] Milosevic's arrest yesterday is also big news.

I've had to speak to Nick Brown, whose reputation has taken a severe knock over the foot and mouth outbreak, and to Michael Meacher [environment minister] to help them finesse their way through it, especially as we have been saying what a catastrophic signal delay would send to the rest of the world. Which is why one month is OK but no more.

Wednesday, 4 April 2001

So far the coverage has been pretty good, with Hague looking weak for suggesting that the election should be delayed even further. He has decided to campaign about foot-and-mouth for the next few weeks so that has politicised the crisis, hopefully at a time when it has reached a plateau and the number of new cases may start to fall. But MAFF [Ministry of Agriculture, Fisheries and Food] is in a complete mess over the statistics and has been putting out over-optimistic figures on the numbers of animals being culled. AC is having to deal with the MAFF press office and be pretty tough with them. The party involvement is fairly modest, other than trying to say that Hague is running scared.

Margaret is treating everybody in the office to a special screening of the *Bridget Jones* movie at the BFI [British Film Institute] tomorrow. A story that Tom Baldwin on *The Times* had within minutes. We voted for it over *Billy Elliot* because everybody had already seen *Billy Elliot*. But it was written up as us preferring a film about London yuppies to one about northern grit!

Thursday, 5 April 2001

On my way to Gatwick to fly out to France for the weekend. We have just been to see *Bridget Jones*. The BBC filmed us all going in for some reason. The grims – Douglas, Alexander, Spencer Livermore, etc. – didn't come, the miserable sods.

Already foot-and-mouth is definitely slipping down the news bulletins. I've suspected for some time that it is actually doing us a favour. It has been soaking up the news and preventing the Tories getting any easy hits for their announcements. Certainly, given the election delay, I think we'd be better off with a continuing sense of crisis for another couple of weeks or so. But I already get a sense that the media are getting bored with it and are ready to move on – although Andy Marr [BBC political editor] told me yesterday that the BBC had consciously decided not to do too much politics for a while to stop the viewers getting bored when the election finally comes.

John Major launched a blistering attack on New Labour and the government in a piece in the *Spectator* that was picked up by the *Telegraph* today, but nobody seems to be following it up as yet. AC dictated some withering comments about him never having got over his defeat at the hands of TB. He wanted us to say it was 'the revenge of the underpants'. [Before he gave up political journalism to work for Blair, Alastair Campbell had derided John Major for wearing his underpants outside his shirt tails. The image had been picked up by cartoonists, etc., and had contributed to Major's poor image. Major had attacked Campbell in the *Spectator* article.] I think AC was taking it all a bit too personally. He was a bit cross with me yesterday because I briefed TB's traditional address to the PLP on the eve of an election campaign to the effect that the Tories wanted to exaggerate the seriousness of foot-and-mouth because they were scared of an election. As soon as I said it – as part of a much longer briefing – I knew I shouldn't have. The BBC mentioned it at lunchtime but it died effectively after that. I said straight away that I knew I shouldn't have said it so that shut AC up fairly quickly. No real damage done.

Most MPs at the PLP meeting seemed okay with the change of date, despite the disruption to their constituency planning. The atmosphere is much calmer. A funny session at PMQs. Hague had been slapped down by the brigadier in charge of providing military support in the foot-and-mouth crisis for saying the army should be given total control. So Dennis Skinner [MP for Bolsover] got up and said the army should be given total control of the Tory Party.

Sunday, 8 April 2001

On my way back to the flat after a very nice weekend in France. I have to be careful as there was a piece in 'Black Dog' [the *Mail on Sunday* diary column] saying I had set a bad example and ignored the advice given to ministers to stay in the country and campaign by going to my 'gîte' in France for a week over Easter. Not accurate, of course, but even so. Steve Richards was staying with us as well as Steve Bassam [Lord Bassam, Home Office minister]. It shows how completely I separate my work life and France. It hadn't even occurred to me that it was against our advice to ministers.

Steve (Richards) said that however difficult Gordon might be he was still head and shoulders above any other potential leader and I agreed. Would I back him for leader after TB? Probably. Not that it would make the slightest bit of difference what I thought!

Wednesday, 11 April 2001

This would have been the day on which we launched our manifesto and I wish it still was, but instead we drift along trying to keep ourselves busy and find things to do. The grid seems to have slotted fairly effortlessly into a May campaign leading up to a June election so there's not much more preparation to be done. A lot of the party staff are going to various marginal seats – mainly by the seaside – to do some canvassing. About half my team are going to Falmouth and Cambourne but I'm not going with them. I will, however, be spending a very long Easter weekend in marginal Hove.

I was cheered up no end last night after there was a meeting to review the party election broadcasts. I wasn't at it but I heard about it afterwards. There was a broadcast based on 'Economic Disaster II' with lots of special effects of shadows being cast over the City of London, etc. It was very expensively produced but has bombed in the focus groups. Mark Lucas then offered to show them 'Son of Satan'. And, lo and behold, everyone loved it. Ed Miliband [Treasury special adviser] was in hysterics, saying, 'This is great. What's wrong with this? We should use it.' Needless to say, Margaret and Mark were delighted.

Tuesday, 17 April 2001

Quiet weekend politically, except for a rash of Tory leadership stories inspired by the idea that Ken Clarke would back Portillo – something he denied today. All quite interesting and obviously bad for Hague. I saw Jim Naughtie [*Today* programme presenter, who was writing a book on Blair and Brown] for a drink tonight. He was trying to get me to talk for his book but I refused. He said the Tories should have been annihilating us in recent months but that they were all preoccupied with what happens after the election.

Wednesday, 18 April 2001

Three weeks to kick-off and marginally more interesting today. A meeting on the manifesto which David [Miliband, responsible for writing the manifesto] admitted didn't contain a mass of exciting new ideas. We discussed how best to sell it. Is it radicalism or incrementalism? TB thinks the best story will be 'an end to Thatcherism', with him boldly saying that this decade is about moving on from Thatcherism to something new. It says a lot about TB's confidence that he's ready to do it, although he may yet decide to water it down. The problem is that the manifesto isn't very exciting so the journalists will just look for what it says on hunting, Lords reform, Section 28 and Europe. I said we should get all those stories out before the election, just as we did with PR. There's not really a problem with it being dull so long as we manage expectations. The pledges and TB's launch speech can carry the story. But we do have to explain what TB meant when he said he wanted a second term which would be far more radical. So where's the beef? We would also have to say why we were asking to be returned with another huge majority if we have such an uncontroversial programme.

Thursday, 19 April 2001

Things are getting a bit busier and it's pretty evident that things are far from ready for 7 June. A quick run through the grid today showed it's actually all over the place. I did a fair bit of work on it today, as well as trying to bolt down a few running stories. My planned trip to Scotland tomorrow has been cancelled because TB wants us at Chequers. The news has been mostly about the Tories' race row. [Three Tory MPs had refused to sign the Commission for Racial Equality's pledge not to exploit race in the election. John Townend, a retiring Tory MP, had blamed immigrants for the rise in crime and Hague had taken no action.] Unfortunately Robin Cook has made a speech, which none of us knew anything about, saying that chicken tikka masala was now the British national dish, etc. It wasn't remotely racist although the Tories still accused him of playing the race card. [Cook had made a thoughtful and powerful speech arguing that 'The idea that Britain was a pure Anglo-Saxon society before the arrival of communities from the Caribbean, Asia and Africa is fantasy,' and asserting the value to Britain of both cultural and racial diversity. I agreed with his sentiments totally but regretted the timing because it gave the Tories something to attack]. But we're getting the better of the row. Even Peter Oborne in the *Spectator* gave us credit for creating a news vacuum so that the Tory leadership row would rumble on.

Hague and Portillo were stupid enough to do a joint doorstep interview in which Portillo said the whole shadow cabinet was backing Hague and Hague just said limply, 'I agree with everything Michael Portillo has said. I have his full support.' Very convincing.

Friday, 20 April 2001

Good meeting at Chequers this morning going through the election plans. Everyone encouraged by the polling, which Philip [Gould] said showed us going into the election in a stronger position than any government since the war. We are only a point or two down on where we were before the '97 election, but then so are the Tories. Stan Greenberg's [American election strategist used by the Democrats in the US and Labour in Britain] expectation is that we will end up on about 44 per cent with the Tories on 33 per cent with a majority of well over 100. Hague and the Tories continue to be seen as weak, with splits and infighting, and Portillo likely to challenge.

TB said he had looked at the right direction/wrong direction ['Is Britain moving in the right direction on crime?', etc.] figures very carefully and thought there were weaknesses, that people thought nothing worked properly in Britain and that we just lurched from crisis to crisis. We needed to show that the country had a lot to be confident about. Primary schools, universities, science, where we are well up the international league tables.

A bit of a debate about when to publish the pledge cards – sooner, to get them well talked about before polling day, or later, so that we could continue to appear 'govern-mental' rather than in campaign mode for as long as possible? I think the latter.

We are getting better hits at the moment for straightfor-ward government stories than we have for ages and we should enjoy it for as long as we can. That's Gordon and Douglas's view too. TB said he wanted the idea out there that he had ordered a very positive campaign and that, with the state the Tories are in, it is more important than ever for us to show what we've achieved and what we're promising.

There was a general agreement that the manifesto was detailed and dull and can only work as an argument, not a source of sexy stories. TB said he had started working on his introduction but all he could think about, with foot-and-mouth going round in his head, was sheep! He wants to get back to rebuilding essentially the '97 coalition and showing that even post-'97 people are continuing to switch to us. We had to show that we had policies that reached out to non-traditional constituencies of support. Margaret said small businesses and the self-employed were important and he agreed. Showing that we have a post-Thatcherite agenda will give us some edge, but we mustn't go back on being New Labour at any stage. We had to acknowledge that asylum was a real problem and show that we were tackling it. He wants Jack to make a big speech on it next week.

Our next objective was to capture 'the future for all' as our agenda – based on aspiration and ambition. We mustn't be pushed into representing 'society' while the Tories represented 'the individual'. We had to stress that individuals did best in a strong society. He wants good Tory-attack stories on their policies to stop them getting momentum in the campaign. There would probably be some credit for Hague because he fights on despite all the shit he has to take. What TB called his 'inner Zen'.

On the way back in the car to Downing Street Sally [Morgan], Pat [McFadden] and I had to listen to Five Live on medium wave, because the radio in the fancy Lexus Philip had laid on for us wouldn't pick up any FM station over 90.0 because apparently they don't exist in Japan! So the driver said, anyway. They were running a thirty-minute discussion on our choice of 'Lifted' by the Lighthouse Family as our campaign song. The guests on Five Live, all music-industry insiders, were dismissive, saying it was safe and bland, etc. They had a Labour MSP on, Frank McSomething-or-other who has a collection of CDs running into thousands, who agreed, and said that 'those people down in Millbank' probably thought it was good music. We had a laugh about it and agreed that if 'Lifted' was a drink it would be Jacob's Creek; if it was an item of clothing it would be Gap chinos; if it was a car it would be a Ford Mondeo; and if it was a politician it would be Tony Blair.

Wednesday, 25 April 2001

On my way home from Ian McCartney's fiftieth birthday drinks, which was great fun. It's been a scrappy week so far, although the polling remains strong and Hague is weakening further. Monday's *Daily Telegraph* splashed with Gordon Brown and Millbank being furious with Cook over his chicken-tikka speech. I spoke to Peter earlier and he was laying into Robin too and says TB is still furious about the speech. It must be awful for Peter – he must think there was every chance that he would replace Robin as foreign secretary after the election if he hadn't had to resign. There are still worries about whether most of the cabinet are capable of doing decent speeches on the 'Next Steps' and the real choice at the election. We have to make sure the election doesn't turn into a referendum on us rather than a choice between us and the Tories. The Tories are trying to get back on to cultural issues like crime and asylum. We've heard it all before, of course.

Sunday, 29 April 2001

Quiet weekend. The Tories still embroiled in a race-related leadership crisis. They didn't try to lay a glove on us over anything – just two weekends before we all know the election is going to be called. Extraordinary.

Wednesday, 2 May 2001

A poll in today's *Sun* says we would have had a majority of 227 if we'd had an election on 3 May. That's despite us not having had a single news conference at Millbank in the last month, or for some time before that. In the past week the Tories have been doing our job for us, embroiled in an ever bigger row over race. Lord [John] Taylor [a black former Tory candidate] accused Hague of weak leadership for failing to discipline John Townend. Another Tory peer, Baroness Flather, who's Asian, piled in while other Tories backed Townend. Hague tried to close it down on Monday by getting Townend to sign an apology, but it still rumbles on. Philip's polling suggests that while weakness and division are damaging Hague, the race issue is working for them among some voters and, no doubt, out of sight of the media, they will be playing it for all it's worth.

Thursday, 3 May 2001

Today would have been polling day. As it is, the media are only just gearing up to any kind of excitement about an election being called next week. TB held a news conference to declare that the foot-and-mouth crisis is as good as over. That was enough to say that politics as normal is back. So, the broadcasters feel they have to carry all three main parties on every story now and Hague is getting coverage, no matter what he says. It's startling what an advantage foot-and-mouth was for us in closing down conventional politics almost totally for the past five weeks.

We continue to debate whether the public are ready for us to go straight in hard and try to annihilate the Tories early on, or whether we need to offer something a bit more inspirational first to justify why we're going out there to ask for another large majority. I've written to the BBC, complaining about the choice of subjects on which they want to hold debates between our front bench and the opposition – too much emphasis on Tory issues like crime and asylum. I gave it to *The Times* and the *Sun* but I wish now I'd pushed it harder as we want a bit of a row over it.

Friday, 4 May 2001

Travelled down to Brighton on the train with Anji tonight. She says she's convinced TB won't stand down for Gordon and that Gordon will never be prime minister. TB has got too much he wants to do, including sorting out Africa. She's still not sure what she will do after the election, but she thinks AC will stay because he loves it so much. I suggested Matthew [Doyle, Labour's broadcasting officer] as a special adviser at Number Ten. She said she thought it was a good idea because he's very good and he would be no threat to AC – which, she says, I have been a bit, and Phil Bassett too, which is why he never lets either of us get any more powerful.

Sunday, 6 May 2001

Phil Webster [*The Times*] said to me today that it looked as if most of this morning's front pages had been written by AC and me and, indeed, they were very good for us. Positive stuff about our manifesto, no stories at all from the Tories apart from one we planted about them taking a foreign donation [not allowed under the party funding rules]. They never fail to live down to their reputation.

AC did a briefing yesterday about tomorrow's political cabinet, which will take a final look at the manifesto and discuss a detailed plan for the campaign. Lots of 'investment versus cuts', the Choice, etc.

I was called into a late meeting at TBWA tonight with Gordon, AC, Douglas, Bob Schrum [American election strategist], etc. It was a pain as I'm so knackered, but it felt good because we are at last under way. We are launching on Tuesday. The Tories may come out with their manifesto before ours – maybe Thursday – which is great for us. They're leading with their chins and giving us permission to attack them. We'll say it's the earliest manifesto launch and the quickest to fall apart. The only risk, expressed by Gordon, is if it gives them an early lift and some definition and detracts from our plan to focus big-time on the economy.

The IFS [Institute of Fiscal Studies] and the media are already saying that taxes will have to go up in the second term. The question is how far we can go in saying we won't put up taxes. We will say that we have a balanced approach of investment, economic stability and targeted tax cuts. We can point out that no sensible government ever goes through every tax and says what it will do with it before an election. The Tories, on the other hand, have an inflation target that will mean higher interest rates and admit they will have higher debt. I've heard the detailed economic text so many times and, while I'm no economist, I've never really followed it completely. So, a lot of our people won't have a hope and we'll have to give them a very simple script and tell them not to deviate from it. It's a bit worrying that we don't have this already or, indeed, a script on asylum or Europe either.

Gordon is reluctant to debate the economy directly with the Tories, or he wants Alistair Darling to do it. I'm not sure it will be that easy. At least once the campaign has officially started we can use Millbank properly and AC can be there. At the moment he won't come there and we don't want meetings at Number Ten because the cameras would get shots of Bob Schrum coming in, etc. Hence TBWA.

Monday, 7 May 2001

TB has decided to attend most of our early meetings at seven a.m. We're concerned to ensure that there's no confusion between what's being said on his bus as it goes round the country and here at Millbank. So the morning meetings will be crucial. The aim will be to have stories every day, positive about us and negative about the Tories. The media demand will be so much higher that we'll need more people to provide strength and depth – key figures will include Patricia Hewitt, Steve Byers, Margaret Beckett and Estelle Morris. On the economy we stick to 'We've got the economy right and that's why we can invest in health and education, etc.' Can't say the tax burden will go up or that it will go down. People will just have to accept that there's no answer to the question because it can't be answered. Apparently at the last election Gordon drew up a list of 250 questions that fitted the same category, impossible to answer, and they were only ever asked twenty of them. We must stick to what we've already said on spending. So we can't, for example, say that the £200 winter fuel allowance will be paid every year.

The political cabinet was given a very good summary by TB of where we stand as we go into the campaign. We have big leads on all the main issues, including asylum. He warned that it will be a far tougher campaign than people thought. There's a lot of cynicism about and, indeed, the Tory campaign is built on it. They will play the underdog and we will be accused of complacency, wanting another landslide, whether we say it or not. The Tories will try to get us to run against ourselves in effect. And the *Telegraph* and other papers will end up by saying that we should be held in check with a much reduced majority. There will only be two possible stories in the first week, either Labour falters or the Tories fall apart. The key campaign message is 'a lot done, a lot still to do, a lot to lose'. Public-service reform will need to be stressed throughout the campaign with a series of speeches. We will have to do a lot of explanation, leading the electorate through what we've done and what we're going to do. The Tories, on the other hand, will be looking for a cultural battle on issues like asylum, Europe, Section 28, etc. Portillo will want to look tough on the economy if only because of the coming leadership election, so we have to box them in by identifying them with cuts.

Prescott reminded people that he was first elected as an MP in 1970 when Labour started the campaign eighteen points ahead in the polls and went on to lose. He said turnout would be a problem but the party was in good spirits.

Gordon said it would need to be a positive campaign so that we establish that we are the party people look to if they care about the future. The Tories will try to learn from GWB [George W. Bush] in America and run on values issues. But GWB didn't allow himself to be distanced from the Democrats on the public services and that's a lesson the Tories haven't learned.

Blunkett warned against alienating young voters by appearing too tough.

Jack Straw made a very strong plea that we should make the positive case for refugees. They weren't popular after the war, the Jews, or in the seventies, Ugandan Asians, but in the end they were always good for the country.

TB said we needed to acknowledge there was a problem with bogus asylum seekers and that we had to show we were dealing with it.

Clare said people were bored and we needed to offer them some excitement.

Chris Smith said only excitement or fear would push up turnout and we didn't have enough of either yet.

Alistair Darling said we needed to remind people of all the things we've done that we hadn't even said we'd do in '97.

TB summed up by saying that we had to be hungry to win. We must go out there and show that we want a mandate for a reason. We should show vision as well as discipline. He said the lesson of the 1970 campaign was that Labour just coasted along and then were surprised to find they had lost.

Tuesday, 8 May 2001

Good first day. TB at a school in Southwark. Far too churchy for my liking and the sketch-writers will take the piss, but it looked better on the box than it did in the flesh. Hague in the street in Watford, looking a bit chaotic and answering questions for Ffion [his wife].

We heard yesterday that Gerry Bermingham will be standing down in St Helens and TB wants the seat for Shaun Woodward. Shaun had wanted to be imposed but there will be a proper selection with candidates short-listed by the NEC. I've told Shaun not to do media until the selection meeting, which will hopefully be on Saturday.

Gordon was transparent in our final strategy meeting with TB at Number Ten yesterday. He wants himself, [Alistair] Darling and Douglas [Alexander] to be the main campaign spokespeople. The rest of us had no choice but to point out that they were all Scottish and all male. He reluctantly agreed that Margaret Beckett could be involved but didn't really want anyone else.

Still not sure when the Tory manifesto will be launched, but it is expected to be either Thursday or Friday. If they don't launch on Thursday we need a big positive story that day so we can go negative when they launch on the Friday. If they do go on Thursday then we do a massive demolition job on their manifesto on Friday morning.

Wednesday, 9 May 2001

The pledge cards go out this afternoon after the last PMQs. We have decided to brand the Tories' manifesto 'The Boom, Bust, Public-service Cuts Manifesto'. They've been campaigning negatively for two days. We are going positive today with our pledge cards and will do a positive press conference on the economy tomorrow, stressing monetary discipline, financial discipline, investment in public services and targeted, not irresponsible, tax cuts. We need to destroy the Tories' credibility on the economy sooner rather than later so it doesn't become a discussion about how we spend the surplus. That was the mistake Al Gore [Democratic Party presidential candidate] made.

TB addressed the PLP today. He thanked them for all their help and co-operation in the first term, and said good relations between the parliamentary party and the leadership were one reason why we were going into the campaign in such a strong position. But he warned them that it would be a fight every day from now until 7 June. We had to expose the Tory campaign for what it was: trying to win power through the back door. He stressed all the positive things we'd achieved like the New Deal, the national minimum wage, Working Families Tax Credit, etc. – all the stuff they like – and said Labour had shown a substantial commitment to the least well-off in society. He said he was looking forward to the campaign because it was a chance to go out and explain what we were in government for.

Thursday, 10 May 2001

Still working on our economic script ahead of the Tory manifesto. The tax cuts they have trailed, including cuts in fuel tax, will push the spending gap back up to near the

£16 billion figure we prefer. Should we cut fuel duty? It would be opportunist to do it during an election and, anyway, the cost is huge. So we'll say that what the Tories are proposing would mean higher interest rates and mortgages going up. Helpful that interest rates were cut by 0.25 per cent at lunchtime today. As TB said at the morning meeting, if you look beneath the Tory manifesto you see the economy at risk. But we are also looking to build a bit of momentum towards the weekend.

Gordon very grumpy over a story in the *Sun* reviving the TB–GB stuff and saying TB was planning to stay on as prime minister and that there was no secret deal to hand over to Gordon.

Friday, 11 May 2001

The Tories launched their manifesto yesterday as we hoped they would. It makes them the issue, even though it went OK for them. There are some errors in their figures that we can save for later in the campaign. The *Guardian* had a leak from our manifesto this morning on repeating our tax pledges from '97. Works well for us. Philip [Gould] says the public view is settled, that we've started and should be allowed to finish what they elected us to do. So our job is to keep the public exactly where they are right now. The phone banks report our vote holding up but with very little excitement among Labour voters.

We did a cheeky one-off poster today of Hague as Just William – 'somebody didn't do his homework'. We stuck it on an ad van and drove it round to where Portillo was speaking. It was in shot behind him so everybody could get a photo and his people made no attempt to have it moved. With enemies like these . . .

Some concern about what the manifesto says about the family. Some ministers who aren't married think it's too strong and an invitation to the media to come after them. TB was asked on GMTV this morning about why childless couples were subsidising families with children through the tax system. He handled it OK by not really answering it. Low inflation and low mortgages help everyone, etc.

Saturday, 12 May 2001

End of the first week and a pretty smooth start, although the media are all saying that the Tories had a much better week than us. Gordon and TB seem happy. Gordon is nervous on tax, which is running hard. He's desperate not to have a debate with Michael Portillo and has instructed me to negotiate a tough deal with the broadcasters over all debates so as to give him some cover. I've agreed to give *On the Record* [BBC1] and *Dimbleby* [ITV] two debates at cabinet level and the occasional one-on-one interview. We've been a bit bullish and said our key campaigners can't just drop everything to appear on their programmes. Fortunately we are doing more news conferences than the Tories so we can say that while we take questions Hague takes cover. Gordon says he'll do Humphrys [who presented *On the Record*]. So I've tried to do a quiet deal with the programme that I hope I can deliver.

We still have a problem of too few women on our platforms. I set up Mo to do a poster launch but then AC said to drop her in case she went off message. Clare stupidly said on *Any Questions* [Radio 4] that our launch at the school was 'odd' and 'surprising' last night.

David Miliband is going for selection as the candidate in South Shields and everybody is really keen to help him. Less enthusiasm for Shaun Woodward: people like Ian McCartney very reluctant to help a Tory who voted against the national minimum wage. Ray Powell is messing around in Ogmore. He wrote a letter to TB saying he was standing down but then he let himself be readopted this morning.

So far I'm having a really good time. Less stressful than I expected, though very long hours. Unbelievable Sunday lobby meeting today. Utterly embarrassing. The hacks are so useless. All they wanted to ask about was whether Peter is advising behind the scenes and whether we were all rowing about the launch. I got very cross with Margaret for letting Matthew Freud, who's a friend of hers, tell the *News of the World* that Geri Halliwell was in our first broadcast without consulting us at all. So AC said we should refuse to give them any pictures and should tell all the other red tops [tabloids] so that's what we did.

Shaun has been having a tough time of it at his selection. Apparently he didn't know who the rugby captain of St Helen's was. I'm surprised he hadn't researched that.

So far the atmosphere inside Millbank hasn't been too bad at all. Team Brown still huddle madly but they can't get away with too much when the office is so open plan – even though they have got themselves a position behind various pillars and cupboards so they are largely out of sight. It's fun having Bob Schrum and Stan Greenberg around: along with Philip they have now become a single entity. As in, 'Where's Bob-Stan-Philip?'

We almost had a major disaster last night when Jim [Godfrey] accidentally emailed a briefing note to the *Express* all about manifesto stories, and which stories we planned to give to whom, etc. They could easily have done us over with a big 'Millbank leak' story but Jim managed to negotiate us out of it brilliantly. They will get a couple of good stories they wouldn't otherwise have had in return for not embarrassing us.

Sunday, 13 May 2001

Planning to kick off week two with a big launch on enterprise and employment. We want to stay positive while saying over and over that the Tory manifesto is unravelling. Once we've launched ours we can do a final breakdown of theirs and show the Choice. Trying to beef up our regional TV and local radio interviews as well.

Monday, 14 May 2001

The polls show us up two points overall after the first week. Up on the economy and on the country moving in the right direction too. On asylum-seekers and on standing up for Britain we're down. The focus groups seem settled and, if anything, are strengthening. People think we deserve a second term. Going positive seems to be helping. We can put the pressure on the Tories for being so negative and offering nothing.

The papers are still full of alleged tensions within our campaign, suggesting that people think Gordon is mishandling it. All wildly exaggerated. Peter had a piece in the *Independent* calling for less of the old media techniques and more substance. *The Times* splashed on a letter of support for us from business leaders. Excellent. Even better, the *FT* had an unnamed shadow cabinet member talking about £20 billion of spending cuts by the end of the Parliament. Obviously Oliver Letwin [shadow chief secretary to the Treasury]. He has form. We should be able to have a lot of fun with this. Letwin is in hiding. We're going after him. I've authorised a 'Wanted' poster – 'Last wherabouts [*sic*] unknown. Reward £20 billion for schools, hospitals and police if this man is stopped.' Lots of coverage for Geri Halliwell and our PEB [party election broadcast]. It was even the third story on the Radio 4 bulletins.

More questions on the media, including the *Today* pro-gramme, about whether TB and Gordon have any informal deal over the leadership. *Today* also did a full ten minutes on Keith Vaz and Geoffrey Robinson. Outrageous.

Douglas is getting touchy. Worried that criticism of the campaign will reflect on him. Actually, the mood in Millbank is very good. No major rows or obvious tensions.

We're looking for ways to be a bit more imaginative in our challenges to the Tories. They still haven't had a single news conference at Conservative Central Office [CCO] so we thought about staging one ourselves outside their front door. Unfortunately they called one today so we scrapped the idea. But when it lasted only nine minutes we put Fraser [Kemp] up in front of CCO for ten minutes to show them up.

Shaun Woodward scraped in by four votes yesterday in his selection. On the second ballot. There are stories saying it was all a fix, which is a bit odd as he so nearly lost. David Miliband is comfortable in South Shields. Future leader of the Labour Party? I hope so.

Jack Straw called me last night. He wants to debate Ann Widdecombe on *Newsnight* tonight. I didn't mention it at the meeting this morning in case Gordon tried to force him to pull out so that Jack would be the first cabinet minister to refuse a debate rather than him. I'll try to finesse it during the day so the debate can go ahead.

Tuesday, 15 May 2001

The Liberal Democrats' manifesto launch. Their spending commitments mean the equivalent of an extra 3p on income tax. We say we welcome their support for health and education spending but that, as usual, their sums don't add up. They can't be trusted on the economy. Not as much in the press about Letwin and his £20 billion as we'd hoped but we can keep it going. At least Andy Marr waved our poster about on the news last night. We say at least Letwin is being honest. Hague wants the tax cuts but won't admit how much it will cost in cuts to public services. Very funny scene before our morning press conference. We had Darling, Beckett, Hewitt, Ian Austin [Gordon Brown's spokesman] and Ed Miliband [treasury special adviser] together for a briefing session and not one of us could recite the government's five economic tests for the euro. We had to get Bill Bush [Downing Street head of research] to find them for us. This was less than ten minutes before the presser was due to begin.

Wednesday, 16 May 2001

Mad flurry last night that came close to farce. We heard via *The Times* that some Tory candidates had signed an advert funded by Paul Sykes [anti-euro businessman] calling for a referendum on Britain's continued membership of the EU. Hague had been asked about it and said his candidates could take whatever view they liked so long as they weren't on the front bench. Gordon got very excited about it and said it was a turning-point in the campaign: the Tories had unravelled over tax and were now unravelling over Europe. Alistair Darling was despatched to do TV and radio clips.

Then Phil Webster [*The Times* political editor] rang me and said it seemed that some Labour MPs had signed the advert too. So I paged Darling and called him back before he did any interviews. Then we discovered there were actually more Labour signatories than Tories and started ringing them. Five out of seven of those named said they hadn't signed it, or made it clear that they had just been saying that they were in favour of a referendum on the euro, which is Labour policy anyway. By this time we had decided it wasn't a story about the candidates but about Hague's leadership – panic in the face of defiance by his euro-fanatics: he ran up the white flag to the extremists in his party at the first whiff of trouble. So we managed to get the story back although it wasn't as big as we had at first hoped.

Meanwhile we have had Adrian McMenamin [press officer] dressed up as Sherlock Holmes outside CCO with two huge bloodhounds searching for Oliver Letwin. Pictures on all the bulletins. The press caught on to the fact that we spelt 'wherabouts' wrongly on the Letwin poster, but it just got it more coverage so that's OK.

AC won a £200 bet by getting the *Evening Standard* to splash today with 'Britney Supports Labour' on the strength of a signed photo to him – she had spelt his name wrong – when she probably had no idea who she was signing it for.

Our manifesto was launched today and went very smoothly. We were all nervous about taking the journalists and politicians up to Birmingham for it. Matthew Parris and others will probably take the piss about the train journey, with us keeping the politicians away from the hacks as much as possible, but they were bound to take the piss out of something.

And I think I may have been a bit too obvious when I offered Martha Kearney [*Newsnight*] and Peter Hayes [Central TV] the first two questions to TB in the presser in return for knowing what they would be. Control freakery and all that. In the end Martha threw in a supplementary about the Dome and Peter asked about the National Football Stadium and why it wasn't coming to Birmingham, so neither was very helpful. Stupid thing to do, really, but AC always asks for it. Gordon looked pretty grumpy that, despite being miked up, he didn't get to answer any questions. But it all looked great.

Thursday, 17 May 2001

Well. Yesterday's entry was written before the whole day started to go pear-shaped. It turned into the most astonishing day of the campaign so far. By the time we all got back to Millbank from Birmingham we heard that TB had been barracked by some woman, Sharron Storer, at a hospital visit in Brum. TB tried to engage her so as to have a private meeting with her indoors away from the cameras but she refused. It looked a bit like a set-up. And then we learned that Jack Straw had been slow-handclapped when he went to address the Police Federation. Some suggestion that they were all a bit pissed after a good lunch. We thought of using the line that they were only able to make so much noise because we had recruited so many new police officers, but decided against it! Jack had made the mistake of trying to be too boastful at the beginning of his speech.

Then word came through that John Prescott had hit a protester in North Wales. We spoke to him and he said an egg had been thrown at him. We couldn't find out exactly what had happened, or how it was going to look on TV, which is just as important, because the pictures were still being driven back from Rhyl, which took ages. Gordon and others wanted us to put out some words in response as quickly as possible. I argued strongly against, saying we should wait until we knew what had really happened. Bizarre having Derry [Irvine, the lord chancellor] and Charlie [Falconer] giving weighty advice. The best legal brains in the country advising on a street brawl. In the end John put something out saying he had defended himself 'as anybody would'. There was a bit of a split in the office between the 'blokes' who thought Prescott had done exactly the right thing, and some of us, including most of the women but also me, who thought you shouldn't react to violence. Adam Boulton took the same line on Sky

News, going completely over the top and saying Prescott would have to resign, etc. It was surreal watching the punch being replayed over and over again on the TV late into the night. Much agonising about what line TB should take at our early presser this morning. TB wanted to say that what had happened to Prescott was unacceptable and that what had happened to Hague [he'd had to abandon a walk-about in Wolverhampton after crowd trouble] was unacceptable, that politicians should be able to make visits without this sort of thing happening. In the end he was brilliant and stuck to 'John is John', which got a lot of laughs.

The polling is still moving our way. At least, it was until yesterday so we'll have to see what impact it all has. The Tories up just one point on the tax question but there's strong movement towards us on investment in public services.

The Tories had a PEB on crime that seems to have broken through. The top issue raised on the phone banks is now crime. When shown any kind of confrontation the focus groups side with angry people against politicians. We mustn't let the election slip back to being a referendum on the government's record. Must stick to the Choice.

Friday, 18 May 2001

The Prescott issue seems to have been contained. Most people seem to think he was provoked and reacted instinctively. The polling shows them split on whether he should apologise. By the end of yesterday his mood had improved a lot and the story was running well. Great on the ten o'clock news. Prescott has refused to make anything that comes close to an apology. He did a good, fairly innocuous interview with Fiona Ross on Scottish Television just saying the incident was 'regrettable'. AC was trying to suggest he should say sorry, but John reminded him that *he* 'never said fucking sorry when he hit Mike White'. [AC had hit the political editor of the *Guardian* in a notorious incident when he was a journalist working for Robert Maxwell's papers just after Maxwell's suicide.] Meanwhile Jack Straw says he'll thump AC if any more stories appear saying David Blunkett is going to replace him as Home Secretary. But Jack was pretty lamentable in media interviews today. Totally unable to get our positive message across. We've known for ages that Hague was going to raise asylum today and he did it with ease. Despite knowing it was coming we completely failed to pre-empt it.

We had two women on the platform at the morning news conference today after having had all men yesterday on Prescott Punch Day.

Saturday, 19 May 2001

The published polls are all showing the Tories slipping further back and us increasing our lead. Huge lead in *The Economist*. Although their poll was done by MORI, who always seem to give us a bigger lead than the other polling organisations. But our own polling is also very good.

We did a focus group with Tory voters last night. Four were switching to Labour because of the economy.

Asylum is still running but it got better for us yesterday as the day wore on. Jack still pretty awful but Barbara Roche [immigration minister] was very good. She set a Europe angle running by saying that the Tory plans could well be illegal under the European Convention on Human Rights.

TB did clips but sounded a bit defensive.

My view was that Hague had actually said nothing new [on asylum] and that where he was in the polls now already took account of the fact that people know he's tough on asylum.

Gordon said he wouldn't do the *Election Call* programme on the BBC on Monday. The Beeb said they would do Portillo instead and when word started to get round the journalists that Gordon had pulled out he backed down. He's now said he will do GMTV tomorrow, which has pissed off *On the Record*. I was trying to keep David Jordan [editor of *On the Record*] as sweet as I could by being reasonable with him, but he's just rung and said I was 'very devious'.

We're getting lots of stories from the campaign on the road of the broadcasters putting microphones on protesters and then getting them to go and confront TB, etc. We're looking at whether to attack them publicly for it or do something behind the scenes to make them back off. It's actually getting quite dangerous sometimes, with scuffles and crowd trouble.

Sunday, 20 May 2001

I'm still thoroughly enjoying the campaign, although it rarely feels as if it has really come to life. One of the papers this morning called our campaign 'a laid-back shambles', which is a bit of an exaggeration. The polls have barely shifted and in so far as they have it has been in our favour.

Gordon's main priority is to protect his own position and avoid any debates on the economy – so Andrew Smith [chief secretary to the Treasury] ended up debating Portillo today and doing very well. The campaign remains far too focused on the economy, although crime managed to run fairly well for us today.

David Hill is proving a huge asset [he joined the team as the main spokesman] although if I was concerned about my status I might worry that he was taking part of my job – but he's doing what he's so good at, which is talking to the hacks, and that's fine by me. Nineteen days to go.

Monday, 21 May 2001

The polls continue to improve but asylum is still playing strongly in the focus groups, along with Europe and crime – all issues that are capable of helping the Tories. Michael Portillo is about to launch his shadow Budget so we are trying to get our lines straight. We will probably call it 'the Tory Boom and Bust Budget', then home in on the NHS. They are budgeting for no new nurses – 'nil by manifesto'.

The hunt for Oliver Letwin goes on and we're sending Andrew Smith to Letwin's constituency in Dorset. Maybe we could even get Paddy Ashdown to parachute in or land by boat. Or possibly a civil-rights demo outside Tory Central Office – 'Set Letwin Free'.

Tuesday, 22 May 2001

Some concern from the focus groups that the tit-for-tat style of the campaign is turning people off. They want more positive talk and a serious discussion of the issues. But we are still seen as the best of two evils. So we will work up some more positive lines on health and education.

Thatcher made her intervention today with a speech alongside Hague in Plymouth. She went off the text of the speech they had issued to say she would never agree to a single currency. We put out some words from Alan Milburn in response but Robin Cook went ballistic. He kept ringing me to say how cross he was, that he hadn't been a bad spokesman on Europe and that if we didn't start putting out his statements he would stop being co-operative and start giving them straight to PA. He keeps wanting to make speeches and it seems to be my job to hold him off. Gordon says he's looking for a fight and we shouldn't give it to him. So why not let him do *Newsnight* and the *Today* programme? Everybody else horrified at the suggestion.

A letter from Margaret complaining about the behaviour of TV crews has been leaked to the *Telegraph* by
Sky, so we've briefed *The Times* and the *Indy* to spike their
guns a bit. No surprise that the broadcasters are defending
themselves against charges of collusion with hecklers, etc.,
saying we haven't substantiated our allegations. The row
is now leading the bulletins, which is not where we wanted
it to be. Douglas and Gordon complaining that they didn't
see Margaret's letter before it went out. The blame game
has started early. Some people want us to up the ante
and start justifying our allegations with evidence. Others,
including me, think we should try to close it down. I took
the most conciliatory line, arguing that the broadcasters
had listened to what we had said and had taken it on
board, and that we should say so. Gordon now seems to
have come round to the point of view I expressed earlier,
that we should have complained jointly with the Tories
and the Lib Dems.

The Yorkshire region people are getting a bit worried
about our Dewsbury defector, Paul McCormick: they seem
to think it could stir up the race issue in an unhelpful way
and have unpredictable effects across the region.

Letwin finally appeared on *News at Ten* last night, but
just in a clip saying the only figure for tax cuts was £8
billion. [After Oliver Letwin's gaffe, Labour had started
using his figure of £20 billion as the extent of the Tory
spending cuts]. Andrew Smith is already down in his constituency so we will just keep up the attack. Several of us
favour our candidate standing down in his seat so that he
would almost certainly be defeated by the Lib Dems but
Margaret is very opposed.

Wednesday, 23 May 2001

Very tense meeting this morning. The most difficult so far in the campaign. Gordon very much on the defensive, firmly restating our lines on tax and why we can't go any further. Stan Greenberg said the A-Bs were slipping on the issue of tax. Everybody very angry that the *Today* programme did a big *Daily Mail*-style European-tax story this morning despite their own correspondent in Brussels, Angus Roxborough, reporting that Commission sources called it 'absolute tosh'. Neil Kinnock's office had done a lot of work on him. David Hill was straight on the phone to them.

No mention at all of education in the bulletins even though we are launching our education manifesto today. Almost all the questions at our news conference were about Europe. AC is worried that three days of Europe now would damage us further, but that seems to be what we're into, whether we like it or not. We all agreed that we need better positive stories on things like education and better ways of getting the story moving through the various news cycles, but we never do anything about it. We've been feeling on the defensive all week.

Some of the internal grumbling about the campaign is getting through to the media. Peter has obviously been talking to Andy Grice [*Independent*], who has written up some unflattering comparisons with the '97 campaign. Margaret has been coming under a lot of pressure from Gordon's people about her letter to the broadcasters. Kevin Maguire [*Guardian*], whom they are very close to, wrote quite inaccurately that I had written it with her. She's getting a bit of a pounding in the press so I made sure I sat next to her at the seven a.m. meeting. Bob Schrum says that if the media are accusing us of being relentlessly negative then we might as well be. Gordon says positive and negative must run hand in hand.

Robin was actually very good on radio and TV this morning, despite everyone's fears.

I'm not the only one around here who has started to feel I just want it to be all over. We're all getting tired and aren't having much fun. We didn't do very well at getting up TB's rejection of Thatcherism. He thinks it's hugely significant but the hacks don't see 'Labour Leader Attacks Former Tory Leader' as a big story. TB seems strangely disengaged from the campaign. His mind seems to be elsewhere. Thinking about the future, maybe. He's almost going though the motions, reading anything that we put in front of him.

Thursday, 24 May 2001

The polls are still stratospheric. But AC and TB (less so!) are into attack mode on the media. Not just yesterday's *Today* programme but the ten o'clock news last night, which led with the Europe story and then had a bizarre piece based on the mad ramblings of [Lord] Tebbit, accusing the security services of infiltrating UKIP [UK Independence Party]. Apparently, according to Tebbit, this was so the Tories would do even worse in the election and so make it easier for us to get Britain into the euro. Nothing on education. But, then, the truth is that our education manifesto contained fuck-all. It goes to show that just because you say education is your story it doesn't guarantee any kind of coverage.

After the reservations in Yorkshire I managed to reduce coverage of our Dewsbury defector to zero on a national level, except for a piece on the *Guardian* website. McCormick was talking to journalists in the constituency and releasing some 'Dewsbury manifesto'.

Channel 4 have had a mole in our press office, one of the volunteers, Zoë, who has been making a video diary.

I've been trying to shrug it off and there hasn't been a lot of coverage. Fairly harmless piece in the *Guardian* today.

I'm having a much bigger row with *Panorama*, who are doing a programme that is just on Labour's record on the NHS on the Sunday before polling day. It seems to go right against the BBC guidelines on impartiality.

Steve Bates [chief press and broadcasting officer] scored a triumph today with an idea to hand out slices of orange and play the *Match of the Day* theme at our press conference so we could accuse the Tories of scoring an own goal at half-time in the campaign: they have just said they wouldn't guarantee not to put up VAT. David Hill and Phil Bassett wanted to play 'It's All Over Now Baby Blue'. It's Bob Dylan's sixtieth birthday. I said no and TB said it definitely mustn't happen.

Strike threats at the post office and on the Tube are a worry. We're trying to get them sorted out behind the scenes as best we can.

Hague has been on *Question Time* and was shite.

Friday, 25 May 2001

Gordon says we must keep reminding people about the economy. When we talk about health and education it must be an economic argument too. The Tories would cut £20 billion from the public services, so vote for the NHS and against £20 billion cuts.

The press is full of unhelpful stories about what's going to happen after the election, reshuffles, etc. The Archbishop of Canterbury has called for a more moral campaign, less backstabbing, etc. We just have to agree with him. We don't apologise for criticising our opponents but we want to be as positive as possible. The media won't let us.

Gordon very concerned about TB's speech tomorrow

on Europe, etc. Asked AC if he could see it but AC said it didn't yet exist – true, as it happens, but Gordon didn't believe it because the speech has been widely briefed. There's a draft by Derry but it's crap and long-winded and will need totally rewriting.

Saturday, 26 May 2001

The office was in a state of mass panic yesterday as TB was getting ready to make his big speech in Edinburgh on Europe/patriotism/leadership. It was being constantly rewritten but all the key players had decided not to go up to Scotland with him. So AC, Pat [McFadden], etc., were all here trying to advise from a distance. Only Bruce Grocott [MP, Blair's parliamentary private secretary] was there to help him on the ground. Bruce is great but he has famously Eurosceptic views! Hilary [Coffman] broke the tension by answering the phone, 'Hello, Speech Crisis Centre.' We could hear Bruce at the other end writing in additions to the text longhand while TB dictated them. The result was that nobody knew exactly what he was going to say on such a crucial issue until he actually got up and delivered it.

Meanwhile we have a new poster, dubbed Wiggy, which I'm against. It shows Hague in a Thatcher wig. Gratuitous, in my view, but AC says it kills Hague dead. Gordon was claiming at the morning meeting not to have seen it but Margaret says she showed it to him.

We had a very, very funny news conference this morning. The hacks ganged up on us to ask why there weren't more women on the platform and why they never answered any of the questions. Then when Estelle Morris started to reply Gordon interrupted her almost immediately to finish the answer! The whole room collapsed and I think it took him a while to realise why.

On a more serious level we are debating at great length how far to go on Europe. TB is in a very confident mood, which is great to see. Hague is saying there are two weeks to save the pound and we're standing up to him. The focus groups last night were still solid but show that people are confused about Europe. They don't understand why we're talking about it now. They don't want the election to be about Europe and are feeling pressured by the Tory campaign. So we need to constantly remind them that they don't need to make up their minds now. There will be a referendum for that. Hague says the pound is sunk if people vote Labour, effectively giving up on the referendum. But Francis Maude [Tory foreign affairs spokesman] says the opposite.

We had a message passed on via Britain in Europe [the all-party pro-European campaign] from Ken Clarke that he won't say anything on Europe to criticise Hague because he is being pushed so hard by the Labour candidate in Rushcliffe [Clarke's constituency]. He thinks he could lose. But there's no evidence that he would say anything helpful even if we did ask our guy to back off. So, after talking to TB, I told our team there to go all out and try to win the seat.

Robin Cook is still very shirty about not being used enough. He rings me constantly, and again this morning to complain that Michael Wills [MP for Swindon North] was on the *Today* programme this morning talking about Europe when he was actually talking about patriotism. It's a bit rich for him to complain when he went to Chevening [the foreign secretary's country residence] yesterday and wasn't even out campaigning. A new battle has opened up with *TW2* [*The World This Weekend*, Radio 4] about TB appearing tomorrow. He is in two minds about doing it but Anji, etc., say he must be allowed some time off, so I told them not to expect him and offered Margaret

Beckett instead. They then leaked the story to the *Observer*. Very stupid of them as he might well have gone on after all and now we can't be seen to be relenting under media pressure.

Sunday, 27 May 2001

Another pretty chaotic day. We had planned it as a day on crime but the news was dominated by racially motivated riots in Oldham. AC texted me to ask if I thought TB should do interviews. I said no: it would look as if we were exploiting the situation for political purposes and doing what we accuse the Tories of – jumping on a bandwagon. At the eleven a.m. meeting most people disagreed with me. But it's just as well he didn't do any because Simon Hughes [Liberal Democrat] made a link between the riots and what the Tories had been saying on race. So the headline would have been 'Blair Intervenes in Race Row'.

Gordon was very grumpy, still smarting over Europe. He called it a 'self-inflicted wound'. And he claimed again not to have seen the Wiggy poster. I told both AC and Derry that I thought it would be seen as gratuitously offensive. John Reid, who is going to unveil it, is a bit nervous about it too. Gordon wants the economy back up as the main issue. He's right to say that the row over the Tory £20 billion cuts has all but evaporated.

A lot of discussion, too, about how to deal with the asylum issue. Margaret says it is still a big problem for us, especially in the South East and London but also in other areas. We may try to get TB to do something on it just on London and the South East media. I think a better idea would be for him to launch our special 'Ambitions for the south-east' document and make sure he mentions asylum.

We had a great election broadcast out tonight, featuring TB very heavily. The Tories, predictably enough, called him President Blair and accused us of a personality cult. They'd kill for a personality like him, of course. The idea was that viewers could phone in afterwards and even talk to TB himself, but BT totally fucked up and hardly any calls got through. We had the cameras in and we were able to put a few real callers through to TB but the rest of the cabinet, whom we'd also wheeled in, ended up getting calls from our own staff in Millbank and the call centre who were told to ring through on internal lines. Except we never told the cabinet who they were talking to so we wouldn't piss them off. Most real callers just got an engaged tone – at least, we hope they did. Even on the internal lines weird things were happening. Mark Bennett [AC's assistant at Number Ten who resigned to work on the campaign] got 'Sorry, the other person has hung up,' and Mark Lucas heard dozens of people all saying, 'Hello? Hello?' It was a real farce, as everybody in the building knew what was going on except the ministers and the TV crews. I had a row with some snotty PR woman from BT who said it wasn't as bad as I was claiming.

A lot of our people, not just Robin Cook but Prescott, Margaret Jay and even John Reid, have started complaining that they're not being used enough on the media. I had a row with David Jordan because *On the Record* trailed that Prescott would be appearing next week when I had already told him it would be Margaret Beckett. Then Prescott told me he wanted to do it so as to wrap up the campaign. So I'll probably end up looking stupid.

Monday, 28 May 2001

Our internal polling shows us on 46 per cent with the Tories on 26 per cent and the Liberal Democrats on 16 per cent. We're up on every attribute and have a ten-point advantage on 'Is Britain going in the right/wrong direction?' TB is up four to 57 per cent approval. Hague down three to 26 per cent. Three per cent of people think Hague is doing 'an excellent job' as leader of the opposition.

Our message in the closing week or so is that there are three reasons to vote Labour – we deserve a second chance, we need a mandate to invest in schools and hospitals, we can't risk the Tories wrecking it. The Tories only talk about the public services and the economy when they are forced into it. They haven't raised either for three weeks.

In France, Jospin is making a very unhelpful speech saying corporate taxes will have to be harmonised in the EU. The Tories are seizing on that.

Tuesday, 29 May 2001

Trying to get back on the economy, but everyone very edgy. We launched our business manifesto to give us a chance to get up stability and economic competence. But Patricia Hewitt said she wouldn't be on the platform at the morning news conference as a patsy who doesn't answer any questions. We talked her round but her train was delayed anyway. Except we can't use that as a reason for her not appearing because transport is part of the business launch. The CBI support us on transport investment. So we had to draft in Tessa Jowell at the last minute. She arrived ten minutes late for the news conference and hadn't seen the words she was due to read.

Gordon wants us to say the Wiggy poster is to illustrate that a return to Thatcherism isn't acceptable to the British people. It's not about attacking Hague when he's down. Hague's policies are more extreme, more right-wing than hers and would lead to £20 billion cuts. He says we have to take the high ground. There's a problem that switchers see the poster and say, 'He's not her,' while our supporters see it and say, 'He is her.' So we're going for a much more low-key poster launch than we had originally planned.

The phone banks report that the euro is coming to the top of the agenda for people calling in. They don't understand our policy and need reassurance about the referendum. We have to keep repeating that there will be no single currency without a referendum. Steve Bates suggests, 'The pound won't go unless you say so.'

There's been a lot of negative coverage about the Jospin speech. We should have engaged more with the story and put Robin Cook up. But when we eventually asked him to do the *PM* programme he was on a train to Budapest.

Gordon doesn't want us to be any more specific than we have been already on the euro, the conditions, the timing or the importance of the referendum. He would rather we weren't addressing it at all but everybody else can see that we have to. We thought the *Today* programme had picked up the story of the phone chaos yesterday. Andrew Gilligan [*Today* programme reporter, later prominent in the row with the BBC over the Iraq war] phoned me to say he had heard from two people inside Millbank that we were using staff to phone through because we didn't get enough calls from real voters. But nothing has been on the programme so far or in the papers. I'm sure it will be soon and I'm surprised it hasn't already.

Gordon and Douglas very unhappy about a piece in the *Independent* saying that no Scot will ever be prime minister because of devolution.

I've been talking to a few people about who might replace Margaret as general secretary. It's pretty clear she'll be gone soon after the election. Pat McFadden said he'd rather put his head in a bucket of warm shit than take over and Matthew Taylor [head of the IPPR think tank, seconded to the campaign team] said he'd rather nail his balls to a moving train.

Unusually AC gave a briefing to the journalists yesterday afternoon on our internal polling. He wants to get up the idea of Tory meltdown. We were accused of doing it to try to get Jospin off the front pages, in which case we failed. The other accusation is that we're over-confident, which is at least partially true. The campaign has become slack, ragged and unfocused. Everybody just wants it to be over.

Still fighting *Panorama* over their NHS programme. The BBC now say they will refer to the other parties but they are insisting that it's perfectly reasonable to make public-service delivery the issue and perfectly fair to examine the record of the party that looks as if it's going to win. We are contesting both the premise and their facts.

Wednesday, 30 May 2001

Polls still looking good. ICM in the *Guardian*, usually the least good for us, shows us with a 19 per cent lead. The Tories are losing ground on all the issues they refuse to talk about, including tax. But they are up a bit on Europe. We seem to have a problem in Kent where we are picking up anger and a feeling that we are not fighting for their interests. We'll switch some resources there. Ian McCartney said he'd heard that the Tories were asking on the doorsteps in Kent, 'Do you feel left out in your own town?'

Gordon still grumpy over talk of euro-referendum timing after TB did a piece in the *Sun*. But we feel we have to keep reminding people that the referendum is their chance to say yes or no. He also says Pat Hewitt messed up on national insurance on TV yesterday, but none of the papers seem to have picked it up.

Hague seems to have realised he's got it wrong. In *The Times* and on *Newsnight* he shifted tack to say the election wasn't the last chance to save the pound. He looked very tired and lacking in confidence. Wiggy has gone down well. Pictures in most of the papers, including the *Telegraph*.

A bit of difficulty at this morning's press conference when Stephen Byers tried to justify our policy of the 'right to request' flexible working hours for mums returning after pregnancy. It seems a daft policy to me and a typical New Labour half-measure.

Thursday, 31 May 2001

A week to go. The Tories have done us a favour by going on the attack over the taxing of child benefit. It gave us the chance to come back at them on all the things we're doing on benefits for parents with children, something we've been trying unsuccessfully to highlight until now.

TB was great on *Question Time* last night. Miles stronger than Hague earlier in the week. Hague was on *Dimbleby* [ITV] last night and wasn't much better. TB's only slight slip was to say that he had voted against fox-hunting when actually he was in Bosnia on the day of the first vote and in Northern Ireland on the second. Fortunately we found that he had voted against it in 1992 when it came forward as a private member's bill. He was barracked on the programme by some rather unattractive-looking farmers who just got angry and ranted so TB got the better of them. Also by a woman whose child needs a bone-marrow transplant, but she was so obviously a total set-up and had already been in the *Sun* saying she was going to ask him about it. So it looked fixed and did the BBC no favours. They were pissed off.

The row with *Panorama* is hotting up. We had agreed to put Alan Milburn [health secretary] on to do an interview. We then got a list of so many detailed and wide-ranging questions that it would be impossible to brief him up on all of them in the middle of the campaign. He flatly refused in any case, quite rightly. He said it would only make news if he fucked up. So, we are debating whether to offer junior ministers or just stall and eventually refuse to offer anybody so they have to use old clips. They were very alarmed when I rang and said we could no longer be sure who we'd offer or when.

More defectors in the news. We had one, Anthony Nelson [a former Tory treasury minister], whom we'd codenamed 'Horatio', but he bottled out. Charlie Falconer had spent the evening with him on Tuesday and he'd said he was nearly ready to do it then. Maybe his daughter, who works at Tory Central Office, talked him out of it. The Lib Dems got a bit of coverage for John Lee, another minister who served under Thatcher, and who has joined them.

Margaret has been refusing even to discuss the plans for the election night party but she finally relented today. It will be at Millbank. She, Matthew Freud and Waheed [Alli] have obviously been planning to invite lots of celebs but hadn't given any thought to the media side of it. We can't afford to look as if we're planning a victory celebration in advance.

Very funny question at a news conference: 'Are Tony Blair and Gordon Brown the Lennon and McCartney of politics?' Gordon looked very awkward and said nothing, but TB came back with 'Which one's Lennon and which one's McCartney?' It seems pretty obvious to me.

Friday, 1 June 2001

No movement to the Tories on any of the polling indicators from the economy to Europe. Our overall numbers are down a little with a small rise for the Lib Dems. The

Tories seem to be adopting the Queensland strategy [used successfully by the right-wing opposition to a popular Labour government in the Australian state elections]. They're saying don't give Labour another landslide. It's the back-door strategy for power. We mustn't let them turn the last few days into a referendum on our negatives. We have to keep on with a positive offer and a positive reason for voting Labour. 'Be Part of It' – make people feel that they're not just spectators at a football match but part of the change that's taking place in Britain.

Mrs T has been talking about the dangers of landslides and an elective dictatorship – a bit rich coming from her. But every time she appears, it's good for us. It looks like she's still pulling the Tories' strings.

Hague did another very bad interview on Sky. But on *Newsround* [BBC1] he seemed to know all the answers about who was number one in the charts and Muggles in Harry Potter!

Our last few days will be about putting schools and hospitals first.

I spent longer than necessary yesterday on the *Panorama* issue. I showed Gordon a letter I wanted to write to the BBC and he said we should get our lawyers involved. So we did. Unfortunately the lawyer, Bill Bush and I all agreed we didn't have a leg to stand on legally. We decided we should just keep the pressure up and probably eventually concede an interview. Gordon then shifted his position completely and said he didn't know why we'd consulted the lawyer and we should just write a letter. Oh, well.

Saturday, 2 June 2001

Attention turning a bit to the Lib Dems. Gordon says we should attack them on the economy and not on public services. When it comes to managing the economy they can no more be trusted than the Tories. They are weak on the pound, on crime and on asylum-seekers.

Still sorting *Panorama*. Looks like John Denham [minister of state at the Department of Health] will end up doing the interview. I'm getting very tired indeed.

Sunday, 3 June 2001

We need to deal with the landslide argument, avoid apathy and get turnout up. We will be putting up posters presenting voting as a positive act. For schools and hospitals. Plus attack the Tories for cynicism: they started off saying, 'Vote for our policies', then 'Vote for some of our policies', then 'Vote for one of our policies' (save the pound), now 'Don't bother voting for our policies, just don't give Labour a landslide.' We need to show energy, hunger, that we want to earn the voters' support. So, lots of activity in the final days.

Panorama have made changes but their arguments are still full of inaccuracies. They had to back down on their central claims when Robert Hill [Policy Unit expert on health] was able to show that their sources were out of date. John Ware [*Panorama* reporter] very angry.

I've been talking to 'Horatio' and he should be making a statement to the PA later to say he'll be voting Labour. He's very pro-euro so we've been trying to pull him back a bit from saying too much. He must say he's only in favour if the economic conditions are right, etc. And it mustn't look as if he's only supporting us because of the euro. It must be about the sound management of the economy and public services.

Monday, 4 June 2001

Latest MORI poll suggests turnout will be 55 per cent. A real worry. How do we get it up? What will bring people out to vote? Schools and hospitals first. Never go back to Thatcherism. Labour is out earning every vote.

One–nil to us on *Panorama*. Denham was brilliant and the papers said the programme had to back down. TB on the defensive on *Newsnight* over the Health Service. Doctors and nurses are saying we promised we would rebuild the NHS in five years. But he points out that we never said it could be done overnight and that we will reach the European average for health spending by 2006/7. He was also attacked on the gap between rich and poor. He said it wasn't really the issue and was accused of not answering the question. 'I'm answering it my way,' he said. Also national insurance and Keith Vaz.

Tuesday, 5 June 2001

The Lib Dem surge seems to be running out of steam. But they are still doing well. The Tories, on the other hand, look totally incoherent. They have no clear message. Their frontbenchers are in complete confusion over what it is they are trying to say. So we must get back to the Choice. It's between Labour and the Tories. There's no point in any more sophisticated messages in the last two days of the campaign. Vote Labour for schools and hospitals. Vote Conservative for £20 billion cuts in public services.

Wednesday, 6 June 2005

Our lead is 21 per cent in the unadjusted figures. Labour 44 per cent, Tories 23 per cent, Lib Dems 16 per cent. On the worst-case adjusted figures, assuming the lowest turnout model, we are 46/29/19. The Tories are going through the floor. We have a twenty-point lead on 'Is Britain going in the right/wrong direction?' In the focus groups we're holding well among working-class women in particular. The energy of our campaign is paying off and we've managed to rekindle the fear of the Tories winning. People loathe Hague and they remember that the Tories are traditionally very good at winning elections. We've been having lots of phone conferences because our team is dispersed all over the country. Lots of calls to mobiles breaking up as people go in and out of tunnels, etc. A lot of confidence. Philip Gould exultant, saying everything he had advised us to do was working, Wiggy was breaking through, etc.

Thursday, 7 June 2001

Polling day. Nothing left to be done in London. I went to Brighton and Hove to canvas in the marginals. Everybody reporting things looking good. Beautiful sunny day and I fell asleep on the beach over lunch. Back to Millbank in the evening feeling, and looking, sunburnt.

Monday, 11 June 2001

Well, it's all over and it feels very strange. I've been feeling a real mix of emotions all weekend. Some pride in what we've achieved – a majority of 167 – some depression or at least deflation that suddenly I'm no longer a part of it. Real excitement about going out to France and getting on with the next stage in my life and some apprehension about how I'm going to make a living. I've been in Brighton over a very sunny weekend being a normal human being again: on the beach, eating and drinking and seeing friends.

Thursday night/Friday morning was strange. Working all night so I couldn't enjoy the party. Gordon shook my hand and said congratulations. I had to throw two people out for having sex in TB's office at two in the morning. I'd gone in there looking for cream for my sunburn and found the door locked. Unfortunately for them it had a window in it.

Epilogue

Labour won the election with a majority of 167, down twelve on four years previously. The swing to the Tories was tiny, just 1.8 per cent, and they made a net gain of only one seat. Labour lost six and the Liberal Democrats gained the same number. It was almost as if the election had never happened. William Hague promptly resigned, soon to be replaced by the hapless Iain Duncan-Smith who was later deposed by his own MPs in favour of Michael Howard.

The electorate had told Tony Blair and his team to get on with the job.

As I boarded a flight for France the Prime Minister was reshuffling his government. Gordon Brown and John Prescott were confirmed in their jobs, although the latter moved to the Cabinet Office and lost responsibility for the Environment and Transport. Robin Cook was demoted to leader of the House of Commons, only to resign later over the Iraq war. Jack Straw took his place as foreign secretary and, as expected, David Blunkett took over the Home Office. Nick Brown left the cabinet but stayed in government for a while longer. Chris Smith was sacked and Peter Mandelson remained on the backbenches running an ultimately successful campaign to be made a European commissioner. Douglas Alexander became a minister of state at the Department of Trade and Industry.

During Tony Blair's second term many of the seeds planted in the years covered by these diaries flourished while others withered and died. Investment in health, education and transport was maintained and the results slowly began to show. The peace in Northern Ireland held but a lasting devolved administration there proved elusive. The Parliament in Scotland and the Assembly in Wales prospered and grew in confidence. The Tories, who had opposed their creation, came round to supporting them. Blair's feud with Rhodri Morgan was forgotten and, in a remarkable turnaround, Ken Livingstone was readmitted to the Labour Party and won a second term as Mayor of London as the official Labour candidate.

There was little or no more talk about proportional representation. House of Lords reform staggered on slowly without Tony Blair conceding elections to the upper house. By the general election of 2005 Britain was no closer to joining the euro than it had been in 2001, and arguably further away than in 1997. The hunting of foxes by hounds was finally outlawed.

Tony Blair announced that the general election of 2005 would be his last as leader of the Labour Party. His reputation had taken a severe knock as a result of the events surrounding his decision to take Britain to war with Iraq in March 2003. In the general election held on 5 May 2005, Labour secured an overall Commons majority of 66.

Acknowledgements

Getting these diaries to the point of publication has not been a straightforward process. The attitude of the Cabinet Office, jealous guardians of the right to publish by any former employee of the government, meant that many people have had to put in a great deal of time and effort surmounting, or finding ways round, the hurdles that were put in our path.

First things first, however. There could have been no diaries but for the opportunity offered to me back in 1998 to observe the Labour government at first hand and from a very privileged position. I will always be grateful to Tony Blair for employing me as one of his special advisers. His good-humour, tolerance and humanity made the three years I spent on his staff not just an unforgettable experience but a thoroughly enjoyable one too. Alastair Campbell, with whom I worked most closely, gets a raw deal from the media. The tougher side of his nature is well documented, but I have yet to meet anybody who has known the man and not liked and admired him. He was a terrific boss and colleague, and his observation that 'life is on the record' gave me some unintended encouragement in putting these diaries into the public domain.

While typing up the manuscript I couldn't help but notice how many of the nicest people I met in politics, and those whom I respected most, feature so rarely, if at all. The reason is obvious. They got on with their jobs diligently, competently and without dramas or histrionics. It would be invidious to name them, and indeed there are too many, but I hope they know who they are and will accept that the absence of their names from the index is a tribute to their talents and not the reverse.

Rebecca Goff, Alison Blackshaw and Mark Bennett deserve special mention. They offered far more than secretarial support in Downing Street and at Millbank. Their wise counsel kept me from making more mistakes than I did and helped protect me from the consequences of those I blundered into.

For obvious reasons I was not able to show the full text of these diaries to anybody outside my publishers during the production process. Fortunately, however, I did get invaluable help from people who were willing to offer their thoughts without the benefit of having read the manuscript. Some must remain anonymous, but I would like to offer particular thanks to Richard Ayre, Anthony Seldon, Matthew Parris and Julian Glover.

Broo Doherty at Wade & Doherty is a first-class literary agent. If she was ever shocked by the murkier worlds of politics and spin doctoring into which I dragged her she never showed it. Her great confidence in the diaries – she was never once put off by any of the setbacks along the way – was a great encouragement.

I had the good fortune to work with a highly professional team of publishers and advisers through Hodder & Stoughton; Hugo Wilkinson, Briar Silich, Fiona McMorrow, Sarah Byrt, Joanne Cash, Hazel Orme and the entire production department deserve heartfelt thanks. My editor, Rupert Lancaster, guided this book to the point of publication with skill, quiet determination and a gift for tactical ingenuity that suggests he could have been equally successful in politics. And yet his insistence on playing straight with all concerned at every stage probably indicates the opposite.

The diary appears here very much as it was written

between 1998 and 2001. The mistakes in it are all mine, both in terms of fact and judgement. As most of the writing was done several years ago, I don't need to make the ritual apology to my partner for putting up with a temperamental author. However, James had to deal with a great deal more when I was a full-time spin doctor and part-time diarist. He tolerated my long absences, irritability and unreliability with extraordinary patience and was a tremendous support throughout my three years in active politics. Without him it would have been much, much harder to keep going.

Index

Adams, Gerry 33
Admiral Duncan, The 102
Adonis, Andrew 28,103
Advisory Committee on the
  Rural Environment 77
AEEU (Amalgamated
  Engineering and Electrical
  Union) 249, 316
Afghanistan 28, 29, 194
age of consent, gay 12, 189
Aherne, Bertie 27, 179
AIDS 172, 214, 273
Alagiah, George and wife,
  Frances 24
Alexander, Douglas 69, 84, 137,
  156, 177, 193, 233, 240,
  258–9, 260, 261, 263, 265,
  267, 271, 293, 296, 297, 301,
  307–8, 311–12, 317, 320, 325,
  329, 333, 339, 347, 356, 365
Alexander Douglas (father) 263
Allan, Tim 8
Alli, Waheed, Lord 33, 154, 359
American Airlines 23
ANC (African National
  Congress) 69
Ancram, Michael 181
Andrew, Prince 26
Annual Report (1999) 129,
  (2000) 235
Any Questions (BBC) 336

Arbuthnott, James 165
Archer, Jeffrey, Lord 100, 133,
  163
Argentina 38
Armstrong, Hilary 164
Ashcroft, Michael, Lord 116, 209
Ashdown, Paddy 3, 28–9, 34, 36,
  40, 43, 44, 50, 52–3, 55, 346
Ask The Prime Minister (ITV)
  277
asylum-seekers 192, 194, 204,
  211, 212, 213, 214, 252, 256,
  295, 315, 326, 327, 328, 330,
  331, 332, 338, 344, 346, 353,
  361
Attlee Government 1945–51 198
Austin, Ian 206, 210–11, 222,
  249, 251, 254–5, 257, 258,
  273, 290, 304, 340
Ayling, Bob 23
Ayre, Richard 5 and partner,
  Guy 24

BA (British Airways) 23
Bailey, Ric 5
Baldwin, Tom 59, 79, 80, 290,
  319
Balls, Ed 63, 148, 188, 288
Bank of England 2, 24, 118, 161
Banks, Tony 56, 130, 132, 174
Barnett Formula 193

Bassam, Steve, Lord 321
Bassett, Phil 107, 127, 195, 329, 350
Bates, Steve 247, 251, 350, 356
BBC (British Broadcasting Corporation) xii, xiii, 1, 2, 5, 6, 9, 16–17, 20, 21, 24, 34, 43, 45–6, 50, 51, 52, 58, 63, 66, 67, 78, 82, 89, 90, 92–3, 94–5, 97–8, 101, 102, 112, 115, 128, 174, 181, 201, 203, 210–11, 212, 231, 246, 277, 286–7, 296, 305, 310, 313, 319–20, 328, 336, 345, 350, 356, 357, 358–9, 360
Beckett, Margaret 2, 11, 21, 38, 40, 90, 124, 147, 202, 309, 331, 333, 352–3, 354
beef, ban on British 175, 176
Bell, Martin 280, 296, 297
Beloff, Michael, Lord 78
Benn, Tony 89, 201, 295
Bennett, Mark 91, 354
Bercow, John 243
Berlin centre-left conference (2000) 275
Bermingham, Gerry 333
Bevins, Tony 67, 71, 180
BFI (British Film Institute) 319
Bickerstaffe, Rodney 252, 257
Billy Elliot 319
Birt, John 43, 82
Black, Eban 278
Blackadder 148
Blair, Cherie 30, 32, 99, 126, 128, 131, 164, 165, 166, 168, 179, 184, 243–4, 277, 279, 304, pregnancy 161, 163, 184, 221, 223
Blair, Euan 234

Blair, Leo (son) 223, 277
Blair, Tony and Africa 329 Annual Report (1999) 129, (2000) 235, asylum seekers 204, 326, 332, 344, Beaconsfield by-election (1982) 169, Cherie Blair 32, pregnancy 161, David Blunkett 45, Britain in Europe 160, Britishness 208, Gordon Brown xi, 3–4, 18, 21, 37, 84, 93, 115–6, 122, 124, 129, 139, 144, 146–7, 152, 185, 190, 242, 251, 261, 263, 308, 322, 329, 335, 339, 350–1, 359, Nick Brown 46–50, Budget (1999) 92, (2000) 208, George W. Bush 304, cabinet meetings 156, 218, Alastair Campbell 12–13, 32, 82–3, 151–2, 155, 194–5, 229, 236, 281, 284, 288, 292, 301–2, 304, 314, 349, CBI (2000) 222, Christmas card (2000) 277, 279, Bill Clinton 99–100, 105, Michael Cockerell documentary 236, Conservative Party 123, 160–1, 196, 214, 258, 266, 284–5, 335, Robin Cook 13, 28, 92, 130, 183–4, 188, 229, 327, crime 76, 284, Daily Mail 223, Ron Davies resignation 40–4, Donald Dewar, 82, 105, 193, Ecclestone Affair 253, education 76, 88, 284, 302, Employment Spokesman x, European Council meetings, Berlin (1999) 89–91, Brussels (1999) 96, Cologne (1999)

114–5, Feira (2000) 273, Helsinki (1999) 209, Lisbon (2000) 232, Nice (2000) 276–7, Pörtschach (1998) 39, Stockholm (2001) 316, Tampere (1999) 152, European Parliament election results (1999) 122, foot-and-mouth disease 328, 'forces of conservatism' 148, fox-hunting 185, 229, 286, 288, 358, fuel protests 250–2, general election (1997) 87–8, general election (2001) 141, 209, 282, 285, 289–90, 308–9, 314, 316, 323–6, 330–6, 342, 349–55, 365, general election date (2001) 217, 279, 305, 315–18, GM food 77, 114, 117, 199, William Hague 161, 224, 276, 279, 286, 326, Peter Hain 235, Hamilton and Wigan by-elections 135–6, hit by tomato in Bristol 283, holidays (1998) 22, 25–28, (1999) 68, 131–3, 135, holiday (2000) 243, homosexuality 41, 48, 102, Anji Hunter 7, 329, interviews on media 56, 72, 93, 97, 100, 101, 115, 126, 141, 184, 277, 282, 336, 352, 358, 362, Iraq 62, Charles Kennedy 314–5, Kosovo 88–9, 92, 95, 98, 105–11, Labour Party 112, 130, 198, Labour Party conference (1998) 31–2, (1999) 143, 147, (2000) 247, 251–3, 255–7, Labour Party donors 281–2, Labour Party spring conference (2001) 302–4,

leader of the opposition 153, leadership style 54, 142–3, 154–5, 237, 326, 355, Leo Blair (son) 223–4, 226, 234, Liberal Democrats 52–3, 74, Ken Livingstone 52, 78, 100, 155, 366, local government elections (2000) 215–6, London mayoral elections 155, 158–9, 162, 187–8, 197–8, 200–2, 205, 212–3, 216–7, 229, Longbridge MG-Rover 88, John Major 16, Nelson Mandela 247, 273, Peter Mandelson 37, 62–7, 77, 96, 100, 120, 124, 152, 263, 292, 298–301, 306, 'Maoist' 157, Tony Martin case 214, Ivan Massow 239–40, 242, media strategy 82–3, 188, 194–5, 210, Millennium Dome 81, 87, 176, Slobodan Milosevic 99, Rhodri Morgan 45, 52, 105, 191–2, 366, 'most dangerous man in Britain' 13, Mo Mowlam 146, 187, 205, 218, 271, Rupert Murdoch 95, 119, 270, nanny 200, NHS 76, 115, 185, 207, 362, Northern Ireland 37, 101, 120, 197, 288–9, Number Ten re-organisation 79, 88, 217, 221, office used for sex 364, Parliamentary Labour Party 320–1, 334, party election broadcast 353–4, political strategy 125–6, 183, 189–90, 221, 266, 295–6, Michael Portillo 286, John Prescott 39, 52–3, 76, 125–6, 155, 250,

Blair, Tony – *cont.*
256, Prescott Punch 343,
Lance Price ix–x, xix–xi,
10–11, 13–14, 17, 32, 75,
94–5, 106, 119, 152, 220,
223–4, James Proctor 128,
proportional representation
38–40, 43–4, 104, 106, 116,
reading glasses 143, religion
25–6, 158, Scottish politics 35,
81–2, 84–5, 101–2, 104–6,
108–9, 135–6, 193, 260, 296,
second term as Prime Minister
323, 365–6, Section 28 194,
sex education guidelines
189–91, single currency 56,
73–4, 79, 100–1, 114, 116,
122–3, 152, 157–8, 176–7,
229–30, 240, 261, 271, 298–9,
357, 'Son of Satan' 316, to
stand down xiv, 366, Sharron
Storer 342, *The Sun* 26, 86,
223, 304, Thatcherism 349,
Third Way 99, 163, travels on
Tube 155, TV debates during
general election 287, visits:
Albania 110, Birmingham
341–2, Bristol 283–4, Bulgaria
110, China 35, Davos 188,
Florence 161, 163,
Gloucestershire 305, Hull 155,
250, Manchester 74, Northern
Ireland 26–7, 29, 55, 92,
120–1, 197, St. Albans 270, St.
Petersburg 200–1, Scotland
71–3, 81–2, 93–5, 101–2, 200,
263, 306, 351, Sedgefield 47,
Slough 215, South-West
England 188, 190, United
States 30–1, 98–100, 304,
Wales 9, 101–2, 305, web-cast
194, Welsh politics 42, 44–5,
105, 191–2, Westlife 298,
301–3, WI speech 226–8, Ann
Widdecombe 123, 256,
Woodward 164, 167–71,
174–5, 177, 179–82, 333
Blank, Victor 264
Blues Brothers, The 50
Blumenthal, Sidney 168, 170
Blunkett, David 2, 45, 89, 105,
117, 126, 130, 133, 156, 162,
188, 189–90, 191, 192, 205–6,
209, 215, 218, 225, 271,
301–2, 344, 365
BMA (British Medical
Association) 150
BNP (British National Party) 86,
296
Boateng, Paul 75, 80
BOC (British Oxygen) 23
'bog-standard comprehensives'
302
Bolland, Mark 54
Boothroyd, Betty 1
Borthwick, Moray 180
Boulton, Adam 67, 342–3
Bowen, Adam 284
Bowie, David 38
Boycott, Rosie 71
Bradshaw, Ben 12, 145, 242, 282,
299, and partner, Neal 24
Bradshaw, David 226
Breakfast (BBC) 128
Breakfast With Frost (BBC) 50,
146–7, 159, 181, 183, 184,
185, 266, 282–3, 286
Bremner, Rory 100, 223, 236
Bridget Jones' Diary 319
Bristol Royal Infirmary 4

Britain in Europe 122–3, 152, 160, 270–1, 352
British Council 52
Brown, Gordon appointed Chancellor 1, Tony Blair xi, 3, 18, 21, 36, 85, 93, 115, 122, 135, 139, 146, 147, 152, 185, 186, 189–190, 242, 251, 261, 263, 304, 312, 329, 335, 350–351, 359, Britishness 190, 208, Nick Brown 50, Budget (1999) 84, 85, (2000) 202, 208, cabinet pay 92, cabinet photo (2001) 285, Alastair Campbell xi, 4, 21, 60, 146, 273, Christmas card (2000) 279, Conservative Party policies 263, 295–6, 299, Robin Cook 143, 148, 188, 270, 327, 346, Donald Dewar 90, 93, 104, 263, Economic Policy Commission 254–5, Europe 56, 350–351, European Council Lisbon (2000) 208, fuel protests 250, general election campaign 141, 194, 209, 260, 285, 290, 312, 325, 330–332, 345, 347–8, 350–351, 353, 355, 357, 360, chairs general election strategy committee 156, 172, 175, 177, 240, 283, 308, 333, health spending 185, 195, 196, 204, 206, 212, Labour Party conference (2000) 257, Labour Party spring conference (2001) 303–304, Ken Livingstone 162, Peter Mandelson 6–7, 36, 62, 66, 85, 124, 177, 237, 261, 268, 276, marriage to Sarah Macaulay 96, 242, 253, media leaks 273, media strategy 212, 257, Millbank 248, National Minimum Wage 11, north-south divide 173, political strategy 104, 122, 152, 196, 215, 260, 273–274, 290, 299, possible leader of the Labour Party 146–147, 210, 321, 329, 356, Pre-Budget report (1999) 160, Prescott punch 342, Lance Price 93, 153, 220, 279, 308, 364, 'psychological flaws' 3, 144, Andrew Rawnsley book 3, 144, 251–253, re-appointed as Chancellor 365, reshuffle (July 1998), 21, *Richard and Judy* 139, Geoffrey Robinson 258, 263, Scottish party election broadcasts 301, Scottish politics 15–16, 53, 69–70, 85, 90–93, 101–102, 109, 268, single currency 45, 122, 203, 222, 230, 270–272, 356, 357, Third World debt 115, Working Families Tax Credit 139
Brown, Michael 107
Brown, Nick 21, 22, 41, 46–52, 58, 142, 285, 305, 319, 365
Brown, Paul 229
Brunson, Michael 65, 201
BSE 77, 175
BT (British Telecom) 354
Budget (1999) 81, 83, 84, 85, 92, (2000) 202–3, 204, 206–7, 208, 212, (2001) 307
Bulger, Jamie 214
Burns Inquiry 229

Bush, Bill 34, 59, 73, 82, 83, 95,
    105, 118, 126, 189, 193, 200,
    248, 340, 360
Bush, George W. 267, 269, 276,
    277, 304, 332
Business for Sterling 249
Butler, David 277
Butler, Sir Robin 264
by-elections, Anniesland 272,
    Ayr (Scottish Parliament) 206,
    Beaconsfield 169, Eddisbury
    111–12, 126, 128, Falkirk
    (Scottish Parliament) 268,
    Hamilton 132, 135, 136–7,
    144, N.E. Scotland (European)
    55, Newark 88, Preston 272,
    Romsey 217, West Bromwich
    272, Wigan 135–6
Byers, Stephen 21, 22, 23–4, 45,
    50, 66, 95, 190, 210, 212, 221,
    229, 250, 252, 271, 279, 294,
    295, 312, 331, 358

Cabinet photo (2001) 285
Call My Bluff 101
Callaghan, Jim, Lord 22, 198
Campbell, Alastair Douglas
    Alexander 258, 271, BBC
    coverage of Kosovo 92–3, 97,
    biography of 137–8, 145,
    Tony Blair 12–13, 32, 83, 146,
    151–2, 155, 194–5, 224, 229,
    236, 281, 284, 288, 292, 302,
    304, 314, 349, Cherie Blair's
    pregnancy 161, David Blunkett
    191, 301–2, 'bog-standard
    comprehensives' 301–2, Nick
    Brown 47–50, 52, Gordon
    Brown xi, 21, 60, 146, 190,
    273, George W. Bush 304,
    Stephen Byers 252, cabinet
    meetings 218, Hilary Clinton
    108, Bill Clinton 163, Robin
    Cook 98, Michael Cockerell
    documentary 236,
    Conservative Party 280, as
    Daily Mirror journalist 344,
    Jill Dando murder
    investigation 176, Ron Davies
    resignation 40–43, Eritrea
    150–51, European Councils
    Cardiff (1998) 9, Feira (2000)
    232, Nice (2000) 274, 278,
    278, Elizabeth Filkin 280,
    choice of election day 318,
    'forces of conservatism' 160,
    foreign policy 89, fox-hunting
    288, fuel protests 268, funding
    for Tony Blair's office 153,
    general election (2001)
    campaign songs 289, date 313,
    318, manifesto 310, planning
    298, speech on Europe 251,
    strategy 259, 312–13, 329,
    337, 348, 351, 'Wiggy' poster
    351, 353, William Hague 74,
    259, Hammond Report 305–6,
    holidays (1998) 75, (1999) 131,
    133, 137, homosexuality 239,
    242, honours list 37, House of
    Lords reform 56, Iraq 63,
    Kosovo 111, Labour Party
    conference (1999) 148, 150,
    (2000) 252, Labour Party
    donors 153, 281, 'life is on the
    record' 141, lobby briefings
    201, 211, 214, 217, 228–9,
    230, 272, 357, London
    mayoral race 186–7, 197, John
    Major 320, Peter Mandelson

6, 21, 60, 63–7, 96, 222, 237, 298, 305–6, Ivan Massow 239–42, media strategy 17, 32, 38, 56, 72, 82–3, 100, 122, 130, 160, 172, 180, 188, 194–5, 199, 236, 259, 265–6, 312, 329, 341, Alan Milburn 252, Millbank 220, 227, 230, 330, Millennium Dome 81, Mo Mowlam 27, 159, 336, Rupert Murdoch 199, NATO 97, 100, Northern Ireland 27, 37, 213, Number Ten re-organisation 210, 217–8, 221, Number Ten press office 70, 153, 195, 200, Oratory School 144, political strategy 35, 124, 190, 202, 221, 229, Michael Portillo 140, post-election plans 329, John Prescott 177, 302, Prescott punch 344, Lance Price ix, x, xix, 4–8, 14, 52, 82, 85, 86, 93, 95, 103, 111, 112, 184, 220, 259, 320, 329, Public Administration Committee 12, Andrew Rawnsley book 255, Geoffrey Robinson 154, 263, sex education guidelines 191, single currency 56, 276, Britney Spears 271, 341, Laura Spence 224, The Sun 37, 86, tax burden 204, tomato throwing in Bristol 284, TV debates during general election 288, Charlie Whelan 53, 68, WI speech 227, Shaun Woodward 165, 166, 169–70, 175, 177, 180, 184
Campbell, Menzies 135, 201

Campbell, Naomi 38
Campbell, Nicky 20, 128, 160
Canavan, Dennis 268, 272
Canterbury, Archbishop of 87, 350
Carey, George 87'
Cash for Wigs' 302, 304
Cashman, Michael 145
Castle, Barbara 22
CBI (Confederation of British Industry) 45, 222, 355
CBS Television 97
Central TV 341
Chandos, Tom 167
Channel 4 187, 241, 349–50
Channel 4 News 12, 26, 78, 241, 254
Charles, Prince and Camilla 57
Chicago Economic Club 99'
chicken tikka masala' speech 324, 327
Child Support Agency (CSA) 16
ChildLine 195
Chirac, Jacques 278
Churchill, Winston 216
Clare, Bill 141
Clark, Alan 14, 59, 140, 141, 264, 280
Clark, David 21
Clark, Wesley, General 98
Clarke, Ken 102, 122–3, 290, 322, 352
Clary, Julian 243
Clelland, David 43
Clifford, Max 161
Clinton, Bill 4, 26, 28, 29, 30–1, 69, 87, 98, 99–100, 103, 105, 109, 110, 139, 145, 163, 267, 270, 277
Clinton, Chelsea 163

Clinton, Hillary 99, 108, 109, 163

CND (Campaign for Nuclear Disarmament) 207

CNN (Cable News Network) 111, 269

Cockerell, Michael 203, 204, 211, 214, 236

Coffman, Hilary 41, 42, 351

Cohen, Bill 99, 109

Commission for Racial Equality 323–4

Committee on Standards in Public Life 11, 264

Commonwealth 172

Comprehensive Spending Review (1998) 15, 20, (2000) 185, 206–7, 234, 237, 238

Conference Arrangements Committee 252

Conservative Central Office 248, 339, 341, 346, 359

Conservative Party conference (1999) 151, (2000) 258–9, donors 2, 116, 289, 329, economic record 3, general election manifesto 246, 329–30, 333, 334–5, 338, general election results (1997) 1, 4, general election strategy 313, 331–2, 343, 346, 355, 359–60, 361, 362, leadership speculation 14, 133–4, 140, 166, 168, 248, 324–5, 327, 332, 340–1, manifesto 329–30, on Lance Price's appointment 7, 9, policies 54–5, 76, 107, 125, 135, 160–1, 164, 165, 192, 207, 214, 275–6, 232, 247, 275–6, 295, race row

323–4, 327–8, tax and spending plans 234–5, 237, 258, 263, 287–8, 295, 299, 307, 308, 309–10, 330, 334–5, 340, 350, 357, 358

Cook, Gaynor 98

Cook, Robin xii, 1, 4, 11, 13, 28, 29, 39, 62, 92, 98, 106, 130, 132, 135, 190, 201, 208, 271, 324, 327, 346, 349, 352, 354, 356, 365, and the single currency 143–4, 148, 183–4, 188, 229, 230, 270, and Gordon Brown 143–4, 148, 183–4, 188

Cooper, Yvette 191, 309

Cordon, Gavin 254

Coronation Street 33, 49

Cranborne, Robert, Lord 56–7, 58–9

Craven, Mike 54, 110, 312

Crimewatch (BBC) 176

Cunningham, Jack 21–2, 75, 146, 151

d'Alema, Massimo 99

da Silva, Reinaldo 43, 54, 57, 61, 69, 238, 299

Dagenham, Ford 219

Dáil, Irish Parliament 27

Daily Express 32, 43, 52, 67, 71, 80, 90, 145, 180, 265, 337

Daily Mail 9, 51, 52, 60, 80, 100, 134, 138, 140, 206, 214, 223–4, 246, 253, 274, 276, 289, 293, 297, 299, 300–1, 312, 348

Daily Mirror 77, 161, 181, 185–6, 199, 205, 226, 244, 259, 264, 266, 312, 318

Daily Record 81–2, 87
Daily Telegraph 25, 44, 46, 80,
　116, 154, 190, 203–4, 206,
　242, 266, 271, 276, 281, 299,
　300–1, 320, 327, 331, 347, 358
Daldry, Stephen 219
Dalgleish, Neal 234
Damazer, Mark 231
Dando, Jill 176
Darling, Alistair 22, 126, 139,
　207, 215, 230, 275, 290, 307,
　308, 330, 332, 333, 340
Davidson, Lorraine 15, 20
Davies, Ron 35, 40–2, 43–4, 45,
　46, 47, 51, 58, 105
Davos Economic Forum 2000 188
Dawn, Liz 33
Defence Review (1998) 11
Delta House 137'
demon eyes' poster 312
Denham, John 66, 361, 362
Dewar, Donald 15, 16, 53, 69,
　72, 82, 83, 84, 85, 86–7, 90,
　91, 93, 104, 105, 121, 137, 145,
　176, 179, 193, 206, 260, 261,
　263, 268
Diana, Princess of Wales 4, 13
Dickson, Niall 86
Dilkes, Phil 179
Dilnot, Andrew 11
Dimbleby (ITV) 336, 358
Dimbleby, David 93
Dobson, Frank 2, 126, 129, 130,
　151, campaign for Labour
　nomination as London mayor
　153, 155, 158, 159, 162, 184,
　186–8, 196, 197, campaign for
　mayor of London 197, 198,
　200, 201–2, 205, 212, 213,
　215, 216

Dobson, Janet 187
Donnelly, Alan 71
Douglas, Michael 207
Dowle, Martin and partner
　Fabricio 52, 53–4, 55
Doyle, Matthew 235, 236–7,
　251, 329
Draper, Derek 17–20, 26
Duncan, Alan 7, 14, 280
Duncan-Smith, Iain 365
Dylan, Bob 350

Eagle, Angela 205
EastEnders (BBC) 186, 312
Ecclestone, Bernie 2, 253'
Economic Disaster II' campaign
　307–8, 311, 322
Economist, The 282, 285, 289
Edge, Simon 6
Edmonds, John 121, 252, 257
El Pais 274
Election Call (BBC) 345
Electoral Commission 310–11
English Nature 77
ethical foreign policy 13
euro see single currency
Europe policy 45, 348, 349, 351,
　352, 353
European Commission 86, 111,
　113, 298, 316
European Constitution 123
European Convention on
　Human Rights (ECHR) 344
European Councils Berlin (1999)
　89, 90–1, Brussels (1999) 96,
　Cardiff (1998) 9, Feira (2000)
　232, Lisbon (2000) 208, Nicc
　(2000) 274, 276, 277, Tampere
　(1999) 152, Cologne (1999)
　114–15, Vienna (1998) 61

European Court of Human Rights 145, 147, 148–9, 243
European Movement 114
European Parliament 54, 71, 179, 272, election campaign (1999) 114, 123, election results (1999) 122, 119–20, 122
European rapid-reaction force 274
Evans, Alun 153, 172, 195
Evening Standard 6, 59, 65, 71, 75, 100, 128, 202, 212, 215, 259, 288, 341'
Excalibur' 59

Fabricant, Michael 304
Face the Nation (CBS Television) 97
Face, The 186
Falconer, Charlie, Lord 60, 63, 73, 87, 107, 109, 113, 114, 123, 127, 129, 133, 171, 196, 217, 229, 244, 262, 293, 300, 301, 342, 359
Fatchett, Derek 107, 108
Faulks, Sebastian 38
FBI (Federal Bureau of Investigation) 30
Ferguson, Sarah, 'Fergie' 26
Field, Frank 21, 22
Filkin, Elizabeth 280, 312
Financial Times 271, 338
Flamingo's Club, Blackpool 34, 40
Flather, Shreela, Lady 328
focus groups 71, 81, 85–6, 87, 120, 138, 195, 288, 322, 338, 343, 346, 352, 363
Foot, Michael 169, 198
foot-and-mouth disease (FMD)

305, 309, 314, 315, 316, 318, 319, 320–1, 325, 328
Football Association (FA) 53'
forces of conservatism' 148, 152, 156, 157, 160, 225, 227
Foulkes, George 293
Fox, Liam 141
fox-hunting 125, 126, 160, 185, 228, 229, 242, 249, 288, 317, 358, 366
Freedland, Jonathan 241
Freud, Matthew 337, 359
fuel protests 249–50, 252–3, 256, 268, 284

G8 106, 122
Gambaccini, Paul 6, 91, 175, 178
Gavron, Nicky 219
gays in the military 136, 145, 148–50
general elections (1970) 332, 333, (1997) x, 1, 288, 324, 325, 331, 332, 335, 348, (2001) xiii, xx, campaign 333–64, date 175, 278, 296, 305, 309, 313, 315–18, 321–2, 323, 327, 334, Labour manifesto 282, 321, 323, 325–6, 329, 335–6, 337, 338, 341, 348, 349, 355, polling day 328, protestors 342–3, 345, result 362–3, songs 247, 289, strategy 193–4, TV debates 286–9, 328, 330, 334, 358–61
General Election Planning Group 174–5, 227, 284, 286, 292, 293
genetically modified (GM) crops 75–6, 78, 223
genetically modified (GM) food

75–6, 77–8, 113, 114, 117, 118, 199
Gilbert's Disease 262
Gilligan, Andrew 356
GMB (formerly General, Municipal and Boilermakers Union) 121, 222, 252
GMTV 128, 336, 345
Godfrey, Jim 235, 236, 238, 251, 311, 337
Gods and Monsters 91
Goff, Rebecca 232, 302, 368
Good Friday Agreement 3, 208
Goodlad, Sir Alastair 111, 126
Gore, Al 267, 269, 276, 283, 334
Gould, Philip 36, 37, 70, 71, 76–7, 81, 85–6, 87, 89, 101–2, 116, 120, 124, 128, 133, 138, 152–3, 157, 160, 195, 202, 209, 228, 232, 233, 237, 278, 288, 291, 301, 318, 324, 335, 363
Government Information Service 12
GQ 243
Grassroots Alliance 26
Gray, Jim 241
Greater London Assembly (GLA) 186, 216–17, 219
Greater London Council (GLC) 162
Green Party 213
Greenberg, Stan 208, 269, 283, 324–5, 337, 348
Grice, Andy 241, 273, 348
Grocott, Bruce 351
Guardian 8, 55, 62, 71, 80, 159, 186, 197, 203, 228, 241, 244, 245, 254, 280, 299, 335, 344, 348, 349, 350, 357

Gummer, John 77
Guthrie, Sir Charles 150

Hague, Ffion 133, 333
Hague, William 4, 14, 17, 18, 37, 58–9, 65, 73, 84, 89, 92, 102, 104, 111, 112, 114, 120, 126, 128, 132, 133–4, 135, 140, 161, 169, 172, 178, 180, 189, 209, 213, 214–15, 224, 227, 235, 239, 243, 248, 256, 259, 270, 272, 274, 275, 276, 278, 279, 284–5, 286, 287, 290, 295, 296, 298, 307, 309, 311, 312, 313, 314, 319, 321, 322, 324–5, 326, 327, 328, 333, 335, 336, 340, 341, 343, 344, 346, 350, 351, 352, 355–6, 357–8, 360, 363, 365
Hain, Peter 235, 245–6
Hall, Phil 11, 48–9, 54
Hall, Tony 231
Halliwell, Geri 337
Hamlyn, Paul, Lord 281
Hammond Report 291, 298, 300–1, 305–6
Hammond, Sir Anthony 291
Hansard 10
Hare, David 38
Harman, Harriet 2, 12, 16, 21
Harry Potter 360
Harvard University 169
Hashimoto, Ryuatro 38
Hastilow, Nigel 284
Hastings, Max 100
Hayes, Peter 341
Hellawell, Keith 147, 196, 200, 205, 209
Henderson, Doug 130
Herald 136

Heseltine, Michael 122–3, 263
Hewitt, Patricia 331, 340, 355, 357
Hill, David 81, 312, 345, 348, 350
Hill, Robert 150, 361
Hinduja brothers 291–2, 293
Hinduja, S.P. 291
Hitchens, Peter 8
Hitler, Adolf 78
Hoddle, Glen 72, 73
Hoey, Kate 131–2, 310
Hollis, Patricia, Lady 16
Holmes, Richard 36
Holmes, Sherlock 341
homosexuality 12, 44, 47, 51, 54, 96–7, 102, 140, 145, 148–50, 189, 164, 192, 205–6, 239, 242
honours list 8, 37
Honours Scrutiny Committee 116, 209
Hoon, Geoff 66, 107, 109, 151, 199, 223, 271
House of Lords reform 22, 31, 35–6, 56–7, 103, 160, 323, 366
Howard, Michael 14, 107, 297, 365
Howarth, Alan 180
Hughes, David 134
Hughes, Simon 164, 353
Humphrys, John 38, 92, 336
Hunter, Anji 7–8, 21, 52, 57, 70, 84–5, 89, 94, 101, 106, 107, 128, 131, 137, 145–6, 154, 176, 187, 200, 225, 226, 227, 239, 240, 242, 244, 255, 258, 270, 297, 305, 309, 329, 352
Hussein of Jordan, King 74
Hussein, Saddam 62

Hyman, Peter 10, 32, 57, 66, 73, 83, 87, 89, 103, 110, 121, 128, 160, 192, 202, 226, 237, 301

ICM 245, 357
IMF (International Monetary Fund) 139, 257
Independent on Sunday 190, 199, 266
Independent 6, 96, 107, 235, 241, 244, 266, 273, 338, 348, 356
Institute of Fiscal Studies (IFS) 11, 330
IPPR (Institute of Public Policy Research) 235, 251, 356
IRA (Irish Republican Army) 124, 190–1, 222, 276
Iraq 61–2, 63, 90, 301, 356, 366
Irvine, Derry, Lord 60, 90, 302, 304, 342, 351
ITN (Independent Television News) 10, 51, 65–6, 67, 93, 102, 135, 147, 201, 246, 303

Jackson, Glenda 130, 153, 161, 185, 187
Jackson, Michael 241
James, Howell 54
Jay, Margaret, Lady 21, 22, 36, 153, 205, 224, 354,
Jenkins Commission 29, 31, 35, 36, 38, 39–40, 43, 44, 56, 316
Jenkins, Roy, Lord 29, 36, 39
John, Elton 164
Johnson, Matthew 179
Johnston, Bruce 25
Joint Consultation Committee 44, 52
Jordan, Bernie 242, 244

Jordan, David 345, 354
Jospin, Lionel 11, 33, 163, 175, 355, 356, 357
Jowell, Tessa 26, 355

Kampfner, John 6
Kaufman, Gerald 188
Kavanagh, Denis 157
Kearney, Martha 341
Keen, Alan 91, 164
Keen, Ann 12, 91, 164–5, 166, 171, 177, 181, 215
Kellner, Peter 59, 128
Kemp, Fraser 108, 142, 282, 285, 339
Kemp, Ross 312
Kennedy, Charles 123, 179, 201, 314, 315
Kevill, Sian 56
Kilfoyle, Peter 142, 146, 276–7
Kinnock, Glenys 213–14
Kinnock, Neil x, 113, 121, 198, 348
Kohl, Helmut 33
Kok, Wim 99, 115
Kosminsky, Peter 274–5
Kosovo 88, 89, 92, 95, 97, 98, 101, 108–9, 111, 112, 114–15, 116, 117, 124, 145
Kramer, Susan 202
Kursk 245

Labour Party xiii, xx, centenary (2000) 198, conference (1998) 31–4, (1999) 145–50, (2000) 247–8, 251–3, 273, donors 153–4, 264–5, 281–2, 302, Economic Policy Commission 254–5, gala dinner (1998) ix, (2001) 310, general election results (1997) 1, (2001) 362–3, (2005) 366, National Executive Committee 20, 333, National Executive Committee elections (1998) 24, 26, 31–2, 33, 45, party organisation 117, 119, relations with Liberal Democrats 39–40, 50, 52–3, 104, 106, 121, 191, 294, Scotland conference (1999) 82, (2001) 306, spring conference (1999) 74, (2001) 301, Wales conference (2001) 304
landmines 13
Langdon, Julia 219
Lapping, Andrew 166
Lawrence Report 79–80
Lawrence, Stephen 79, 80, 87, 278, parents 278
Lee, John 359
Lennon, John 359
Letwin, Oliver 338, 339–40, 341, 346, 347
Levy, Michael, Lord 281
Lewinsky, Monica 4, 87, 91
Lewis, Julian 153
Liberal Democrats 31, 36, 39–40, 44, 52–3, 74, 104, 105, 106, 107, 121, 191, 202, 272, 280, 294, 296, 297, 316, 339, 347, 354, 359, 362, 365
Liddle, Helen 35, 36, 53, 70, 72, 82, 84, 104, 108, 292, 293, 303
Liddle, Roger 14, 17–19, 39, 103'
Lifted' 326
Lighthouse Family, the 326
Lilley, Peter 140
Livermore, Spencer 233, 259, 265–6, 320

Livingstone, Ken xiv, 34, 52, 54, 56, 59, 71, 75, 76, 78, 89, 100, 146, 155, 366, as mayor of London 219, campaign for Labour nomination as London mayor 158–9, 161–2, 182, 184, 185–7, 197, campaign for mayor of London 197–8, 200–2, 205, 213, 215, 216–17

Lloyd, Tony 130

lobbyists 26, 311, 312

local government elections (2000) 196, 212, 215, 216–17, 218, (2001) 305, 309, 315, 318

London Police Authority 153

Longbridge, MG-Rover 88, 210, 216

Lucas, Mark 276, 322, 354

Macaulay, Sarah 242

MacDonald, Gus, Lord 22, 176

Macintyre, Donald 97, 121, 226–7

Macpherson Report 278

MacShane, Denis 107, 238

Maguire, Kevin 348

Mail on Sunday 29, 32, 54, 55, 100, 142, 181, 200, 219, 223, 230, 238, 274, 321

Major, John 4, 15, 16, 74, 133, 195, 226, 263, 280, 320

Manchester United 95

Mandela, Nelson 247, 256, 273

Mandelson, Peter advisor to the ANC 68–9, 74, appointed Northern Ireland secretary 151, Tony Blair 36, 63–7, 77, 96, 100, 120, 124, 152, 263, 300–301, 306, Gordon Brown 6–7, 36, 60, 63, 66, 85, 177, 237, 263, 268, 276, 318, George W. Bush 276, Alastair Campbell 6, 21, 60, 63–7, 96, 222, 237, 298, Robin Cook 327, European Commissioner 298, 299, 365, general election planning 131, 141, 177, 232, 235, 237, 239–40, 249, 258, 267–8, 317, chair of General Election Planning Group 159, 174–5, 227, general election strategy 260, 337, 338, 348, Hammond Report 306, Hinduja brothers 294, Northern Ireland Secretary 185, 194, 209, 222, 226, John Prescott 8, 23, 271, Lance Price 4, 6–7, 9, 22, 23, 36–7, 154, 237–8, 261, 299–301, rehabilitation after second resignation 305–6, resignation as Northern Ireland secretary 297–301, resignation as Trade and Industry secretary 62–9, 71, 263, Geoffrey Robinson 154, 264, 276–7, sexuality 22, 41–3, 53–4, 55, 57–8, 61, 96–7, 136, 137, 264, single currency 39, 45, 222, 229, 237, 270–71, 275, Shaun Woodward 164, 170, 171

Marr, Andrew 220–1, 320, 340

Marsden, Gordon 8, 12

Martin, Tony 214

Mason, Angela 150, 164, 205

Massow, Ivan 172, 239–40, 241–2, 249, 296–7, 317

Match of the Day 350

Maude, Francis 160, 234, 277–8, 287, 352

Maxwell, Robert 344
May, Brendan 164
May, Sir Robert 77
McAleese, Mary 27
McCartney, Ian 61, 112, 130, 132, 136–7, 162, 171, 196, 209, 327, 336, 357
McCartney, Paul 359
McConnell, Jack 260, 301
McCormick, Paul 307, 347, 349
McDonagh, Margaret 32–3, 71, 117, 132, 159, 162, 182, 218, 220, 226, 227, 231, 232–3, 235, 240, 249, 264–5, 275, 281, 290, 297, 301, 311, 312, 313, 316, 317, 319, 322, 325, 337, 347, 348, 351, 353, 356, 359
McFadden, Pat 34, 94, 104, 108, 158, 200, 224, 231, 232–3, 240, 265, 301, 326, 351, 356
McGowan, Alasdair 149
McGuinness, Martin 37, 60
McKellen, Sir Ian 91
McLeish, Henry 260, 286, 293, 303, 307
McMahon, Peter 121
McMenamin, Adrian 341
McSmith, Andy 138
McTaggart, Fiona 19
McWhirter, Ian 121
Meacher, Michael 19, 78, 319
Meale, Alan 130
Media Monitoring Unit 180
media strategy 72–3, 82–3, 154–5, 157, 172–3, 266, 267–8, 313, 336
Menem, Carlos 38
Metropolitan Police 46, 79–80, 165
Meyer, Sir Christopher 87

Michael, Alun 41, 42, 44, 45, 46, 55, 71, 78, 105, 130, 191, 292
Michael, George 14
Milburn, Alan 66, 151, 205, 212, 241, 271, 279, 295, 301, 346, 358–9
Miliband, David xix, 10, 17, 32, 70, 76, 112, 113, 118, 310, 323, 336, 339
Miliband, Ed 304, 322, 340
Millar, Fiona 161, 294
Millbank xiii, 2, 16, 24, 112, 120, 121–2, 131, 137, 141, 156, 194, 220, 223–4, 226, 228, 229, 230, 231–3, 235, 237, 239, 240, 248–9, 251, 258, 265, 267, 268, 279–80, 282, 285, 290, 291, 297, 301, 302, 304, 308, 311, 313, 314, 326, 327, 330, 331, 337, 339, 342, 354, 356, 359, 363, 368
Millennium Dome xiv, 23, 81–2, 87, 118, 129, 175–6, 183, 184, 192, 256, 290–1, 341
Milosevic, Slobodan 88, 92, 95, 98, 99, 105, 111, 114, 147, 318
Mirror Group 264
Monks, John 120, 121
Monopolies and Mergers Commission 95
Morgan, Piers 161, 185, 205, 264
Morgan, Rhodri 41, 42, 44, 45, 46, 52, 78, 105, 191–2, 196, 366
Morgan, Sally 29, 30, 52, 61, 76, 105, 112, 162, 187, 219, 229, 236, 239, 240, 326
MORI (Market and Opinion Research International) 274, 344, 362

Morris, Dick 275
Morris, Estelle 309, 331, 351
Morris, John 130
Morris, Nigel 244
Moss, Kate 38
Mowlam, Mo 2, 11, 18, 19,
    26–7, 30, 33, 50, 92, 112, 127,
    130, 133, 146, 151, 156, 157,
    159–60, 162, 166, 173, 176,
    183, 184, 185, 186–7, 190,
    191, 194, 196, 197, 202, 205,
    207, 209, 218, 219, 221, 241,
    247, 266, 271, 336
Murdoch, Rupert 13, 95, 119,
    270, 286
Murphy, Paul 27
Murphy, Phil 180, 218, 220, 227,
    229
Murray, Jo 310'
Mystic Meg' xv

National Changeover Plan 79,
    80, 203
National Executive Committee
    see Labour Party
National Football Stadium 341
National Minimum Wage 11–12,
    24–5, 118, 173, 304, 334, 336
NATO (North Atlantic Treaty
    Organisation) 93, 97, 98, 100,
    101, 106, 109, 111, 114, 117,
    124, 130, 132, 149, summit,
    Washington 98, 132, 149–50
Naughtie, Jim 322
NEC see Labour Party, National
    Executive Committee
Neill Committee see Committee
    on Standards in Public Life
Neill Report 35
Neill, Patrick, Lord 10–11

Nelson, Anthony 359, as
    'Horatio' 361
New Deal 44, 123, 161, 173, 252,
    334
New Statesman 182, 183, 218,
    285
New York Stock Exchange 31,
News at Ten (ITV) 24, 290, 347
News International 45, 95, 228,
    238
News of the World 11, 43, 46,
    48–50, 54, 243, 254, 278, 337
Newsnight (BBC) 17, 19, 41, 56,
    90, 123, 126, 128, 259, 339,
    341, 346, 357–8, 362
Newspaper Press Fund 13, 101
Newsround (BBC) 360
Newton-Dunn, Bill 272
NHS 2, 15, 16, 76, 118, 134, 143,
    184, 185, 295, 346, 362
Nice Treaty 278
Nine o'Clock News (BBC) 93,
    102
Norris, Steve 163, 172, 212, 213,
    215, 313
Northern Ireland Assembly 225,
    266
Northern Ireland negotiations 3,
    16, 26–7, 29–30, 55, 92, 93,
    108, 111, 115, 118, 124, 154,
    162, 185, 194, 208, 213, 222,
    226, 288, 366
north-south divide 172–3

O'Brien, Mike 291
Oakley, Robin 21, 45, 65, 115,
    220
Oasis 277
Oborne, Peter 137, 145, 228, 324
Observer 3, 17–18, 19–20, 72,

91, 138, 141, 144, 145, 246, 290–1, 312, 353
Official Secrets Act xvii
Omagh bomb 26–8, 29
Omen, The 311
On The Record (BBC) 210–11, 336, 345, 354
Ondaatje, Christopher 281–2, 283, 285, 289, 310'
Operation Turnout' 175
opinion polls 31, 95, 154, 160, 230, 245, 250, 251, 254, 255, 266, 274, 278, 284, 295–6, 314, 324–5, 327–8, 338, 343, 344, 345, 349, 354–5, 357, 359, 362–3
Orange Order 19
Oratory School 144
Oxford University 11, 224–5
Oxford, Bishop of 312

Paisley, Rev. Ian 37
Panorama (BBC) 231, 350, 357, 358–9, 360, 361, 362
Parkinson, Cecil 14
parliament recalled 27, 29–30
Parliamentary Commissioner for Standards 280, 312
Parliamentary Labour Party 106, 108, 122, 229, 266, 273, 320, 321, 334
Parris, Matthew 41, 51, 107, 341
party election broadcasts 213, 296, 310–11, 322, 337, 338, 343, 353–4
party political broadcasts 231, 246, 248, 252, 276
Pascoe-Watson, George 225
Patten, Chris 111–12, 113, 139–40, 157, 170, 185

Paxman, Jeremy 38, 56, 90
Pensioners Forum 257
pensions policy 215, 252, 254–5, 256, 257
People 71, 102, 297
Philip, Prince 133
Phillips, Trevor 56, 153
Pienaar, John 9
Pinochet, General Augusto 36–7, 38, 39, 55, 59, 60–1
Plaid Cymru 105
Platell, Amanda 133–4, 276
pledge cards (1997) 2, 285–6, (2001) 282, 308, 325, 334
PM programme (BBC) 90, 264, 356
Police Bravery Award 13–14
Police Federation 205, 342
Pope, Greg 110
Porter, Shirley, Lady 11
Portillo, Michael 1, 14, 102, 140–1, 142, 196, 234, 235, 267, 274, 276, 286, 287, 322, 324, 325, 332, 335, 336, 345, 346
Powell, Jonathan xvii, 16, 30, 34, 39, 47, 59–60, 64–6, 75, 88, 102, 114, 121, 140, 153, 157, 168, 170, 203, 217, 219, 237
Powell, Lucy 123
Powell, Ray 336–7
PR Week 232, 233, 251
Pre-Budget Report (PBR) (1999) 156, 160, (2000) 268
Prentice, Bridget 144
Prescott, John xii, xvii, 1–2, 8, 22, 23, 24, 27–8, 39, 44, 52–3, 54, 68, 69–70, 76, 78, 89, 96, 108, 110, 124, 125, 126, 127, 129, 130, 132, 133, 136–7,

Prescott, John – *cont.*
138, 147–8, 153, 155, 162,
171, 172, 176, 177, 187, 193–4,
224, 243, 244, 245, 246, 249,
250, 256, 258, 259, 271, 293,
301–2, 312, 332, 342–4, 354,
365, the punch 342–4
Prescott, Michael 311
Press Association (PA) 6, 8, 16,
180, 254, 264, 346, 361
Press Complaints Commission
25, 49
Price, Glen 17
Price, Joe 262
Price, Lance Douglas Alexander
258–62, BBC 5, 46, BBC
Correspondent 1, 2, 5, 6, 94,
313, Tony Blair 5, 75, 94, 95,
96, 98, 100, 103, 139, 175, 220,
255–6, 265, 283, Nick Brown
46–52, Gordon Brown 93,
153, 220, 279, 308, 364,
Alastair Campbell 4, 5, 6, 7,
14, 52, 82, 85, 86, 92, 93,
95–6, 103, 111, 112, 113, 184,
200, 221, 259, 320, 329,
commentator 107,
Conservative Party 102, Robin
Cook xii-xiii, 132, 352,
decision to resign 5, diaries 2,
6, Evening Standard 6, house
in France 224, 230, 233, 262,
265, 266, 281, 319, 363,
general election (1997) 1,
(2001) date 318, planning 232,
row with broadcasters 347,
350, 356–9, 361, 362, general
election strategy 225, member
of General Election Planning
Committee 159, Gilbert's

Disease 262, government
policy 103, William Hague
112, Hammond Report 306,
Kosovo 92, 98, Labour Party
Director of Communications
220–22, 223–4, 226, 230–33,
leak of party political
broadcast 246, Oliver Letwin
338, lobby briefings 213, 217,
Nelson Mandela 256, Peter
Mandelson 4, 6–7, 9, 22, 23,
36–7, 154, 237–8, 260,
300–301, media strategy
112–15, 302–3, Millbank 258,
ministerial performance 117,
mother and father 24, 174,
new role at Number Ten 104,
112–13, 125–6, 153, 155, 195,
217–18, New Statesman 285,
Oxford University 225, policy
presentation 89, John Prescott
xii-xiii, 22, 70, 125, 127, 133,
138, 244, 245, Prescott punch
343–4, race 324, 353, reshuffle
in Scotland 109, security
vetting 7–8, 19, 20, sexuality
44, 47, single currency 157,
special advisor at Number Ten
4, summer campaign (1999)
131–7, Sunday Express 82, TV
debates during general
election 295, Charlie Whelan
68, 'Wiggy' poster 351, 353
Price, Miles 262
Price, Tracey 17
Proctor, James xiii, 9, 12, 17, 20,
34, 55, 58, 59, 61, 84, 85, 86,
94, 113, 128, 197, 220, 231,
244, 262, 266, 267, 269, 272,
277, 316

Proctor, Jonathan and Cathy 231
Prodi, Romano 316
Progress 20, 235
Progress 249
Proms, the 24
proportional representation (PR) 28–9, 31, 32, 33, 34, 35, 39–40, 44, 54–5, 106, 116, 119, 183, 216, 314, 315–16, 323
Public Administration Committee 12
Punch 53, 54, 58, 154
Purnell, James 34, 103, 143, 219
Putin, Vladimir 200, 201
Puttnam, David 174

Queen, HM 87
Queen's Speech (1998) 55, (1999) 137, 147, 156, 162, (2000) 276'
Queensland strategy' 360
Question Time (BBC) 89, 117, 125, 200, 210, 279, 295, 350, 358
Quinn, Carolyn 6
Quinn, Lesley 137

Race Relations Bill 174
Radio Clyde 82
RAF 10
Rafferty, John 83, 84, 176
Rantzen, Esther 174, 195
Raphael, Adam 289
Rawnsley, Andrew 3, 144, 163, 251, 252, 253, 255
Raynsford, Nick 146, 155, 215, 219
Redgrave, Corin son 174
Redwood, John 165, 256

Register of Members' Interests 62, 265
Reid, John 70, 76, 92, 104, 108, 109, 135, 137, 145, 146, 189, 241, 248, 250, 280, 285, 286, 292, 353, 354
Reiss, Charles 65
Richard and Judy (ITV) 72, 73, 139
Richard, Ivor, Lord 21
Richards, Steve 183, 190, 266, 321
Rimington, Stella 263
Robertson, George 2, 11, 29, 89–90, 99, 130, 132, 136, 146, 149
Robinson, Geoffrey 7, 21, 62–4, 65–6, 131, 153–4, 244, 257, 258, 264–5, 277, 312, 339
Robinson, Tony 148
Roche, Barbara 204, 344
Rollason, Helen 38
Ross, Fiona 343
Rothermere, Jonathan, Lord 100
Routledge, Paul 7, 62, 251, 285
Rowley, Alex 53
Roxborough, Angus 348
Royal Court Theatre 219
Royal family 158
RUC (Royal Ulster Constabulary) 140, 185
Ryan, Conor 218, 220

Sainsbury, David, Lord 76, 77, 281–2, 285
Salmond, Alex 72, 85, 91, 92, 93, 101
Sands, Sarah 25
SAS 251
Saving Private Ryan 98

Sawyer, Tom 10
Scadding, Andrew 296
Scargill, Arthur 296
Scholar, Michael 63
Schröder, Gerhard 11, 33, 99
Schrum, Bob 269, 329, 330, 337, 348
Scotland Yard 46, 165
Scotsman 121
Scottish Executive 107, 121, 189, 222–3, 260, 261, 286, 301, 307
Scottish General Election Planning Group 286, 293–4
Scottish Parliament 15, 84, 90, 193, 206, 268, 307, 366, election results (1999) 104, 105, 118
SDP (Social Democrat Party) 167, 169
Section 28 164–6, 168, 170, 172, 175, 188–9, 191, 194, 205–6, 323, 332
Sedgemore, Brian 182
Seldon, Anthony 157
Sellafield 22
Serbia 89, 106, 117
Sergeant, John 6, 45
sex education guidelines 189, 205–6
Sherman, Jill 75
Shevas, Anne 218
Shore, Peter 35
Short, Clare xii, 156, 199–200, 219, 295, 309, 332, 336
Siena, Archbishop of 25
Sierra Leone 219, 251
Simpson, John 92, 94–5, 97–8
Simpson, Kieran 49–50, 51
single currency 3, 13, 14, 29, 35, 39, 45, 56, 71, 73–4, 79,
100–1, 114, 116–17, 119, 122–3, 138, 143–4, 152, 155, 157, 177, 183–4, 188, 203, 222, 229, 230, 237, 240, 249, 261, 271, 286, 298–9, 340–1, 346, 349, 356, 357, 361, 366
Sinn Féin 11, 37, 226
Six o'Clock News (BBC) 43, 90, 93, 115, 246
Skinner, Dennis 321
Sky News 67, 93, 180–1, 228, 246, 342–3, 347, 360
Sky Television 95
Sloman, Anne 43–4, 90, 115, 128, 231, 296
Smith, Andrew 104, 210–11, 307, 345, 346, 347
Smith, Chris 19, 22, 91, 150, 205, 242, 332, 365, and partner Dorian 91
Smith, Godric 6, 8, 10, 22, 23, 75, 131, 195, 213, 217–18, 221, 225, 228–9, 230, 236
Smith, John 108
Smith, Lesley 310
Smyth, Martin 208
Snow, Jon 38
SNP (Scottish National Party) 16, 55, 71, 72, 81, 85, 101, 136, 144, 287, 296
Soames, Nicholas 280
Social Exclusion Unit 173
Social Market Foundation 174
Socialist Labour Party 296
Soley, Clive 63, 273, 298, 318'
Son of Satan' 311–12, 316, 322
Sopel, Jon 7
Spears, Britney 271–2, 341
Spectator 55, 320, 324
Spellar, John 149

Spence, Laura 224–5
Spice Girls 16
spin xv–xvi, 33, 87, 139, 152,
   161, 207, 221, 228, 236, 238,
   243
spin doctors xii, xiii, xv, xvi, 9,
   32, 63, 80, 81, 184, 227, 313
Standards and Privileges
   Committee 280
Steel, David, Lord 193
Stephanopoulos, George 103
Stevens, John 46, 165
Stonewall 145, 150, 164, 205
Storer, Sharron 342
Strang, Gavin 21
Strategic Communications Unit
   (SCU) 8, 95, 107, 112, 121,
   153, 172, 195, 226, 229, 277
Strathclyde, Thomas, Lord 59
Straw, Jack 1, 4, 30, 35, 38, 39,
   40, 43, 55, 60, 79, 80, 102,
   117, 123, 124, 126, 130, 147,
   152, 173, 181, 205, 209, 218,
   221, 222–3, 271, 285, 301,
   306, 311, 332, 339, 342, 344,
   365
Street-Porter, Janet 199
Streisand, Barbra 248
Strozzi, Prince and Princess 25
STV (Scottish Television) 343
Sun xv, 13, 26, 37, 38, 51, 62, 67,
   69, 80, 86, 95, 131–2, 134,
   148, 155, 161, 177, 181, 214,
   216, 223, 225, 240, 242, 244,
   249, 271, 274, 276, 286, 293,
   302, 304, 307, 318, 327, 328,
   335, 357, 358
Sunday Business 210
Sunday Express 32, 43, 68, 82,
   205

Sunday Mirror 266, 312
Sunday Telegraph 116, 266, 281,
   302
Sunday Times 43, 102, 176, 228,
   273–4, 283, 294, 302, 312'
Switch' xix, 26, 128
Sykes, Paul 340

Talk Radio 128
Tate Modern 219–20'
Tax Bombshell' campaign (1992)
   288
Taylor, Ann 21, 90, 189
Taylor, Damilola 279
Taylor, John, Lord 327–8
Taylor, Matthew 15, 356
TBWA 232, 233, 237, 240, 248,
   308–9, 329–30
Tebbit, Norman, Lord 44, 188,
   349
Temple-Morris, Peter 11, 12
Ten o'clock News BBC 343'
Thank You' campaign 270
That's Life (BBC) 174
Thatcher, Margaret, Lady 60,
   95, 107, 133, 134, 146, 151,
   152, 164, 211, 346, 351, 359
Thatcherism 224, 323, 325, 349,
   355, 362
Third Way Conference, Florence
   161, 163
Thomas, Mark 187
Thompson, David 81
Thurwell, Neville 49
Times, The 16, 22, 46, 59, 75,
   79, 80, 97, 125, 134, 144,
   159, 228, 240, 243, 244, 266,
   278, 290, 291, 297, 313–14,
   319, 328, 329, 338, 340, 347,
   357–8

Today programme (BBC) 24, 28, 33, 58, 68, 78, 92, 116, 135, 162, 199, 240, 250, 253, 322, 339, 346, 348, 349, 352, 356
Tory Reform Group (TRG) 181
Townend, John 324, 328
Transport and General Workers' Union (TGWU) 252
Trimble, David 111, 208, 222
TUC (Trades Union Congress) 120, 250
Turnbull, Sir Andrew xvii
Twigg, Stephen 1, 12, 145, 207, 242
Tyson, Mike 222–3

UKIP (UK Independence Party) 349
Ulster Unionist Council 222
Ulster Unionist Party (UUP) 111, 124, 208, 226
UN (United Nations) 31, 89, 111, 209, 219
UNISON 252
Upton, Jonathan 229, 231
US Presidential election (2000) 267, 269, 277, 283
UTV (Ulster Television) 101

Vaz, Keith 109, 175, 261, 293, 294, 297–8, 312, 339, 362

Wade, Rebekah 161
Walter, David 296
Walters, Simon 181
Ware, John 361
Warner, Nigel 166
Watts, John 302
Webster, Phil 97, 313–14, 329, 340
Wegg-Prosser, Ben 7, 19–20, 57, 62–3, 64–5, 67, 68, 69, 134, 280, 306
Welfare Reform Bill 110, 160
Welsh Assembly 42, 191, 366, election results (1999) 104–5, 118
Westlife 298, 301, 302, 303
Westminster Council 11
Whelan, Charlie 6–7, 37, 53, 62–3, 65, 66, 68, 139, 144, 154, 206, 257, 262
White, Michael 344
Whitton, David 263
WI (Women's Institute) 226–8, 229
Widdecombe, Ann 123, 125, 256, 287, 339
Wiggy poster 351, 353, 355–6, 363
Wills, Michael 208, 352
Wilson, Sir Richard 47–8, 50, 240, 263–4, 288
Winning, Cardinal 158
Winston, Robert, Lord 184
Wintour, Patrick 72
Wishart, Ruth 263
withholding tax 96
Womack, Sarah 180
Woodhead, Chris 44
Woodward, Camilla 164, 170–1, 178–9 192
Woodward, Lesley 181, 182
Woodward, Shaun 164–72, 173–4, 175, 176, 177, 178–82, 184, 194, 195–6, 209, 239, 242, 317, 333, 336, 337, 339
Working Families Tax Credit 118, 123, 129, 139, 161, 173, 252, 334
World At One, The (BBC) 17, 90
World Cup 9, 10, 16

World This Weekend, The (BBC)
130, 295, 352
Wright, Peter 100

Yates, Paula 252
Yelland, David 13, 62, 67, 69,
131